Bodies
of
Meaning

SUNY series
in
Radical Social
and
Political Theory

Roger S. Gottlieb, Editor

Bodies
of
Meaning

Studies on Language, Labor, and Liberation

David McNally

State University of New York Press

Published by
State University of New York Press, Albany

✓
© 2001 State University of New York

For information, address State University of New York Press
90 State Street, Suite 700, Albany, NY 12207

Production by Michael Haggett
Marketing by Anne M. Valentine

Library of Congress Cataloging-in-Publication Data

McNally, David.
Bodies of meaning : studies on language, labor, and liberation / David McNally.
p.   cm.
Includes index.
ISBN 0-7914-4735-9 (hc : acid-free paper) — ISBN 0-7914-4736-7 (pb : acid-free paper)
1. Body, Human—Social aspects.   2. Body, Human (Philosophy)   3. Postmodernism.
I. Title.

HM636.M35 2000
306.4—dc21   00-027106
10 9 8 7 6 5 4 3 2 1

For Sue

CONTENTS

Acknowledgments   ix

Note on Citations   xi

Introduction   1

1 Nietzsche, Darwin, and the Postmodern Fetish of Language   15

2 Forgetting the Body: Linguistic Economies from Saussure
   to Derrida   45

3 Bodies that Talk: Sex, Tools, Language, and Human Culture   79

4 Body, Speech, and History: Language and Materialism in
   Voloshinov and Bakhtin   111

5 Corporeal Reason: Language, History, and the Body in
   Walter Benjamin's Dialectics of Awakening   161

Conclusion   229

Notes   235

Index   271

ACKNOWLEDGMENTS

Having labored on this book for a number of years, I owe thanks to many people. For ongoing intellectual stimulation around issues related to language and critical theory, I wish to acknowledge the many students who have participated in my graduate seminar, "Marxism and the Philosophy of Language," at York University. Thanks also to Susan Buck-Morss, Peter Ives, and Alan Sears who read parts of the manuscript in draft form. I also wish to acknowledge the encouragement of Ellen Meiksins Wood who, a number of years ago, persuaded me to commit some of my ideas on these matters to paper. I would like, in addition, to thank Mike Haggett, Michael Rinella and Anne Valentine, all of SUNY Press, for their valuable assistance. As always, my children, Adam and Sam, deserve special mention. And so, last but not least, does Sue Ferguson who, in addition to reading the manuscript and offering valuable commentary, was a constant source of encouragement and support throughout all stages of its preparation. For that, and for so many other reasons, I dedicate this work to her.

NOTE ON CITATIONS

Because a number of works are cited frequently in the text, the following abbreviations will be used. Full references are provided in the endnotes.

AC   Friedrich Nietzsche, *The Anti-Christ*
AH   Mikhail Bakhtin, "Arthur and Hero in Aesthetic Activity"
BC   Walter Benjamin, "A Berlin Chronicle"
BGE   Friedrich Nietzsche, *Beyond Good and Evil*
C   Karl Marx, *Capital*, vol. 1
C3   Karl Marx, *Capital*, vol. 3
CGL   Ferdinand de Saussure, *Course in General Linguistics*
CP   Walter Benjamin, "Central Park"
D   Friedrich Nietzsche, *Daybreak*
DM   Charles Darwin, *The Descent of Man*
DN   Mikhail Bakhtin, "Discourse in the Novel"
EC   Friedrich Nietzsche, *Ecce Homo*
EN   Mikhail Bakhtin, "Epic and Novel"
F   Valentin Voloshinov, *Freudianism: A Critical Sketch*
FC   Jean Baudrillard, *For a Critique of the Political Economy of the Sign*
FM   Pavel Medvedev, *The Formal Method in Literary Scholarship*
FTCN   Mikhail Bakhtin, "Forms of Time and Chronotope in the Novel"
G   Karl Marx, *Grundrisse*

GI   Karl Marx and Frederick Engels, *The German Ideology*
GL   Jacques Derrida, *Glas*
GM   Friedrich Nietzsche, *On the Genealogy of Morals*
GT   Jacques Derrida, *Given Time: I. Counterfeit Money*
GS   Friedrich Nietzsche, *The Gay Science*
ID   Sigmund Freud, *The Interpretation of Dreams*
IP   Walter Benjamin, "Images of Proust"
K   Walter Benjamin, "Franz Kafka"
MPL   Valentin Voloshinov, *Marxism and the Philosophy of Language*
N   Walter Benjamin, "N [Re The Theory of Knowledge, Theory of Progress]"
OG   Jacques Derrida, *Of Grammatology*
OGTD   Walter Benjamin, *The Origin of German Tragic Drama*
OMF   Walter Benjamin, "On the Mimetic Faculty"
OPP   Walter Benjamin, "Outline of the Psychophysical Problem"
OS   Charles Darwin, *The Origin of Species*
OWS   Walter Benjamin, "One-Way Street"
P   Jacques Derrida, *Positions*
PC   Walter Benjamin, "Paris, Capital of the Nineteenth-Century"
PDP   Mikhail Bakhtin, *Problems of Dostoevsky's Poetics*
PHND   Mikhail Bakhtin, "From the Prehistory of Novelistic Discourse"
PSEB   Walter Benjamin, "The Paris of the Second Empire in Baudelaire"
RHW   Mikhail Bakhtin, *Rabelais and His World*
S   Walter Benjamin, "Surrealism, The Last Snapshot of the European Intelligentsia"
SEC   Jacques Derrida, "Signature, Event, Context"
SG   Mikhail Bakhtin, *Speech Genres and Other Late Essays*
SM   Jacques Derrida, *Specters of Marx*
TE   Jean Baudrillard, *The Transparency of Evil*
TI   Friedrich Nietzsche, *Twilight of the Idols*
TPEI   Thomas Keenan, "The Point Is to (Ex)Change It"
TPF   Walter Benjamin, "Theological-Political Fragment"
TPH   Walter Benjamin, "Theses on the Philosophy of History"
UM   Friedrich Nietzsche, *Untimely Meditations*
WP   Friedrich Nietzsche, *The Will to Power*
Z   Friedrich Nietzsche, *Thus Spoke Zarathustra*

INTRODUCTION

This book begins with a polemic. It originates in a sharp critique of the tendency of major social theorists to abstract language from human bodies and their social practices. But this book is more than a polemic. It also develops a materialist approach to language that builds upon some of the most profound and original work within critical social thought. So, while trying to show where Friedrich Nietzsche, Ferdinand de Saussure, Jacques Derrida, and others have gone wrong, it also draws on the work of theorists like Mikhail Bakhtin, Valentin Voloshinov, Walter Benjamin, and upon feminist and Marxist thinkers inspired by them, to trace an alternative route to exploring questions of language, power, and resistance. As much as it may irritate and provoke many adherents of post-structuralism and deconstruction, then, this book is also meant to give them food for thought. And for those exasperated by the esoteric jargon of the new idealism, these studies are meant to show that it is possible to tackle some of the key questions raised by the linguistic turn in philosophy and social theory without sacrificing intelligibility, a concern for real social practices, or a commitment to emancipatory politics.

One overarching argument runs through these pages: that postmodernist theory, whether it calls itself post-structuralism, deconstruction or post-Marxism, is constituted by a radical attempt to banish the real human body—the sensate, biocultural, laboring body—from the sphere of language and social life.[1] As a result, I argue, these outlooks reproduce a central feature of commodified society: the abstraction of social products and practices from the laboring bodies that generate them. What one critic has said of the post-structuralist theory of Jacques Lacan—that the body is "that very 'something' which it cannot recognize as a

1

thing and still preserve its disciplinary integrity"—can in fact be said of the whole field of postmodernist thought.[2] The extra-discursive body, the body that exceeds language and discourse, is the "other" of the new idealism, the entity it seeks to efface in order to bestow absolute sovereignty on language. To acknowledge the centrality of the sensate body to language and society is thus to threaten the whole edifice of postmodernist theory.

This claim will encounter an immediate objection. After all, talk of the body is everywhere in postmodernist discourse. We have desiring bodies, performative bodies, cyborg bodies. Yet, there is something curiously attenuated about the postmodern body. It has been de-materialized, relieved of matter, biology, the stuff of organs, blood, nerves, and sinews. Even desire is commonly abstracted from the body, reduced to a metaphysical drive to overcome ontological "lack," our incompleteness as beings. Sensible needs—for food, love, sex, and shelter—are not countenanced in this discursive space. The postmodern body is thus constituted by a radical disavowal of corporeal substance. And just as it leaps out of nature, so it catapults itself beyond history and society. Liberated from biology, anatomy, physiology, social class, gender, and ethno-racial identity, the postmodern body is free to invent itself. A plaything of the imagination, it can assume any shape and size, any age or location, any identity its creator chooses; it is as one feminist critic puts it, "no body at all."[3]

There is something a bit anxious, then, about postmodernist body-talk. It is as if the "others" of linguistic idealism—nature, materiality, corporeal substance, social labor—were to be exorcised through invocations of the word "body," as if rhetorical rituals could linguistify the body, turn it into the empty stuff of post-structural linguistics. To the degree to which something called a body figures on the postmodernist stage, it is the *body as text*, something which can be "rewritten," constructed through discourse, by disembodied Western intellectuals.[4] Human bodies with an evolutionary history have no place here. Nor does the laboring body of social history, the body that strains with the sweat of coffee-picking, that turns stiff from the routines of the assembly line, that grows chaffed and swollen with the labor of scrubbing and cleaning, that breaks down from repetitive motion at the keyboard. Denied the postmodern intellectual's ostensible flight from embodiment, such bodies find that the materiality of real sites of oppression—the sweatshop, the coffee field, the brothel, the mine, and mill—is not so easily deconstructed. Whatever the postmodern body may be, it has little to do with the lived bodies of the vast majority.

Rather than truly breaking from the "philosophy of consciousness" that has dominated Western philosophical thought, the new idealism has produced a subordination of body to mind, of nature to culture, as extreme as any to be found in older forms of idealism. And as with all idealisms, this latest version works feverishly to banish whatever won't fit its schema. Postmodernist theory rigorously patrols its linguistic space, fending off incursions by anything that smells of nature, biology, corporeality. Here we can see why the post-structuralist substitution of language—whether it's called "sign," "text," "writing," or "discourse"—for mind is much less radical than it may at first seem. True, consciousness is now brought into contact with underlying structures (like those of the language system) which shape and define it. But those structures are themselves de-materialized and disembodied. Cut off from nature and material human practices, the formal structures of language are given an amazing power of determination with respect to the world we inhabit. Jacques Lacan, for instance, declares as unabashedly as any old-style idealist: "It is the world of words that creates the world of things."[5] And this basic position—that language or discourse constitutes our bodies, our world and our selves—is a staple of much postmodernist theory. True, it is not always put so baldly. Yet, Derrida's assertion that the emergence of structural linguistics "was the moment when . . . everything became discourse" is really another version of the same proposition, as is Judith Butler's claim that "to return to matter requires that we return to matter as *sign*."[6]

Like its predecessors, linguistic idealism involves the subsumption of concrete entities and relations—bodies, objects, social practices—under a set of conceptual abstractions. Yet, the very materiality of matter and bodies resists this absorption into the sign. The anxious efforts of thought to master the material world run up against the irreducibility of its objects. Inevitably, the postmodernist totalization of language collapses under the weight of its impossible project: to make everything language and, thereby, to make language everything. After all, to banish the body, to repress it, as the new idealism does, is not to eliminate it, but merely to forget it. And, inevitably, what has been forgotten lives a ghostlike existence within postmodernist thought. In its efforts to banish biology and corporeal substance, postmodern idealism simultaneously creates for itself "an unspeakable threat—the body of nature," as Vicki Kirby puts it.[7] The natural body is still there, after all, even if theory does not register its presence. And the same applies to the laboring body. Somebody is still working in factory, field, office, and mine. Someone is still birthing children, nursing, feeding, tending, and caring for them. Somebody still cleans the streets and the toilets, attends to the elderly and infirm, makes the cup of coffee and the pot of rice. Bodies are still gripped by hunger, scarred by homelessness, wracked by disease. A theory which effaces these realities simply occludes these bodies and their labors—but it does not eliminate them. Indeed, as Karl Marx and Sigmund Freud have taught us, what has been repressed invariably returns, even if in unrecognized forms. Despite capital's claim, for instance, that, as money, it and it alone produces wealth, laborers rise up time and again to disrupt this claim—and thereby to challenge the abstractions which cover over the realities of people in mines and fields, on assembly lines, bound to sewing machines in sweatshops and homes. Similarly, as psychoanalysis reminds us, despite the neurotic's efforts to forget the pain that has marked his or her personality, the trauma returns with enormous force, albeit in the disguised forms of latent dream-wishes, neurotic habits, and repetition compulsions.

Central to the critical materialism that informs this book, then, is the insistence that the concrete bodies, practices, and desires, which have been forgotten by idealism, perform a return of the repressed.[8] Invariably, these things
return in devalued form, as "the excrescences of the system," as the degraded and
discarded elements of refuse which "show the untruth, the mania, of the systems
themselves."[9] The task of critical theory is to produce a knowledge built out of
these excrescences, a knowledge derived from attending to the fragments which
have escaped the imperial ambitions of linguistic idealism. And this means
starting from the body—that entity which is radically outside the theoretical
edifice of the new idealism and whose presence threatens its integrity. And it
means doing so while attending to the differences—of gender, class, sexuality,
ethno-racial identity, and more—which mark and define these bodies. But if our
project is one of emancipatory materialist critique, then begin from the site of
bodies we must.

A central feature of bourgeois thought, after all, has been its othering of the
body and its embodying of the other. Proletarians, women, Blacks, the colonized:
these groups of the oppressed and exploited have long been assigned the category of the body by dominant discourses. The bourgeois outlook demeans the
laboring body as an object of grotesque and repulsive processes, the site of
biology, instinct, sweat, and desire. Indeed, those considered corporeal beings
have been regularly treated as a different race of humans. Granier de Cassagnac,
in his, *Histoire des classes ouvrieres et des classes bourgeoises* (1838), for instance,
claimed that proletarians were a subhuman class formed through the breeding
of thieves with prostitutes. In the same register, Henry Mayhew's, *London Labour
and the London Poor* (1861), divided the whole of humanity into two distinct
races: the civilized and the wanderers. Those of the latter race, proletarians and
the poor, were defined by their inability to transcend the body and its libidinal
impulses and desires. Mayhew refers disparagingly to their "love of libidinous
dances," their "passion for stupefying herbs and roots," and the "looseness of
their notions of property," among other vices.[10]

Bourgeois culture is constituted in and through a process in which bodiliness
is ascribed to outcast others. "It could be said as a broad generalization," write
two ethnologists, "that bourgeois culture was like an organism with a hidden
body. The body was there, to be sure, but its existence was persistently denied
by the head. Bourgeois culture was spiritual, not physical."[11] Bodies appeared
outside bourgeois society, therefore, as attributes of foreign or alien social types.
These non-bourgeois others, these "people of the body," to use Himani Bannerji's
wonderful expression, were feminized, racialized, and animalized; they were
constructed as members of a radically different race, sex, and species.[12] With the
creation of the capitalist world market through dispossession of the European
peasantry, colonial plunder, and the trade in human beings, whole categories of
racialized and sexualized groups of the laboring and dangerous classes were
invented. Africans, Orientals, women, the Irish, Jews, homosexuals, prostitutes,

and the laboring poor of Europe—all of these became people of the body. Discourses of class, gender, race, and empire thus intersected, positioning reason, culture, civilization, and mind on one side of the divide, and animality, uncontrolled sexuality, and the laboring body on the other. The discourse of colonialism pathologized whole peoples by constructing them as pure, brute bodies. As Frantz Fanon put it in an older rhetoric, for the colonial world view, "the Negro symbolizes the biological."[13] Similarly, the procreative body the pregnant, birthing, nursing female body, was equally degraded, treated as a site of natural, biological processes which belong to the animal more than the human. All of these bodies underwent simultaneous processes of sexualization and degradation. Of course, bourgeois discourses have to admit the body at some stage of the game. But they do so by "cleansing" it of the sweat of labor and the blood of menstruation and childbirth. The bourgeois body is a sanitized, heroic male body of rational (nonbiological) creatures: it does not break under the strain of routinized work; it does not menstruate, lactate, or go into labor; it does not feel the lash of the master's whip; it does not suffer and die. The bourgeois body is, in short, an idealist abstraction.

The bourgeois and postmodern (non)body has its sociohistorical roots in the way capitalism radically separates intellectual from manual labor. Management, supervision, and intelligence are positioned on one side of a class divide, while labor, physical hardship, and the body are situated on the other. Mind is de-materialized, while the body is de-subjectivized, reduced to a mere thing. This dualism is a product of the twofold opposition between use value and exchange value, on the one hand, and concrete and abstract labor on the other that Marx identifies at the heart of the commodity. I return to this issue in more detail in chapter 2. But for the moment, let me note that commodities become exchangeable to the degree to which the capitalist market abstracts from their concrete, useful, sensible characteristics and reduces them to interchangeable quantities of human labor in the abstract. In entering into exchange, Marx notes, all the "sensuous characteristics" of the commodity "are extinguished." Commodities become nothing more than an objectification of an abstraction—abstract human labor—stripped of all the concrete characteristics of the labor that actually produced them.[14] This abstraction is expressed in the exchangeability of commodities with money. On the market, diamonds and coffee, iron and cotton, books and condoms, word processors and bread (and the concrete labors that went into producing them) become interchangeable units of the same intangible stuff—abstract human labor—which expresses itself in money. The commodity thus contains an internal opposition: on the one hand, it is a sensuous material object capable of satisfying specific human needs and produced by specific acts of labor; on the other hand, it appears on the market with a price tag which announces that it is no different from any other commodity, since its identity consists only of a given sum money (its price). One result of this is that a unique conceptual structure—the exchange abstraction—comes to govern the dominant forms of thought in capitalist society. In a society whose reproduction is secured through socioeconomic laws which abstract from the concrete and sensuous characteristics of labor and its products, the dominant mode of thinking about things is one of universalizing abstraction. What Hegel calls abstract universals—general concepts denuded of all concrete particularities, stripped of all empirical content—emerge as the standards of scientific thinking in and about society. The exchange abstraction effected by the capitalist market becomes the fundamental form of bourgeois thought.[15] The ruling conceptual paradigm thus reproduces the opposition between abstract and concrete labor in the form of a radical opposition between head and hand, mind and body. Indeed, in the epoch of emerging capitalism, workers were regularly described *as* "hands"—farmhands, dockhands, hired hands. For most bourgeois thought, this class opposition is configured as one between nature and culture. Nature is posited as the strictly determined realm of matter, animals, bodies, women, the colonized, and proletarians. Culture on the other hand, is figured as the domain of mind and language, of the autonomous, self-creating bourgeois male. The new idealism associated with post-structuralist linguistics simply reaffirms this dualism in the oppositions language/world and language/body.

To be sure, the dualism mind/body maps onto a multiple sets of oppositions: capitalist/worker, white/black, man/woman, straight/gay, metropolitan/colonial. Moreover, there are complex interrelations among these oppositions as they emerge in the concrete sociohistorical contexts of actual societies at particular points in space and time. As a result, these oppositions intersect with one another in manifold ways that complicate the social geography. Post-structuralism and deconstruction often enjoy "playing" with these oppositions, showing how they can be interrogated and parodied. Yet postmodernists tend to accept these oppositions as unchangeable, as part of the text which defines and constrains us all. Their very play with the dominant categories—their irony, parody, and self-mocking—is derived from and celebrates the oppositions which make this exuberant activity possible. In this respect, the new idealism travels a similar route to that taken by much postmodernist art: endless enjoyment in playing with the commodity sign. Yet, as one commentator has pointed out, this passion for playing with the commodity sign often makes it "difficult to distinguish, among postmodernist artists and post-structuralist critics alike, between *critics* of the reification and fragmentation of the sign and *connoisseurs* of this same process."[16] Ironic play with the commodity form becomes a substitute for a critical theory designed to assist its overthrow.

All too often, post-structuralism and deconstruction partake of a positivism which insists that there *really is* nothing beyond the fetishes of the commodity—no bodies, no concrete labors, no real struggles of resistance which might be the basis for an emancipatory project. Consequently, as I demonstrate in chapters 1 and 2, postmodernism is trapped within the antinomies of bourgeois thought. And this, needless to say, has political implications: not simply is there nothing outside the text, as vulgar deconstruction puts it, there is also nothing outside and beyond the commodity form.[17] That, of course, is the partial truth sedimented within postmodernism: its tacit recognition that we live in a totalizing system, that of the commodity, which really does efface individual subjectivity. But this "truth" is also a token of the falsity of postmodernism since the commodity becomes total only through an immense process of abstraction and forgetting. What defines a critical theory is that it attends to what this total system represses and forgets, thereby holding open the possibility of a different order of society. This does not involve a celebration of contingent particularity, however, so much as a search for those fragments of the totality that oppose its totalizing logic.[18] In glibly denying that there is anything beyond the system— or, the other side of the coin, in celebrating a fictitious contingent particularity utterly outside the social whole—postmodernism takes up a thoroughgoing conformism. And, despite certain protestations on these points, Derrida affirms such an interpretation with his announcement that he "would hesitate to use terms such as 'liberation'."[19]

For the new idealism, there is no way out of the linguistic forms of thought or the social relations characteristic of Western capitalist society. And this applies directly to the foundational dualism of bourgeois thought: the mind/body opposition. While the new idealism has reconstructed this opposition in terms of the dualism language/body, its basic thrust remains unchanged: an effort to make language everything, the body nothing, or, what amounts to the same thing, to create "a language-body" which gives birth to everything else.[20]

So determined is postmodernist resistance to any independence of the realm of the material, of the body and nature, that it denounces as "essentialist" all efforts to turn to real bodies, to uncover the corporeal bases of social life. One of the objects of this book is to demonstrate that this charge is misguided. To talk about human bodies and the practices in which they are immersed need not entail treating the body as a timeless object of nature. The human body, as I hope to show, is inherently historical. True, bodies have a relatively fixed biological constitution. But the evolutionary history of the human body also involves the emergence of cultural practices and social history. To talk meaningfully about the human body is to talk about bodies that are the site of dynamic social processes, bodies that generate open-ended systems of meaning. It is, in other words, to talk about relations of production and reproduction, about languages, images of desire, technologies, and diverse forms of sociocultural organization. All of these things operate on the site of the body and its history. This is not to say they create the body. It is to insist, however, that they extend and modify bodily existence and experience. The constants of bodily existence take shape through manifold and pliable forms of social life. This is what it means to describe the human body as an indeterminate constancy; and it's what it means to talk, as I do across these studies, about *historical bodies*.[21] For historical bodies are, I shall argue, both linguistic and laboring ones. "To describe a body as historical," writes Terry Eagleton, "is to say that it is continuously able to make something of that which makes it. Language is in this sense the very index of human historicity, as a system whose peculiarity is to enable events which transgress its own formal structure."[22]

The idea of the human body as historical has important roots in the thinking of three major theorists: Charles Darwin, Marx, and Freud. It was Darwin who blew apart the idea of species as unchanging products of divine creation. By demonstrating that the human body was a product of natural history beginning with the earliest forms of life, Darwin demolished doctrines which tried to hive off humans and their minds from the rest of nature. In so doing, he de-essentialized the human body by immersing it in the time of natural history. Left there, however, Darwin's theory was susceptible to a conflation of human history with natural history (and the mechanical materialism such a view entails).[23] Worse, it could be vulgarized so as to naturalize structures of social inequality. Marx provided a materialist way out of this dilemma by showing that, while human history is continuous with natural history, it also involves a crucial discontinuity. The emergence of cultural, language-using, toolmaking primates introduced a new order of temporality, the time of human history. This temporality does not transcend natural time, it mediates and supplements it, introducing different orders of determination. Marx's great contribution in this area was to show how the time of human history was shaped by the forms in which human productive activity is regulated by systems of social labor. The way labor is organized becomes central to the histories of laboring bodies and their extensions. Finally, Freud adds to this mix the history of the libidinal body. Freud sees the body as a site of drives for love, happiness, social attachments, and erotic fulfillment whose frustrations and satisfactions produce complex histories, products of conscious narratives, and unconscious wishes. Since trauma, fantasy, language, and desire are constitutive of it, this erotogenic body is not reducible to the life-history of the physiological body; its experience is simultaneously organic and psychic. Nevertheless, contrary to postmodern versions of psychoanalysis, the erotogenic body is always an organic one, even while it is something more than that: the human being invariably confronts "the exigencies of life," as Freud puts it "first in the form of the major somatic needs."[24] As does Marx, Freud tells a story of how history becomes alienated from the bodies that produce it, of how these histories become forms of domination and repression, rather than of gratification and contentment. One task of critical theory is to indicate how these psychic and cultural histories relate to the history of capital and of labor's struggles, often far from fully conscious, to be liberated from the circuit of the commodity. To this end, in chapter 5, I take up Walter Benjamin's remarkable attempt to bring Freud and Marx together in his theory of the dream-images of commodities.

Both Darwin and Freud, however, subscribed to a liberal materialism with its roots in bourgeois philosophy. As a result, despite the radical thrust of their thought, they tend to naturalize existing relations of class, gender, and race and dominant forms of sexuality, family, and the state.[25] Marx's critique of the reifying tendencies of bourgeois thought—of its propensity to naturalize historically created forms of social life—is vital to critically reconstructing the Darwinian and Freudian notions of the historical body. For this reason, Marx's brilliant analysis of the fetishism of commodities figures centrally in much of the argument throughout this book. Nevertheless, both Darwin and Freud probed fundamental aspects of the history of the body which were not Marx's object of study. An adequate account of language, the human body, and its history thus needs to begin with the three historical bodies anatomized by Darwin, Marx, and Freud respectively: the evolutionary body, the laboring body and the libidinal body.

As should now be clear, an historical body must also be understood as a signifying body, a body which generates and is shaped by systems of meaning. Meanings are not produced by disembodied and ahistorical systems of signs (as they are for Saussure). Instead, meanings begin from the body—in coordinated movements of hand, face, tongue, larynx, as these exist in relation to other bodies—and they carry expressive, emotional and libidinal charges, not just communicative messages. But the bodies from which these emerge are already inserted in history, society, and systems of meaning. Even where meanings are objectified at high levels of abstraction—in sign systems, novels, currencies, dress codes, or digitized systems of information—they are always attached to human bodies, reinscribing them within language and history. Body and meaning thus interpenetrate in dialectical movements through which each makes the other. With Bakhtin, then, I share the view that we are invariably dealing with "bodies of meaning"—meanings which are embodied in real material forms and bodies which are sites of meaning—and that "one cannot draw an absolute distinction between body and meaning in the area of culture."[26]

Working with this notion of "bodies of meaning," this book investigates language in terms of the models of the historical body developed by Darwin, Marx and Freud. This is not a study devoted to their work, however. Darwin is discussed in chapter 3 simply in relation to evolutionary accounts of language, while Marx figures largely in my critique of Derrida and in terms of his impact on the thought of Voloshinov and Benjamin. Indeed, Freud barely appears in the text until its final chapter where I read Benjamin's analysis of commodified culture in terms of the Freudian theory of dreams. Readers of this book will, I hope, come away with some new appreciations of Darwin, Marx, and Freud and what they might teach us about language and history. But this is not a book about their work. Rather, it is a study of language, labor, and the body which turns to theorists who have engaged their work.

Perhaps this is now the point to anticipate an objection and close off a misunderstanding. My argument is not that critical social theory ought to shift its attention from language to the body. There are good reasons for being interested in language and its connections with power and resistance. My argument is that we ought to think about language *through the body*; that any attempt to understand language in abstraction from bodies and their histories can only produce an impoverished knowledge. In the face of the rarefied abstractions of the new idealism, I believe it is crucial to accent the body, indeed to exaggerate it. I share with Bakhtin, therefore, the idea that any productive confrontation with idealism must begin one-sidedly. Critical materialism involves a determined effort to undermine the sovereign pretensions of language and mind. And it does so by forcing the disembodied abstractions of idealism into contact with what has been marginalized, repressed, and debased. This means, as with Bakhtin, that the high must be brought low, language and mind forced into contact with hands, bellies, buttocks, and genitals. In the grotesque realism of the body celebrated by Bakhtin, theoretical and political renewal can only come from below: via a movement through the realm of the debased and degraded "material bodily lower stratum." And the same applies, I argue, to the new idealism which is so anticorporeal and antimaterialist that it must be brought low, dethroned, degraded, and brought to earth. As Bakhtin puts it:

> Degradation here means coming down to earth, the contact with earth as an element that swallows up and gives birth at the same time. To degrade is to bury, sow, and to kill simultaneously, in order to bring forth something more and better. To degrade also means to concern oneself with the lower stratum of the body, the life of the belly and the reproductive organs.[27]

My readings of thinkers like Nietzsche and Derrida are undertaken in this spirit. I acknowledge the materialist impulses located within their work, but I see these as subverted by crucial idealist moves, especially with respect to language. Following Bakhtin, I attempt to expose these idealist moves by forcing them to confront the bodies they have left behind. I do so in the conviction that the renewal of critical theory begins from the site of the grotesque body in labor, the body immersed in the world of material things. This entails, as I try to show in chapter 5, Benjamin's insistent move "toward the realm of things as the strongest threat to the dialectic of self-consciousness."[28] The sovereign pretensions of language and mind (which take the form of the self-creating dialectic of self-consciousness) must be undone via a journey through the brute realm of bodies and things. Beginning from the excrescences of idealism, critical materialism constructs a radically different account of language and thought—and their relation to labor and liberation. Thus, after having worked through a critique of Nietzsche, Saussure, Derrida, and others in chapters 1 and 2, I turn in chapter 3 to the body and its lower strata, the very bases of thought and language. Feet, hands, pelvis, genitals all figure in my account of the natural history which led to the emergence of language-using primates. That a book on language and social theory should concern itself with such matters will elicit charges of "biologism," "naturalism," and "essentialism." Yet these anxieties in the face of biology and animality must be challenged if we are to undermine the idealist contempt for real bodies that runs through postmodernist theory. At the same time, this intermediate chapter on the evolutionary history of the human body prepares the way for a return to language and social history—but a return which bears the imprint of its immersion in the natural history of the body. Again, I want to insist that the body is not our point of termination. I am not serving up a simple inversion of the language/body opposition by valorizing the body over and against language. Rather, I hope to destabilize this dualism by showing how the body passes over into language and language into the body. With Bakhtin, then, I embrace Rabelais' attempt "to return both a language and a meaning to the body . . . and simultaneously return a reality, a materiality, to language and to meaning."[29] Indeed, I argue that these dialectical reversals are at the very heart of an emancipatory theory and practice.

Yet, it will fairly be objected, haven't I committed myself to an essentialism of the body that effaces gender and sexual difference? In talking about "the body" in a generic, non-gendered way, aren't I ignoring what so much feminist theory has tried to teach us: that we are not all of the same body, that the female body (and some female bodies more than others) experiences a unique sort of repression within the dominant relations of modern society? My response to these questions is twofold. First, a growing current within feminist theory is taking up many of the concerns with embodiment and the materiality of social practices that form my point of departure; this book engages such work and seeks to contribute to it.[30] Second, it is part of my argument, in common with some important work in feminist thought, that in order to talk meaningfully about the human body we cannot circumvent those female bodies—maternal bodies—to which we all ultimately trace our origins. But this argument, too, invites misunderstanding. Let me briefly clarify the way it shapes the studies that comprise this book.

The bourgeois body, as I've suggested, is an idealized, heroic male body. It is the body of the aristocratic warrior-king. Since ancient Greek philosophy, this body has been liberated from labor. And it is equally liberated from women. This dual separation—from labor and from women—is fundamental to the aristocratic vision of the male body that characterizes the dominant discourses of Western thought. The heroic male body—repository of wisdom, courage and virtue—does not experience the ardors of labor, be they those of childbirth or manual work. Indeed, for Plato, the aristocratic male body is to be freed from the realm of sense experience itself, so as to enter the sphere of mathematical and formal reasoning, of knowledge uncontaminated by sensible contact with the things of the empirical world. The ideal body-image that dominates bourgeois thought, where the separation of intellect from body reaches its apogee, is thoroughly abstracted from birth and death, sweat and labor, menstruation and lactation.[31] As a case in point, during the nineteenth century, British imperialism regularly retired its colonial administrators at age fifty-five. Consequently, as Edward Said remarks, "no oriental was ever allowed to see a Westerner as he aged and degenerated, just as no Westerner needed ever to see himself, mirrored in the eyes of the subject race, as anything but a vigorous, rational, ever-alert young Raj."[32] The discourse of imperialism distills the bourgeois contempt for real bodies. Ideal bodies are white, male, non-laboring and non-libidinal; real bodies are nonwhite, female things, beastly objects of labor and erotic desire.[33]

The ideal male body owes its being to no one else. It is absolutely, indeed maniacally, autonomous. It acknowledge no dependencies. In the first instance, this view reinscribes the fetishism of money-capital. After all, at the heart of bourgeois economics is capital's claim to absolute self-sufficiency; capital insists that it gives birth to itself, creates itself out of itself, without any mediation by labor. Corresponding to this myth of self-sufficient capital is the myth of the hyper-rational, autonomous male. The autonomous bourgeois male body does not originate in the body of an other, it gives birth to itself through the thought products of its own mind. By constructing an unrecoverable language-body at the origin of life and discourse, post-structuralism retraverses this circuit around the female body, the body of the mother, the nursemaid, the domestic. The post-structuralist hostility to all discussion of "origins," in fact, substitutes language for any other origin. Yet this is really nothing more than another philosophical effort to efface the female body. As Kelly Oliver observes: "From Socrates as midwife to a pregnant Zarathustra, philosophy is full of attempts to forget the connection between woman and life. The latest attempt to forget might be the poststructuralist scoff at the 'nostalgia' for origins."[34]

Throughout chapters 1 and 2, therefore, I undertake a return to the forgotten female body. I argue that Nietzsche and Derrida in particular try to construct a myth of the self-birthing male, and I endeavor to show how this is connected to their fetishistic views of capital. I insist that a reinstatement of the body within critical theory must begin with the maternal body—understood in both its biological and social senses—as the body which subverts the myth of male autonomy by exposing its dependence on an other and its relation to social labor.[35] In so doing, I try to bring together Marx's critique of the fetishisms of the commodity, money, and capital with feminist work on the maternal body. Along with a number of recent interventions in feminist thought, I share the view that the maternal body is the starting point of our collective body since it speaks to the shared biology and history of all of us.[36]

At the same time, I resist both the reduction of the female body to maternality and the idealization of the figure of the mother. The maternal body to which we are all ultimately connected is about aggression as much as love, and it is inscribed by orders of oppression. As much as this body must be named and acknowledged, we cannot afford to idealize it if we are to be true to the scars of history. Furthermore, the maternal body is also a productive (and not merely a reproductive) one. In chapter 3, I draw upon recent anthropological work which highlights the economic and culture-building labors of women by restoring gathering (as opposed to hunting) to its central role in human cultural development. My argument is not that women ought simply to be identified with the maternal body. It is, rather, that we need to return to those bodies most ruthlessly degraded and exiled by bourgeois thought—among them maternal bodies—if we hope to overturn the anticorporeal bias of the dominant forms of thinking about language and society. By showing that all of us are related to (and have been dependent upon) maternal bodies, I mean to affirm the corporeality of *spirit*, of the heroic, culture-building labors which the dominant tradition has ascribed to a disembodied, aristocratic, male intellect. And this involves recovering all the forgotten and degraded laboring bodies which are the hidden basis of idealist abstractionism. The maternal body simply—but crucially—provides a universal point of entry into our material and social embodiment. It allows us to see the irreducibility of the laboring body and to grasp the "body-as-matrix" of social relatedness.[37]

There is, however, a very real theoretical and political danger in all of this— the danger of setting up a utopian image of reconciliation, of the reintegration of mind and body, male and female, manual labor and intellect. All such impulses need to be resisted because, as Walter Benjamin warned, they reconcile us to a world which knows no reconciliation—a world of exploitation and misery, of suffering and pain. Language/mind and the body *are* radically separated within capitalist society. The body, as debased instrument of labor, is in fact subordinated to the abstracted and disembodied rationality of capitalist production. These are separations and subordinations theory cannot wish away. To attempt a theoretical reconciliation, a reintegration of language and the body, is to abstract emancipatory theory from a debased reality. Moreover, the setting up of a utopian image today invariably draws upon the association of woman with nature and the undefiled.[38] This idealization of woman as the other of a debased world in fact affirms the facts of female oppression. For Benjamin, the way around this is to turn to the brute material facts of our world—to ruins, corpses, scenes of death and destruction—in order to force the utopian impulse into the closest contact with a world of pain and ruination. Any redemptive impulses on the part of theory, in other words, must emerge through immersion in the brute facts of a suffering world.

One gets intimations of this in the powerful work of Columbian sculpture-artist Doris Salcedo. Witnessing and remembering those whose lives have been shattered and broken by government-sponsored terror, Salcedo's sculptures knit together bits and pieces of furniture such as chairs and tables, with animal bone and human hair. In this way, she evokes the material embodiment of people and things which can be so disturbingly disrupted by violence and terror. As one commentator describes her work, "Plates, clothing, buttons, zippers and bones are grafted, compressed and compacted into the surfaces of pieces of furniture. Chairs are covered by a fine skin of lace as if seared into wood, bones are embedded into the side of a cabinet, a spoon forced between the seams of wood of a kitchen bureau. We may say the furniture appears wounded, both physically and psychically."[39] In her recent work, Salcedo has taken to weaving human hair around pieces of furniture (in one remarkable piece the hair binds a baby's crib to a table) as if to indicate the fragile but essential connections between bodies and things which have been brutally and violently severed. The merest bits of bodies and things thus evoke the rich structure of embodiment without which there is no life.

Benjamin's profound theory of language, history, and the body works in a similar register. Drenched in embodiment, his work nonetheless refuses utopian images of whole bodies, of bodies reconciled with the natural and social worlds. In the fifth and final chapter of this study, I explore Benjamin's original theory of language, commodities and dreams of liberation. I argue that his work represents one of the most important resources we have for developing a critical materialist account of language which takes up issues of class, gender, and the body. Moreover, Benjamin's central political concern—for liberation from the rule of capital—is one which I share, and one which informs the political ethos that animates this book. Ultimately, I argue, the debates about language which have dominated social theory in recent decades dovetail with debates about the possibilities for anticapitalist liberation. By rigorously avoiding the real corporeal body, I suggest, postmodernist theory cannot possibly contribute to an emancipatory politics. For what could it mean to talk of liberation in the absence of real bodies and their labors and desires? What makes Benjamin so important is his insistence that liberation involves a return of language to the body, indeed, to a language *of* the body. At the same time, as I have intimated, such a return is a problem of practice, a practice informed by the explosive contact of memory with the future. And such a remembering of the body-which-is-yet-to-be opens up the most fundamental question of human existence. As Benjamin puts it in an essay on Kafka: "In every case it is a question of how life and work are organized in the human community."[40] When all is said and done, that is the central thesis of this book: that the question of language is a question of the body. And that all body questions are questions of life and work—and the prospects for their liberation.

1

NIETZSCHE, DARWIN, AND THE POSTMODERN FETISH OF LANGUAGE

A sign hovers at the threshold of contemporary social theory. This sign is an elusive thing. It laughs, it wails, it mocks its pursuer. If apprehended it turns silent, it vanishes like a ghostly apparition. It has a name, this sign: Friedrich Nietzsche. But does this name unlock an identity? Or do we find behind this name merely more names, more signs, in an infinite movement that knows neither beginning nor end?

The elusive Nietzsche, the Nietzsche who resists identity, the thinker behind whose mask one finds yet more masks, predominates among recent readings of the work of this most influential of German philosophers.[1] There is much that can be learned from such readings—not the least of which concerns the sensibilities of intellectuals caught up in "the postmodern condition." I have something to say about these sensibilities in the next chapter. For the moment, however, I wish to explore a different issue, one which takes us to the heart of a problem with much recent social theory: its evasion of the Darwinian challenge that provoked so much of Nietzsche's writing.

For here I detect something of a symptomatic silence, an avoidance that hints at a resistance. Read Michel Foucault, Gilles Deleuze, Jacques Derrida, and their followers when they discuss Nietzsche. The near total absence of Darwin's name is striking. This contrasts with many earlier readings. I take just two examples from the literature. First, Walter Kaufmann: "Nietzsche was aroused from his dogmatic slumber by Darwin, as Kant had been by Hume a century earlier." Second, R. J. Hollingdale: "Kant's philosophy was an answer to the challenge of British nihilism—and so was Nietzsche's. The adversary this time was Charles Darwin."[2] Darwin loomed large in the Nietzsche interpretations of Kaufmann, Hollingdale, and others. Today he can at best be found in the margins of Nietzsche studies. Yet, as deconstruction reminds us, any theoretical discourse is haunted by what it has marginalized; its ordering categories invariably refer, even if only negatively (i.e., by avoidance), to those it has excluded. What haunts postmodern Nietzscheanism, then, when it refuses to read Nietzsche through his response to Darwin?

Let me offer an hypothesis: the current avoidance of Darwin's impact on Nietzsche is a sign of the resistance of much social theory to the biological, the bodily, the "animal" in human beings. Post-structuralism, deconstruction, and their offshoots read Nietzsche within the framework of modern philosophies of consciousness, theories which attempt a radical separation of consciousness from its embodiment in beings who are the products of millions of years of natural evolution. Yet Nietzsche, I hope to show, resists such a reading. After all, Nietzsche is the first great figure in the history of philosophy to attempt to wrestle with, think through, and absorb the revolutionary impact of Darwinism.[3] In so doing, he moved the body to the center of his reflections on human beings, history, and society. By ignoring this dimension of his thinking, post-structuralist and deconstructive readings have radicalized the idealist aspects of Nietzsche's thought. There *is* a powerful idealist impulse running through Nietzsche's work; indeed it might be said ultimately to flatten out his thought, to eliminate its inner tensions. But this idealism coexists with, and struggles against, a materialism heavily indebted to Darwin. It is this Darwinian provocation that makes Nietzsche's assault on the philosophy of consciousness so powerful. And it is the avoidance of Nietzsche's Darwinian-materialist impulse that blunts the critical edge of much modern-day Nietzscheanism and reduces it to a largely harmless idealism.

DETHRONING CONCIOUSNESS: HOW NIETZSCHE TURNED DARWIN AGAINST PHILOSOPHY

Immanuel Kant's philosophy encapsulated for Nietzsche all that ailed modern thought. For in his monumental effort to preserve knowledge and truth, Kant had so delimited the scope of knowledge as to shake philosophical certainty to its foundations. "Despair of the truth," wrote Nietzsche, is the danger that "attends every thinker who sets out from the Kantian philosophy."[4] Why was this so?

As students of philosophy are taught, Kant was responding to the challenge laid down by David Hume, according to whom the experience of human beings in the world cannot provide a sufficient basis for formulating universal truths.

No amount of individual experience with objects can ever prove the truth, for example, of Newton's law of gravitation. The fact that my limited experience gives me occasion to believe this law to be true does not constitute a philosophical proof. All that experience provides is a basis for associating certain ideas with sensations and experiences in such a way as to produce "common sense" assumptions about the world in which we live. But commonsense assumptions and beliefs are not the same thing as incontrovertible and universal truths. Philosophy should thus forsake the search for eternal truths and rest content with working out commonsense principles for everyday life. Problems such as the nature of space, time, and causality are simply beyond the bounds of knowledge. Skepticism is the only rigorous, philosophical attitude toward such issues.

In his effort to resist thoroughgoing skepticism, Kant makes an enormous concession to Hume: he grants that the human mind can never have genuine knowledge of the way things are *in themselves*, independent of human experience. But, insists Kant, we can understand some of the universal properties of the mind itself. With this maneuver, Kant turns the quest for knowledge away from the world of things and back toward the knowing subject. Kant's is thus a "philosophy of consciousness" in the strict sense. His philosophy eschews the quest for knowledge of things outside the mind; instead he turns mind back on itself, pushes consciousness toward systematic self-reflection in order to attain knowledge not of things in the world, but merely of the mind's capacity for knowledge.[5] Granting Hume's claim that the finite existence of the individual can never exhaust the infinite possibilities of experience in the world of things, Kant seeks nonempirical objects of understanding, objects constituted by the mind. By abstracting from everything external to the thinking subject, we will arrive, he claims, at "objects" of knowledge which are pure products of the human mental apparatus. While Hume may have been right to reject the possibility of mind fully understanding things in the world, his failure was in not considering the case in which "the understanding might itself . . . be the author of the experience in which its objects are found."[6]

Kant calls his approach a "transcendental" one; his search is for knowledge that transcends the limited, partial, finite experience of the world available to any individual. To this end, he seeks knowledge of the universal structures of the mind, the knowing subject, which are the conditions of all experience of things in the world. Independent of and prior to any possible experience, such knowledge is *transcendental* since it transcends the world of empirical things and events. "I entitle *transcendental*," he writes, "all knowledge which is occupied not so much with objects as with the mode of our knowledge of objects." It is a condition of such a science of knowledge that "no concepts be allowed to enter which contain in themselves anything empirical."[7] Kant's critique of "pure reason" is thus radically divorced from sensible experience. It can make no claims about entities in the world, about "things-in-themselves." Things in the world are not the province of philosophical knowledge. Kant thereby rejoins an ancient philosophical tradition which separates the realm of the senses, the body, and everyday being-in-the-world from the realm of true thought. Yet, as Nietzsche sees, Kant's tortuous effort to save philosophy in fact ushers in its downfall.

This downfall is entailed in the extreme move through which Kant simultaneously humbled philosophy and tremendously exaggerated the independence of mind. The result is a form of idealism which collapses under its own weight. On the one hand, Kant has declared that philosophy can provide us with no knowledge of the world of objects, the senses, and everyday experience. But this can only induce a "despair of the truth" and "a gnawing and disintegrating skepticism and relativism," Nietzsche believes, since philosophy has now renounced its claim to understand existence (UM, 140). At the same time, Kant's exaggerated claim for human consciousness—that the understanding can know itself—is simply unsustainable. The understanding cannot know itself precisely because it is not "the author" of its own experience. Consciousness, as Darwin has shown, is a product of organic evolution; originating in the preconscious, in the empirical world, mind can never get to a point before that origin where it might be the author of the whole of its own experience. To treat consciousness as autonomous and self-determining is thus the wildest of metaphysical delusions.

This line of argument is key to the brilliance of Nietzsche's polemics. Nothing is a source of such freshness, originality, and vigor as his effort to think through the implications of Darwinism for philosophy. As this claim is at the heart of my reading of Nietzsche, and similarly central to my criticism of his reading by theorists like Martin Heidegger, Deleuze, Foucault, and Derrida, let me pause briefly here to review the relevant background.[8]

During the mid-1870s, Nietzsche undertook a significant intellectual reorientation. Putting into question what he saw as the naive antimodernism which had characterized his earlier thought, he plunged into a study of modern "scientific" currents such as positivism and Darwinism. A central role in this reorientation was played by Paul Rée, an enthusiastic Darwinian who sought to explain morality through the prism of natural evolution. In 1875, under Rée's influence, Nietzsche read some of the works of Ernst Heinrich Haeckel, a biologist and philosopher at the University of Jena, who had become a zealous popularizer of Darwinism.[9] "Nietzsche," Hollingdale writes, "accepted the fundamental implication of Darwin's hypothesis, namely, that mankind had evolved from the animals in a purely naturalistic way through chance and accident." In Darwin's theory of natural selection as a blind, law-governed process that had no goal or purpose, Nietzsche found a view of "evolution freed from every metaphysical implication."[10] And he was quick to grasp that this antimetaphysical outlook had explosive consequences for philosophy.

Yet Nietzsche soon realized that the truly revolutionary impact of Darwinism—which he registers with sparkling prose in *The Gay Science* (1882)—had been missed even by most of its adherents. He poured particular scorn on those who thought that moral philosophy could emerge unscathed, even strengthened, from its contact with Darwin. As early as his *Untimely Meditations* (1873–76), for example, he vigorously attacked the theologian David Strauss who, in *The Old Faith and the New* (1872), had attempted to reconstruct "faith" and morality in terms of a materialism heavily indebted to Darwin. Nietzsche condemns Strauss' effort as timid, cowering, insipid. Having embraced Darwinism and scientific materialism, he contends, Strauss should have seen his obligation to "take the phenomena of human goodness, compassion, love and self-abnegation, which do in fact exist, and explain them from his Darwinist presuppositions." Instead, he chose to "flee from the task of *explanation*" (UM, 29–30).

Nietzsche proceeds to turn Darwin against this alleged Darwinist. "An honest natural scientist, " he asserts, "believes that the world conforms unconditionally to laws, without however asserting anything as to the ethical or intellectual value of these laws." Since Darwin has shown that "man" is "a creature of nature and nothing else," it is incumbent upon the moralist to explain the emergence of morals from the premoral, of culture from nature. To presuppose that natural laws have ethical and intellectual value is the crudest dogmatism. A consistent scientific materialism must account for the origin and genealogy of morals in terms consistent with natural laws. Strauss' performance is dishonest and cowardly because he refuses to tell his readers what should follow from his scientific and materialist premises—that Darwinism announces the death of God and morality: "he does not dare to tell them honestly: I have liberated you from a merciful God, the universe is only a rigid machine, take care you are not mangled in its wheels! This he dares not do: so he has to call in the sorceress, that is to say metaphysics" (UM, 31, 30–31, 33). Nietzsche sees himself as the thinker who dares to make this announcement, who is willing to embrace scientific materialism all the way through to the end of metaphysics and the old morals. In the process, he finds that he can turn Darwin against Kant's efforts to preserve morality and truth from radical skepticism (or nihilism).

Kant, after all, had called upon the human mind to fully understand itself by developing absolute, universal knowledge about its own capacity to know. Yet, this attempt to turn human understanding into a complete realm of knowledge (self-knowledge) unto itself is, says Nietzsche, simply preposterous. It results in a "ridiculous overestimation and misunderstanding of consciousness." After all, consciousness is merely "the last and latest development of the organic." The task of the true thinker, one who dares really to think in the aftermath of Darwin and the death of God, is to recognize that "the human and animal past, indeed the whole primal age and past of all sentient being continues in me."[11] The independence and self-containment that Kant tries to grant to consciousness and knowledge shatter against the hard rock of Darwinism. The organs of knowledge are of a physical, corporeal nature. They are part of the empirical world, the world of things-in-themselves. Kant's attempt to free them from the realm of the empirical is nothing but dogmatic idealism since knowledge itself must be understood in the first instance in biological terms: "In order for a particular species to maintain itself and increase its power, its conception of reality must comprehend enough of the calculable and constant for it to base a scheme of behavior on it. The utility of preservation . . . stands as the motive behind the development of the organs of knowledge." It follows that "all our categories of reason are of sensual origin: derived from the empirical world." With this in mind Nietzsche proposes as a maxim to philosophy: "to start from the *body* and employ it as guide."[12]

Kant fails to consider the possibility that consciousness might be an adjunct, and not a particularly sophisticated one, of bodily needs and drives. He does not consider mind, ideas, knowledge from the standpoint of their utility for a species driven by the exigencies of self-preservation. Indeed, he has not entertained the possibility that his own philosophical inquiries might express something of the natural, organic history of the species. "It is high time," Nietzsche writes, "to replace the Kantian question, 'How are synthetic judgments *a priori* possible?' by another question, 'Why is belief in such judgments *necessary?*' "[13] Nietzsche proceeds to subject the evolution of ideas to Darwinian analysis. Just as nature produces random variations (mutations) in a species, only a few of which survive in the rare event that they improve an organism's adaptation to its environment, so "over immense periods of time the intellect produced errors. A few of these proved to be useful and helped preserve the species: those who hit upon or inherited these had better luck in their struggle for themselves and their progeny" (GS, 169). This is straightforward Darwinian reasoning (although, as I show in chapter 3, it is wrongly applied). Nietzsche makes no assumptions about "progress" or "improvement" in the evolution of a species; he eschews all teleological talk about a direction or rationality to natural selection. Those intellectual variations, or "errors," which proved helpful to the reproduction and survival of some members of a species and their offspring have tended to be preserved. The human organism is itself the product of an immemorial history of deviations from earlier forms. All we can say about these "errors" is that they have proved useful; human beings have made the mistake, however, of supposing such useful ideas to be true in some transcendent sense. But usefulness to a species is no indicator of objective truth.

Not only does Nietzsche turn the force of his Darwinian argument against the illusion of truth, he also uses it to attack prevailing notions of morality. Just like the idea of truth, so, he tells his reader, "your judgment 'this is right' has a pre-history in your instincts, likes, dislikes, experiences, and lack of experiences" (S, 263–64). Indeed, as he puts it in *Daybreak* (1881), "the beginnings of justice, as of prudence, moderation, bravery—in short, of all we designate as the *Socratic virtues* are *animal:* a consequence of that drive which teaches us to seek food and elude enemies."[14] Just as consciousness emerges out of the preconscious, morality grows out of the amoral, the struggle for existence. It, too, must be understood as something useful which has cloaked itself in deceptive guise. Yet the errors, illusions, and deceptions that consciousness has created for itself about "truth" and "morality" must themselves have been useful to human survival. Consequently, to think against such notions is both difficult and dangerous, for it means that the thinker will attempt to break away from, and live without, illusions that have over millennia proved useful, perhaps necessary, to human survival. This is one meaning of Nietzsche's statement that Darwin's ideas constitute a doctrine that is "true but deadly" (UM, 112). But there is more to it than this. For Nietzsche is also deeply worried that Darwinism represents a powerful buttress to Judeo-Christian ethics, democracy, socialism, feminism, and their cult of the poor and "the weak." This fear about the social and political impact of Darwinism creates terrific tension in Nietzsche's attitude toward the author of *The Origin of Species* and accounts for the many "anti-Darwin" statements in his writings and notebooks.[15]

Already, at the time of his *Untimely Meditations*, Nietzsche took up what he considered "deadly" about Darwinism: the radical historicizing of modern thought that Darwin signals. No longer is it possible to take "man" as a self-sufficient point of departure for thought. Man has dissolved into the history of the organic, and the beginning point of that history recedes endlessly. "Contemplation of history," writes Nietzsche, "has never flown so far, not even in dreams; for now the history of mankind is only the continuation of the history of animals and plants; even in the profoundest depths of the sea the universal historian still finds traces of himself as living slime." The consequences of this historicization of thought about humans and the world are dizzying: the collapse of all foundations, the slide of "man" into a history without beginning or end. Prior to Darwin, man had a place and a time; man was the highest form of life, the rational animal, the thinking being, the creature standing next to God. Now those foundations have collapsed, the horizon of man has disappeared. All temporal coordinates are gone, human beings no longer know their place in the universe or their time in the history of life. Everything is flux, the chaotic, purposeless becoming of matter, a nonsensical churning of primordial slime. Nietzsche believes he is unique in his capacity to stand in the center of this historicizing storm. He presents himself as the thinker who can bear the questions thrown up by Darwin's destruction of the human temporal horizon, his dissolution of man into infinite time. In *The Gay Science*, he provocatively poses some of these questions: "How could we drink up the sea? Who gave us the sponge to wipe away the entire horizon? What were we doing when we unchained the earth from its sun? Whither are we moving? Away from all suns? Are we not plunging continually? Backward, sideward, forward, in all directions? Is there still any up or down? Are we not straying as through an infinite nothing? . . . God is dead. God remains dead. And we have killed him" (GS, 181). By murdering God, man has created a vacuum in which he, the murderer, can himself become a god. The values of life, existence, being, no longer rest with God, they are up to man. But man wants to duck this terrifying responsibility, he wants to avoid taking God's place. Talking of the murder of God,

Nietzsche asks, "is not the greatness of this deed too great for us? Must we ourselves not become gods simply to appear worthy of it?" And he answers his questions with the observation " 'I have come too early' . . . This tremendous event is still on its way, still wandering; it has not yet reached the ears of men" (GS, 182).

It takes extraordinary intellectual and moral courage—a willingness to stand in the flux of infinite time, without foundations or certainties, and to legislate one's own values—to bear the weight of this world without foundations, argues Nietzsche. It requires exceptional individuals, individuals who have broken with the "herd instincts" which have preserved the species—hard, severe individuals who will throw their survival into jeopardy by renouncing the habits of the herd. History has reached a moment of truth, a crisis-point, at which the preparation of rare individuals—a new breed of masters, thinkers, statesmen, and warriors— is required. Yet at this moment of need, Darwinism preaches its stupid, plodding message of species-preservation, a message which discourages the preparation of a new breed.

"The kind of history at present universally prized," says Nietzsche in the *Untimely Meditations*, "is precisely the kind that takes the great mass-drives for the chief and weightiest facts of history." This is producing a society in the image of sniveling Christians and "socialist dolts," a society which preserves the majority— the weak who cannot bear the death of God—while extinguishing the strong and exceptional. Darwinism buttresses the slave instincts and herd morality and diminishes the rare breed by encouraging the writing of history "from the stand- point of the *masses* and seeking to derive the laws which govern it from the needs of these masses, that is to say from the laws which move the lowest mud- and clay-strata of society." For Nietzsche these masses and their history deserve contempt: they are of value only "as instruments in the hands of great men; for the rest, let the Devil and statistics take them!" (UM, 113)[16]

AGAINST DARWIN: "WILL TO POWER" AND NIETZSCHE'S IDEALISM

One reason for Nietzsche's polemics against Darwin has to do with the enor- mous weight Darwinism assigns to cooperation in the evolution of species, most notably humans. This emphasis on cooperation conflicts sharply with the so- called Social Darwinist idea to which Nietzsche was deeply attached—"the survival of the fittest," the notion that the strongest members of a species will predomi- nate. Nietzsche seems to have been well aware that this is not the thrust of Darwin's argument; he recognizes the tremendous importance the author of *The Descent of Man* attached to speech, language, cooperation, and social organiza- tion in human evolution. Over and over again, Nietzsche challenges the idea that self-preservation is the driving principle of natural selection. In place of self-preservation, he installs his principle of *will to power*: "Physiologists should think before putting down the instinct of self-preservation as the cardinal instinct of an organic being. A living thing seeks above all to *discharge* its strength—life itself is *will to power*. " Physiology and the theory of life, he writes elsewhere, have robbed science of a "fundamental concept, that of activity." By focusing on adaptation of organisms to their environment, "the essence of life, its *will to power*, is ignored."[17] True, he concedes, some members of the species, the weaker sort, do express their will to power by adapting to their environment, by seeking merely to survive rather than create. But the will to power is manifest differently by weak and strong members of a species. The weak strive for unity and cooperation, they seek to discipline the strong to the needs of the herd; the strong, on the other hand, promote disunity, differentiation, solitariness (WP, 346).

For millennia, claims Nietzsche, human history has been a story of the victory of the weak over the strong, herd-instincts over individualism, slave morality over aristocracy, the subjugation of the rare and exceptional to the vulgar and common.[18] But today, in the aftermath of the death of God, the development of hard, courageous individuals ready to accept the challenge of thinking against truth and morality requires reversing this state of affairs, subjugating the weak to the strong, breaking slave morality, and establishing a new race of masters. And Nietzsche does not shrink from spelling out the politics of his attack on slave morality, socialism, and democracy. "We simply do not consider it desirable that a realm of justice and concord should be established on earth," he declares. Such a society would be a banal, mediocre "realm of leveling and chinoiserie." He continues: "We count ourselves among conquerors; we think about the necessity for new orders, also for a new slavery . . . " (GS, 338). It is necessary to redraw sharp lines between rulers and ruled, masters and slaves. And this means a new aristocracy: "Every enhancement of the type 'man' has so far been the work of an aristocratic society—and it will be so again and again—a society that believes in the long ladder of an order of rank and differences in value between man and man, and that needs slavery in some sense or other" (BGE, 201).[19]

Yet the establishment of a new aristocracy and a new slavery will not be the accomplishment of any conventional politics. Nietzsche's political thinking becomes increasingly apocalyptic as he imagines scenarios in which millennia of herd-thinking and slave morality might be overturned. Such an overturning presupposes "upheavals, a convulsion of earthquakes, a moving of mountains and valleys, the like of which has never been dreamed." When this happens, politics and war will become one, and "there will be wars the like of which have never been seen on earth. It is only beginning with me that the earth knows *great politics*."[20] This political perspective, Nietzsche's "aristocratic radicalism," is evaded in most recent scholarship.[21] Similarly ignored is the way in which he employs the concept of the will to power in order to maintain key elements of Darwinism while breaking from its deadly, leveling implications. Yet this inattention is curious; it signals a desire to avoid the biological and materialist impulses animating so much of Nietzsche's work.

What Nietzsche attempts is to out-Darwin Darwin, to use naturalistic, biological reasoning—albeit of a metaphysical sort—to arrive at radically different conclusions about evolution and modern society. That is why he takes such pains to dispute the principle of self-preservation (which he suspects in part to be true). In *The Gay Science*, for example, he attacks "Darwinism with its incomprehensibly one-sided doctrine of the 'struggle for existence' "(GS, 292).[22] Self-preservation, he insists, is simply the form the will to power takes among the weak. "All the sick and sickly instinctively strive after a herd organization," he insists. But do not be fooled, Nietzsche cautions. The sick and the weak are acting just as aggressively when they unite and foster herd-morality, as are the strong when they try to break away from society by defying its rules. "The great and small" are always struggling over superiority, but for the small this means promoting the doctrine of self-preservation and the "moral" duty of the few, the strong, to the preservation of the many (GS, 292). The few, the rare, the strong and exceptional can assert their struggle for superiority, their will to power, only by rejecting herd-instincts, slave morality, the doctrine of self-preservation. In their place, they must affirm separation, differentiation, self-overcoming, the order of rank, a new nobility.

Darwinism thus stands condemned for the leveling implications of the principle of self-preservation. To accept this principle is to assign a single purpose to all human "types" which could then be shown to lead to unified languages, moral codes, and modes of social cooperation. Nietzsche wants to show that slave morality, herd instincts, democracy, and socialism are not the outgrowth of a unifying biological principle. To this end, he mobilizes a metaphysical biology that substitutes the chaotic principle of will to power for the unifying doctrine of self-preservation. And on the basis of this principle, he affirms that there are different drives and impulses animating the behavior of the weak and the strong, the lower and higher types. But how is it possible that the human "types" should be so different as to have fundamentally different biological drives? Nietzsche circumnavigates this problem by declaring that every human body consists of a multiplicity of conflicting and competing drives and impulses. The body itself is chaotic, it is not unified at the instinctive level. The apparent "unity" or "identity" of a human type is the product of the dominance established within the individual of one drive over another. But why this struggle for dominance within the body? Because life is will to power, self-overcoming, the drive for superiority. Nietzsche claims that will to power is the meta-instinct animating all the "lesser" drives and passions. However, the majority of humankind flees this corporeal chaos, this struggle within their bodies and minds; they try to stabilize a sense of self and seek the reassurance of the herd. In so doing, they affirm self-preservation and herd-life as the form of their will to power.

Will to power, in other words, is not a unitary drive, but a chaos. There is, of course, a monism of sorts here. But it is the monism of difference, division, competition, the drive for domination. Amidst the chaos of conflicting drives within the individual—a chaos in which each instinct seeks dominance—one or another of these drives must win predominance (however temporarily). There is, in other words, a system of dominance, or as Nietzsche calls it, an "aristocracy in the body," based upon ruled and ruling drives and passions. The lower types are those in whom the instinct for unity and herd-life has prevailed, while the higher types are those whose bodies and characters are ruled by the drive for separation and differentiation, for surpassing and overcoming the herd-like mass. Nietzsche often seems to believe that both impulses are necessary for life (we are reminded here of the tension between Appolonian and Dionysian that runs through his thought beginning with *The Birth of Tragedy*). But the danger for modern humans is that the creative, life-generating energies of the few will be suffocated by the stabilizing, herd-like tendencies of the mob. While the herd may be necessary to the formation of a stable society, they are analogous to the inert matter to which the sculptor gives form and life: mere material for the form-givers, the artists, and creators. The problem, however, is that the highest types are today the most fragile, their existence is the most imperiled by a society based upon "organized herd instincts" and the "timidity of the weak." And this is why "man as a species is not progressing," since the higher types are being wiped out by the herd (WP, 364).

The overwhelming weaknesses of Nietzsche's argument here should be self-evident. Defiant assertion replaces serious argumentation; he hectors, he exclaims, he declares, he bullies. His persuasive powers retreat behind agitated proclamations: this is truth, he exclaims, because I so declare it.[23] Indeed, the whole notion of the will to power violates the materialist premises he mobilizes against Kant by invoking a mechanism of evolution which is itself not explicable in evolutionary terms—the very move for which Nietzsche attacked Strauss.[24] Ironically, it is this flimsy doctrine of will to power which has moved to the center of the new Nietzscheanism, the post-structuralist/post-modernist Nietzsche of recent years.[25]

The Nietzsche embraced by postmodernists is the thinker who, turning away from a dialogue with natural science, resorts to highly charged rhetorical moves. His philosophy then becomes an aesthetic and political construction, one designed to overpower its readers. At these moments, Nietzsche's texts turn most ironical; he mocks the very notions of evidence, explanation, and truth; he presents his claims as simply the most powerful and courageous expressions of will to power available to humankind. I can't "prove" my point, he seems to concede, but I can impose it. This requires philosophizing "with a hammer;" it means that each of his books should function as "a grand declaration of war."[26] After all, there is no truth of the matter, there is only the self-affirming will to truth and power; and he, Nietzsche, intends to prevail in the battle of wills to truth.

Nietzsche's move toward this sort of grandiose self-assertion, which gets increasingly pronounced in his last writings, is merely a more dramatic and ironic version of the flight "from the task of explanation" for which he attacked Strauss. For this reason it is worth pausing to inspect the line of argument Nietzsche does advance. And this means resisting the rhetorical spell of his highly charged declarations by asking what he actually tells us about the will to power.

In opposition to what he takes to be "Darwinian" accounts of morality, Nietzsche informs us that knowledge of the present-day utility of an organ teaches us nothing about its origin. The fact that moral codes can be shown to be useful today in preserving social organization, does not mean that they originated for this purpose. "The 'evolution' of a thing, a custom, an organ" he writes, "is thus by no means its *progressus* toward a goal" (GM, 77; see also WP, 343, and D, 125). Yet, as one commentator has pointed out, "this is pure Darwin"— if we subtract "Nietzsche's characteristic huffing and puffing about some power subduing and becoming master."[27] Only strict adaptationism, or what Stephen Jay Gould has described as "cardboard Darwinism" believes that biological structures and organs were formed for present purposes. Indeed, this would be to write the history out of natural selection. As Gould explains, strict adaptationism

> . . . wallows in the most serious logical error of historical reconstruction, the same error that sinks sociobiology—the equation of current utility with historical origin, or the idea that we know why a structure evolved once we understand how it works now. . . .

> The fallacy of inferring historical origin from current utility is best expressed by noting that many, if not most, biological structures are co-opted from previous uses, not designed for current operations. Legs were fins, ear bones were jaw bones and jaw bones were gill-arch bones. . . .[28]

Indeed, as Gould points out elsewhere, Darwin recognized that the "oddities and imperfections" of organisms were the best proof that they had developed over long periods of time, that they had a history. If every structure and function seemed perfectly to "fit" the needs of the organism, then this would buttress ideas about their design by a creating intelligence, a god. "But, Darwin reasoned, if organisms have a history, then ancestral stages should leave remnants behind. Remnants of the past that don't make sense in present terms—the useless, the odd, the peculiar, the incongruous—are the signs of history."[29] So, Darwin was at pains to distinguish utility from origin.

Yet, Nietzsche's confusion on this point might be forgiven, as it is a quite commonplace misunderstanding of Darwinism. But his confusion is not innocent. In rejecting cardboard Darwinism, Nietzsche is really trying to smuggle in his claim that will to power is the driving force of natural selection—not successful adaptation to an environment (what he calls "self-preservation"). In order to replace all the mundane, herd-like talk of "utility" with his doctrine of self-overcoming, he shifts to a voluntarist view of natural selection which is indebted to the tired-old Lamarckian notion of the inheritance of acquired characteristics.

It is instructive in this regard that one of the few references to biological thought in contemporary Nietzscheanism appears in Gilles Deleuze's *Nietzsche et la philosophie*. Discussing the will to power, Deleuze notes that Nietzsche preferred the evolutionary theory of Jean-Baptiste Lamarck to that of Darwin. Whereas Darwin saw the driving force of evolution in the "wholly reactive" principle of adaptation to environment, Lamarck posited "a truly active plastic force" of a higher order than adaptation. Indeed, Deleuze remarks that Nietzsche held this active, transformative force to be the "noble" principle of evolution (while adaptation represents its base principle). Evolution is thus driven by two different forces: a noble, active, and energizing one on the one hand, and a slavish, reactive, stabilizing one on the other.[30] As we have seen, these two forces are themselves for Nietzsche just different modes of will to power, the modes appropriate to different human types. At no point does Deleuze inquire further as to the meaning of Nietzsche's Lamarckianism. But its purpose is made quite clear in *Beyond Good and Evil* where Nietzsche tells us that "one cannot erase from the soul of a human being what his ancestors liked most to do and did most constantly." This is clearly a claim on behalf of the Lamarckian idea that members of a species can inherit behavioral characteristics developed by their ancestors, that is, that acquired traits can be biologically transmitted. "It is simply not possible," he continues, "that a human being should not have the qualities and preferences of his parents and ancestors in his body..." (BE, 213, 214).[31] It is the last three words which are crucial here: *in his body*. After all, there is nothing especially radical about the suggestion that acquired traits might be *culturally* transmitted from one generation to the next. Indeed, as Gould has suggested, there is an important sense in which "human cultural evolution is Lamarckian—the useful discoveries of one generation are passed directly to offspring by writing, teaching, and so forth."[32] But Nietzsche's claim is a more radical one: that these traits are biologically transmitted, that the individual inherits them in his body. But why should this be so important to Nietzsche?

Nietzsche needs the Lamarckian idea in order to develop an *aristocratic biology*. Were he simply to assert that acquired traits—moral codes, behavioral characteristics, dislikes, preferences, languages, arts, trades, world views—could be culturally transmitted, then he would have to accept that in principle all individual members of a species might have access to a common cultural stock. But by insisting that acquired characteristics are biologically inherited, he is able to claim that the species contains two "types" and that these types are close to the point of differentiation into two identifiably different species—or, as he often prefers, different "races." Indeed, immediately after the sentence in which he claims that an individual can inherit the qualities and preferences of his ancestors "in his body," Nietzsche writes: "this is the problem of race" (BGE, 214). And this enables him to produce his severe diagnosis of what ails "European man": race-mixing, the inter-breeding of types encouraged by democratization. As a counterforce, Nietzsche advocates the breeding of a new race/species of men. But to be bred, the "higher type" must also exist, and Nietzsche insists over and over again that this is the case. In the *Untimely Meditations*, he suggests that these higher types represent a break from animality: "They are those true men, those who are no longer animal, the philosophers, artists and saints: nature which never makes a leap, has made its one leap in creating them" (UM, 159).

But, while nature is creating a higher human type, "the democratic mingling of classes and races" and the associated "intermarriage of masters and slaves" is undermining nature, producing "an age of disintegration" in which "human beings have in their bodies the heritage of multiple origins."[33] Culture is thwarting nature, democratic mingling and intermarriage are preventing the biological transmission of the highest cultural possibilities. This is why "the order of rank" must be restored: the higher biological types cannot differentiate themselves from the herd if democratic leveling continually mixes races. The task therefore is breeding (WP, 501). So taken by this idea is Nietzsche that he declares, "I write for a species of man that does not yet exist: for the 'masters of the earth'." He goes on to advocate "international racial unions whose task will be to rear a master race" (WP, 503, 504). This perspective animates Nietzsche's manifesto, *Thus Spoke Zarathustra*. Indeed, he suggests there that "superman" (or "the overman") stands to man as man does to the ape: "*I teach you the Superman.* Man is something that should be overcome. . . . What is the ape to men? A laughing-stock or a painful embarrassment. And just so shall man be to the Superman: a laughing-stock or a painful embarrassment" (Z, 41–42).

But note the injunction in this passage: man is something that *should* be overcome. Nietzsche is not invoking an automatic process of natural selection which is bringing about the emergence of a new species from the species "man." On the contrary, he is positing a task, a challenge: the overcoming of man. This signals the voluntarism running through the whole of his argument in this area, a voluntarism which dovetails with his Lamarckianism. For Nietzsche suggests that the higher types must create themselves—and he means this quite literally. Recall the passage from the *Genealogy of Morals* in which he criticizes modern science because it has "robbed" physiology of "a fundamental concept, that of *activity*." Recall as well his emphasis on activity over adaptation and reaction. Nietzsche wants to resist mechanistic images of evolution which overestimate "the influence of 'external circumstances' " (WP, 344). It is his purpose to raise activity, the will, the drive to create oneself, to unimagined heights. To this end, he contrasts man-the-product-of-nature with man-the-self-creator.[34] Whereas members of the herd are governed by their sense of submission to natural laws, the higher types obey only their own laws, they are self-legislators,

self-creators. Indeed, this is what Nietzsche means in commending active nihilism: after the death of God, the majority have chosen the illusion of natural
morality, but a minority understand that there are no grounds for universal
moral codes. Recognizing this, they have taken upon themselves the most
dangerous task—to live without foundations, to become their own foundation,
to accept the responsibility for creating themselves. And this can only mean
stretching out over the abyss, living in the nothingness that exists in place of
God, and becoming "those we are—human beings who are unique, incompa-
rable, who give themselves laws, who create themselves" (GS, 266). Nietzsche's
call to create is also an injunction to destroy. The self-creators must wage war
against the suffocating forces of the herd so that "there should be more and
more war and inequality among" men (Z, 124–25). In this "war," in this battle
to restore rank, to differentiate types, to break the new men away from the
herd, many will die. Indeed, death on a mass scale would be an indicator of the
progress of life (GM, 78).

Putting aside what is politically objectionable about it for the moment, all
this talk of supermen, higher types, self-creation, and grand politics encounters
a crucial theoretical problem: how is this hyper-voluntarism to be maintained on
the basis of a materialist critique of idealism? Having emphasized the bodily, the
sensual and the corporeal against Kant, how is Nietzsche to sustain the idea of
a new species creating itself? He can do so only by radicalizing the voluntarist
and idealist elements in his thought.

This becomes especially clear when we consider the way in which Nietzsche
starts to dissolve the body into interpretation. Having used materialism to debunk Kant and his followers, he dramatically shifts gears. Kant, as we have seen,
acknowledges that he can make no claims about the truth of things in themselves, he accepts that thinking subjects can only see the world through the
perceptual and cognitive lenses with which they are endowed. All experience of
things outside ourselves, therefore, involves a translation of the raw data of
experience into terms that our faculties of knowledge can process. In Nietzsche's
terms, the Kantian position means that humans have no alternative but to *interpret* sensations from the world outside themselves. But Kant argues that this
need not be the case when the human mind attempts to know its own universal
structures of perception and cognition. While there is always a mismatch, a lack
of correspondence, between the human mind and objects outside it, this does not
apply to mind reflecting on itself. There we find a correspondence, indeed an
identity, between the subject and object of knowledge. Nietzsche, as we have
seen, disputes this claim. By showing that the mind is governed by bodily drives
it doesn't plan or direct, Nietzsche deprives it of the autonomy to understand
itself. Even in trying to understand itself, mind must interpret something it
doesn't create—the bodily drives and impulses that motivate the will to know.
Try as he might, Kant can never escape the fact that all striving for knowledge
involves a finite and relative act of interpretation.

Kant goes off the rails, in other words, when he tries to find a sphere of pure facts, a realm free of interpretation where objects and their concepts coincide. Yet, "facts is precisely what there is not," Nietzsche exclaims, "only interpretations." And this is because knowledge is tied up with existence. "Our apparatus for acquiring knowledge," he proclaims, "is not *designed* for 'knowledge'"; it is driven, after all, by need, interest, passion. All we can legitimately say is that our apparatus for acquiring knowledge is useful to human preservation, but this entirely begs the question of truth. What we call truth, argues Nietzsche, is merely a way in which the will to power overcomes the chaos in its midst, imposes an order on sensations, and provides a stable framework for life: "interpretation is itself a means of becoming master of something." It follows that "knowledge works as a tool of power" (WP, 267, 273, 342, 266).

Yet, this line of argument dissolves Nietzsche's materialist emphasis on the body. Once everything is reduced to interpretation (as will to power), nothing can escape this reduction. How could Nietzsche halt interpretation once it gets to the body, how could he claim to find a solid foundation on which the whole interpreting, commanding, and surpassing activity of will to power could be grounded? Must not the body itself be an interpretation, a product of will to power? Nietzsche seems to have reckoned with the force of these questions. And when he is most wound up about will to power, he does not shrink from the radical idealism their answers entail.

Nevertheless, Nietzsche's embrace of the "everything is interpretation" position is far from consistent. And for good reason: its anchoring in the body is what imparts such a powerful charge to his critique of idealism. That is why his argument so regularly gravitates back to the body. It is understandable, therefore, when commentators present Nietzsche as arguing that all interpretations "are the result of unconscious instinctual operations."[35] Indeed, at the very moments when his thought is moving toward an extreme idealism, Nietzsche often shifts toward a hard (or vulgar) materialism that emphasizes eating, diet, digestion, the bowels. Perhaps sensing that he risks blunting the cutting edge of his radical insistence on physiology and the body, he tries to hold together the absurd idealism of the will to power that overcomes everything and makes its world, and a hard, physiological materialism. In this mode, he will often try to link the will to power to the body by treating true genius as a return to instinct, and herd morality as antibiological (see WP, 243, 33).

It is clear that a theoretical conundrum confronts Nietzsche in this area. Put simply, his commitment to will to power as self-overcoming must contend with the problem of the self and the role the body plays in anchoring it. After all, if "the total character of the world . . . is in all eternity chaos" (GS, 168), then what justification is there for assuming that anything resembling a *self* endures across the temporal moments of meaningless, chaotic becoming? Nietzsche seems dazzled by this question, at once recognizing its force while trying to evade its unrelenting logic. So, in a polemic against "the despisers of the body" in *Thus Spoke*

Zarathustra, he asserts: "I am body entirely and nothing beside." And he continues further into the same chapter: "Behind your thoughts and feelings, my brother, stands a mighty commander, an unknown sage—he is called *Self*. He lives in your body, he is your body" (Z, 61, 62). This insistence on a relative stability, coherence, and identity of the bodily self is the solution favored by Alexander Nehemas in his influential study, *Nietzsche: Life as Literature*.[36] It is, to be sure, an attractive solution, one that minimizes the idealist dynamic of Nietzsche's doctrine of will to power. It is also, however, a less than fully convincing one. Consider, first, the overwhelming evidence of Nietzsche's critique of the notion of the "subject." Nietzsche tells us that "to posit an interpreter behind the interpretation" is an "invention," a "hypothesis"; he describes the idea of the subject as "the fiction that many similar states in us are the effect of one substratum." Similarly, he attacks the "false observation" that "it is *I* who do something, suffer something, 'have' something"; and he maintains that there is "no subject but an action." Indeed, Nietzsche's view is that the very idea of the subject is a metaphysical illusion produced by grammar and speech (WP, 267, 269, 294, 337; BGE, 24; TI, 48). Thus, we are returned to the same problem: what self does the will to power overcome, if the self is an illusion, if everything is chaos, multiplicity, nonidentity? Henry Staten captures the force of this dilemma when he asks, in light of Nietzsche's attack on the concept of a preexisting self, "in what sense could one then speak of 'appropriating,' 'becoming stronger'? Who or what is it that would grow, appropriate, satisfy its will to power? If there is to be a sensation of growth, there must be a *substratum* of change." Yet, as we have seen, Nietzsche attacks the whole idea of such a substratum, the notion of some existential-experiential level at which a being can be said to persist in any kind of meaningfully unified sense. However, as Staten notes, "only if it retained some sort of 'memory' of its previous state could it feel that it had increased; in that case it would retain some form of identity with the previous state and no radical self-surpassing would have taken place."[37]

It is important to be clear about what is at stake here. Nietzsche's doctrine of will to power is designed to overcome the vacuum created by the death of God; it is meant to enable the higher types to "become gods," as he puts it in the *Gay Science*. For this reason, it is inadequate to reduce his concept of self-overcoming to commonplace ideas about self-development. Nietzsche is concerned to create a higher type capable of living with permanent flux, chaos and becoming, a type that can survive in the midst of nothingness. To this end, the human type itself must be overcome and a higher race of "supermen" ("overmen") created. And, given that everything is chaos, this means that these new men will *become* infinite change and chaos. Their identities will become nonidentities; they will transcend everything fixed and stable. But this poses a problem for their effort to legislate values, to rule the world by creating a "meaning" for life. After all, to draw up a new set of rules or a new moral system is to attempt to bring movement to a standstill. If the new men are to create new meanings, therefore, these cannot take the form of a code or a new set of moral tables; they can be nothing more than the act of creation itself. Indeed, that is the new meaning: never-ending self-creation. The new men will *be* change itself, they will endlessly create themselves, they will never *be* themselves. Yet, as we have seen, this radical dissolution of identity creates major problems. In steering away from anchorage in any substratum that could sustain a self, Nietzsche's doctrine starts to cross over into mysticism. Once he has dissolved the self and its body into the activity of interpretation, he has no way back to a "self" that overcomes itself. And this threatens to subvert his whole doctrine. For this reason, he veers back sharply from time to time to "the body," even though he has made a nonsense of such a notion.

We can see Nietzsche struggle with this problem in one of his most influential works, *The Genealogy of Morals*. In the First Essay of that book, he contends that every moral code, "every table of values, every 'thou shalt' known to history or ethnology requires first a physiological investigation and interpretation rather than a psychological one." He picks up this theme again in the Third Essay where he argues that the principle underlying slave morality and the Judeo-Christian ethic is resentment (*ressentiment*). And resentment, he insists, has itself a "physiological cause"; perhaps, he suggests, it lies in "some disease of the *nervus sympathicus*, or in an excessive secretion of bile, or in a deficiency of potassium sulphate and phosphate in the blood, or in an obstruction in the abdomen which impedes the blood circulation, or in degeneration of the ovaries." It doesn't matter that the individual experiences his resentment as the result of a "psychological pain"; this is "*not* the fault of his psyche but, to speak crudely, more probably even that of his belly." Yet, just when he is engaged in this most reductionist kind of materialism, Nietzsche pulls up abruptly and ends this section claiming that even with "such a conception" as the physiological one he has just outlined, it is still possible to "be the sternest opponent of all materialism" (GM, 55, 127, 129; see also GS, 186, 193).

There is only one way in which these crudely physiological arguments might sustain an antimaterialist stance: by absorbing the body into consciousness. And this is exactly what Nietzsche does in the final sections of *Genealogy*. Talking, for example, of the context in which Europe will come to know "two centuries" of turmoil and convulsion, he describes all of this happening "as the will to truth gains self-consciousness"(GM, 161). Indeed, that is the only way to dissolve the body into interpretation: by making the instinctive drive for power, truth, and mastery something that the self-conscious individual wills, to arrive, in other words, at will willing itself. The higher types are thus said to make themselves. In so doing, they "create" their own bodies too—by imposing an interpretation on them and by making themselves masters whose acquired traits can be passed on to their offspring.

Nietzsche's argument in this area rejoins his early aestheticism, particularly as manifest in *The Birth of Tragedy* with its memorable statement that "only as an aesthetic phenomenon are existence and the world justified"—a statement which he commends in his "Attempt at a Self-Criticism" (1886).[38] True, Nietzsche wants to say that the higher types, the self-creators, bursting with life and Dionysian energy, are especially attuned to their emotions and instincts (e.g. TI, 83). But, having dissolved everything into interpretation there is little sense in which he can preserve instinct and emotion as raw data that are not themselves simply interpretations. After all, will to power wills everything—body, instinct, taste, values. As Eric Blondel has argued, for Nietzsche "the will to power is interpretation to which everything 'is led back'." And it follows from this that, notwithstanding all the talk of the body and sensuality, "the images of physiology provide not a foundation for materialism, but a metaphysics of the will to power as interpretation."[39] And this metaphysics of will to power ultimately defeats Nietzsche's materialism. Despite his efforts to restrain his metaphysics, to tie it to the body and to instincts, the logic of his idealism ultimately prevails. Perhaps nowhere is this more apparent than in *Thus Spoke Zarathustra* where he tells us that "the spirit now wills its own will" (Z, 55). What is crucial about the higher types is not that they will a specific goal, as this would be to limit themselves, to tie themselves to a finite objective, which would in turn have to be overcome. The key to the higher types is that they have the will to will.[40] Genuine willing is thus indifferent to the content of what is willed. Nietzsche's is an aesthetics of form over content, a formalism writ large. The goal of a creative act is the act of creation itself. The true artist does not aspire to create something outside himself (and for Nietzsche it *is* a him); no, the true artist seeks simply to create . . . himself. The self-creating self is Nietzsche's ideal. And the solipsism of this position is transparent: "in the final analysis one experiences only oneself" (Z, 173). Little surprise, then, when Nietzsche endorses an explicit narcissism. He is only being consistent, after all, when he writes: "And do you want to know what 'the world' is to me? Shall I show it to you in my mirror?" (WP, 549–50)

This can only mean that the higher types make their own bodies—through language. By writing their own stories, giving shape and form to themselves, willing the interpretations that shall be their lives, the higher types write their own bodies. Rodolphe Gasché has captured the logic of this position, albeit uncritically. Discussing *Ecce Homo*, he points out that it "is nothing other than an attempt to constitute a body for oneself, by writing oneself in granite words." In elaborating upon the meaning of this claim, he refers to "Nietzsche's written body," to his "book-body" (i.e. the body that is written into being through his books), to his "text-body," and he describes the Nietzschean project as a drive "to make oneself a body of signs."[41] These formulations nicely capture Nietzsche's move to absorb the body into language—his own language to be precise. And this absorption of the body into language is all about radically differentiating the self from others, all about the elimination of alterity. This entails, as Gasché puts it, "a spiritual gestation," a project of "giving birth to ourselves as our own type," a work that continues "until we give birth to our body as something completely *mine* which belongs to no one."[42] Whatever else this might be, it is clearly a radical linguistic idealism, one that involves a leap out of biology, the material fact of our birth, our history, and our inherence in others.

The individual experiencing himself, never outside himself, but always overcoming himself—that is Nietzsche's ideal. There is a disquieting logic to this ideal: it culminates in what has been called a "sadomasochistic subjectivity."[43] For self-overcoming must overcome everything inside and outside the self—others, moral codes, the world, the body, its own history and identity. One aspect of this has been grasped by postmodernist commentators: the idea of the self as an endless play of self-creation. But there is a more troubling side that such commentators generally ignore: the aggressiveness, harshness, and anger that Nietzsche's will to power directs toward the self. The flip side of the narcissism of the will that "experiences only itself" is a rage against everything about that self that is tied to a body and a history, everything that "roots" the heroic individual, that ties and connects him to others, everything that gives him an identity: body, history, social relations, memory. Genuine self-commanding and self-obeying involves "a real mastery and subtlety in waging war against oneself." Having overcome the herd, having rejected others—except as means to their own self-creation—the noble spirits confront the most difficult task: not to be contained by their own finitude, their own limited "selves." And it is this— Nietzsche's aggressive desire to break through his own body and self—which would seem to account for his surprising fascination with "the ascetic priest" in *The Genealogy of Morals.*

While readers of *Genealogy* usually pick up quickly on Nietzsche's critique of ascetics as despisers of the body, they less readily grasp another movement at work in this text: its extreme admiration for those who really can live ascetically, for those who can make themselves in defiance of their bodies.[44] In the Second Essay of *Genealogy* Nietzsche argues that conscience is the product of a war against the body, the result of "a forcible sundering" of the human being from its "animal past" (G, 85). Yet, Nietzsche abruptly turns rhapsodic about this development. The joy the ascetic achieves through self-repression and self-control, through "delight in imposing a form upon oneself," is the result of a "strange new beauty and affirmation." And this delight of "the self-denier, the self-sacrificer," he says, "is tied to cruelty" (GM, 87–88). Nietzsche returns to this theme in the Third Essay of the work where he claims that philosophy would not have been possible "without ascetic wraps and cloak," without "the peculiar, withdrawn attitude of the philosopher, world-denying, hostile to life, suspicious of the senses, freed from sensuality." Extolling the accomplishments of the ascetic for whom "pleasure is felt and *sought* in ill-constitutedness, decay, pain, mischance, ugliness, voluntary deprivation, self-mortification, self-flagellation, self-sacrifice," he claims that we here encounter "a discord that wants to be discordant, that *enjoys* itself in this suffering and even grows more self-confident and triumphant the more its own presupposition, its physiological capacity for life, *decreases*" (GM, 116, 117–18). These are tremendously charged passages. A will that wants to become master "not over something in life but over life itself"—is not this the model for Nietzsche's higher type? And does not his description of a will that "grows more self-confident and triumphant" as it denies "its own presupposition"—its body, its "physiological capacity for life"—fairly glow with admiration? Not surprisingly, Nietzsche goes on to tell us that "this ascetic priest, this apparent enemy of life, this *denier*—precisely he is among the greatest *conserving* and yes-creating forces of life" (GM, 120–21). It is to the eternal credit of asceticism that it created a meaning for life; the ascetic's "aversion to life," after all, "remains a *will*" (GM, 163–4). Self-denial as affirmation: this is the force of Nietzsche's argument concerning the will to power. So threatening is the modern situation, so dangerous is the task of stretching out over the abyss, of affirming nothingness, chaos and flux as one's identity, that the most extreme self-denial is required. Self-overcoming emerges as self-abnegation, as ascetic denial of the very presupposition of life—the body.

Moving in this register, Nietzsche radicalizes that moment in his thought which flees from the body and animality. In the third of his *Untimely Meditations*, he asserts that "As long as anyone desires life as he desires happiness he has not yet raised his eyes above the horizon of the animal." Unlike humans, animals "suffer from life and yet do not possess the power to turn the goad of life against themselves and understand their existence metaphysically." Turning the goad of life against themselves is the task of the higher types, and this involves "the redemption of nature from the curse of the life of the animal." In this vein, he describes "true men" as *"those who are no longer animal, the philosophers, artists and saints"* (UM, 157, 159). "Those who are no longer animal" . . . those who overcome "the curse of the life of the animal"—here again we encounter the ascetic ideal. And it reemerges even in *The Anti-Christ*, that work most devoted to Nietzsche's attack on Christianity where he insists that "the most spiritual human beings, as the *strongest*, find their happiness where others would find their destruction: in the labyrinth, in severity towards themselves and others" (AC, 188). Surely it is this ascetic ideal that motivates Zarathustra's dictum, "deeper into pain" (Z, 175). And just as surely, this ascetic revolt against animality and the body is integrally connected to Nietzsche's misogyny, his hatred for woman, mother, birth. But before turning to that question, it is worth noting how the reading of Nietzsche that has been especially influential in postmodernist circles—that of Martin Heidegger—extends Nietzsche's revolt against biology and animality.

Heidegger was well aware of Nietzsche's attention to the human body. But he insisted that those who read Nietzsche's discussions of life and the body in biological terms are caught up in an "illusion" according to which "the biological element is taken to be what is unique and real."[45] For Heidegger, the organismic character of the body is something animalistic and inessential; the body must be understood metaphysically. With this assertion, he then undertakes to detach Nietzsche entirely from Darwinism: ". . . all Darwinistic thought processes must be extruded. Above all, Nietzsche's idea of viewing man and world as such primarily from the perspective of the body and animality in no way means that man originates from the animal and more precisely from the 'ape'—as if such a doctrine could say anything about man at all!"[46]

This passage is typically Heideggerian in its substitution of grandiose declaration for reasoned argumentation. Let us, however, briefly consider Heidegger's claim that Nietzsche "in no way" means to suggest "that man originates from the animal and more precisely from the 'ape' " in light of a single passage from *Daybreak*. There Nietzsche writes: "Formerly one sought the feeling of the grandeur of man by pointing to his divine *origin:* this has now become a forbidden way, for at its portal stands the ape, together with other gruesome beasts . . ." And for those who want to suggest that man can escape from his animal origin, Nietzsche has a dismissive retort: "The becoming drags the has-been along with it: why should an exception to this eternal spectacle be made on behalf of some little star or for any little species upon it! Away with such sentimentalities!" (D, 32) Heidegger thus stands condemned for sentimentality—and rightly so. But there is something else at work here: Heidegger's "embarrassment over the human body," as Michel Haar puts it.[47] In his perceptive examination of Heidegger's reworking of Nietzsche's theory of art, Haar has shown that Heidegger attempts to liquidate the active and bodily characteristics of artistic creation. Haar documents Nietzsche's commitment to the idea that art involves physical sensation, an intensification of bodily strength and pleasure, and his view that sexual energies are sublimated in artistic production. But Heidegger will have none of this: "When Heidegger does allude— and with embarrassment—to inescapably biological conditions, such as intensified bodily strength, pleasure, sensuality, animal well-being, or, more rarely, malaise, he always attempts to bring them back to the psychic, or else to show that they must be 'restrained, overcome and surpassed'."[48] Indeed, this is merely one point at which we encounter a recurring Platonism in Heidegger's thought, a Platonism that has been inherited by much postmodernist theory. For all his railing against Socrates and Plato for having participated in the forgetting of Being which allegedly characterizes Western philosophy, Heidegger's reading of Nietzsche (and his philosophy more generally) shares with Plato a *forgetting of the body.*

And this forgetting of the body is accomplished by a radical demarcation of human from animal. In his 1934–35 course on Friedrich Hölderlin, for example, Heidegger announces that "the leap from living animal to speaking human being is as great as, or greater than, that from lifeless stone to living being."[49] Elsewhere, he informs us that our ears, eyes, and hands have nothing essential in common with animal organs; indeed, he insists that animals do not hear, see, or touch—at least not in the real sense (which has nothing to do with the body). With respect to ears and hearing, for example, Heidegger instructs us that

> We hear when we are "all ears." But "ear" does not here mean the acoustical sense apparatus. The anatomically and physiologically identifiable ears, as the tools of sensation, never bring about a hearing, not even if we take this as an apprehending of noises, sounds and tones. Such apprehending can be neither anatomically established nor physiologically demonstrated, nor in any way grasped as a biological process at work within the organism.[50]

On a number of occasions, Heidegger also insists that animals do not "see."[51] He similarly maintains that the hand is not really (essentially) a bodily organ, and that it has nothing to do with the "hands" of other species: "In the common view, the hand is part of our bodily organism. But the hand's essence can never be determined, or explained, by its being a bodily organ which can grasp. Apes, too, have organs that can grasp, but they do not have hands. The hand is infinitely different from all the grasping organs—paws, claws, fangs—different by an abyss of essence."[52]

Note in this passage, first, the reappearance of the ape who has haunted a previous passage, the ape whose familiarity with the human might be deduced from a reading of Nietzsche. Observe, secondly, that the human hand is said not to be significantly but, rather, *infinitely* different from the "grasping organs" of animals. And note, finally, that this infinite difference of hand from grasping organ is measured in terms of a difference "by an abyss of essence." The human body, its organs, its sense experience have nothing—literally nothing—in common with animal life for Heidegger. Little surprise, then, when we are told in *Being and Time* that "the ontology of Dasein . . . is *superordinate* to an ontology of life."[53] Whatever may be said to characterize *Dasein* (the human being in its essential constitution) it is not its existence as a living being. That, after all, would be to connect the human with the animal, to associate "man" with the ape.

All these themes are rehearsed in Heidegger's *Letter on Humanism,* a text which has enormously influenced post-structuralism. Taking up the problem of "the essence of man" in the *Letter,* Heidegger rejects the idea of man as "the rational animal," and he leaves little doubt that it is the association with animality that he finds most disturbing about this concept. By characterizing him as the rational animal, "we abandon man to the essential realm of *animalitas,*" he writes. Yet the human being, or ek-sistence, as Heidegger now describes him, "can also never be thought of as a specific kind of living creature among others." Moreover, the human body provides no opening for seeing man as a "living creature," since it "is something essentially other than an animal organism." Thus, although living creatures are "in a certain way" close to us, they are "at the same time separated from our ek-sistent [human—DM] essence by an abyss."

Once again we encounter the abyss that opens up every time Heidegger finds himself in the region of the animal and the ape. And here, too, we encounter the emotive resonance of Heidegger's distaste for human animality, as in his reference to "our appalling and scarcely conceivable bodily kinship with the beast."[54]

It is hard to imagine traveling a greater distance from those moments in Nietzsche's thought which insist on our corporeality. Unlike the author of *The Gay Science,* Heidegger is in anxious flight from the human body and the animality it entails. That is why Heidegger seizes upon—and radicalizes—those moments of Nietzsche's thought which extol war against the limits to self-making that the body represents. It is this Nietzsche—the idealist who substitutes a metaphysics of self-overcoming for the corporeal materialism that elsewhere animates his thinking—who has been embraced by postmodernist thought. And it is this Nietzsche who, as I have intimated, also attempts to banish women from the sphere of the self-creating men of the future.

There is nothing new in pointing out the antifeminism and misogyny running through Nietzsche's writings.[55] Yet, as recent commentators have perceived, Nietzsche's remarks on women, as on so much else, vacillate sharply. On the one hand, he denigrates women as inferior, as lower types whose talk of rights, equality, and emancipation deserves scorn. On the other hand, he registers an awe, indeed a fear, of women, who he posits as smarter, more cunning, and more dangerous than men. Nietzsche's awe is driven in part by his fascination with women as mothers, as those who give birth to human beings. Discussing love between men and women in *The Gay Science,* for example, he argues that men and women love differently. For women, love means "total devotion." Every woman wants to give herself totally to a man; a man—at least a genuine man—simply wants to take this devotion, to own it. In love, woman is a slave and man a master (GS, 318–19). Love is a sort of war between the sexes (EH, 267). Yet, these warring parties are driven to procreate, to produce heirs. And, as Nietzsche hints, this means each is using the other as a means to their own reproduction. Let us listen closely to the following passage: "Has my answer been heard as to how one *cures* a woman—'redeems' her? One gives her a child." So far, this is traditional male chauvinism. But he continues: "Woman needs children, a man is for her only a means: thus spoke *Zarathustra*" (EH, 267). This exceptionally interesting passage comes after a diatribe against the notion of "equal rights" for women. But after telling us that love is war and that one cures a woman by giving her a child, he then tells us, invoking Zarathustra, that woman uses man as a means—a means to bear children. And this would seem to be what Nietzsche has in mind when, earlier in this section, he asserts that "the state of nature, the eternal war between the sexes" gives woman "by far the first rank."

Nietzsche recognizes that, on his own argument, males are "a means" for the reproductive strategies of females—and it is hard to miss the idea here that women are the true masters, treating men as means to their will to power. The problem for Nietzsche is that sexual reproduction involves a part of the male being "taken" by and "incorporated" by the female. But what does this do for the self-sufficient male's will to power, the will to power that overcomes every dependency, everything that might try to limit and define it? Can man ever overcome his dependence on woman—both the woman who gave birth to him and the woman who bears "his" (are they truly *his*?) children? Indeed Nietzsche's warning that "the perfect woman tears to pieces when she loves" (EH, 266; see BGE, 170) expresses the fear that if a man "gives" himself to a woman, a part of him will be taken, broken off. "Woman," Nietzsche warns, "is indescribably more evil than man; also cleverer" (EH, 26).

This fear of woman—that she will seduce man into giving up part of himself, that she will "tear" him apart—seems to account for Nietzsche's advice against sexual intercourse (GM, 111; WP, 431–32). The true artist creates something which is a pure product of his own will: his self. He does not produce anything which involves losing a part of himself in woman, in the finite world of things. As Henry Staten points out, "the logic of Nietzsche's discussion here is that of Diotima's discourse in the *Symposium*. . . . The production of the ideal work is a way of avoiding the transit of Eros through the body of the female, thus of avoiding mortality, of gaining immortality."[56] Indeed, Nietzsche's discussions here exude womb envy; he invokes the image of the artist as pregnant with . . . himself. Consider, for example, his advice against intercourse. Nietzsche tells us that "it is not chastity when an athlete or jockey abstains from women." No, abstinence is about something higher than chastity, it is about art: "Every artist knows what a harmful effect intercourse has in stages of great spiritual tension and preparation." Indeed, it is the "'maternal' instinct" of the artist that "ruthlessly disposes of all other stores of energy, of animal vigor, for the benefit of the evolving work" (GM, 111). The true artist, just like a mother, diverts sexual energy (animal vigor) into the creation with which he is pregnant. Nietzsche's texts are replete with the imagery of self-birth, as in the following passage: "one emerges again and again into the light, one experiences again and again one's golden hour of victory—and then one stands forth as one was born, unbreakable, tense, ready for new, even harder, remoter things" (GM, 44). It comes as no surprise, then, when Zarathustra tells himself that he will have to create his own children: "For one loves from the very heart only one's child and one's work; and where there is great love of oneself, then it is a sign of pregnancy. . ." (Z, 181).

Love of oneself leads to pregnancy, to the bringing forth of one's own children. Nietzsche's idea of self-overcoming is founded, as Peter Sloterdijk has argued, on the notion that the human subject must suppress "the horror of its own birth." For the fact of our birth, of which our body bears the marks, signals our dependence on something outside ourselves—mother, woman, history, body, society. This is why Sloterdijk talks about the Nietzschean "rage of self-birth"; the subject that aspires to will itself always comes up against a limit, an origin

outside and before itself, for which it cannot assume authorship. The aggressiveness we have noted in Nietzsche, the sadomasochistic subjectivity we have observed, describes that movement in which the (male) subject tries to originate
itself, give birth to itself, and collapses periodically into rage against woman, his
limit.[57]

Jacques Derrida's commentary on Nietzsche, while picking up on some of
the motifs in his imagery regarding women, seems strikingly oblivious to this
movement in his thought. Derrida seizes upon the idea that "Nietzsche is the
thinker of pregnancy which, for him, is no less praiseworthy in a man than it
is in a woman." But, when he claims that for Nietzsche woman "engulfs and
distorts all vestige of essentiality, of identity, of property," he grasps just one of
Nietzsche's moves.[58] For what woman destabilizes is the artist-philosopher's drive
to make himself. Woman, most notably as mother, represents the higher type's
origin in something "lower" than himself, in a body, a life, a history that is other
than the self. Woman is thus a limit, a finitude that cannot be overcome—unless
one authorizes a leap into a myth of self-origin. More than this, the idea that
woman is also a subject (and not just a natural limit on male subjectivity)
threatens the whole antinatural, anticorporeal thrust of Nietzsche's doctrine of
self-creation and self-overcoming.

Nietzsche exhibits, therefore, the same ambivalence about women that he
portrays toward the body. On the one hand, he acknowledges the "truth" about
the body—that it is the origin of consciousness, will, and so on—and that
(among other things) woman represents the body from which we have all come.
He is fascinated and enticed by the tremendous "power" that woman/body
represents. At the same time, he is equally repulsed since this woman/body
represents a limit to will and its power. For that reason, he returns again and
again to that limit, skeptical that it can be overcome, yet determined to take the
leap, to transcend any fixity, origin, truth, or identity that woman and the body
represent. Therein lies at least one source of his fascination with asceticism, with
disavowal of woman and the body. Yet, can one live fully inside oneself? Is not
Zarathustra regularly drawn back to the crowd, to followers, to children and
women? Acknowledging this, Nietzsche affirms absolute separation as the hard-
est, most severe calling, the only way to live without identity, or stability. Yet this
affirmation, based on his concepts of will to power and eternal recurrence, is, in
his own terms, thoroughly contrived and unconvincing.[59]

One of the Nietzsches with whom we must contend, then, is the (post)modern
mythmaker who conjures away the natural and social world with his myth of
self-creation and self-overcoming. As Allan Megill points out, "Nietzsche is
articulating an idealism far more radical than anything to be found in
Hegel. . . . His myth is in fact a form of mysticism, a purely individualistic, even
solipsistic creation." Like Plato, who he repeatedly attacked, and with a similar
aristocratic gesture, Nietzsche repeatedly turns his back on the world of the
body, the senses, and everyday life. In place of personal and social embodiment

he substitutes an abstract, disembodied, self-generated (male aristocratic) mind-body. Consequently, the world of Nietzsche's myth "utterly lacks the structures necessary for social life. It ignores, that is, the natural and social needs of humankind for the unconstrained freedom of the artist."[60] In the final analysis, Nietzsche's aristocratic hostility to democracy, leveling, and slave morality, along with his flight from woman and the body, torpedoes the materialist impulse at work in his engagement with Darwin and natural science. The result is an idealist metaphysics that forfeits its critical charge. What we are left with is the Nietzsche of postmodern fame, the metaphysician who turns his back on the body and sensuality—and on the language of everyday life.

LANGUAGE AND "THE METAPHYSICS OF THE PEOPLE"

Fashionable readings of Nietzsche see him first and foremost as a theorist of the illusory and metaphorical nature of language. According to some of Nietzsche's early unpublished writings, rather than representing the world, language *constructs* it by using concepts to order and stabilize the flux of our experience. Language in this view is a set of metaphors designed to give the appearance of "being" to the endless becoming that is life.[61] In Nietzsche's later writings this theme connects with the Darwinian idea that language emerged because of its usefulness to human beings. Language is thus perspectival for Nietzsche, it reflects a view of the world from the perspective of members of a species intent on survival. Rather than expressing real relations among humans and objects in the world, the "metaphysics" of subject, verb, and predicate that constitute the grammatical structure of language is metaphorical, it is the comparison of things in the (objective) world with our (subjective) experience of them. The problem for thinkers who seek truth, therefore, is that they must disavow the ostensible "truths" of language in order to transcend its limits. Yet, they can only do so from within the universe of language, since consciousness itself comes into being in and through language. In this sense, then, the true thinker turns the metaphysics of language against itself; he or she attempts the paradoxical task of expressing that which language cannot say.[62]

In rebelling against the stabilization and institutionalization of experience that language represents, genuine thinkers try to express aspects of reality that elude ordinary language. The political impulse here—which has been evaded in most of the recent enthusiasm for Nietzsche—has been nicely summarized by J. P. Stern. Describing how Nietzsche condemns ordinary language "as an aspect of the institutionalization of all individual experience," Stern comments:

> And here we come to an all-pervasive and, I think, unacceptable limitation of Nietzsche's thinking: he is fundamentally uninterested in, and often undiscriminatingly hostile to, what we may

call, *the sphere of association.* By this I mean that in all his philosophizing he has nothing really positive to say about, and much
suspicion of, all those human endeavours—in society, art and
religion, in morality, even in the sciences—whereby single discrete insights and experiences are transfixed, stabilized and made
reliable by means of rules and laws and institutions.[63]

This hostility to the sphere of association culminates in an aristocratic aestheticiza-
tion of language. For Nietzsche is not simply interested in attacking "truth," he
is particularly keen to criticize the truths of the herd which he finds embedded
in language. This becomes especially clear when we turn to his most sustained
treatment of language in *The Gay Science.*

Here Nietzsche links consciousness and language directly to communication. Consciousness, he insists, is of social origin, it *"has developed only under the
pressure of the need for communication."* Indeed, "consciousness is really only a net
of communication between human beings . . . a solitary human being who lived
like a beast would not have needed it" (GS, 298). Language and consciousness
are for Nietzsche, as for Marx, species-specific capacities which develop from the
needs of human beings for particular kinds of communication. But for Nietzsche,
the defect of consciousness and language is precisely that they are social (herd-
like) not individual (solitary and pure). Nietzsche wants to separate something
that is impure and corrupt (communicative consciousness) from something that
is pristine (solitary existence). "Consciousness," he writes, "does not really belong
to man's individual existence but rather to his social or herd nature." And because of this, consciousness and language enable us to express "what is not
individual but 'average'." The more Nietzsche pursues this line of argument, the
more he counterposes the individual to the social, the unique to the average, the
essential to the derived. Consciousness misrepresents the existential experience
of the individual by translating it into what is average and communicable. What
is communicable is fallen, distorted, impure: "whatever becomes conscious becomes by the same token shallow, thin, relatively stupid, general, sign, herd
signal; all becoming conscious involves a great and thorough corruption,
falsification, reduction to superficialities, and generalization" (GS, 299–300).

It follows that "everywhere language is sick" since, as soon as people "unite
for a common work, they are seized by the madness of universal concepts" (UM,
214, 215). These universal concepts liquidate the unique elements of individual
experience (a special problem for the higher types), and they impose the metaphysical structure of herd life on all experience. The problem for the true thinker
is to resist "the seduction of language (and of the fundamental errors of reason
that are petrified in it)" (GM, 45; also TI, 48). Yet, how is this seduction to be
avoided? How is the rare individual to express himself without using language
and the "metaphysics of the people?" After all, if "the speaker has already *vulgarized*
himself by speaking" (TI, 93), doesn't it follow that the only solution is to

disavow communication by refusing to speak? Certainly, Nietzsche often suggests as much; at such moments, Zarathustra turns silent. At other times, he hints that it might be possible to devise a new language, a language at the limits of ordinary speech, which would openly challenge the stability of all meanings, including its own. Such a language would be a sort of music, it would incorporate screams and silences, it would disavow communication as its goal. "By reaching the nocturnal heights of tone and intensity," notes one commentator, "language ceases to appear as an instrument of communication."[64] And yet, Nietzsche hopes to communicate; like Zarathustra, he cannot bear silence and total isolation. But, if he is not to vulgarize himself, he cannot speak to his contemporaries, he must speak to those who are yet to come, to those who might breathe a different air and speak a new language. *Thus Spoke Zarathustra,* he declares, is a book "with a voice bridging centuries." Its words "reach only the most select" (EH, 219–20). Perhaps some of its readers are being prepared today—that is an open question—but Nietzsche will speak in a new voice, use a new language, and risk being understood by no one: "The time for me hasn't come yet; some are born posthumously" (EH, 259). It is extremely painful to imagine being born after one's death. Yet this is a pain Nietzsche must endure. At times he goes so far as to suggest that speaking only to himself is the ideal toward which he strives. He regularly acknowledges, however, that such an experience is unbearable: "No one talks to me other than myself, and my voice comes to me as the voice of a dying man. . . . With your help I shall deceive myself about my loneliness; . . . For my heart . . . compels me to talk as though I were two."[65]

"To talk as though I were two"—is this the myth that Nietzsche needs? Is it the beautiful illusion that sustains him as he tries to find a voice that speaks the incommunicable? Certainly he hints that this is so. Yet, Nietzsche knows this is a myth. Either his desire to communicate would vulgarize his thought and his meanings, or the esotericism of his language would condemn him to having no listeners. After all, if his language was in fact radically new, then translation into the language of the ordinary would not be possible.[66] For this reason, the schizoid solution beckoned: to be his own listener, to speak a language that communicates to no one. "For me—how could there be an outside-of-me? There is no outside" (Z, 234). This absolute interiority is the summit of Nietzsche's idealism. And it is the ultimate secret of his philosophy of language.

Nietzsche constructs here a classic example of what Louis A. Sass has called "languages of inwardness." In his study of the relationship between schizophrenia and modernist art and literature, Sass identifies three trends in schizophrenic speech which characterize modernist languages of inwardness: desocialization, impoverishment, and autonomization. Desocialization refers to the prioritizing of "inner speech," the treatment of language not as a means of communicating with others but as a medium for the self-expression of uniquely private experience. With the term "impoverishment," Sass intends the move toward a kind of

self-centered speech, often telegraphic and elliptical in nature, and denuded of
rich references to a shared context of meaning. Finally, autonomization involves
"a new recognition of the independent nature of language, an acknowledgment
of its existence as a system imbued with its own inherent mysteries and forms
of productiveness."[67]

In Nietzsche, the first two trends—desocialization and impoverishment—
are thrown into sharpest relief. His antipathy to the sphere of association dovetails with a distaste for communication. It is in the writings of the "post-Nietzscheans"
that the third trend—autonomization—reaches its pinnacle. Nowhere is this
clearer than in the structuralist and post-structuralist appropriations of Saussure's
linguistics which posit language as a system bereft of human agency—an autonomous structure which speaks through us. True, people do engage in speech
acts for Saussure and his followers. But this has nothing fundamentally to do
with the operation of language as an autonomous and self-reproducing system.
In embracing—and radicalizing—this reified notion of a language system, post-
structuralism unwittingly theorizes language in the image of the commodity
form. As Marx reminds us, the commodity-form involves the radical separation
of the concrete, natural, and sensuous characteristics of things (their properties
as use-values and products of concrete labor) from their social being in the
sphere of market exchange as repositories of an abstract, immaterial substance
called "value" (which manifests itself in money). And this contradiction at the
heart of the commodity—between its concrete existence on the one hand and its
abstract social being on the other—gives rise to a unique kind of fetishistic
thinking which "forgets" the concrete labors that go into producing things. Post-
structuralist theories of language—which separate language from speaking subjects—move entirely within this fetishistic circuit, one we encounter both in
Saussure's linguistics and Derrida's deconstructionism. Like Nietzsche's metaphysics of the will to power, these theories are constituted in and through a
forgetting of the body.

2

FORGETTING THE BODY:
LINGUISTIC ECONOMIES FROM
SAUSSURE TO DERRIDA

> As in political economy we are confronted here by the notion
> of *value:* both sciences deal with *a system for equating things of
> different order*—labor and wages in one, and a signified and a
> signifier in the other.
>
> —Ferdinand de Saussure, *Cours de linguistique générale*

It is a curious fact of intellectual history that in postwar France the posthumous
lectures of a cautious Swiss linguist, Ferdinand de Saussure, should have been
rewritten as a radical philosophy of difference and the undecidability of meaning. Some argue that the Saussure who has come down to us as the father of
post-structuralism is a counterfeit.[1] But such a claim immediately plunges us
into the churning currents of deconstruction. After all, if we are to believe
Jacques Derrida, in the case of language, as in economics, it is impossible to
differentiate the counterfeit from the real. Meanings, be they of verbal statements or bank notes, are not fixed; they vary across contexts. Every time a
statement is reiterated it enters a new context and takes on new meaning. Yet,
no particular version of a statement is any more or less true than another, they
are just different. Moreover, argue Derrida and his followers, there is no "original" context to which we can return to recover a first meaning of a text. I can
no more go back to such a context than I can return to the past of my grand-
parents and experience it as they did. Their past can only exist *for me*, and the
same is true of all past linguistic statements and meanings. Consequently, there
is no assured way to demarcate statement from restatement, original from copy.

    The same is said to be true of the (post)modern economy in which new and
derivative forms of money—such as paper currencies, checks, instant debit cards

and electronic funds—all function just like the "real" thing. In principle, counterfeit money is no different from these derivative forms of money; indeed, so
long as it circulates (i.e. is taken for the "real" thing), counterfeit performs all the
functions of money. And since the very meaning of counterfeit is that it is taken
for the real thing (otherwise it is withdrawn from circulation as a fraud), it
follows that the real and the counterfeit are always in circulation, forever exchanging with one another, to the point that they are interchangeable, identical
in their difference.[2]

It is fitting that issues of money, currency and exchange should emerge as
we begin to discuss Saussure. For one of the most interesting features of Saussure's
linguistics is his use of economic concepts to construct a science of language.
Saussure hoped to use the concept of "value" to illuminate relations among
linguistic signs. But in so doing he entangled himself in a fetishistic economics
of language. Astute reader that he can be, Derrida sees some of this. But Derrida
also resists moves to defetishize. Intrigued by the movements of specters, spirits
and fetishes, he refuses any move toward the real, toward the embodied practices
which underwrite spectral movements. And, as we shall see, this refusal of
defetishizing critique undercuts efforts to use deconstruction as critical theory.

And here I caution the reader. Tracing the movement of Derrida's arguments can be a frustrating task. Derrida delights in word play and allusion, he
relishes the obscure and the inscrutable. This has led some readers to conclude
that deconstruction is simply nonsense. I do not share this view. I detect a
reasonably consistent set of core positions in Derrida's writings. Indeed, translated into the language of contemporary social theory, Derrida emerges, I argue,
as the exponent of a view of contemporary capitalism that is widespread in left-
leaning intellectual circles. For Derrida promotes the idea that we have entered
a new era—a post-industrial information economy—in which speculative capital
buzzes the globe in micro-seconds unhampered by the limits once set by nature,
geography, transportation systems, or rebellious laborers.[3] This economic theory,
I suggest, is of a part with his economics of language. My critique of Derrida
on language intersects, therefore, with a critique of postmodernist theories of
late capitalism—theories which fetishize the movement of financial capital, inflate
capital's autonomy from labor and productive activity and, in so doing, down-
grade the prospects for an emancipatory politics. All of this comes back, I argue,
to a view of language and economics that short-circuits the realities of the body.

Banishing the Body and History: Saussure's Science of Language

One of Saussure's abiding concerns is with defining the object of linguistic science. To this end, he separates formal properties of language that can be studied

scientifically from those that are messy, many-sided, heterogeneous. This leads him to construct a set of dualisms, largely based around distinctions between form and content. The following Table sets out some of these key oppositions:

SAUSSURE'S OPPOSITIONS

Formal property	Content
Langue (language system)	Parole (speech)
collective	individual
homogeneous	heterogeneous
synchronic (ahistorical)	diachronic (historical)

Saussure argues that linguistics studies the formal properties of a (static, unchanging) language system, rather than the ever-changing characteristics of language as manifested in speech. Indeed, linguistics arrives at its object of study—the language system—only through a systematic abstraction from its dynamic, living elements: human bodies, concrete individuals and actual speech utterances:

> Taken as a whole, speech is many-sided and heterogeneous; straddling several areas simultaneously—physical, physiological, and psychological—it belongs both to the individual and society; we cannot put it into any category of human facts, for we cannot discover its unity.

> Language, on the contrary, is a self-contained whole and a principle of classification. (CGL, 9.)

Saussure's definitions of language are often of a largely negative character; the language system, he suggests, is what remains once we eliminate vocal organs, phonation, and speech from our considerations. He informs us that "the vocal organs" are "external" to language, that "language exists independently of phonetic changes" (as the latter "affect only the material substance of words"), and that "the activity of the speaker" has "no place in linguistics" (CGL, 18). Language is speech dematerialized and dehistoricized, speech stripped of its entanglement in the bodies and lives of real historical actors. Or, put in Saussure's own stark terms, "Language is speech less speaking"; it is "a form and not a substance" (CGL, 77, 122).

Post-structuralists have had little quarrel with these initial methodological moves. In their search for structures, discourses, texts and codes independent of human actors, they have retained Saussure's formalist abstractionism. One of the most remarkable things about Derrida's critique of Saussure, for instance, is his charge that the Swiss linguist *failed* to emancipate himself adequately from the presence of the human voice. Derrida accuses Saussure of "phonocentrism," with centering his linguistics on speech. The exile into which Saussure tries to send the human body, vocal organs, communicating individuals, and their histories is not the problem; Derrida's complaint is that this banishment is not thorough-going enough. In an important respect, Derrida has reason to complain. After all, one of the more interesting things about the lectures compiled in the *Course in General Linguistics* is the regularity with which Saussure returns to some of these banished elements. A lengthy appendix to the introduction, for example, deals with phonology and the physiological mechanics of speech (CGL, 38-64) and at a number of points in the text Saussure emphasizes that all linguistic change and evolution is speech-driven (CGL, 18-19, 70-76, 140, 165, 168). Indeed, in one passage, he claims "speaking is necessary for the establishment of language, and historically its actuality always come first" (CGL, 18).[4] Why then does he believe that his abstraction of language from speech is theoretically defensible? The answer has, at least in part, to do with his use of economic models in defining the central concept of linguistics—the sign.

Signs, Saussure tells us, combine two elements: a signifier (or sound image) and a signified (or concept). In English, the sign *dog* entails both a specific sound image and the concept appropriate to that acoustic image. In Saussure's view, sound images are meaningless without associated concepts, just as concepts are non-entities without sound images which accompany them (CGL, 65-6). But just as signs are internally differentiated (between signifiers and signifieds), so they are externally differentiated, that is, each sign is different from every other. In other words, just as we have the internal relation signified/signifier which constitutes the sign, so we have the external relations sign1 . . . sign2 . . . sign3 . . . sign4 . . . which are equally definitive of any sign. Saussure tries to capture these external relations with an economic logic. What concerns him here is not the meaning, but rather the *value* of a sign, i.e., its relation to a system of signs. Saussure insists that there is no necessary relation between signifier and signified: there is no natural connection between the acoustic image created when we produce the sound *dog*, and the concept dog as it refers to a certain four-legged mammal, just as there is no such connection between this concept and the sound image *chien* which designates the same concept in French. The relationship between these two elements of the sign is "arbitrary" (CGL, 67-68). Nevertheless, these arbitrary elements form a system of linguistic values. In sorting through this issue, Saussure develops what has been described as his "most radical innovation in linguistics"—his concept of value.[5]

Saussure seems to have adopted a neoclassical economic view according to which commodities have no intrinsic value. Value, then, is a purely differential and external relation; it refers to the ratio at which commodity A exchanges for commodities B, C, D, and so forth. A pair of shoes, for example, will exchange with so much wheat, or steel, with so many bottles of wine, or pens or books.

Outside of these relations, a commodity has no value. Its value is determined by those exchange relations which, as we shall see, can also be expressed in a common measure or monetary unit. Value, in other words, is exchange value, or price when expressed in monetary terms.

Saussure proceeds to suggest that the world of signs is constructed much like this world of commodities. Starting from the premise that the world is experienced as an ever-fluctuating mass of sensory perceptions and ideas, he argues that signs enable us to introduce ordered relations into our experience of the world. Again, a twofold movement is at work. Signifiers slice up the sound spectrum in order to create differentiated units of sound, just as signifieds (concepts) partition the chaos of ideas generated by our sense perception (CGL, 111-113). In dividing up the chaos of sound and thought into discrete units (which combine as signs), language systems make conceptual thought possible. But, on their own, these units (signs) have no value; only as elements of a system do they acquired value. In other words, each sign is defined by its presence in a system; outside of such a system, these units are without value and meaning, they denote nothing. The value of a sign, in other words, is determined by the fact that it is *not* the other signs with which it forms a system. It follows that the value of a sign is defined *differentially,* that is, by its difference from the other signs in the language system. "Signs function, then," says Saussure, "not through their intrinsic value but through their relative position." And again: "the concepts are purely differential and defined not by their positive content but negatively by their relations with the other terms of the system. Their most precise characteristic is in being what the others are not" (CGL, 118, 117).

Like commodities, then, or at least like Saussure's notion of commodities, a sign has a relative value or value-in-exchange which derives from its difference from other units of the system. This is the context for his famous claim that "in language there are only differences" (CGL, 120). This passage, and others like it, have created enormous excitement in structuralist and post-structuralist circles. That it rests on the most vulgar sort of economics has, regrettably, not drawn much notice. Moreover, this and similar statements have been inflated into grand ontological statements of a sort that Saussure regularly resisted. But before proceeding to these points, let us examine Saussure's economic reasoning a bit further.

Setting up the problem of external relations among signs in his lectures, Saussure pauses to invoke general economic principles. "Even outside language," he informs his audience, "all values are apparently governed by the same paradoxical principle." And he proceeds to spell out this principle:

They are always composed:

1. of a *dissimilar* thing that can be *exchanged* for the thing of which the value is to be determined; and

2. of *similar* things that can be *compared* with the thing of which the value is to be determined (CGL, 115).

To illustrate this point, Saussure tells us that a five-franc piece can be exchanged for a dissimilar thing, like bread, or that it can be compared with similar things of the same system (e.g., one-franc pieces), or with a similar thing from a different system (e.g., a dollar). Since this muddled piece of reasoning has gone largely unremarked (and has been repeated in many quarters), it is worth pausing to unpack it.

Saussure is telling us that the paradox of the principle of exchange, which governs all systems of value, is that I may compare a thing with other things that are similar to it, or with things that are dissimilar to it. If I give a five-franc piece to the baker and receive a loaf of bread in exchange, we have an exchange of dissimilars (money for a commodity). On the other hand, if I go to the bank and exchange a five-franc coin for five one-franc coins or some coins of equivalent value on a dollar standard, we then have an exchange of similars (money for money). But note some of the assumptions that Saussure has smuggled into his "general economics": we take a market economy for granted; we assume the existence of a general equivalent (or money form); we then take the general problem to be the value of money, in this case a five-franc piece (and not of commodities); we further suppose a number of national currencies. Saussure thus starts us off in a fetishized world dominated by money and commodity exchange which are naturalized as the general forms of all economy. Little surprise, as we shall see, that Derrida, having started from inside Saussure's system, ends up telling us there is no escape from the circuit of capital. But before turning to Derrida, let me pursue the way in which Saussure's reified economic categories play havoc with his notion of linguistic value.

One of the best commentaries on Saussure's confused ideas about linguistic values, David Holdcroft's *Saussure: Signs, System, and Arbitrariness*, demonstrates how the notion of purely differential value breaks down. Holdcroft argues that differences cannot be purely negative, they must entail contrasts of some unique and meaningful sort. To illustrate the point, he takes the signifieds "chair" and "three" and claims that, while different, "intuitively they are not opposed terms," that is, they do not form an opposition that assigns a meaningful value. He contrasts this difference (between chair and three) with those between hot and cold, Tuesday and Sunday, male and female. Rather than signs being defined purely negatively (by sheer difference), he suggests that we would do better to see them as defined only by certain relevant differences (or oppositions). Indeed, he argues, without this distinction we would not be able to define any positive values to signs and would be "adrift in a sea of differences without any principle of relevance."[6] But the whole point about commodity production in capitalist society is that it is not governed by concrete considerations of the uniquely useful characteristics of products of labor. Capital is indifferent to the concrete character of the commodity and its capacity to satisfy specific needs. That it is wool, steel, microchips, bread, or books matters not one bit. Commodity exchange really does abstract from these "relevant differences." Yet, a model of linguistic value derived from these uniquely abstracting features of capitalism results in a thoroughly impoverished theory of language.

For this reason, Saussure tries to escape this empty formalism which results in "a sea of differences without any principle of relevance." He argues that we drift in a sea of differences only so long as we contemplate signifiers and signifieds separately. Once "we consider the sign in its totality, we have something that is positive in its own class. . . . Although both the signifier and the signified are purely differential and negative when considered separately, their combination is a positive fact" (CGL, 120). Now, Saussure's reasoning here is far from clear. What he seems to intend is that, taken separately, the sound-image "dog" and the idea "dog" are purely differential; once combined into a sign, however, and compared to other signs, they have a positive value within the sign system we call language, that is, they demarcate a part of the world of referents as pertaining to that particular sign. Put simply, there is a positive correspondence between the sign "dog" and that animal (as distinct from others) which we intend in English when we use this word. While there is something commonsensical about this claim, it is not clear how it flows from the discussion of the value of the sign. The problem here is that Saussure cannot make the move that Holdcroft suggests above: determine which differences constitute *relevant* oppositions (which might enable him to move from relevant difference to positive value). For this would be to conceive of the language system not in terms of formal differences, but in terms of those differences that are important for the conduct of human life, that is, in terms of concrete human activities. The distinction hot/cold, for example, is a relevant and meaningful one for the everyday life of humans in a way that the distinction chair/three is not. Formally, however, both distinctions are the same. Only when we admit human beings, with their senses, needs and desires, into the discussion can we make the sort of distinctions that Holdcroft proposes. But, having banished human beings, their bodies, vocal tracts, gestures, voices, social organizations, and histories from the discussion, Saussure cannot draw relevant distinctions. And one reason he cannot get out of this conundrum—in which his formalist concept of difference makes the introduction of positive linguistic values implausible—has to do with the fetishized economic concepts he employs. We can see this by revisiting the "paradoxical principle" that characterizes all economy for Saussure.

Recall Saussure's paradox of an economic or linguistic sign that can be exchanged for a dissimilar thing (e.g., five francs for bread), or for similar ones (a five-franc piece for five one-franc coins). But why should this twofold principle be taken to apply to all forms of economy? Why, for instance, should we even introduce money into the discussion? As most economic theories acknowledge, simple barter is also a possibility. Indeed, Adam Smith's *The Wealth of Nations* begins with the example of a "primitive" economy in which beavers are exchanged directly for deer without the mediation of money. Smith, like most classical political economists, then proceeds to conceptualize money in terms of the exchange of commodities. Saussure sees none of these issues; he makes no effort to justify the elements of his economic analogy. Instead, he simply and uncritically begins with that entity—money—which represents the pure form of exchange abstracted from its concrete particularities (i.e., the sale and purchase of specific goods). Indeed, in the examples he uses to illustrate his "paradoxical principle," it is the value of money (not of specific commodities) that is at issue. To resolve the problem of money and its value, Saussure would have to move from the abstract form of exchange (money) to its concrete constituents and elements (and the historical forms they assume). That is, he would have to show how the exchange of commodities for money (and vice versa) can be derived from the social relations of commodity exchange. Economic theories that fail to do this end up in a fetishism that attributes the value of money to some material property (e.g., the physical attributes of gold) or some purely subjective construction (e.g., the enchanting power of gold, or an arbitrary social convention). The critical move made by classical political economy is to root money in commodity exchange, and from there to move to commodity production, to laboring activity itself—as Ricardo tries to do with his labor theory of value (which is critically developed and transformed by Marx). But having made money an eternal feature of all economic relations, Saussure closes off such a move. Consequently, he cannot explain precisely what needs to be explained: why relations among producers take the increasingly reified form of interactions among things expressed through the movements of a single thing (money). By taking money as a universal feature of all economies, Saussure cannot derive it from a specific social form of labor. And the same thing is true for his analysis of language. The pure form of language—the language system—floats detached from speech and discourse, just as the pure form of exchange—money—remains disconnected from the rudimentary elements of economic life. As a result, he is reduced to empty propositions of the sort that characterize vulgar economics: "language is speech less speaking"; "language is a system of pure values"; "in language there are only differences"; "language is a form and not a substance" (CGL, 77, 80, 120, 122). These are textbook examples of abstraction of the formal features of a system from the concrete social relations that animate them. This formalist abstractionism leads, as it does in vulgar political economy, to empty propositions of the sort: "The true and unique object of linguistics is language studied in and for itself" (CGL, 232).

Yet, there is a logic that drives these increasingly empty propositions: the fetishism of the commodity form—and its crystallization in money—taken as an entity in and of itself. Indeed, it is this inverted logic that Marx probes throughout *Capital*. The key to grasping the logic of capital, Marx argues, is to follow the movement by which concrete laboring activity takes progressively more abstract forms. For capitalism is based upon the systematic transformation of concrete acts of labor (the specific and unique work activities that people perform) into elements of human labor in the abstract—measurable and interchangeable bits of homogeneous labor. This has to do with the fact that the economic metabolism of capitalism is governed by the principle of exchange, not use. Commodities exchange, moreover, not according to their concrete usefulness—otherwise water would be expensive and diamonds cheap—but according to the labor-time necessary for their production. Yet it is not the *actual* labor-time involved in production which determines this value-in-exchange (otherwise the slowest, least efficient producer would get the best prices). Rather, the *average* (or socially necessary) labor-time required determines value. The value of a good is thus determined by an averaging operation which abstracts from concrete labor processes, from the actual laboring activity in which individuals have engaged. The mechanisms of capitalist production and exchange ignore the unique and unrepeatable moments of productive life-activity in order to reduce each moment of labor to a quantum of universally interchangeable human labor in general. And this abstract human labor is represented (and measured) by money. Capitalism is thus an economy in which the value of things seems to be determined by something which is a non-thing, something abstracted from the world of commodities which confers value upon them—money. As a useful object and a product of concrete labor, the commodity is without (exchange) value—literally valueless—unless it can be translated into money.[7] This is what Marx means when he writes that a commodity is "a thing which transcends sensuousness"—its value to the capitalist has nothing to do with its concrete sociomaterial properties as, say, a table; instead, it has value only as a repository of abstract labor which can, via its exchange with money, be transformed into other commodities.[8]

The domination of economic life by money is an index of the unique forms of alienation that characterize capitalist society, among the most important of which is that people do not know the social value of the labor they perform until it is translated into its abstract (socially validated) form. And this translation is effected through the medium of money. By stamping a price on things, money declares how much abstract human labor is congealed in a commodity. As a result, money—the general form of exchange—seems to drive the whole system.

As the capitalist market economy becomes increasingly self-reproducing, money more and more comes to the fore as a social power. Rather than a mere means of exchange, it becomes the end in itself of all production and exchange. This give money, says Marx, a "seemingly transcendental power."[9] An inherent property of commodities—that they are in principle endlessly exchangeable with all other commodities—now seems to be a characteristic conferred on them by money.

Money is thus the material incarnation of the abstraction inherent in the value relation. In money the commodity "transcends sensuousness," it takes a form—the abstract, interchangeable form of value—entirely separate from its sensuous characteristics as a particular sort of good, composed of specific materials and fashioned by unique acts of concrete labor. As Elaine Scarry has pointed out, capitalism involves a dislocation in the structure of creation in which human artifacts become "internally referential," that is, they deny reference to the human acts from which they emerged and refer only to themselves.[10] It seems, in other words, as if commodities establish their own values by interacting on the market: the obscured social relations between different acts of concrete labor assume "the fantastic form of a relation between things."[11] In appearing to sever any connection between labor and value, the commodity takes on a fetish character, seemingly endowed with a life of its own. And this fetishism can take extreme forms—nowhere more so than in interest-bearing capital where money appears to beget money without the mediation of any act of human labor, thereby generating a fetish of self-birth, of money which gives birth to itself and its offspring: "In interest-bearing capital, therefore, this automatic fetish is elaborated into its pure form, self-valorizing value, money breeding money, and in this form it no longer bears any marks of its origin. The social relation is consummated in the relationship of a thing, money, to itself."[12] As Marx goes on to note, "vulgar economics" celebrates this "pure fetish form" of capital as essential truth.

It should now be clear that Saussure's notion of linguistic value is imbued with the formalist abstractions of the capitalist economy, indeed with some of its most fetishized appearances. Saussure's claim that "language is a form and not a substance" mirrors a central feature of the capitalist economy: that things have value not because of their concrete, useful characteristics, but because of their exchangeability with other units of abstract human labor. Moreover, Saussure, too, assumes that the exchangeability of signs resides in "a system of pure values," not relations among acts of human labor and, therefore, that language is "a form and not a substance." Just as a commodity "transcends sensuousness" in the capitalist market, so language for Saussure transcends the sensuous reality of speech.

In making these claims, I recognize that Saussure's economics of language does not consistently map onto classical economic models with signs functioning as commodities and language-system as money. Saussure's treatment of the issue is too confused and incoherent for such a mapping operation to tell the whole story. What I am suggesting is that a logic of economic concepts drives Saussure's basic categories, one based upon fetishistic notions of money and commodities. Only an anti-fetishistic economic model—a dialectical critique of political economy and its concepts of commodity and money—could have provided an escape from this formalist abstractionism.

Ironically, my argument has been vindicated by Paul Thibault who, in *Rereading Saussure*, has tried to rescue the author of the *Course in General Linguistics* from charges of idealism. In a lengthy and confused attempt to link Saussure with Marx, Thibault asserts that "the creation of values in the language system is homologous to the emergence of what Marx called the 'general equivalent' in the exchange of commodities."[13] Despite his intent, Thibault here confirms the reification I locate at the heart of Saussure's system. After all, to equate the general phenomenon of linguistic value with the specific role of money (as general equivalent) in capitalist economy is to treat a phenomenon appropriate to capitalism as a general feature of language. Indeed, Thibault makes this move by enlisting the analysis of the Italian linguist Ferruccio Rossi-Landi who similarly tried to employ Marx's value concepts, designed for the critical analysis of capitalist social relations, as general concepts of linguistic science. Rossi-Landi makes the universal claim, for instance, that "words and expressions are used . . . primarily according to their exchange value."[14] In so doing he too models language on the capitalist market—and thereby commits the same error that plagues Saussure.

We can now see why Saussure's linguistics are so susceptible to the sort of criticism advanced by V. N. Voloshinov in *Marxism and the Philosophy of Language* and developed throughout the writings of Mikhail Bakhtin (which will be discussed in chapter 4). Voloshinov argues that the appropriate objects of study for Saussurean linguistics are dead languages, languages from which speech really has disappeared. A dead language truly offers the prospect of a "finished monologic utterance" that can be anatomized outside the connective tissue of ongoing, incomplete, and unfinished utterances, that is, outside of living speech. Just as fetishistic economics deals with commodities, money, and capital torn from their connections to living labor, so formalist linguistics deals with a dead thing which it calls language:

> In reifying the system of language and in viewing living language as if it were dead and alien, abstract objectivism makes language something external to the stream of verbal communication. This stream flows on, but language, like a ball, is tossed from generation to generation. In actual fact, however, language moves together with that stream and is inseparable from it. Language cannot properly be said to be handed down—it endures, but it endures as a continuous process of becoming.[15]

This line of argument opens onto a thorough-going deconstruction of Saussurean linguistics (what Voloshinov calls "abstract objectivism"). Voloshinov's critique does not deny the systematic features of language, but it defetishizes them by insisting upon their inherent relation to speech, to concrete verbal utterances in actual sociohistorical contexts. Moreover, Voloshinov is not interested in simply inverting the Saussurean opposition of language-system and speech by valorizing activity over system. Rather, he intends to dissolve this opposition into a dialectic of form and content. This, as I show in chapter 4, is an enormously promising critical move. But it is one that is refused by Derrida's deconstructionism which instead radicalizes Saussure's abstraction from speech, the voice, embodied human subjects, and their histories.

JACQUES DERRIDA, PHILOSOPHER
OF FICTITIOUS CAPITAL

Let me begin with some disclaimers. In what follows, I do not pretend to offer a detailed commentary on Derrida's *oeuvre*. My interest here has to do with some features of Derrida's economics of language. Furthermore, while much of what I have to say will be deeply critical of Derrida's views, I do not believe that deconstruction is wholly uninteresting. Indeed, critically reconstructed, there are elements of deconstruction that can be seen to develop the Marxist critique of "immediacy" according to which the forms in which phenomena appear cannot be an adequate basis for knowledge. At times, Derrida's commentaries seem to follow the sort of insistence one finds in Marx, Georg Lukacs, Theodor Adorno and Maurice Merleau-Ponty on the necessarily mediated character of all phenomena. These theorists all insist that no phenomenon can be adequately grasped in its immediacy; instead, it is the task of dialectics to reconstruct the way in which "things" are socially and historically constituted, mixed with and mediated by activities and processes that appear "external" to them. Derrida's famous insistence that writing is prior to speech is, in part, an effort to make the same point, to demonstrate that meanings do not originate in speech acts but, instead, refer back to an infinite web of prior (and future) speech acts, contexts of meaning and their inscriptions (all of which is meant to be subsumed by the concept of "the text"). This deconstructive proposition might be said to open onto a sort of negative dialectics (Adorno), or what Merleau-Ponty described as "hyperdialectic"—an analysis which stays within the mediations and movements of one thing into another, a dialectic which, in refusing to jump outside the jolting movement of things, rejects claims to absolute, reified knowledge. "From the most superficial level to the most profound," writes Merleau-Ponty, "dialectical thought is that which admits reciprocal actions or interactions . . . even more that each of these relations leads to its opposite or to its own reversal, and does so by its own movement." And this dialectical movement cannot be called to a halt, or registered in a set of axioms: "It is essential to it that it be autocritical—and it is also essential to it to forget this as soon as it becomes what we call *a philosophy*. The very formulas by which it describes the movement of being are then liable to falsify that movement." Dialectical thought thus disavows the absolute sovereignty of concepts: "In thought and in history as in life the only surpassings we know are concrete, partial, encumbered with survivals, saddled with deficits."[16]

At times, deconstruction seems close to this sort of dialectical critique. Indeed, a number of theorists have followed these deconstructive moves in order to develop a reading of Derrida in which his concepts of writing and the trace are meant as reminders of the inescapably material character of language and thought. Some who read Derrida in this way also see his thought as intersecting with that of Marx.[17] While acknowledging the fruitfulness of some of these readings, I would argue that they fail to come to terms with the linguistic idealism that permeates Derrida's thought.[18] After all, Derrida regularly takes his distance from critical theory. He contends that anti-fetishistic thought (like that of Marx) is defeated by its commitment to an underlying truth, a "pure" phenomenon that has been distorted and obscured but which might be recovered through the work of defetishization. In fact, Derrida condemns even the critique of immediacy for imagining it can produce more adequate or truthful descriptions of phenomena. And this has to do, as I argue below, with the thoroughly fetishized view of language he adopts—one that makes the very notions of defetishization and dialectical critique absurd. "For Derrida," as one sympathetic commentator puts it, "there has never been anything but fetishism."[19] Yet, rejection of defetishizing critique entails a disavowal of embodied human activity. As a result, when it comes to dealing with issues of economy—of the organization of human activities for purposes of social and material production and reproduction—Derrida tries to slip away from anything that hints of laboring bodies. Instead, he becomes entranced by interest-bearing capital, capital that begets capital of itself, and by its most rarefied form: credit or fictitious capital. And this entrancement is of a piece with his views on Saussure's linguistics.

Derrida's critique of structural linguistics focuses on Saussure's attempt to introduce positive values into language. Much of the argument is driven by his charge that the Swiss linguist was guilty of "phonocentrism," of centering his linguistics around speech and the human voice. Derrida's main argument in this area has been challenged elsewhere.[20] I wish to focus my attention on a different problem: Derrida's discussion of the sign. The central issue here is his rejection of Saussure's attempt to derive positive values from signs which are differential in nature (i.e., defined by their differences).

What is radical about Saussure, according to Derrida, is his claim that "in language there are only differences." This claim, based on the notion that signifiers and signifieds endlessly refer to one another but never to any fixed or positive meaning, ostensibly destabilizes Western metaphysics and its assumption that there is an order of Being that might be known by thought. However, Saussure allegedly undermines this radical move when he suggests there are positive values in language. In so doing, he attempts to freeze the endless "reference from sign to sign" by positing an invariant structure that transcends every sign and confers a value on each of them. Within Saussure's linguistics, then, lurks the notion of a "transcendental signified," a concept which is a positive value unto itself, something outside the differential play of reference that determines the value of all signs. Derrida holds that, when Saussure tries to move from difference to positive values, he repeats Kant's search for transcendental knowledge, for knowledge of invariant features of the universe of knowing subjects. Put in economic terms, Derrida charges Saussure with trying to construct a *gold standard*, a universal equivalent separated off from the endless reference of one commodity to another. Rather than having to refer infinitely to all other commodities—a movement in which we never arrive at a fixed value (or price)—a gold standard enables that movement to be halted; now goods need only measure themselves against that item (gold) which, separated from the play of difference, defines all values. Similarly, argues Derrida, the idea of a transcendental signified—a determined measure of linguistic value—removes signs from their endless referral to one to another by endowing them with positive values and fixed meanings.[21]

Derrida intends to engage in a "de-construction of the transcendental signified" (OG, 49) by showing there is nothing, no thing-in-itself, that can escape representation by signs. There is, in short, nothing we might access behind signs or outside of representation: "From the moment that there is meaning there are nothing but signs" (OG, 50). Language is a sign, the sign "sign" is a sign, indeed, even *the thing itself is a sign*" (OG, 49). With these arguments, Derrida hopes to reinvigorate Saussure's original claim, prior to his move toward positive values, that in language there are only differences. And since there is no reality beyond language, since there is nothing outside representation, it follows that in being there is only difference as well. This is the position he tries to capture with his concept of *différance*.

I have already spoken somewhat inaccurately, however, since the point of Derrida's concept of *différance* is that he seeks to capture nothing with it, since there is nothing out there waiting to be captured beyond the infinite reference of one sign to another. *Différance* is not a conventional philosophical category, rather, it is a concept designed to trace a movement that is never really there in any substantial sense, that is, the differentiating movement that makes differences possible. Here, Derrida hints at the question that dominates Heidegger's philosophy: why is there something, not nothing, why are there beings (which partake of Being) rather than nothingness? The same question applies to language. Without differences, there would be no signs. Everything would then be the same—which is to say nothing. Without difference, then, no beings, entities, signs or language. All of these presuppose difference. But what founds difference? According to Derrida, as beings defined by difference, we can never answer this question much as we are compelled to pose it. We know that for things to be different (rather than all the same), there must be some condition that makes this possible. This is a condition prior to difference, but one which cannot be thought outside of, or prior to, difference (by thinking creatures who differ from some of those entities they think about).

Différance is the name Derrida gives to that condition of all difference. It is, in other words, the name of something that cannot be named. *Différance* is not, it is nothing, no-thing; it is the negativity, the no-thing, which founds linguistic differences. In this sense, it is Saussure's "form without a substance," except that form cannot be taken as a thing, an entity, or a structure. *Différance* might be said, therefore, to be the movement of form-ation of linguistic differences, "the formation of form" (OG, 63). As soon as we ask the question "what is *différance*?" we are already within *différance*, within language and the play of differences that *différance* makes possible. *Différance* is what is there before language—except that we can never know where (or what) that "there" is. Since it is in language that we talk about and interrogate *différance,* we are talking about something that makes this talk possible in the first place. Once we talk about *différance,* we are back into the endless play of reference; so *différance* is both undecidable (as all signs are for Derrida) and the very condition of possibility of that undecidability. This condition of possibility of difference leaves traces within language, in the very differences which constitute language. We can know something of *différance,* therefore, only in the referential movement of one sign to another.[22] And this is to say that our knowledge is a flow, a movement that traces a movement.

Lest I soon discourage my readers from continuing, let me endeavor to bring this discussion back to our central concerns of the moment. Let me show how this line of thought involves Derrida in economic assumptions whose unpacking may make all of this somewhat more digestible. In an interview devoted to this question, Derrida informs his interrogator that "there is no economy without *différance,* it is the most general structure of economy" (P, 8). But if this is so, Derrida would seem to be saying all economy is founded by a movement that is nothing, a movement without identity or meaning, a movement that is purely negative. But does Derrida really want to say that there are no positive values within economic life, no foundational activity, no praxis or labor that grounds economic relations?

The answer here is "yes," although it is a more complicated "yes" than might at first be apparent. In an important early essay entitled "Signature Event Context," Derrida argues that every sign carries within it the "structural possibility of being severed from its referent or signified."[23] To illustrate his point, he uses the example of the statement "The sky is blue," and points out that this statement can be uttered and understood even if no one, including the person who utters it, can see the sky, and even if it is patently untrue (indeed, even if it is a lie). The statement is thus a functioning part of language in the absence of a referent (a genuinely blue sky) to which it might be said to correspond. Now, from this example (which is full of confusions) Derrida draws the conclusion that signifiers can function even if they signify (refer to) nothing, that is, even if they are "severed" from a referent.[24] And he goes on to argue that because a statement can be reiterated in "infinitely new contexts"—for example, we can repeat the statement "the sky is blue" even when it is raining, snowing, or when we are imprisoned in a dungeon from which we cannot see the outdoors—it follows that every sign is potentially "a differential mark cut off from its alleged 'production' or origin" (SEC, 320 318). Every statement is capable of being severed from a referent, detached from its original site of production, while still functioning within language. This for Derrida demonstrates the folly of the whole idea of reference, of the very notion that signs refer to something and that they have a reasonably stable meaning. If "the sky is blue" can be a meaningful linguistic statement in the absence of a referent, concludes Derrida, then language is a self-referential system. In principle, then, there is no reason to prefer the statement "the sky is blue" when this is verifiably so, to the same statement uttered in a different context. Language suspends reference, it does not require something extra-linguistic.[25]

Let me see if I can now bring this discussion back to *différance* and the economy of language. In the last footnote to his *"Différance"* essay, Derrida makes an intriguing reference to Heidegger. Relating his concept of *différance* to the Heideggerian notion of Being, Derrida quotes Heidegger's claim in *On Time and Being* that "Being proves to be destiny's gift of presence, the gift granted by the giving of time."[26] Here, Derrida introduces an idea that will loom increasingly large in his later writings: that the fact of our being given life, the fact of having "time on earth" as the saying goes, eludes reason and all forms of human economy. The inexplicable fact that we live—that there is being rather than nothingness to use Heidegger's expression—is a "gift" that we take, a gift we receive from Being without any expectation it will have to be repaid. The gift is thus something completely outside the movement of human economy. Whereas the latter is based upon notions of exchange (giving in order to receive), the gift is simply given without anticipation of a future receipt. And here we encounter a seeming paradox: the gift of life is the condition of all economy (without life there is no economy); at the same time, the logic of the gift—giving without any notion of receiving in turn—escapes all economic logic according to Derrida. In developing these ideas, most systematically in *Given Time: I. Counterfeit Money,* Derrida clarifies his model of human economy in a way that illuminates his notions about language and politics.

Given Time: I is organized around the contrast between the gift and the economic circuit. Economics describes a circular movement: an individual gives an item in anticipation of receiving something in return. Just as a circle always returns to its point of departure, so a good of some sort always returns to a giver. All giving is thus a form of exchange, a giving in order to receive. This applies even to the gift-giving that has played such an important role in pre-capitalist societies. Taking issue with anthropological studies which see precapitalist gift-giving as eluding the economics of exchange, Derrida argues that even the individual who merely desires the satisfaction of giving happiness to another still wants something for him- or herself. Indeed, as soon as a gift appears *as a gift,* it negates itself. For, if a gift entails an obligation on the part of its recipient, even the obligation of acknowledging the gift, it constitutes a debt (the recipient owes gratitude, recognition, future payment). But then it is no longer a gift; it is instead inscribed within the economic circuit of exchange (giving in order to receive). A true gift would have to be immediately forgotten; were it to be remembered, it would entail obligation and thus reenter the economy of exchange.[27]

Now this argument involves a dramatic conclusion: human subjects cannot give gifts. After all, subjects exist to the extent to which they remember their "selves," to the extent to which they construct themselves narratively through time. Subjects know what is theirs: their lives, memories, histories, what "belongs" to them as subjects. To exist in time is to be in the economy of debt and exchange, to be in the circular movement in which things re-turn. But the gift is a rupture within this economy, and hence a rupture within time. Any "gift" within time immediately negates itself; the very fact of its being remembered (of existing as something you gave to me or I gave to you) inserts it into the economy of debt, obligation, and exchange.

As soon as human subjects differentiate themselves from others, they enter into economic relations, relations of property. Subjects calculate, they assess who and what they are and what belongs to them, and by doing so they differentiate their selves from others (they calculate what is proper to themselves, i.e., their own proper-ty). This includes the calculation that they are generous gift-givers. To see oneself as such is a property calculation, a calculation of oneself as commanding something (awe, gratitude, respect, etc.) as payment for who or what one is (in this case a gift-giver). The economy of the subject is an economy of calculation, of balance sheets, of credits and debts, of what one owes and is owed in turn. It follows, then, that *subjects are capitalists,* calculators intent upon being paid back with interest. And since subjects are constituted in and through language for Derrida, language too must be a system of calculation, a capitalist system.

"Language is as well a phenomenon of gift-countergift, of giving-taking—and of exchange," Derrida writes (GT, 81). After all, in language I name myself, I *give* my words, I exchange my words with yours. Language is thus a field in which selves are constituted and enter into exchange. And moving on to the example of writing, Derrida ascribes a capitalist logic to signing one's name. In so doing, I claim words, a text, a part of language as mine, as my property. And I expect something in return. By signing my name I construct a debt, I enter into a relation in which you, my reader, owe me something as payment for what I have written. In creating my product (which I sign), I expect payment with interest, with a surplus value: "As an identifiable, posed, bordered subject," says Derrida, "the one who writes never gives anything without calculating, consciously or unconsciously, its reappropriation, its exchange, or its circular return—and by definition this means reappropriation with surplus-value, a certain capitalization. We will even venture to say that this is the very definition of the *subject as such.* One cannot discern the subject except as the subject of this operation of capital" (GT, 101).

Yet, something always escapes the economy of the circle, some things are never returned, some things are endlessly, infinitely disseminated, contends Derrida. As much as I assert my claims, defend my property, remember my gifts and what is owed to me, it is also the case that some of what I circulate does not return, not everything I expend flows back to me. Where my words, my texts, my "gifts" do not stay within the economy of exchange, we might be said to touch upon the *death of the subject,* the limits of the subject's intentions and calculations. In reading a text I have written, for example, a reader may find a meaning I did not intend; indeed, a reader may claim to find a meaning I vigorously disavow. Yet, this is a gift of sorts, something I did not plan to offer, but which the reader received nonetheless. Circulating alongside the "gifts" I have offered up for exchange, in other words, are meanings I did not authorize, meanings I do not claim or accept (indeed which I might disown). But they are there because my offering exceeds me—and in so doing it exceeds the exchange economy (GT, 101-2).

This excess, that which was unauthorized, that which was not meant to circulate, could be a gift. And this returns us to the problem of money ("We can no longer avoid the question of what money is," [GT, 59]). For money is what validates something within the exchange economy. Money is the general equivalent that stamps everything with a price and announces its value, i.e., how much must be paid for it. But what about those things for which payment was not demanded? What of those elements of my text which I did not authorize but which circulate nonetheless? As an author I can claim they are counterfeit, that they are not my meanings and do not bear my signature. But where does the authentic end and the counterfeit begin? How do I know, for example, if my version of Saussure is real or counterfeit? More troubling, perhaps, when a reader interprets my text in ways I disavow, how can I stop this "counterfeit" from circulating? How do I demonstrate that they have misread me? And if I operate in a discursive field in which alleged "counterfeits" circulate alongside authorized meanings, how do I know the difference? When Nietzsche writes "I have forgotten my umbrella" in an unpublished manuscript, by what standard do I disregard this as a philosophical statement, while accepting the validity of other unpublished remarks (as I have done in chapter 1), or even of published ones?[28] For Derrida, all such distinctions are specious since all economies function on the principle of credit: we take words, texts, or currencies on faith. We take the change we are given after a purchase at the shop on faith; we spend these bills and coins and in so doing recirculate them without having first verified their authenticity. And we exchange and circulate words, letters, texts in the same way: "Everything is act of faith, phenomenon of credit or credence" (GT, 97).

It should be clear that this argument converges with Derrida's critique of Saussure's attempt to construct positive values for signs. Just as he sought to destabilize signs, so Derrida intends to destabilize all economies of meaning by showing that unauthorized meanings circulate within the economy of language. And this requires that he take up the question of money. Recall my question above where I asked by what "standard" I might differentiate true from counterfeit readings of a text. To pose the question could be said to involve the search for a stable system which orders all exchanges and stops the endless reference of one sign to another. But we live beyond the gold standard, beyond a universal equivalent and a transcendental signified, argues Derrida. We live "in the age of value as monetary sign" (GT, 124). Money now takes the form of paper currencies, checks, credit cards, and electronically coded signatures (GT, 110, 129). There is nothing fixed and stable that anchors all these dematerialized forms of money. Like the sign, money lacks a referent, it has broken away from a material foundation. Different forms of paper, even bits of electronic information, circulate on credit—just like my text. Counterfeit money, fraudulent signatures, and bad checks also function as "real" money since they facilitate exchanges. It follows that counterfeit money *is* money (GT, 153).

Since forms of money circulate without any referents, it can be said that capitalism, driven by credit and speculation, now operates without any necessary material foundations. Just like literary fiction, capitalism is a system in which the counterfeit cannot be differentiated from the real. The link between fiction and capitalism is important here. For credit, says Marx, is "fictitious capital." And fictitious capital, dematerialized money which circulates on credit, is for Derrida the purest form of all economy. Indeed, counterfeit money is the very truth of capital: "Counterfeit money can become true capital. Is not the truth of capital, then, inasmuch as it produces interest without labor, by working all by itself as we say, counterfeit money?" (GT, 124) In modern capitalism, in other words, capital can be created without material processes, without labor, even without (real) money. Thus, capital can issue "from a simulacrum, from a copy of a copy (*phantasma*)" (GT, 161).

Here Derrida's argument intersects with postmodernist theories of simulation which depict ours as a virtual economy based on the dissemination of images and their copies. According to writers like Jean Baudrillard, in our society the distinction between the real and its representation has dissolved, as signs and images have displaced things. If classic capitalism involved a shift from the production of use-values to the production of exchange-values, this was later superseded by a shift from exchange-value to sign-value. People now buy products for what they signify—images of happiness, health, beauty, eroticism, status. The connection of these images to real, material things is accidental at best. Perhaps inevitably, Baudrillard took this analysis a step further and proclaimed that commodity-signs refer only to themselves. Just as post-structuralist linguistics maintains signs do not refer to anything except other signs, so postmodernist social theory depicts an economy driven by sign-values independent of all external reference. No longer do we seek refuge in signs because of something to which they refer (happiness, beauty, etc.). Instead, we are automatically absorbed into the endless process by which signs refer to themselves. The purpose of any sign-system is, for post-structuralism, purely internal: it merely follows its own code. And this logic is now transferred to the ostensible postmodern society of simulation. What matters today is simply that the system keeps growing, that it continually reproduces itself. The point of the Xerox machine is not that it copies some particular thing, but that it copies to infinity. There is no point to television, Disneyland, theme parks, advertisements—they simply are what they are. In the cybernetic, digital economy of the computer, the microchip, the fax, the VCR, and fiber optics, we move within a circuit in which, like a photocopy machine, copies produce copies of copies. We are all now just copies in an infinite spiral of copying, of simulation: "You are no longer either subject or object, no longer either free or alienated—and no longer either one or the other: you are *the same* [like any copy—DM], and enraptured by the commutations of that sameness."[29]

While it is Baudrillard who most provocatively develops these arguments, similar theses inform Derrida's thinking. In *Specters of Marx* we are told, for example, that today more than ever "the political-economic hegemony, like the intellectual or discursive domination, passes by way of techno-mediatic power." As a consequence, claims Derrida, we urgently need to come to terms with "the new speed of apparition . . . of the simulacrum, the synthetic or prosthetic image, and the virtual event, cyberspace and surveillance, the control, appropriations, and speculations that today deploy unheard-of powers."[30] Derrida hints strongly throughout *Specters* that he subscribes to a number of postmodernist theses concerning virtuality and hyperreality. Moreover, many of his arguments, especially his criticisms of Marx's concepts of labor and use-value, rehearse arguments developed much earlier by Baudrillard.

In *For a Critique of the Political Economy of the Sign*, Baudrillard informs us that in modern society "use value no longer appears anywhere in the system." Later, in *Symbolic Exchange and Death*, he announces: "The end of labor. The end of production. The end of political economy." Finally, in *The Transparency of Evil*, he maintains that we now find ourselves in "an economy freed from 'Economics' and given over to pure speculation; a virtual economy emancipated from real economies."[31] Let us probe the connections between these claims.

Baudrillard's assertion that use-values have disappeared is based on a fundamental confusion. He argues in *For a Critique*, for example, that Marx's concept of use-value entails some notion of "pure" or natural human needs which are not socially mediated or constructed (FC, chap. 2). This is a dubious claim, to say the least. After all, Marx criticized Ludwig Feuerbach precisely for naturalizing human beings, treating them as products of nature not history. The *German Ideology* takes Feuerbach to task for focusing on sense experience to the detriment of sensuous *activity*. Extending this argument to the question of needs, Marx and Engels claim that what makes human beings historical creatures is the development of new needs: "the satisfaction of the first need . . . leads to new needs; and this creation of new needs is the first historical act." From here, they go on to insist that human production is always twofold, i.e., both a natural and a social relation.[32] Elsewhere, Marx explicitly attacks bourgeois political economy for trying to differentiate natural needs from artificial ones. Such a distinction reduces people to abstractly natural (i.e., nonhistorical) creatures whose true needs are simply biologically given, and thus indicates the "desperate poverty" of the bourgeois economic view of human beings.[33] For

Marx, history entails the development of new needs, new sensibilities, new modes of perception and experience: "the cultivation of the senses is the work of all previous history."[34]

Why, then, does Baudrillard so misread Marx on this point; why does he attribute to him the very (bourgeois economic) position he criticized? The answer seems to be that he wants to assimilate the (post)modern economy to the post-structuralist model of language. Just as signs refer only to other signs (and not to anything extra-linguistic), so Baudrillard insists that commodity-signs do not refer to use-values that transcend them. Incorrectly linking the notion of use-value to the idea of natural needs, he concludes that a society driven by consumption in order to satisfy ostensibly false, artificial or constructed needs would be a society beyond use-value and hence beyond the categories of Marx's analysis of capitalism. Since we now consume commodity-signs in order to acquire an identity, to become an object of desire, it follows for Baudrillard that we ourselves have become signs without referents, detached signs circuiting within a sign-system, or more accurately a system of copying, of simulation, with its own imperatives and its own code.[35]

The utter socialization of the real, its complete immersion in the circuit of the sign-system, means for Baudrillard, the transition to the "hyperreal" where the "real" is the copy of a copy, the simulated effect of a machinery of simulation—a simulacrum. Television, film, and video do not represent (or misrepresent) real events; there is no reality beyond their virtual constructions. When Baudrillard announced that "the Gulf war did not happen," he meant it—there was no reality outside what we saw on our television screens.[36] The age of simulation signals the end of any distinction between events and their representations. And this brings us to more endings: "the end of the scene of the historical, the end of the scene of the political, the end of the scene of fantasy, the end of the scene of the body."[37]

It is not my intent to work through all the levels of confusion and poor theorizing that characterize this sort of apocalyptic commentary. What interests me here is the idea that the body has disappeared, and that its disappearance has to do with money having become "hyper-realized." For Baudrillard, capital (if it should any longer be called that) has reached a point of hyper-autonomization. Speculative funds, money circuiting without reference to production, now constitute the pure form of capital, a self-moving non-substance that has no purpose other than its own endless reproduction. This unending flow of money has no effects, it does nothing. It is not about the appropriation of surplus-value, but, rather, involves "a sort of ecstasy of value, utterly detached from production and its real conditions: a pure, empty form" (TE, 27, 35). Within the new orbital society in which everything and everyone circles without a center of gravity, endlessly copied "money is now the only genuine artificial satellite. A pure artifact, it enjoys a truly astral mobility; and it is instantaneously convertible.

Money has now found its proper place, a place far more wondrous than the stock exchange: the orbit in which it rises and sets like some artificial sun" (TE, 33).

The end of labor, the end of history, the end of political economy and the body—all these endings are functions of the detachment of satellites from their centers of gravity. While Derrida does not engage in the same sort of apocalyptic sociological commentary that preoccupies Baudrillard, he arrives at similar conclusions. Like Baudrillard, Derrida believes that money has broken away from all reference, and he, too, rejects the idea that there is something substantial, some living process, which underwrites the simulated movements of images and specters. Marx is faulted, therefore, for wanting to exorcise the spectral forms capital assumes; he is impugned for trying to show that there are real bodies, real acts of labor that underpin these ghostly apparitions: "Marx continues to want to ground his critique or his exorcism of the spectral simulacrum in an ontology. It is a critical—but pre-deconstructive—ontology of presence as actual reality and objectivity. This critical ontology means to deploy the possibility of dissipating the phantoms . . . and of bringing this representation back to the world of labor, production and exchange" (SM, 170).

For Derrida, defetishizing critique is a metaphysical illusion based on pre-deconstructive ideas about "the real." This is especially so today when capital "produces interest without labor" (GT, 124). Nothing grounds the simulacrum of money, there is no distinction between counterfeit and real, there are no foundations. All of this sounds very radical. Whereas Marx hoped to banish the fetishes, to theorize a practice of liberation from enslavement to specters, Derrida has moved beyond all this. He knows the specters are real, or, rather, that everything is a specter, a ghostly image that haunts our waking lives. Marx thus stands condemned for his "pre-deconstructive" ontology. But are things really so simple? Isn't there something a little too easy about all this? Isn't there something curious about the haste with which Derrida exiles laboring bodies, bodies in pain, and the experiences to which they speak—among other things the experience of class?

FETISHISM AND THE LANGUAGE OF COMMODITIES: MARX VERSUS DERRIDA

It might be helpful to look at these issues in terms of the theory of fetishism. Especially instructive here is Thomas Keenan's deconstructive reading of Marx's discussion of the fetishism of commodities.[38] Keenan explores at length Marx's famous formula for a simple exchange relation in which twenty yards linen = one coat. The key to this formula according to Keenan is that concretely different things (like linen and coats) are replaced by equatable abstractions—words. Only in their replacement by words do concretely unique items become exchangeable:

"A coat is not a house, and they have nothing in common, just as Achilles is not a lion. Their substitution occurs only when their uses or things disappear and return as ghosts, different but alike to the extent that they are all *unfassbar* . . . or more precisely, words." In the next sentence, Keenan describes Marx's theory of fetishism as taking a "linguistic turn" as it moves from things to words (TPEI, 174). He then goes on to suggest that the problem of "what is to be done" opened by the question of commodity fetishism "is figured as a problem of reading and writing" (TPEI, 184).

What Keenan offers here is a linguistified theory of fetishism. Fetishism occurs with the entry of things into language; it is as words, rather than concrete things, that products become commodities capable of being exchanged. Like Derrida in *Specters of Marx*, Keenan insists that fetishism is always there. Just as language is always there before the thing (whose difference from other things presupposes language/writing), so the possibility of exchange is always there. There are no pure things prior to language, and there are no pure use values prior to exchange. Keenan refers to this as "simulation in advance"—things are always ready to be named, the possibility of being named inheres in them (TPEI, 184). Similarly, Derrida says that "the commodity-form began before the commodity-form," it was always there as the possibility things have of being exchanged, which is why we have always had capitalism (SM, 160). But before we buy into this linguistified theory of fetishism in which economic relations are conflated with the post-structuralist model of language, let us look more closely at what Keenan has done to produce this reading.

Discussing Marx's idea that commodity exchange involves abstraction from the concrete, useful characteristics of things, Keenan writes: "In abstraction—the operation that readies the things for exchange, that makes them exchangeable, and that exchanges them—not an atom of use value remains. Nor is anything left of the labor that has produced them, no thing but a strange residue" (TPEI, 173). Two pages later he continues: "What 'allows' exchange to happen is neither the labors nor the uses nor the things themselves but their abstracts, abstractions, operating as tokens (practical necessities) in a relation" (TPEI, 175). These abstracts or tokens, as we have seen, are words. It is words that bring things into relation, that abstract them and replace them by tokens; it is language that fetishizes in substituting words for things. Now, whatever this might be, it is not Marx's argument. Keenan "reads" *Capital* in a way that dramatically elides the very conceptual distinction Marx held to be crucial: that between concrete and abstract labor.[39] By repressing this conceptual distinction, by silencing it, Keenan gets the effect he wants: he banishes labor from the discussion of fetishism. Note, for instance, the two passages I have cited above in this paragraph. In the first, Keenan announces that when things exchange nothing is left "of the labor that has produced them." In the second, he asserts that "the labors" involved in producing things have no more to do with exchange than do their uses. Yet, in any responsible reading this is demonstrably not what Marx says.[40]

Marx tells us that commodities have a twofold character: they are use-values (objects of utility) and exchange-values. Use-values, Marx proceeds, do not determine exchange-values. It is not the usefulness of things which governs their values in exchange (otherwise air would have a high exchange-value and diamonds a low one). Exchange-value is determined in abstraction from the use value of a thing, an abstraction in which "all its sensuous characteristics are extinguished."[41] At the same time, such abstraction also extinguishes the unique, concrete features of the labor that produced the commodity. When commodities enter into exchange, then, this involves an abstraction from the unique characteristics of the weaving, spinning, joining, baking, and so forth, that produced them. These discrete, concrete acts of labor "are all together reduced to the same kind of labor, human labor in the abstract" (C, 128). What counts on the market is not the unique work involved in producing a commodity, but how that labor stacks up against and compares with the totality of social labor. Concrete labor counts, in other words, simply as a quantum of total social labor. And this requires that it be translated into the socially necessary labor-time that dominates production and exchange, that is, that the market abstract from the concrete work that went into making it and that it assess it as so many units of homogeneous (abstract) social labor.

As a result, commodities all have "the same phantom-like objectivity, they are all merely congealed quantities of homogeneous human labor, that is, of human labor-power expended without regard to the form of its expenditure" (C, 128). This abstract labor is no mental abstraction; it is the real social form of labor in modern society. Capitalism entails a very real abstracting process in which concrete labor is translated into quantities of homogeneous, interchangeable bits of abstract labor. (As Marx makes clear later in *Capital*, this abstracting movement becomes generalized where labor-power itself has become a commodity.) It follows that commodity fetishism is not constituted for Marx by a "linguistic turn"; it is not about linguistic tokens coming to replace use-values. Instead, Marx is describing a real social form of production which systematically abstracts from concrete labor and *compels* its translation into abstract labor. And he is not detaching exchange value from labor, as Keenan suggests. Value is not a sign freed from all reference. On the contrary, value is tied to human labor: without concrete labor there can be no abstract labor. But the connection between the two involves a complex and abstracted process of mediation. This is why Marx can write, "Human labour power in its fluid state, or human labour, creates value, but is not itself value. It becomes value in its coagulated state, in objective form" (C, 142). But this phantom-like objectivity of value must express itself in a material form, it is not self-referential; it must pass through some body in order to take form. Indeed, this is precisely what happens when we utter the formula twenty yards of linen = one coat. In this formula, the value of linen finds embodiment in the coat: "In its value-relation with the linen, the coat . . . counts therefore as embodied value, as the body of value." This, says Marx, is "the language of commodities" (C, 143): value expresses itself by assuming a material form through translation into the body of something outside it (another commodity). The language of commodities—like all languages for Marx—is a language of bodies. But capitalism abstracts from these bodies, from specific use values and the laboring subjects who produce them. And this is the secret of money—a secret Saussure and Derrida fail to interrogate.

In the first instance, money is the bodily form of value, it is that "other" through which commodities express themselves. Unlike the coat in the formula above, money is a general equivalent. It exchanges not just with a single commodity (e.g., linen), but with the entire world of commodities.[42] But in principle it is no different than any commodity (like a coat). In offering its body up as a universal equivalent, a money commodity offers the concrete labor that went into producing it as "the expression of abstract human labour" (C, 152). No matter how abstracted things become, the exchange between money and a commodity always entails exchanges of labor. What happens with money is that the abstract labor inherent in every commodity finds "an independent form of value." The twofold opposition internal to the commodity—between use-value and exchange-value, concrete labor and abstract labor—now finds an "external expression" in the relations between concrete particular (commodity) and abstract universal (money) (C, 181). On the basis of this argument, Marx insists that money is not a mere symbol, not simply a token or word that stands in for a thing:

> Money is not a symbol, just as the existence of a use-value in the form of a commodity is no symbol. A social relation of production appears as something existing apart from individual human beings, and the distinctive relations into which they enter in the course of production in society appear as the specific properties of a thing—it is this perverted appearance, this prosaically real, and by no means imaginary, mystification that is characteristic of all forms of social labour positing exchange-value. This perverted appearance manifests itself merely in a more striking manner in money than it does in commodities.[43]

Before proceeding further, let us pause to note how this passage blows apart Derrida's view that Marx simply wants to dissipate the phantoms and specters—the fetishes—of capitalist society. Fetishes are real for Marx—"prosaically real" as he puts it above—because human agents really are dominated by the abstracted forms assumed by their social relations. Dialectical critique demonstrates the relationship between fetishism and alienated conditions of life, but it cannot make them disappear—which is a practical task. But all theory is vulgar which takes the reified forms of appearance as self-evident (and inevitably self-reproducing) by failing to show their roots in a specific form of social organization. Thus, when Derrida describes "the truth of capital" in terms of its ability to produce "interest without labor, by *working all by itself* as we say" (GT, 124), he reproduces the very fetishism Marx exposed, that inversion by which powers are projected onto capital which in fact derive from its domination over living labor.

Indeed, one of the most explosive arguments developed by Marx in the manuscripts that make up the third volume of *Capital* occurs where he argues that interest-bearing capital predominates in vulgar economics because it is the purest fetish, that form of capital which appears to escape any connection to human labor. Because productive capital often needs access to money capital (to borrow in order to finance investment), the surplus value generated by wage labor is generally divided between interest (payment to money capital) and entrepreneurial profit.[44] While the source of interest is surplus labor, this connection is deeply obscured. Interest seems to accrue to money by virtue of some magical property of money itself. As a result, interest-bearing capital gives rise to the most extreme fetishism:

> Capital appears as a mysterious and self-creating source of interest, of its own increase. . . . In interest-bearing capital, therefore, this automatic fetish is elaborated into its pure form, self-valorizing value, money breeding money, and in this form it no longer bears any mark of its origin. The social relation is consummated in the relationship of a thing, money, to itself. . . . The fetish character of capital and the representation of this capital fetish is now complete.[45]

This form of capital, Marx continues, is "a godsend" for "vulgar economics, which seeks to present capital as an independent source of value" (C3, 517). Vulgar economics now finds a basis for constructing a "science" of economics which offers up a fetishized technical account of how things called land, labor, and capital generate their own forms of revenue (rent, wages, and interest respectively). A social theory of capitalism is now supplanted by a naturalistic model of the conditions of economic life. The apologetic economist never asks how it is that land comes to have a value, or how capital breeds interest out of itself without any mediation by labor. Instead, vulgar economics serves up another version of the myth of "self-birth." Determined to deny its origins in an "other"—in this case labor—capital claims the capacity to give birth to itself and all its offspring. "Any mediation disappears," writes Marx, in the mania of self-birthing capital, capital that begets interest of itself (C3, 956). In crude bourgeois economics, capital becomes a raging Nietzschean, an insatiable will to power that denies all otherness, that refuses to acknowledge its "origin" in labor, and that claims authorship of all the conditions of its existence. It is instructive that Derrida should embrace this form—capital which "produces interest without labor"—as "the truth of capital." For in promoting this view, in representing such fetishism as an advance upon Marx,

Derrida joins Nietzsche in repressing an origin that points toward a life-giving body, a body in labor.

It is in this light that we can make sense of Derrida's treatment of fetishism in *Glas*. Derrida there rejects defetishizing critique because to defetishize presupposes a truth, a decidable entity for which the fetish is a substitute. Antifetishistic critique is said to entail the "truth of a 'privileged' transcendental," a signifier that is not a signified, something that stands outside the serial movement of infinite reference. The problem with "what has always been called fetish, in all the critical discourses" is that these imply "the reference to a nonsubstitutive thing . . . a decidable value of the fetish."[46] Defetishizing critique presupposes decidability, it presumes that we can declare some things to be real and others to be fetishes. In rejecting decidability, Derrida opts for the position that everything is a fetish. Marx is naive, therefore, in supposing that dialectical critique can tease out the real within the fetish. In place of this naive metaphysics of truth—which does a disservice to Marx, as we shall see—Derrida works his account through Freud's concept of the fetish.

Freud's theory begins with the idea that a fetish develops when a little boy tries to deny what he has discovered—that his mother is "castrated," that she lacks a penis. Having once believed in the maternal phallus, the little boy is anxious that he, too, should not lose his penis, that he not be castrated. One way of alleviating this anxiety is to deny his mother's castration by setting up a substitute—a fetish object—for the missing phallus. Thus, when the fetishist later displays an obsession with women's feet, shoes, or undergarments, he is really clinging to a substitute for the maternal phallus. The fetishist, for Freud, is one who denies sexual difference, who attributes a phallus of sorts to a woman. But there is a curious ambivalence here: the fetishist simultaneously affirms and disavows the reality of female castration. Were it a straightforward case of denial, no substitute would be necessary; the boy would simply believe in his mother's phallus. But having discovered the reality of his mother's castration—a knowledge he prefers to disavow—he seeks to restore the maternal phallus in an indirect way, and thereby to live with both knowledge and its denial. The use of a fetish-object entails a simultaneous acknowledgment and denial of female castration. Implicit in this ambivalence about sexual difference is a sort of auto-castration; in denying sexual difference the fetishist must also repress the knowledge that he has something (a penis) that his mother lacks. Moreover, auto-castration also removes the terror of the discovery of female castration. If it is his own castration that the boy most fears, he eliminates that horrifying prospect by denying his own penis ("you can't take from me what I haven't got"). "In very subtle cases," writes Freud, the construction of the fetish embraces this sexual ambiguity by "covering up" sexual difference. Freud takes the example of a man who wears an athletic support belt that hides his genitals. Here "the distinction" between male and female genitalia is erased—and with it the threat and reality of castration.[47]

Derrida prefers this discourse of fetishism because it works on the terrain of undecidability and in so doing breaks out of the binary opposition of truth and fetish. In Derrida's reading, the fetishist erases sexual difference by becoming both male and female, and hence neither one nor the other. Because he is both castrated and not castrated, the fetishist moves in "an economy of the undecidable" (GL, 210). Castration figures for Derrida as a metaphor for "cutting through to a decision." And such acts of cutting through operate within the economy of difference where things are divided up, separated, differentiated, and distinguished as in language (where there are only differences). By destabilizing sexual difference, the fetishist moves outside the economy of sexual difference. Derrida thinks this happens in Nietzsche's texts too, especially when Nietzsche announces that he is a woman, that he is pregnant, that truth is a woman, that women love him, and so on. For Derrida, Nietzsche is a Freudian fetishist, one who dresses up like a woman in order to destabilize truth and identity.[48]

In making this argument, Derrida assimilates woman to the undecidable, he uses woman to deconstruct the obsession with decidability that characterizes philosophy. But as a number of feminist critics have pointed out, Derrida thereby treats woman as something outside of economy, culture, language, and philosophy. And this is to make woman an empty form—like *différance,* writing, the trace, or the gift—which lacks substance and specificity. As Kelly Oliver writes, "If woman or the feminine is valued because it is undecidable, then it is valued for what it is not. Woman is still not valued for what she is; she is not valued for her specificity. She is valued as a metaphor for the impossibility of any specificity." And given the bias of Western philosophy," erasing sexual difference amounts once again to erasing the feminine."[49]

Indeed, once he has tried to erase woman and sexual difference, Derrida can then follow Nietzsche's move toward self-birth. This theme weaves in and out of *Glas* as he takes up the idea of the mother as the text that always follows us as it precedes us. Whatever I write, however much I try to give birth to something entirely new, something of the text which frames my work, which makes my work possible in the first place, remains. Language, writing, textuality always precede and exceed me, just as something of my mother remains with me. And this inescapability of my mother—my implication in something, some*body* that is other than me—signifies my death since it erases my boundaries. But just like the fetishist, Derrida hopes to erase this (m)other, to assimilate her to himself: "I call myself my mother who calls herself (in) me. . . . I call my mother to myself, I call my mother for myself, I call my mother in myself, recall myself to my mother" (GL, 117). In making himself his mother, Derrida absorbs her, takes this other into himself, and then becomes his mother by giving birth to himself: "I give birth to myself (*Je m'accouche*), and I write myself (*je m'écris*) because of that" (GL, 193).

Luce Irigaray's *Marine Lover of Friedrich Nietzsche* argues that both Nietzsche and Derrida want to erase birth, that they seek to banish the mother, the feminine, the body, and the earth. To this end, they construct a "language-body" by making language, not the maternal body, the site of our birth: Nietzsche and Derrida want "life to be engendered from a language-body alone."[50] The body is thus linguistified, assimilated to language, its radical alterity denied. But Irigaray insists that there is something *prior* to language—which these philosophers wish to evade. Read in this light, the post-structuralist hostility to all talk of "origins" takes on a new complexion; it emerges as yet another in a long line of efforts to evade the maternal body. As Kelly Oliver suggests, "From Socrates as midwife to a pregnant Zarathustra, philosophy is full of attempts to forget the connection between woman and life. The latest attempt to forget might be the post-structuralist scoff at the "nostalgia" for origins."[51]

DIALECTIC AND MATERIALISM: FROM FETISHES TO HUMAN PRACTICE

This criticism brings us to Derrida's ostensible materialism. Occasionally, the founder of deconstruction has flirted with describing his method as a materialist critique of Western philosophy. And some of the most interesting work in deconstruction has followed up these hints by suggesting that Derrida's concepts of writing and the trace are reminders of the irreducible materiality of history which cannot be subsumed by thought.[52] Suggestive as such work is, it runs up against Derrida's evasion of materiality. After all, Derrida regularly states that his "materialism" has nothing in common with any notion of matter that includes "values associated with those of thing, substantial plenitude, content, referent, etc." (P, 64). What are we to make of this remarkable claim? After all, as Richard Harland notes, "it is an extraordinary redefinition that can leave matter stripped of any suggestion of reality or referent or even *thing*."[53] Yet, this is the price of Derrida's linguistification of life, his modeling of deconstruction on a radicalized concept of linguistic difference. Derrida's interrelated theories of language and the postmodern economy of signs subvert whatever materialist impulses might be identified within his thinking. The result is an idealist critique of idealism. True, Derrida wants to destabilize the totalizing pretensions of idealism. But he is unwilling to do this by degrading it, by forcing the thought-objects of idealism into contact with the world of bodies and things. As a result, his critical operation—if it can be called that—merely retraces the circles of idealism. And this is what accounts for the apparent parasitism of deconstruction, a parasitism that Derrida often celebrates. As much as he mocks the totalizing pretensions of philosophical idealism, Derrida refuses to move outside that framework; instead he merely gestures at its "others" which can only be assigned elusive names. But by resisting any move outside the circle of conceptuality, by repudiating any orientation toward referents or things outside thought, deconstruction evinces a sort of theoretical repetition compulsion: it is drawn back over and over again to the site of a wound—the banishment and forgetting of bodies and objects—which it compulsively avoids. Despite the materialist orientation of some who have taken up Derrida's approach, its hostility to all talk of origins or foundations which set limits to conceptual thought leaves deconstruction endlessly circuiting within the sphere of disembodied ideas. And it renders its critique of idealism empty and tedious.

In contrast, critical materialism—the dialectic of materialist critique—begins from the priority of the object. It does so not to hypostasize the dualistic separation of subject and object since this is a token of an antagonistic society, one in which hand and mind, labor and thought, have been separated and opposed to one another. Materialist critique begins from the struggle against idealism—against the subordination of nature and the world of bodies, objects and labor to subjectivity. And it does so not in order to invert this order of hierarchy, but to "abolish" it.[54] Starting from the standpoint of objects, of the non-conceptual, materialist critique resists all idealist moves to absorb the object into concepts. "Materialism," insists Horkheimer, "maintains the irreducible tension between concept and object and thus has a critical weapon of defense against belief in the infinity of mind." As a result, materialism "challenges every claim to the autonomy of thought."[55] It is in this spirit that I have employed the Bakhtinian strategy of degradation, a strategy designed to undermine the sovereign pretensions of thought by vigorously asserting the priority of bodies and objects. Seen in these terms Derrida's criticism of idealism merely feigns a materialist turn to objects. By avoiding bodies, matter and things, it encloses itself within the philosophy of consciousness and rejects the materialist injunction that thought "throw itself to the objects."[56]

Contrary to naïve criticisms, the materialist insistence on holding to objects, on acknowledging that they always exceed the powers of thought, is not a call to reductionism. For the turn to objects can only mean situating critical thought on the plane of practical human activity—in the midst of the dialectic of subject and object and the movements through which they pass into (but never absorb) one another. After all, "the sensuous world," insists Marx, "is not a thing given direct from all eternity, remaining ever the same, but the product of industry and the state of society." The world of objects is the world of objective human activity. At the same time, "in all this the priority of external nature remains unassailed"; otherwise we would be making the fetishistic error of equating a part (humankind and its history) with the whole of the objective world.[57]

This returns us to Marx's notion of defetishizing critique. For Derrida's hostility to defetishization can now be seen as a refusal to affirm anything outside of language-thought. When Derrida criticizes Marx for trying to bring fetishes "back to the world of labor" and for betraying a preference "for the living body" (SM, 170, 141), he resists that critical operation which shows that language and money do not give birth to themselves. In Derrida's economy of fictitious capital, our birth into language is detached from our origin in the bodies of others in much the same way that money-capital is treated as self-generating, without an origin in labor. In both cases, it is bodies that are repressed—*laboring bodies* to be precise.[58] This is the sense in which Marx's theory of fetishism *does* entail a certain sort of decidability. Not that Marx believes fetishes are simply false; on the contrary, as I have indicated, they are the necessary forms of appearance of alienated forms of life.[59] Nevertheless, Marx seeks to show that these fetishes can be undone—through the practical activity of changing society. And this requires a move from philosophy to a theory of practice which traces the connections of spirits, specters, and fetishes to the practices of living bodies—and which, in so doing, dispels myths of self-birth.

Too often, Marx's move here is read as if it involves a naïve assumption about an unchanging stratum of existence, a universal metaphysical principle (what Derrida calls a "transcendental signified") that is the secret to all riddles. It has become commonplace to suggest that Marx's materialism, with its insistence upon the irreducibility of labor, entails a reductionism which reduces everything to a "foundation," an invariant principle designed to explain all social phenomena. Certainly, mechanical notions of base and superstructure have often produced exactly this sort of analysis. A responsible reading indicates, however, that Marx was interested not in reductionism, but in showing that problems of philosophy and politics come back to questions of *practical human activity*. Marx seeks not to reduce phenomena to a thing called "the base" or "the economy," but, rather, to tease out the way in which all social phenomena refer to human practice and to their specific social processes and dynamics in a given historical context: "Where speculation ends, where real life starts, there consequently begins real, positive science, the expounding of the practical activity, of the practical processes of development of men. . . . When the reality is described, a self-sufficient philosophy (*die selbstandige Philosophie*) loses its medium of existence (GI, 43)."

It is here that Marx's critique poses such a radical challenge to conventional philosophy. By challenging its aspiration to make itself "self-sufficient," historical materialism forces philosophy into contact with that "other" that precedes it: human practico-material activity and its prehuman foundations. This is why Marx's thought works with a concept of historical bodies. And it is also why, when post-structuralists historicize human beings, when they attack naturalistic accounts of human life, they are picking up a theme already developed by Marx, but without Marx's insistence that the self-making in which humans engage is always structured by our embodiment and our history.

This last point is decisive. When Adorno writes that "dialectics is the consistent sense of nonidentity," he is getting at the fact that while humans are historical beings engaged in processes of self-making, we can never be entirely understood in terms of self-creation.[60] There is always something that precedes and exceeds human activity just as there is always something outside of thought.

The non-conceptual precedes and exceeds the conceptual, material life exceeds language and thought. Itself a product of objective life, thought can never entirely exhaust the complex richness of objects. Whereas idealism seeks to absorb all of objective life into the self-movement of thought, historical materialism recognizes that we are bound to processes and histories we did not authorize, that something always escapes our self-knowledge and our self-making, that we are never entirely identical with life itself (and, therefore, that we can never give birth to ourselves). Much as humans make themselves, in other words, they do so according to imperatives they have not authorized, on the basis of conditions (codes, "texts") to which they have not given birth. When Marx and Engels write that the first premises of human life involve "the physical organisation" of individuals (GI, 43) they are setting a limit to their dynamic theory of human self-development; the materialist conception of history entails the idea that human beings are also the products of natural history, a history involving billions of years of organic evolution. Marx's enthusiastic (but not uncritical) embrace of Darwinism registered his enduring commitment to limiting the arrogance of thought. While thought might try to understand a process of organic evolution of which it, too, is a product, it could never give rise to that process. *The Origin of Species* thus represented an insult to all the totalizing pretensions of thought; it humbled the human mind and, like Marx's historical materialism, called on thought to return from the heavens to the earth. It should come as no surprise that modern idealism rages against Darwinism, even if it does so in the brilliant and provocative form of Nietzsche's ambivalent anti-Darwinism. For "rage," Adorno notes, "is the mark of each and every idealism." Despite that rage, however, "it is not true that the object is a subject, as idealism has been drilling into us for thousands of years, but it is true that the subject is an object."[61]

Marx's insistence that thought return to earth, that it acknowledge its imbrication in practical human activity, that it give its due to the historical body, also represents a challenge to deconstruction and all forms of post-structuralism. This is curious given Derrida's recognition of the disquieting impact of Darwinism on philosophy. He writes in *Glas*, for instance, that "of the three wounds to anthropic narcissism, the one Freud indicates with the name Darwin seems more intolerable than the one he has signed himself. It will have been resisted for a longer time" (GL, 27). Yet Derrida does not pursue this point. He suggests occasionally that deconstructing the "difference" between "man" and "animal" is a move philosophy vigorously resists, but he does not investigate this line of thought either. Moreover, there are good reasons for seeing the "gift" which figures so prominently in Derrida's thought as the unacknowledged, unreturnable, nonrepayable gift of life itself. Life is something we are "given" without reason, something which, in escaping all human economies, is outside of logic and reason, beyond any human accounting. The gift of life is something that exceeds and escapes philosophy while also defining and determining it. This is why Derrida returns so often to "chance," to the inexplicable fact of life. After all, chance, not teleological necessity, is what dominates Darwinism. Life on our planet need not have happened, and once it arose it need not have taken the forms it did. Only through the random intersection of geological, climatological, and biological factors did humans emerge. Were the process to be restarted on its original conditions, it is improbable that humans would again develop. The fact of life is something for which philosophy can never account, it is a happening that determines philosophy while eluding its grasp. It is a limit that thought can never reach.

This would seem to be what Henry Staten has in mind when he writes that "my own view is that deconstruction and everything else are ultimately contained in Darwin's tale."[62] Yet, Derrida never takes us into the region of this tale, and his failure to do so does not appear to be a refusal to broach the inexplicable. For, on occasion, he does approximate this region, only to turn abruptly away. In a little-discussed essay, he acknowledges that "the language of bodily organs and functions would thus in turn be a set of symbols referring back to an even more archaic language, *and so forth*. This being so, it would seem logically flawless to consider the organism as a *hieroglyphic text*, deposited in the course of the history of the species." But Derrida refuses this move. He argues that this would entail "turning the object-text into a substance" or a "dead symbol."[63] Yet, as I have argued with respect to Marx, it should in principle be possible to trace out a movement, a process of formation that is not a reified substance, and to say something about its structures and dynamics. Such a move would allow us to show the inherence of human language in "the language of bodily organs and functions" without reducing it to these. And this move is vital if we are to avoid the regular collapse into idealism that characterizes deconstruction.

Derrida's refusal to investigate origins amounts to an evasion of bodies, their births, and their roots in an organic world that precedes and exceeds them. The result is an increasingly empty clunking about in a philosophy of consciousness. As Peter Dews notes, whereas Adorno and Merleau-Ponty respond to the collapse of the philosophy of consciousness by moving " 'downstream' toward an account of subjectivity as emerging from and entwined with the natural and historical world," Derrida moves " 'upstream,' in a quest for the ground of transcendental consciousness itself."[64] As a result, he becomes enamored of entities—fetishes—which leave their bodies and deny their inherence in history and the realm of practico-material relations. Derrida thus gives us language detached from bodies, money detached from labor—in short, beings engaged in self-birth. Darwin and Marx, like Freud, are two of the great debunkers of myths of self-birth. They insist that origins matter and that their recognition is decisive to humbling the arrogance of mind. In challenging idealist denials of origins, Darwin and Marx draw us a radically new picture of language and its inherence in bodies and their histories.

3

BODIES THAT TALK: SEX, TOOLS, LANGUAGE, AND HUMAN CULTURE

Bodies talk. Watch a child gesticulate as it struggles to form a word, observe someone gesturing while talking on the telephone, attend to the amazing range of physical motions that occur when someone speaks. Do all of this and you become aware of a cascading movement of tongue, hands, larynx, facial muscles, eyes, jaws, and more. Listen to neurologists, speech therapists, and others and you quickly learn that there is much more bodily activity that is not directly observable. Spend any time studying the complex physiology of speech and language and it becomes increasingly difficult to accept the rarefied tone in which language is discussed in most social theory. Bodies talk. But bodies that talk have not appeared magically on this planet. Talking bodies have evolved. And we can make some sense of that evolution—*if* we are prepared to engage seriously with the findings of modern Darwinism.

To engage with Darwinism is no easy thing. In addition to being wracked by controversy, evolutionary biology is also plagued by dubious political currents (often dressed up in the guise of "sociobiology"), which seek to reify existing hierarchies and modes of domination by locating their sources in our genes. Too often, however, this has led critics to turn away from the field of controversy by dismissing the sciences as a whole and even, in the case of much postmodernism, treating them as pure fictions of modernist imaginations. While it is good counsel to attend to the one-sidedness and ideological segmentations of the sciences, we are ill-served by a relativism that treats all theories, from creationism to Darwinism, as equally valid stories. Rather than dismissing scientific knowledge, we need to integrate its partial truths into a more comprehensive and many-sided account by way of critique.[1] Moreover, critical theory can only gain by building upon the work of critics who have used evolutionary biology to expose and debunk racism and sexism, often with devastating results.[2] In refusing to engage important work in the natural sciences which bears directly upon their concerns, social theorists fall prey to dualistic separations of nature and culture, animal and human, body and mind. As Vicki Kirby puts it: "To prohibit any mention of biology as inappropriate to critical theory, a stance that permeates much contemporary discourse in cultural studies, is a frightened reflex that only reinvests in the prescriptive determinisms."[3]

In his manuscripts of 1844, Marx suggested that the divergence of philosophy and the natural sciences had been to the detriment of both. He proposed to bring the two together in a theory which would be both historical and materialist: "Natural science will then abandon its abstract materialist, or idealist, orientation, and will become the basis of a *human* science."[4] In the early history of the Frankfurt Institute for Social Research, Max Horkheimer expressed a similar aspiration with his insistence that "materialism requires the unification of philosophy and science."[5] Later critical theory has suggested that notions of unification may be too simple. As a result of the damage done to both philosophy and the natural sciences through their separation, they cannot simply be added together since, as Theodor Adorno regularly reminded us, damaged pieces do not add up to a whole.[6] The social and intellectual conditions for the reconciliation of philosophy and science through their mutual transformation are, however, absent today. For present purposes, I propose a more modest operation: to route a social theoretic discussion of language through the domains of evolutionary biology, paleontology, and anthropology. By pushing social theory into contact with these "others," I hope to materialize the discussion of language. I hope also to show that there are indispensable findings of various sciences which, however partial and one-sided they might be, cannot be circumvented by a social theory interested in the embodied character of human life and the consequent materiality of social practices. My account begins where it must—with Darwin himself.

DARWIN'S DANGEROUS IDEAS, 1: NATURAL SELECTION

The powerful resistance within Western intellectual culture to the theory of natural selection has often been noted. So extreme is this resistance among some writers of postmodernist persuasion that their disavowal of everything biological implies a sort of "new creationism," which radically separates humans from the realm of natural history.[7] While some part of this anti-biologism may arise from insidious distortions of Darwin's theory by right wing ideologues, much of it stems from hostility to the anti-teleological materialism that is central to the Darwinian enterprise. For *The Origin of Species*, as Marx noted, dealt "a deathblow... to 'teleology' in the natural sciences."[8] Yet, this verdict will surprise those who misunderstand Darwin as a teleologist for whom evolution entailed ineluctable progress. Given the prevalence of this misunderstanding, it may be worth starting with some clarifications in this area.

To begin, a qualification: I am interested here in the core propositions of Darwin's theory of natural selection, propositions which he often tried to soften rhetorically. As Adrian Desmond and James Moore argue, Darwin was frightened and disturbed by the ideologically radical implications of his theory—so much so that he held back from publishing his ideas for twenty years.[9] A respectable country gentleman of Whig persuasions, Darwin knew his ideas represented a frontal assault on the ruling view that all hierarchies in nature and society were divinely ordained on the principle that some (the higher types) should rule while others (the lower types) should serve. In attacking the doctrine of the separate creation of species, in maintaining that all life forms have a common origin, Darwin was engaged in a "leveling" operation that could only be construed as an attack on authority. To avoid inciting opposition on political grounds, he sought to dull the cutting edge of his theory by packaging it in terms less threatening to his middle- and upper-class audience. So radical were the implications of his theory, however, that this dulling operation was never more than partially successful.

Darwin's radicalism emanated from his attack on the dominant world view at a crucial point: its claim for the separate creation of all species of life on earth. Knowing that his theory removed this linchpin of the ruling ideology, Darwin recoiled from publicly presenting his opinions. To the botanist Joseph Hooker, he wrote that revealing his views on the mutability of species was like confessing a murder: "I am almost convinced . . . that species are not (it is like confessing a murder) immutable," he confided.[10] Indeed, only in *The Descent of Man* (1871), twelve years after he first published his revolutionary theory in the *Origin*, did Darwin take credit for this accomplishment. Even if he had somewhat exaggerated the force of natural selection, he wrote, "I have at least, as I hope, done good service in aiding to overthrow the dogma of separate creations."[11]

And just as he had not trumpeted this conclusion in *Origin*, so he had avoided the question of human origins there. Only a cryptic comment near the end of the book suggested that, as a result of the theory of natural selection, "Light will be thrown on the origin of man and his history."[12] But this was the rub. Not only had God not created the whole range of species we find on earth, neither had he created humankind. The human species had evolved from predecessors in much the same way as every other life form. In one fell swoop, humanity lost its special status. This conclusion is couched in cautious and detached prose in his published writings. But in his private notebooks and personal correspondence, Darwin often made his point in a mocking style fully conscious of the scale of his heresy: "Our ancestor was an animal which breathed water, had a swim bladder, a great swimming tail, an imperfect skull, and

undoubtedly was an hermaphrodite! Here is a pleasant genealogy for mankind,"
he informed one scandalized friend.[13] Darwin's Notebooks B and C written in
1837 and 1838, more than twenty years before the publication of the *Origin of
Species*, are replete with passages which register his subversive claim that humans
were not separately created. "People often talk of the wonderful event of intellectual man appearing," he writes in one passage,"—the appearance of insects
with other senses is more wonderful."[14] It is worth noting too that Darwin
explicitly rejects the idea that humans (or any other species) represent some kind
of "progress" over others: "It is absurd to talk of one animal being higher than
another. We consider those, where the intellectual faculties most developed, as
highest.—A bee doubtless would [use] . . . instincts." And again: "In my theory
there is no absolute tendency to progression."[15]

Darwin's theory pivots on the assumption that the stunning array of life
forms we see in the world arose from a common source as a result of variations
that proved favorable to the survival and reproduction of diverse organisms.
Heritable variations that improve the survival and reproductive success of members of a species are passed on to their descendants, resulting in new forms and,
under some circumstances, in new species. Life forms thus experience continual
processes of change based upon the preservation among descendants of favorable
variations inherited from their predecessors. Since life involves difficulties in
subsisting and in producing offspring which survive, species evolve (and in some
cases give rise to new species) as a result of variations that prove to be of
"adaptive" value, which help them better survive and reproduce in a given environment (OS, 115).

Darwin floundered, however, when it came to the mechanics of heritable
variation. Only the modern development of Gregor Mendel's work on genes,
and subsequent research on DNA and RNA, enabled biologists to identify the
mechanisms that drive variations and mutations within organisms and, thereby,
to construct a new synthesis of evolutionary and genetic biology (usually described as "modern Darwinism"). In specifying how variation occurs, modern
Darwinism filled a crucial gap in Darwin's original theory and moved on to
firmer ground in rejecting teleological notions of extra-natural forces that guide
the evolutionary process. Modern Darwinism sees a self-replicating code of life
that undergoes random, purposeless, and undirected variation. Many variations
are not preserved among life forms (their bearers finding them less adaptive in
the struggle to survive and reproduce), but some, being favorable, are inherited,
leading to greater diversification of forms of life. Central to modern evolutionary
biology, therefore, is the idea of a self-replicating code which occasionally produces a chance or random mutation. As one commentator notes, at least two
properties are necessary if something is to be a unit of natural selection: "First,
it must be able to reproduce itself (more strictly, of course, copies of itself); it
must be self-replicating. Second, it must have the good luck not to replicate
absolutely faithfully but to make occasional slight mistakes."[16]

Yet, as these formulations indicate, evolutionary biology is prone to atomistic and mechanical formulations of the sort that give rise to ideas like "selfish genes."[17] Such concepts offer up a picture of the biological world in which organisms and environments are merely passive entities used by genes in their "selfish" drive to reproduce (from which point it often seems a short leap to suggest that selfishness, competition, war, capitalism, and male domination are all in our genes). Yet, as Richard C. Lewontin explains, "genes can *make* nothing," they are not the uniquely determining units of biological (never mind social) life. Genes are long sequences of nucleotides crucial to the production of proteins. Yet the process of producing proteins is not magically driven by genes alone: "proteins cannot be manufactured without both the gene and the rest of the machinery. Neither is more important." In short, genes must be "read" and their instructions acted upon (and modified) by other parts of the "machinery" of living organisms. There is not a relationship of mechanical causality here (gene determines organism) but, rather, a more complex kind of interaction which is not reducible to one of its elements (the genes). "If anything in the world can be said to be self-replicating," explains Lewontin, "it is not the gene, but the entire organism as a complex system."[18]

A focus on the organism as a complex system is crucial to any meaningful notion of evolution since natural selection operates directly on bodies (or "phenotypes"), not genes. What natural selection "favors" are complexes of physiological features (e.g., a hand with an opposable thumb capable of intricate manipulation of objects) that involve a bundle of interrelated genes, or genotypes. Rather than mapping onto specific body parts, genes drive a number of interrelated physiological and behavioral characteristics of organisms; they have multiple (and interrelated) not singular effects on an organism. In *The Origin of Species*, Darwin draws attention to many "instances of correlation" in which various features regularly appear together: "cats with blue eyes are invariably deaf.... Hairless dogs have imperfect teeth... pigeons with feathered feet have skin between their outer toes" and so on (OS, 75). These are all examples of multiple and interconnected genetic effects. Natural selection cannot "know" any of this. It simply favors certain kinds of genetic changes by "selecting" phenotypic features that affect the survival and reproductive prospects of an organism. Natural selection, in other words, is not simply a story about genes. It is about the physiological and behavioral characteristics of organisms and the relationship of these to genetic change.

Moreover, as Levins and Lewontin show in their polemic against "vulgar Darwinists," genes operate variably in different environments.[19] In addition, environments themselves are not static; they are teeming with a multitude of organisms, each one changing and modifying the environment in subtle and complex ways. The successes and failures of one species will often radically affect the conditions of others. Darwin pictured this interconnectedness of forms of life when he described plants and animals as being bound by "a web of complex relations." In the *Origin*, he takes a single example: the dramatic changes brought about by the enclosure of several hundred acres of land in Staffordshire (which kept cattle off this land), and the introduction of a single species of plant (the Scotch fir). The results, explains Darwin, involved the flourishing of twelve new species of plants and six insectivorous birds (which means that the effects on insects must have been quite dramatic). The only reasonable conclusion is that species intersect "in ever increasing circles of complexity" (OS, 123-25). Organisms *do* adapt to environments, but they also constitute and transform environments. Each new adaptive move triggers environmental changes which favor further adaptations, and so on. Sometimes changes are dramatic; other times they involve delicate shifts in the "web of complex relations" that constitutes actual environments. Recognizing this, many biologists now depict natural selection as a continuous process taking place all the time, not simply during episodic disruptions of long periods of stasis.[20] This more dynamic view of natural selection returns us to the problem of natural *history*. And it underscores at least three key points.

First, if the environment is continually changing, then there is a selective premium on behavioral flexibility or adaptability. Members of a species who can discover new ways of feeding or breeding will be favored during periods of environmental stress and change. While some of this will be phenotypically given—a longer or deeper beak, for example—some changes will also involve new forms of behavior and activity which are not instinctually precluded. Indeed, it appears that "instincts are malleable," as Jonathan Weiner has put it, drawing on a wide range of evidence concerning birds in the Galapagos. Observing birds that bred with members of other species during periods of swift environmental change, he argues that even things as allegedly fixed as sexual instincts can change. Whereas successful breeding across species may be very rare (and largely unsuccessful) much of the time, there are also periods of environmental change in which it is favored.

Second, the dynamic view puts a greater weight on the selective value of species being able to learn from their environments, register new problems, discover new solutions, and pass these on to other members of their species, particularly their offspring. In *The Evolution of Culture in Animals* and *Life Cycles*, John Tyler Bonner demonstrates not only that animals can learn, but also that the knowledge attained by individuals can be passed on to other members of the species.[21]

Finally, the more dynamic and historical view of natural selection reinforces a point often made by Stephen Jay Gould: that natural selection is strongly conditioned by history. Rather than being able to design a body part or a phenotypic effect as an ideal solution to an environmental problem, natural selection must work by modifying what has come before. For this reason, biological evolution often involves odd and peculiar sorts of "rejiggings" of existing structures. Like a tinkering artisan, natural selection must work with what is at hand.

Gould offers the panda's thumb as a case in point, reminding us that it is not really a finger at all, but rather a unique structure that evolved from a bone which is normally a small part of the wrist. The result is "a somewhat clumsy, but quite workable, solution" to the panda's need for an opposable digit.[22]

Evolutionary theory thus entails a rich view of *natural* history. On top of this, the emergence of language- and tool-using primates introduces a new order of temporality: human history. Contrary to dualist theories of nature and culture, however, I do not hold that human history catapults us out of the realm of biology. Instead, human history superimposes new orders of determination upon those of natural history. This involves complex processes which extend the capacities of human bodies through technology, language, and social organization. But these are new structures of embodiment, not supersessions of the body. In the materialist conception of history, therefore, biology is seen "as a set of potentialities and insuperable necessities," not a set of rigid genetic determinations.[23] To drop biological determination entirely out of account, however, is to depict culture as a leap from embodiment which introduces an "abyss" between humans and animals. A non-dualistic materialist account of language and culture will have to attend to their bases in natural selection. But before turning to language and culture, it is necessary to discuss an oft-neglected aspect of Darwin's theory—his concept of sexual selection.

DARWIN'S DANGEROUS IDEAS, 2: FEMALE SEXUAL SELECTION

Few aspects of Darwin's theory have been so dismissed by evolutionists as his theory of sexual selection. One reason for this seems clear: despite a number of equivocations, Darwin put an overwhelming stress on *female* sexual selection, that is, on the choice of male sex partner by females of a given species. Noting that in species after species—of insects, fish, birds, amphibians, reptiles and mammals—males were more brightly colored, and that these colorings often made life more dangerous (since their bearers were easier prey for predators), Darwin ascribed to female sexual selection a quite considerable power. How else, he asked, might we explain something as ornamental and extravagant as the peacock's tail or the antlers of the reindeer unless we ascribe to them an advantage in being selected for sex by females of the species? Darwin's attribution of an active sexuality to the females of many species bordered on the heretical. It was vigorously opposed by the co-discoverer of natural selection, Alfred R. Wallace and has been rejected by a long line of evolutionists who attribute near-total power to natural selection.[24] Where sexual selection was admitted, it was attributed to males. Thus, Karl Groos in his turn of the century book, *The Play of Animals,* expressed the orthodox opinion when he wrote that "seldom or never does the female exert any choice. She is not the awarder of the prize, but rather a hunted creature."[25] Darwin, too, lapsed into traditional Victorian ideas about the aggressiveness of males and the passivity of females. Yet, these conservative leanings could not undercut the radical implications of his claim that in most species it was "much rarer" for males to select females as sexual partners than vice versa (DM, 1:263). While acknowledging that males often fought one another for females, he resisted the simple idea of male conquest: "in a multitude of cases the males which conquer other males, do not obtain possession of the females, independently of choice on the part of the latter" (DM, 1:262).

One weakness in Darwin's account of female sexual selection is its lack of any real explanation as to the advantageous characteristics females might be selecting; he didn't see that in choosing on "aesthetic" grounds, females might be selecting less "trivial" features in the male (since ornamentation, coloring, song, or size might be indicators of some other characteristic). It is instructive, for instance, that nest-building by male birds is an integral part of their sexual display for choosing females. While male size, coloring, and singing appear also to be selected for, these may all be signs of the physical capacity and behavioral willingness of males to make a "paternal investment" in their offspring (by way of vigorous protection of the young and their provision with food).[26] Nor should we neglect evidence that females in many species prefer to mate with those who provide food. In some cases, the food is the male itself: the orb-weaver spider, for instance, eats her mate while he is copulating with her.[27] Thus, while female sexual selection may be triggered by "aesthetic" signs—bright colors, long feathers, pleasing songs—these often correlate with capacities to provide food or protect offspring from predators. Moreover, when we look at chimpanzees, the species which is biologically closest to humans, we find considerable evidence that "females prefer males that associate with them in parties, who groom them, and who share food with them."[28]

Discussing sexual relations among chimpanzees may seem a peculiar twist in a book on language. But there is good reason for anthropologists, evolutionary biologists, linguists, and psychologists to pay special attention to the study of chimpanzees: chimps and humans developed from a common ancestor sometime between five and eight million years ago, quite a short time in the four billion years of natural evolution on earth. Moreover, since humans share over 98 percent of their genes with pygmy chimps, natural selection produced some momentous changes with quite minimal genetic modifications. Study of the genetics, physiology, social organization, and culture of chimps should thus give us important indications as to those developments in hominid evolution (the evolution of bipedal primates) that account for some of the unique features of modern humans. Not surprisingly, since language is often identified as distinctively human, much attention has been devoted to the linguistic capabilities of chimps. Rather than treating language as *the* distinctively human feature, however, I believe we ought to see it as one part of a package of evolutionary changes within the hominid line, as part of a *biocultural matrix* that distinguishes our species. Put simply, if language is intimately bound up with our bodies, then it will also centrally involve the way hominid bodies and behavior changed with respect to sex, reproduction, child-rearing, food gathering, toolmaking, social organization, and cultural learning.

FEET, FOOD, TOOLS, SEX, AND THE EMERGENCE OF HUMAN LANGUAGE

The dualistic mind-body schema that dominates Western thought has often focused on the emergence of mind and its organic foundation, the brain. Yet, an increasing number of commentators in biological anthropology see the growth and development of the human brain as consequence, not cause, of other crucial changes. Dissenting from the "brain-centered" approach, Stephen Jay Gould argues that "the great punctuation in human evolution" was bipedalism. "Upright posture is the surprise, the difficult event, the rapid and fundamental reconstruction of our anatomy," he states. "The subsequent enlargement of our brain is, in anatomical terms, a secondary phenomenon, an easy transformation embedded in a general pattern of human evolution."[29]

Gould would seem to have a compelling body of evidence on his side. Bipedalism required major anatomical changes, particularly to the structure of the hominid foot and pelvis, but also to the hand, respiratory apparatus, and rib cage. Since the modes of activity these changes imply entailed losses—decreased access to trees to escape predators while moving on two legs around the savanna and problems of heat and dehydration while away from the shade trees provide—they must also have involved considerable gains in finding means of subsistence. The long-standing idea that the shift to bipedalism was driven by a major environmental change—dramatic contraction of forests and the growth of open grasslands or savannas—has encountered a whole series of empirical difficulties. It now seems more likely that our increasingly bipedal predecessor of three or four million years ago still spent much time in the forests, while also using improved bipedal locomotion to forage more widely in search of berries, seeds, small animals, and possibly larger animals that had been killed by other species.[30] In any case, bipedalism could not have been a viable adaptation without major changes in social behavior such as food sharing and cooperative child-rearing.[31] Once viable, however, the shift to bipedalism as the principal form of locomotion opened up new anatomical and behavioral possibilities. In particular, as numerous commentators have pointed out, bipedalism "freed" the hands for purposes other than movement through the trees or on the ground. In the first instance, this would suggest an increasing use of the hands for carrying objects—leaves or shells full of water, seeds, fruit, and berries, children (in the case of mothers at least), small game, parts of the carcass of large animals, containers, sticks (as both weapons and digging tools), and stone tools. Such uses for the hands would have favored anatomical changes that improved carrying and object manipulation (perhaps especially for tool use and toolmaking).[32]

At the same time, greater facility at using and fashioning tools (containers for carrying, digging sticks, stone artifacts for cutting), and at throwing rocks and sticks at small game and predators would have made it possible for bipedal, tool-using hominids to exploit a wider range of resources. This suggests reinforcing selection for both bipedalism and hands capable of greater dexterity. In addition, the active uses of the hands might have provided an impetus to increasing use of vocal communication to supplement gestures (and to changes with respect to the physiology of vocalization). In any case, it seems clear that substantial changes in the "mode of life" would be implied by these anatomical and physiological changes.

To see this, let us begin with the evidence of chimpanzees.[33] Chimps engage in a foraging way of life. Moving around in small groups in search of plant foods, they eat in an overwhelmingly individual and on-the-spot fashion: he or she who finds, consumes immediately. Thus, although chimps live a highly social existence, foraging and feeding are largely solitary. There are a few important exceptions to this, however. First, mothers regularly provide food to their offspring. Second, there is some food sharing by adult males with adult females. Finally, meat, a fairly rare item in the chimpanzee diet, is quite regularly shared—especially with older males, close kin, and females in estrus. Chimps are also tool-users and rudimentary toolmakers. They modify sticks in order to probe for termites, ants, and honey; they use leaves to soak up water in tree holes; they employ stones to hammer tough-skinned fruits; and they wave and throw sticks and rocks to scare other creatures, or to hunt animals.[34]

Turning now to human hunter-gatherer societies, as they are most commonly described, we can make some of the following generalizations. First, gathering—not hunting—is the central economic activity: the bulk of calories people consume comes from gathering plant food (nuts, roots, vegetables). In economic terms, hunting is a "high risk" activity, groups of men regularly returning empty-handed. Recent assessments of gathering highlight the central economic role of women in such societies: for the !Kung of the Kalahari desert, for example, 60 to 80 percent of diet is provided by women's gathering activities. Second, so proficient are humans at gathering that adults "work" considerably fewer hours than do wage-laborers in a modern capitalist society. This leaves a large amount of time for "leisure" activities and social interactions. Third, although subsidiary to gathering, hunting plays an important role in economic and social life. While providing a small proportion of calories consumed, meat is widely shared among people in the band; it involves some of the most overt forms of altruism.[35] Gathering-hunting societies, as they might more appropriately be called, also involve regular tool-use and toolmaking. Containers for carrying, rather than weapons for hunting, may have been the crucial innovation; they would have opened up the possibility of concentrated gathering followed by group eating (involving at least women, children, and older males).[36]

With the growing efficiency of gathering, hunting may have become a more distinct activity. While gathering, women and men with containers and digging sticks could have used their sticks for opportunistic hunting of small burrowing animals. Similarly, the throwing of stones to injure or kill larger animals—something observed in chimps—might also have evolved as a gathering-related activity. Increasing skill at these forms of hunting alongside greater efficiencies in gathering could have provided an impetus to more and more specialization in organized hunting (which need not have been an exclusively male pastime).[37] If these speculations are valid—and they have the support of a growing body of anthropological literature—then it makes sense to suggest that ancestral homi-nids had a "mixed economy" based upon gathering, hunting and food sharing. This hypothesis appears considerably more persuasive than earlier "man the hunter" models of hominid evolution with their emphasis on men as carnivorous killers; it incorporates important findings of the "woman the gatherer" model without denying that hunting, sharing of meat, and food sharing generally, played a key role in hominid social development.[38] Indeed, it may be, as Richard Leakey has argued, that "sharing, not hunting or gathering as such, is what made us human."[39] But what is the evidence for food sharing? And why should it have become such an important part of the hominid adaptation?

Exploration of archaeological sites at Koobi Fora shows combinations of artifacts and animal bones which indicate that, by about two million years ago, hominids shared food at a "central foraging place."[40] This is unquestionably a unique behavioral adaptation. But why should it have evolved? Here, I would suggest, we are returned to questions of child-rearing, hominid sexuality, and female sexual selection.

Human infants, as has often been noted, are born "prematurely." Compared to most newborn animals, even newborn primates, human infants are remarkably dependent. They have no capacity to function independently and their matura-tion toward rudimentary skills in this regard is remarkably slow. There are good biological reasons for this. As natural selection favored bigger brains—for rea-sons I discuss below—it also favored "premature birth." In light of anatomical changes to the pelvis associated with bipedalism, hominid infants must be birthed after about nine months if their heads are to get through the female birth canal with a minimum of complications. In terms of their development, however, "human babies are born as embryos, and embryos they remain for the first nine months of their lives."[41] The main reason for this is brain related: at birth the brain of a rhesus monkey is 65 percent of its final size, chimp brains are about 40 percent of final size, while human infants have attained only 23 percent of brain growth.[42] At point of birth, infant skulls are soft and not fully formed and an enormous amount of the brain's growth must happen outside the mother's womb. This is growth that would otherwise happen inside the womb (in the absence of infant skull/maternal birth canal complications). The unique helplessness of human infants is a consequence of being birthed at an early point in developmental terms. Then, because large brains are favored by slowing down developmental patterns (which involves "neotony," the retention by adults of juvenile features like relative hairlessness, smaller jaws and canines, playfulness and rapid learning), these premature infants also have a prolonged childhood and require substantial and sustained care, attention, protection, and food provision from adults. The predominant biological pattern is for care for the young to be assumed overwhelmingly (but by no means exclusively) by females. But primates, especially chimps, do show some meaningful degree of male care for offspring. And there are good biological reasons for suggesting that female hominids favored mating with males who would make a considerable contribution to care for the young.

At its most basic level, sex entails the reproduction of genes. But it is not enough for genes to reproduce themselves in a new individual; those individuals also need to have a reasonable chance of surviving. One solution to this problem is to produce a very large number of newborns, a few of whom survive; another reproductive strategy is to produce few offspring but to "invest" considerable time and energy in protecting and rearing them (thereby creating a higher survival rate). Mammals have evolved in line with the latter strategy. Primates show particularly long periods of infancy and none more so than humans. Given these facts, it would have been in the interest of those hominids who birthed offspring to find ways of eliciting the assistance of sperm providers.[43]

In saying this I am not trying to reduce hominid sexuality to sex for reproduction. Primate sexuality is immensely variable. Some species tend more toward monogamy, others toward promiscuity; some show comparatively little interest in sex, while others are extraordinarily sexual. Same-sex relations, masturbation, child sexuality are all widespread in the primate world. It is instructive, however, that while chimpanzee females are promiscuous, copulating with a very large number of males, they also tend to favor cooperative males who share food, groom their partners, and attend to the young.[44] Indeed, during consortships, when females engage in repeated copulation with a single male at a distance from the rest of the group, they bring their infants with them. To do so they must have good reason to believe their offspring are safe with a male who is probably not their father. By selecting males who regularly returned with food to share, who groomed them, and who groomed, protected, and played with their young, females could have exercised a powerful selective force greatly beneficial to the survival of helpless infants.[45] When we also consider sibling involvement in looking after the young, and the importance of the mother-son relation in chimpanzees, it becomes clear that mothers would also be encouraging altruistic and cooperative behavior (especially toward younger siblings) in their male offspring. Both biological and cultural factors would have reinforced cooperation, food sharing, and willingness to care for the young.[46] Food sharing (and cooperative activities related to toolmaking to which I return below) would thus owe a lot to the sexual choices of females reinforced by the child-rearing practices of mothers.

Let's now consider the gathering-hunting and food sharing society in terms of its cognitive implications. To begin, take the intellectual skills required for effective and efficient gathering. In the first instance, this involves fairly intricate "cognitive maps." Clearly, these would include spatial maps, especially as bipedal hominids collecting food in containers extended the range of their gathering activities. But cognitive maps would also have entailed increasingly sophisticated perceptions of time; gatherers must be attentive to the time of year when they will find certain kinds of plant food, and the seasons or time of day when they might best encounter specific animals at feeding sites. All of this requires special forms of memory. On top of this, gatherers must be able to read various signs in their environment—such as animal tracks, or dry leaves as indicators of tubers beneath the ground. It is likely, therefore, that this mode of life would entail a selective advantage for long-term topographic memory. Related to this is a second point: the mental and behavioral aspects of the "postponed consumption" characteristic of gathering. Recall that chimpanzees consume the food they collect on the spot. Gatherers, however, do exactly what the word implies: they collect food, postponing personal consumption for more socially organized consumption at a later point in time. The gathering way of life thus involves more sequentially differentiated acts of production and consumption which are linked in temporally mediated ways. Finally, as I show below, the growth in hominid brain size may be directly related to the increasing size (and complexity) of social groups. This has important implications for cultural behaviors such as toolmaking, social organization, and language. Let's begin with toolmaking.

Toolmaking, Thought, and Language

Discussing technology in *Capital*, Marx argues that Darwin's "attention to the history of natural technology, i.e., the formation of the organs of plants and animals" should be supplemented by an equally serious attention to the history of human "productive organs."[47] Marx conceives of technology as a set of material, social, and intellectual extensions of the human body. Among other things, this suggests the inherently "cultural" character of technology and its close association with language. But what do we actually know about early hominid tools?

One of our difficulties is that wooden tools do not survive over millions of years. Our evidence begins, therefore, with the stone tools that appear quite suddenly in the fossil record about 2.5 million years ago and are associated with larger-brained hominids. By the time our human ancestors often known as *homo habilis* appeared, roughly two million years ago, tools seem to have become a systematic part of the hominid way of life: they show considerable forethought and preparation, using materials that could only have been acquired by traveling several miles. A gathering and toolmaking mode of life would have required more intensive and extensive childhood learning, prolonged adult-child bonds, food sharing, and dissemination of technological, environmental and social knowledge, and skills.[48] Not surprisingly, *habilis* had a larger brain than its predecessors (between 600 and 750 cubic centimeters compared with 400 to 550 ccs for those known as australopithecines).

But it is not simply brain size that is the issue here. Perhaps equally important is the increase in brain areas (particularly the neocortex and the prefrontal cortex) devoted to motor skills, memory, foresight, and communication.[49] Much as certain phenotypic adaptations were crucial—changes in the hand, foot, and pelvis, growth and reorganization of the brain, and "neotonic" changes in rates of maturation which favor a prolonged childhood or extended "preadult" learning period—these would not have resulted in the new behavioral complex of tool-using hominids without the sociocultural changes that made intensified and extended social learning possible. We are talking, then, of a new kind of sociobiological complex characterized by "biocultural feedback": new behaviors such as food-sharing, tool-using, and greater learning of social and technological skills by the young (and the attendant efforts to teach by adults) would favor biological changes conducive to these new cultural adaptations. This implies a complex of reinforcing cultural adaptations consisting of tool-making, planned gathering, hunting, food sharing, learning, greater use of memory and foresight, and increased social cooperation and communication. All of these would have required the increased intelligence (and larger, reorganized brains) associated with object-manipulation, more complex social organization (including food sharing and male caring for the young), and the communication and transmission of skills and information. Indeed, *homo habilis* soon replaced its smaller-brained (though, in at least one case, larger and stronger) australopithecine ancestors; and the next hominid to appear in the archaeological record about 1.6 million years ago— *homo erectus*—crossed yet a new threshold in these areas.

The first and most obvious change with *erectus*, who has been described as "the first distinctly human species," is the considerable growth of the brain— initially to about 900 cc, or a 20 percent increase, and then to about 1100 cc, or nearly 80 percent of the brain size of modern humans in the case of late *erectus*.[50] But equally significant is the stunning development of new and more sophisticated tools, known as the Acheulean tool kit. Whereas students of archaeology today can be taught quickly and through simple observation to make the "Oldowan tools" used by *homo habilis* they need months of training to become proficient at making the Acheulean tools that *erectus* created. *Erectus* was also tremendously successful in evolutionary terms, managing to spread through much of Africa,

India, western Asia, and large parts of Europe, making the environmental adjustments required, and persisting with essentially the same tool kit for a million and a half years. Moreover, with late *erectus*, we find evidence of cooperative hunting of large game, continuous use of fire, and relatively stable central foraging stations.[51]

What can we say about the forms of practical activity in which *erectus* would have engaged? To answer this, we need to resist modern tendencies to separate mind and hand, mental and manual labor. Among other things, one of the most distinctive human characteristics is the large part of our brains devoted to coordinating motor activity associated with the hands.[52] Human practical activity—*praxis*—involves a unique relationship between conscious intelligence and bodily activity, a relationship whose central feature has to do with the way we direct our bodies according to planned activity. While our hominid predecessors were not fully human in this sense, they had embarked upon a path of biocultural development in which we can see the rudiments of human *praxis*.

The conscious use of physical materials to alter the environment involves an ability to differentiate self and world in ways that favor *mediated activity*, i.e., activity characterized by the use of intermediary objects (such as tools) to affect the environment to determined ends. More than this, Acheulean tools show a greater standardization. While all toolmaking involves a response to the inherent properties of the materials themselves, we see here a greater capacity to shape these materials to general patterns. Perhaps more important is the way *erectus* created tools (handaxes in particular) for the purpose of toolmaking. There are good reasons for thinking this move is distinctive to hominids. While many other species engage in forms of toolmaking, it appears that only hominids have created specific tools for the manufacture of other tools.[53] With *homo erectus*, then, we observe the development of new and more complex forms of mediated activity, including the making of tools with tools. This suggests some form of language may very well have been in place—though probably not anything like modern speech. Yet, while it constituted a highly successful adaptive complex, this set of technological and cultural skills did not display any particular propensity toward improvement. For about 1.5 million years, the Acheulean tool kit underwent little innovation. Then came the cultural and technological explosion of about 40,000 years ago which was preceded by a growing technological and cultural sophistication.

Between 500,000 and 150,000 years ago, a new, larger-brained hominid species made its appearance in the fossil record. Known as *archaic homo sapiens*, this species had brains in the range of 1,200 to 1,400 cubic centimeters, and produced some refinements to the Acheulean tool kit. Then, between 100,000 and 40,000 years ago, a new archaic form of *homo sapiens* appeared—the so-called Neanderthals. During the same period, anatomically modern humans also emerged. But it was about 40,000 years ago that a quite dramatic "creative explosion" took place. New stone technologies based upon production of blades developed, as did the use of new materials such as antler, bone, and ivory; perhaps 20,000 years ago, small geometric tools known as "microliths" appeared. This period also saw a proliferation in the number and types of tools (as many as 130 different tools have been identified), the joining of parts to make tools (hafting of a wooden handle to an axehead, for example), regular technological improvements, and cave art. Tools, jewelry, and art all offer evidence of a developing "aesthetic" sensibility, and heightened symbolic abilities.[54] There seems little doubt that language and toolmaking had come together in a new behavioral constellation characterized by more complex forms of intellectual reflection, planning, and use of memory, all of which would account for the cultural explosion of the Upper Paleolithic era. In making these points, I do not mean to suggest that language represented an unprecedented cognitive leap. While possessing powerfully new emergent properties, fully human language could only have evolved on the basis of cognitive and communicative powers that had developed throughout hominid evolution; language could only have emerged among creatures whose bodies and cultural behaviors were prepared for it.

KNOWING BODIES: GESTURE, LABOR, AND THE EMERGENCE OF LANGUAGE

One of the defining features of fully human language is its amazing *generativity*. From a finite set of words and a small set of grammatical rules people can create an infinite number of utterances. As Noam Chomsky has repeatedly urged, any competent human language user possesses a powerful capacity to create sentences she has never before encountered.[55] This generative capacity of language seems to be integrally connected to human capacities for creative invention. With this in mind, a growing number of evolutionists propose that fully human language is a fairly recent development in hominid evolution, probably having emerged within the past 150,000 years. After all, they reason, hominid technology was largely unchanging for a period of well over one million years (from about 1.6 million years ago to roughly 300,000 years ago). And this suggests a form of intelligence lacking the generativity of propositional language.[56] Moreover, after groups of *homo erectus* migrated from Africa to Europe and Asia, their Acheulian tool kit regressed: handaxes and cleavers entirely disappeared. While the problem in the first instance may have been the absence of adequate raw materials for their construction, the complete disappearance of these tools suggests that *erectus* may have lacked the cognitive and communicative capacities to maintain a technocultural tradition in the absence of means for its material expression.[57]

A growing number of evolutionists thus hold that fully human language emerged fairly recently in hominid evolution. This hypothesis plays havoc with a central maxim of much contemporary linguistic and social theory: the idea that conceptual thought is impossible outside of language. After all, if fully human language emerged within the last 150,000 years, then this conflation of conceptual intelligence with language would seem to be untenable. Maxine Sheets-Johnstone gets right to the heart of the problem: "prominent people in a variety of disciplines . . . maintain that short of language there are no concepts. Were these people correct, ancestral hominids would have been cognitively disadvantaged to the point that many behaviors—stone toolmaking, caring for injured individuals, or even big-game hunting with all the intellectual abilities it presupposes—would hardly have been feasible undertakings."[58]

It is a bit much to imagine that the manufacture of Acheulean tools, formed to a uniform pattern and displaying aesthetic qualities, did not require conceptual thought. Moreover, it makes no sense in evolutionary terms to propose that fully human language emerged other than on the foundations of prelinguistic forms of conceptual thought. Put simply, unless we advance some kind of creationist explanation, we have to see language as involving new emergent capacities whose roots lay in prelinguistic forms of *praxis* and intelligence. To be sure, fully human language may have made possible new cognitive capacities; nevertheless, it must also have facilitated improved ways of doing things hominids were already doing.

Other evidence also indicates that human intelligence can exist in the absence of language. Merlin Donald, for instance, draws our attention to the case of Brother John, a fifty-year-old member of a religious order, who for twenty-five years experienced epileptic seizures. While he remained conscious throughout these seizures, Brother John lost his ability to use and process language. Despite this, he had full recall of these episodes. And during such seizures his understanding was unimpaired, as was his ability to communicate in the absence of language. During one episode, Brother John indicated to a desk clerk where to look in his passport for information required to complete his hotel registration—despite his incapacity to read the passport or the registration slip at the time. In the absence of language processing, in other words, his practical knowledge and gestural abilities remained intact. As Donald points out, this case confirms studies of deaf mutes who did not have a common language yet "had normal praxic skills and were usually employed as domestics or in the trades, jobs that for the most part demanded a level of social and manual skill that was uniquely human." Donald concludes that "the human brain, without language can still record the episodes of a life, assess events, assign meanings and thematic roles to agents in various situations, acquire and execute complex skills, learn and remember how to behave in a variety of settings."[59]

The fact that practical knowledge—understanding the purpose of a hotel registration form, a menu, a passport, or the tasks of a job—can persist without language and speech, and that the same is true for gestural communication, strongly suggests that large parts of the human brain are wired for forms of extra-linguistic knowledge. Where language and speech centers of the brain are working normally, these systems may all interact; but where language and speech shut down, other forms of knowledge persist. This is what evolutionary theory— with its insistence that previous "gains" will tend to be conserved—should lead us to expect. The appearance of fully human language did not displace prior cognitive and communicative abilities, but built upon them. It follows that language is not identical with cognition or conceptual thought.

Precisely this observation is at the heart of the developmental psychology of Lev Vygotsky. Building on early studies of chimpanzees and children prior to language acquisition, Vygotsky argued for prelinguistic forms of "practical intelligence" embodied in the use of tools to explore and shape the environment. Vygotsky's studies suggested that language and practical intelligence (especially "mediated activity" with tools) develop independently in early childhood. Their convergence, in the course of the child's discovery that everything has a name, sets off a new developmental path along which names for things increase memory and the ability to plan activities. Vygotsky does not conflate language and practical intelligence. Each is a distinctive cognitive activity with roots in animal behavior; what is uniquely human is the form of their convergence.[60] Especially noteworthy in this regard is a body of recent research which sees the development of children's "combinatorial abilities" between about twelve and thirty months of age as characteristic of new capacities in a wide range of areas: language, motor imitation, play, social interaction, and problem-solving. Just as children begin to combine words into multiword utterances, so they combine objects in building towers, replacing puzzle pieces, and so on.[61] The convergence of language and practical intelligence would seem favorable to combinatorial activities in the spheres of *praxis*, language, and social interaction.

All of these issues return us to human bodies and minds. One of the great strengths of Darwinism is its resistance to mind-body dualisms. Darwin sees brains as developing from nervous systems; he sees bodies as acting, emoting, and thinking with greater or lesser degrees of complexity. Moreover, because he sees natural selection as conserving those bodily adaptations that are most useful (along with some which are not overly deleterious), he is predisposed to seeing the bodies of all species as encoded with information. Bodies represent a storehouse of adaptations that reflect struggles with environments—legs, beaks, genitals, wings, hands, and so on all embody histories of environmental learning. Since learning capacities build upon this embodied information, any materialist discussion of knowledge, learning, and intelligence must begin with bodies. And here evolutionary theory finds a point of contact with those currents in phenomenology which emphasize the embodied character of experience and thought. Sheets-Johnstone, for instance, attempts a synthesis of Darwinian and phenomenological approaches, arguing that the phenomenology of embodiment developed by Maurice Merleau-Ponty can join evolutionary theory by recognizing the body through which we open onto the world (and through which the world opens within us) as a "Darwinian body," the product of millennia of natural selection. If we are going to insist on the embodied character of our being-in-the-world (and the world's being-in-us), she suggests, then we need to recognize that these bodies of ours—including that part we call "mind"—evolved out of the experience of species reacting to their environments. Human thought and language must first be understood phenotypically—as entailing bodily changes which made possible favorable cognitive, communicative, and behavioral hominid adaptations. This means seeing knowledge and language initially from the site of the body and its evolution. And it means underlining the primacy of practical experience, of *doing*, in the evolution of thought and language. It follows that, however much they introduce novel capacities, thought and language are continuous with more basic hominid praxic abilities: "Ancestral hominids whose discoveries and practices are integral to our humanness were *non*human. If they did not think, how is it that we do? By divine intervention? By chance genetic mutation? Given the comprehensive evidence for organic evolution, the most likely answer is that thinking evolved hand in hand with doing."[62]

This approach also helps clarify what it means to talk about *embodied knowledge*. A number of commentators have pointed out the importance of "image schemata" in organizing our perception of the world and our activity within it (indeed, Merleau-Ponty developed this insight from the findings of gestalt psychology). Image schemata refer to recurring patterns in our lived experience of space, time, objects, and their relations. In exploring many of these patterns, including "containers, balance, compulsion, blockage, attraction, paths, links, scales, cycles, center-periphery," and others, Mark Johnstone insists they are not transcendental categories of the understanding, but evolutionarily formed structures that fit the experience of certain types of organisms in specific sorts of environments.[63] Pattern recognition is not simply about the "mind" organizing perceptual data into coherent wholes; rather, it is about the whole organism perceiving patterns that facilitate the coordination of its motor activity in the world. Such patterns are meaningful structures for organisms of a particular size with specific features (eyes, hands, legs, central nervous system, etc.), specific senses, and unique capacities (bipedalism, object manipulation, frequent sexual interaction, and so on). Meanings, then, are not the result of arbitrary mappings of concepts onto the world; instead, they derive from corporeal representations that inform the activity of organisms in the world. The human (and hominid) body is thus a "semantic template," a site upon which meanings emerge in the course of practical activity.[64]

This position challenges the Saussurean notion of the arbitrariness of language and meaning. There is a fairly trivial sense in which Saussure is right: the specific acoustic signifiers we use ("cat," "foot," "hammer," etc.) have a purely conventional relationship to the concepts to which they refer. This is what "arbitrariness" refers to in the early parts of Saussure's lectures. But this trivial observation is not what most commentators have in mind when they talk about the arbitrariness of language, nor is it all that Saussure intends. Saussure proceeds to suggest that language is based upon a mental operation according to which the continuum of experience is divided arbitrarily into objects of thought, and it is this position that has been taken up and radicalized by deconstructionists in particular.[65] Precisely this idea of the arbitrariness of language and conceptual thought is destabilized by notions of bodily image-schemata and corporeal representation. For these concepts indicate the manifold ways in which the world of our experience is not organized arbitrarily by thought, but, instead, is deeply rooted in corporeal representation. More than this, they drive home the extent to which language itself is rooted in the body. Human language could only have evolved in accordance with the constraints and capacities of hominid perceptual and motor systems. Language is built upon the same semantic template that structures our bodily experience.

A further point needs to be made in this regard. An important program of neurological research developed by Antonio Damasio and his colleagues indicates that human reason cannot function adequately if the ability to "feel" one's own body is seriously impaired. Damasio's work starts with the problem of individuals who have suffered damage to areas of their brains where reason and emotion seem to intersect (various regions of the prefrontal cortices), yet whose linguistic and cognitive abilities are intact. Despite their ability to understand language and abstract thought, such individuals tend to be incapable of adequately organizing their lives because they lack the concrete "feelings"—about their own bodies, about others, and about the consequences of their actions—that enable them to make sound decisions. After all, we regularly receive background information from our body's motor systems that allows us to monitor basic life needs—hunger, breathing, danger, and so on. Where "emotional" centers of the brain are damaged, however, rational decision-making will break down—even if abstract cognitive and linguistic capacities are unimpaired. In Damasio's terms, such individuals lack the "somatic markers" that are essential to monitoring information about their socio-physical being. Once again, we see the way in which "higher" mental functions like language and conceptual thought are not self-sufficient. Where "lower" mental processes are impaired, rational decision-making will suffer—especially as it concerns bodily needs, relations with others, and future consequences of present actions. Again, from an evolutionary viewpoint, Damasio's findings are not surprising. Long before language and conceptual thought, hominids must have been able to process a wide range of information from their bodies and the wider environment. Indeed, in the absence of information provided by these "lower" processes, the "higher" ones are entirely inadequate to effective functioning in the human world. When those primordial processes which *mind* our bodies are damaged, "higher order" mental processes are rendered functionally inadequate.

The insights we get from bringing Darwinism together with phenomenologies of the body and new work in neurology are further extended when we turn to some important recent research on gesture and sign language. Until about thirty years ago, most linguists denied that sign languages were genuine languages. One main reason for this is that many gestures are obviously far from arbitrary: we often observe a resemblance between sign and referent, a sort of mimetic relationship between the sign and the thing indicated. Yet, rather than conclude from this that sign languages are not true languages, we might do better to question the assumption that language involves a purely arbitrary sign system. In *Gesture and the Nature of Language*, Armstrong, Stokoe and Wilcox do this with great success by showing that manual gestures contain the basic elements of syntax—subjects, verbs, and objects—and of systematic relations among them. From this observation they develop a hypothesis that offers an original and compelling solution to a major problem in understanding the evolution of language: the leap from words to grammar or syntax. After all, if language originated in speech and naming, in attaching spoken words to objects, events, and properties of the world we inhabit, how might creatures employing names have made the jump to the highly abstract operation of talking about complex relations among subjects, objects, and actions? The gap here seems almost unsurpassable. It requires a considerable leap of faith to assume that a set of concrete words like "snake," "fire," "stick," "hurt," and so on could readily give rise to the abstract representations involved in subject-verb-object relations. Observation of gesture suggests a solution since many gestures consist of an integrated series of movements indicating a particular action in relation to various subjects and objects (e.g., "You, throw the rock at the rabbit"). Now, if fully human language built, at least in part, upon gestural communicative abilities, then syntactic properties could have emerged through analysis—by decomposing gestures into their elements—rather than through the synthetic act of moving from individual words to rule-governed relations among subjects, objects, and verbs.[66] When we begin to think about language origins in more corporeal terms, we can see fully human language as having built upon forms of bodily expression and communication that are anything but arbitrary—since they derive from the shape and capacities of our bodies and objects in the world.

This returns us to the question of the sort of intelligence that is essential to human language. I have argued that language could only have been of value for creatures whose minds were "ready" for it. And if syntax—the combination of words into rule-governed relations to produce meaningful statements—is at the heart of human language, then we confront an obvious question: what sort of intelligence might have already possessed some of the abilities that are necessary to syntactic modes of expression?[67] This question directs us to hominid toolmaking cultures since these possess some of the fundamental features of linguistic thought, features which have been described as "constructional intelligence" or "combinatorial ability."

Drawing upon developmental psychology and studies of ape and human toolmaking, Kathleen Gibson has argued that "human intelligence is inherently constructional in nature." Humans, she claims, "break perceptions, motor actions and concepts into small component parts and then combine and recombine these parts into higher order constructs."[68] Gibson points out that ape and human toolmaking are distinguished in precisely this area: unlike humans, apes do not use heat, adhesives, knots, or weaving to permanently join two or more separate objects. In fact, what apes seem to lack are those toolmaking schemes which emerge fairly late in the development of human children, schemes which require simultaneous awareness of several objects and spatial relations.[69] Humans possess cognitive abilities that make possible more complexly meditated tool-making and tool-use—particularly the manufacture of tools as specialized instruments for making other tools and the creation of permanent structures by joining two or more parts together. This vastly increased constructional capability (and the increasingly mediated sense of spatial and temporal relationships it entails) also distinguishes fully human language from language use in apes.[70]

We are back once again, then, to the issue of generativity. For the distinguishing feature of human tool use is the human ability to generate a growing number of complex and sophisticated structures that require intermediate stages (and particular tools of assembly appropriate to these stages) *en route* to construction of the completed object. The use of a tool to make a tool prefigures an essential feature of human language: that unit activities are meaningful only in the context of a composite product. Tools that are helpful only at intermediate stages of construction are effectively meaningless on their own, just as a single unit of sound (a phoneme) is meaningless outside of a word, which is itself often meaningless outside an entire utterance. Now, given what we know about hominid toolmaking, it seems clear that the cognitive abilities necessary for making Oldowan and Acheulian tools (abilities which exceed those of apes) would have put into place some of the cognitive structures necessary for language.

But before the reader assumes I am making a technicist argument about the priority of toolmaking in an evolutionary account of language, let me return to a point I have touched on previously: the uniquely social character of human toolmaking and tool-use. Hominid toolmaking is not simply quantitatively distinguished, i.e., by its degree of mediatedness or complexity. There is a qualitative difference here too: the cooperative organization of human toolmaking as a social process. Peter Reynolds, for instance, contrasts toolmaking by humans and chimps in the following terms: "One chimpanzee does *not* dig the hole in the termite nest while another prepares the stick. One chimpanzee does *not* provide a termite stick for another to use. One chimpanzee does *not* hold one end of the stick while the other strips the bark—unless it is planning on grabbing it away."[71] Human toolmaking, on the other hand, is based on what he calls "heterotechnic cooperation" where at least two people anticipate the action of the other(s) and perform a complementary action in order to produce a result that could not be achieved by a single individual performing the actions in a series. "Thus, human technology is not just 'tool use,' and not just 'cooperative' tool use, but tool use combined with a social organization for heterotechnic cooperation" which is usually organized by a "face-to-face task group."[72]

Humans are the species whose members engage in cooperative heterotechnic toolmaking and who possess the whole complex of social, linguistic, and cognitive skills this entails. Consistent with my argument to this point, Reynolds claims these are "coevolutionary developments"—parts of a sociobehavioral complex that only make sense together. On the cognitive side what stands out is the construction of polyliths from differentiated parts; on the side of the social, it is the differentiated and coordinated task group (a cooperative group using a division of integrated tasks) which is most distinctive. By insisting on the uniquely social character of human toolmaking, Reynolds resists the methodological individualism that impoverishes so much cognitive theory. Most theories of human cognition "typically take the isolated craftsman as their point of departure. . . . Heterotechnic cooperation, however, requires the *integration* of individual minds into a larger, cooperative framework."[73] Individual activity exists as a moment of social praxis; its sociality is constitutive, not something added on. Marx, too, makes this point when he argues that human production always involves organized social relations: "a certain mode of production . . . is always combined with a certain mode of cooperation."[74] While the technical means and the social relations of production are analytically distinct, they are components of a complex. The cognitive properties of human toolmaking only emerge for a species with highly interdependent forms of social organization—which is to say, for a species for whom cooperation has proved advantageous. If chimpanzees lack polylithic constructional abilities, this will have to do with their forms of social life: "chimpanzees lack polyliths because they lack the social organization that normally mediates such physical relationships."[75]

When evolutionists try to link language and toolmaking—in itself a legitimate move—they often err by treating toolmaking in excessively technical and cognitive terms.[76] Especially problematic is the way such theories tend to *desocialize* language and toolmaking by treating them as individual cognitive skills. Yet, studies by Robin Dunbar suggest that intelligence is intimately connected to the size and complexity of social organization. Dunbar shows that the size of the neocortex (that part of the brain most associated with "thinking") in monkeys and apes increases with the size of social group, not with the size of the ecological niche over which the group ranges. He proposes that large groups tend to be unstable unless individuals can attend to many dyadic (one-to-one) relationships—which requires enlarged memory and the ability to understand and negotiate complex social interactions.[77] Dunbar's work thus points to ways in which the cognitive skills involved in heterotechnic toolmaking presuppose social intelligence developed for complex relations in large groups. Polylithic constructional intelligence is not possible for intelligent creatures (like the great apes) who have not developed the sociocognitive skills required for cooperative behavior in large and complex groups. Moreover, these skills appear to be crucial where kinship relations are of special importance given prolonged dependence of children on their mothers, on other adults (including males), and on older siblings. Dunbar further proposes that as social group size exceeded that in which grooming could mediate social relations, language became necessary (providing vocal rather than directly physical reassurance).[78] Language, therefore, could be said to be bound up with the cognitive and social skills involved in understanding how things—physical materials, tools, and social relationships—"fit together" and with the skills necessary to actually putting them together.

These considerations return us to the question of learning. It seems clear that neotonous development (the retention of child-like features) and prolongation of childhood were driven by the selective advantages accruing to individuals whose brains developed over a longer period and whose potential for learning was thereby enhanced. We often forget, however, just how important the imitative skills of human children are to learned behaviors, and just how unique they are: "Although other primates exhibit imitative skills . . . they pale in comparison to the preschooler and even the preverbal child. . . . The human infant, an imitative generalist, is capable of a wide range of feats—duplicating vocal maneuvers, body postures, actions on objects, and/or completely arbitrary and novel acts."[79] This wide-ranging mimetic capacity may be connected to the generativity of human language and toolmaking. Indeed, the fact that other primates have not developed toolmaking cultures—where new techniques are routinely imitated by others, generalized, regularly passed on to the young—seems related to the limits of their imitative abilities. Apes and monkeys have little capacity to model their own activity on the observed actions of another.[80] Certainly, these primates do not understand the intent behind a pointing gesture when, for example, a person wants to direct another's attention to a specific object, action, or location.[81] Yet human children come to understand the communicative intent of such a gesture at around fourteen months: they quickly learn to follow the gesture or gaze of an adult. The limited abilities of apes and monkeys to learn through imitation may derive from their lack of a sense of another as a distinct agent (a "you") like themselves.

It is vital to remember that the most fundamental material of *mimesis* is the human body itself. Most imitation involves a replication of bodily movements: walk, facial, and manual gestures, and so on (the other key medium of imitation is the voice, to which I shall return shortly). Imitation requires sophisticated neural maps of the body so that we can learn to perform quite intricate physical feats (e.g., hitting a moving rabbit with a small rock, using a bat to hit a curving baseball moving at ninety miles per hour, driving a car, skating at high speeds on thin metal blades), feats which are generally beyond the capabilities of other primates. To learn such skills humans rely upon much more detailed neural maps of their own bodies than are available to other primates; indeed, this highly developed body sense may be essential to a fully human sense of self.[82] Humans are terrific imitators partly because they are able to map the detailed movements of another individual onto their own bodily actions. This requires unique motor skills and consciousness of self and other. Rather than imitate a handful of behaviors to which they are biologically predisposed, humans are capable of an extraordinarily wide range of imitative behavior; we are, as Meltzoff puts it, "imitative generalists."[83] When we turn to gestural communication, then, we need to see it not as a discrete skill, but as a specific outgrowth of mimetic capabilities—the use of hands to model real world events—which underpin fully human language in general. Indeed, this seems the logical conclusion of cases like that of Brother John, where mimetic skill survives, including the capacity for gestural communication, despite impairment of symbolic language.

Mimesis would also have played a tremendously important role in hominid social organization since it entails a sophisticated sense of self and other and their interrelations. In order to imitate the actions or behavior of another, I must be able to understand our similarities and differences, and to do so simultaneously. I must, in other words, be able to see that these others are moving distinct parts of *their* bodies—hands, eyebrows, feet, buttocks, etc.—and to map the movement of *my* body in a similar fashion. Much social behavior also involves distinct bodily gestures—handshakes, kisses, removing hats, nursing babies, standing, sitting, sending sexual signals, and so on.[84] Imitative behavior, especially among children, is simultaneously corporeal, cognitive, and social. Our capacity for self-cued mimetic behavior, to use Donald's term, can thus be seen as a crucial capacity without which human toolmaking, social cooperation, and language would not be possible.[85]

Language Sings the World: The Emergence of Speech

I have been arguing for a much more corporeal sense of language and its roots than is customary in social theory. Among other things, I have insisted that gesture is central to language. Yet, this does not commit me to the view of some theorists that language and speech originated directly in gesture.[86] However important it is to emphasize the gestural and corporeal dimensions of language and speech, it seems probable that fully human language has *both* vocal and gestural roots. Nevertheless, speech has become the predominant form of human language, and this fact must be explained. Once again, I begin with Darwin whose discussion of these issues remains remarkably relevant.

Aware of the importance of gesture, Darwin speculated that the use of the hands for other purposes (carrying, toolmaking, and so on) would have favored speech since vocal communication can be conducted while the hands are otherwise engaged. But left here, this is a question-begging account. After all, if evolution largely builds upon existing structures and capabilities, how did it

magically prepare the mouth, tongue, larynx, and so on for speech? Darwin's
answer is simple enough: speech did not emerge in one fell swoop, but was
preceded by less developed forms of vocalization. In particular, Darwin suggests
that hominids probably used cries to express emotions. Monkeys, he points out,
use cries as danger signals. Even for language-using humans, vocal cries are
often more emotionally expressive than words: "Our cries of pain, fear, surprise,
anger together with their appropriate actions, and the murmur of a mother to
her child, are more expressive than any words" (DM, 1:54). This is an especially
significant point, more so than Darwin probably realized. For he is suggesting
that vocalization may have been used by hominids principally for purposes of
emotional expression; moreover, he identifies the mother-child relation as one in
which vocal communication would predominate.

We have seen that the prolongation of childhood dependency—especially
reliance upon the mother—is a central feature of hominid evolution. The survival of human infants depends upon eliciting food and care from others, principally their mothers. Vocal communication, especially crying, is obviously crucial
here. But there is more to it than that. Human babies make an enormous range
of sounds; they are unique among primates in babbling. Much of this babbling,
which imitates the rhythm of speech, clearly involves attachment behavior—
communicative interactions through which the mother-child bond is formed
(alongside bonds with other adults and siblings).[87] Indeed, studies show that
newborn human babies respond preferentially to their mother's voice, suggesting
a prenatal familiarization.[88] Given the centrality of oral gratification in the life
of human infants, much of this vocalization may be especially pleasurable. Babbling and speech, like breast-feeding, help cement attachment between child and
mother (and/or other caregivers). By eliciting the attention of caregivers, smil-
ing and babbling create a vocal bond which helps insure care and safety. Speech
thus constitutes a social bond which makes certain forms of separation possible.
Language—the "mother tongue"—emerges as a means by which the child maintains a new kind of oral connection to its mother or primary caregiver while its
autonomy develops. As one psychoanalytic commentator puts it: "Speech is on
the one hand a means of retaining a connection with the mother as well as a
means of becoming separated from her. The child who suckled at the mother's
breast now replaces this by introjecting a new liquid of the mother—sounds."[89]
Rather than being merely a preparatory phase toward something else (speech),
babbling could be said to have selective advantages in its own right: the child
who babbles, who in so doing attracts the attention of a caregiver and draws her
into "conversation," is more likely to receive care. Employing the organ with
which the child first discovers pleasure and explores the world—the mouth—
babbling exhibits a predisposition toward vocal expression, especially for the
expression of emotions.

While Darwin pays little attention to the mother-child relation, he is quite
attentive to another area in which vocalization is prominent: sexual relations.

Offering evidence from the behavior of insects, spiders, fish, seals, lions, cattle, and a number of primate species, he concludes that "a strong case can be made out, that the vocal organs were primarily used and perfected in relation to the propagation of the species" (DM, 2:330). He draws attention to the overwhelming evidence that "love calls" are used throughout the insect and animal words to attract sexual mates; he is especially struck by the rhythmic character of "love songs," speculating that the perception and enjoyment "of musical cadences and rhythm is probably common to all animals" (DM, 2:333). Vocal expression (babbling and mating songs) permeates what are arguably the most important emotional and social interactions in hominid life: adult-child bonds and sexual relationships. Psychoanalytic suggestions that adult love replicates feelings and experiences from infant and childhood relations with caregivers (predominantly mothers) might be especially pertinent in this regard, implying a common association of orality and vocalization with emotional intimacy and connection.[90] Vocalization would thus have had vital selective advantages independent of language and speech—in terms both of eliciting maternal/caregiver attention and attracting sexual partners.

There are many indications that vocal communication permeates the social life of primates. Drawing upon a seven-year study of the vocal sound system of gelada monkeys—including analysis of one thousand hours of vocal sequences—Bruce Richman claims that "the community life of gelada social groups is immersed in sound."[91] He shows not only that vocal communication is widespread, but also that geladas engage in long sequences of coordinated calling where one member of the group responds to the calls of another by synchronizing its responses. This sort of coordinated vocalization is highly musical, operating according to rhythmic call-and-response patterns. Much gelada vocalization is a form of *contact calling*, as monkeys out of visual contact with each other use sound to locate other members of the group. These vocal cries help individuals to map their position in relation to other members of the group. Yet, contact calling is only one part of coordinated vocal expression. Geladas seem to want to "answer" one another, regularly anticipating (and uttering) the next sound that another will make in their rhythmic sequence: "These attempts at synchronization with upcoming sounds are so frequent that they seem to be part of the drive to be in constant phatic contact with other voices of the group."[92] In short, vocalization seems to be about social connection in the widest of senses. Interestingly, other studies suggest that "vocal forms of reconciliation" can sometimes be as important as grooming among chacma baboons.[93]

Richman's study hints that rhythm may be intrinsic to primate social organization. In synchronized vocalization, individual members of the group try to decipher vocal rhythm and sound sequences in order to fit their voice into the group song. While evidence of similar dispositions toward rhythm is widely found among animals and birds, no species has anything approximating the human propensity for rhythm.[94] Here again, we observe a sort of preadaptation for fully human language. Human rhythmic abilities, which are central to *mimesis* (e.g., the coordination of a sequence of bodily movements in order to imitate) might well have provided some of the neural machinery necessary to syntax, to the fitting together of different bits of vocal information into meaningful utterances:

> If human speech developed in a social context similar to that of gelada many-voiced vocal displays and human choral singing, this could explain why such an extremely complex syntax actually did develop. A complex syntax of rhythm (necessary for controlling the production of vocal displays) could have developed solely under pressures to produce more and more elaborate and complex co-ordinated vocal displays. . . . The semantic use of this complex rhythmical syntax could have come later, much later.[95]

Even without operating as a speech system, vocal sound would have been integrally involved in bonding, sex, love, memory, and social and environmental mapping. Evolutionary selection for speech would have found intricate systems of vocalization already in place.

An evolutionary account of language also plays havoc with the widespread trend to define spoken language in strictly propositional (and thus nonexpressive) terms. Employing abstract cognitive models, much linguistics seeks to radically separate the propositional aspect of language (verifiable statements about persons, things, actions, and their relations) from the expression of emotional states. Yet, not only was vocalization principally a means of emotional expression, it may very well have been used in concert with gesture in order "to lend affect to the hand-signing process."[96] To imagine that speech emerged as a discrete system separate from an older language of emotional expression is simply untenable. As Sheets-Johnstone points out, such a view reintroduces a series of dualisms (mind/body, human/animal, propositional/expressive) in which language-speech is abstracted from the texture of emotional life by relegating "an older expressive system to pure bodies, which is to say to mindless, nonrational, nonhuman animals."[97] In fact, it is quite possible that it was a simultaneously "emotional" and "cognitive" activity—play—that figured in the development of speech. After all, *playing with vocal sounds* to imitate things in the wider environment (dangerous animals, thunder, snakes, etc.) would have gone some way to expanding the range of vocal signification. Darwin intimated as much when he wrote that "language owes its origin to the imitation and modification, aided by signs and gestures, of various natural sounds, the voices of other animals, and man's own instinctive cries" (DM, v 1:56). The roots of speech might then lie in the "interplay" between *mimesis* and vocalization.

Once the ability to construct sounds to refer to extra-linguistic objects was sufficiently developed, there is no reason why a syntax already governing gesture and/or song could not have been used for words. As we have seen, gesture, toolmaking, and music all involve syntaxes of a sort, as unit activities are coordinated to produce a meaningful complex. And clearly speech has some advantages in this regard. As Darwin suggests, vocal communication would have been increasingly advantageous as the hands were employed for other purposes (carrying, toolmaking, gathering, hunting). The remarkable efficiency of speech for high speed transmission of information would also have made vocal communication advantageous. So attuned have humans become to the perception of speech sounds that we can hear them at a rate of about twenty-five segments per second, compared to between seven and nine items per second for nonspeech sounds.[98]

While elements of vocal language, especially for emotional expression, may have existed for a very long time, it seems likely that a recognizable speech system emerged within the last 100,000 years of hominid evolution (and perhaps within the past forty-thousand years). Whether this involved anatomical changes that facilitated wholly new forms of phonemic language, or whether small changes in neural organization made possible new uses for existing capacities is an open question.[99] But it seems clear that the "cultural explosion" of the Upper Paleolithic—ritual burial, jewelry, cave art, proliferation of new technologies and their regular improvement, and so on—was indicative of profound changes in cognitive life and material culture. And, given the depictive nature of early art, it is probable that a major increase in symbolization played a central role here. By enabling the use of symbols to represent things, fully human language made it possible for humans to extend the limits of memory by creating an "external" system for retrieving and disseminating information.

Once vocal language took off, its effects would have stimulated a tremendous increase in the symbolic vocabulary. The possible range of vocal utterances is effectively infinite. Moreover, "phonological invention and communication" do not "interfere with other major ongoing brain activities, like locomotion, skilled manual behaviors, orientation in space, and visual perception."[100] By making it possible to undertake symbolic communication while engaged in a wide range of activities, an increasingly vocal language system would have had major effects on creativity. And this underlines the major differences between human and primate toolmaking: "it is the ability to use symbols which . . . transformed anthropoid tool behavior into human tool behavior." By constructing a cultural system of reference, signification, and generation of meanings, symbols created a "world of ideas" with "a continuity and a permanence."[101] This, I would suggest, is the key to the human propensity to maintain and develop *productive forces*, understood as a complex of technologies, modes of cooperation, and forms of intelligence. It is only with the emergence of fully symbolic language that we enter into human history—and the development of productive forces—and the new order of temporality whose dynamics are the object of Marx's materialist conception of history.[102]

LANGUAGE AND LABOR: BEYOND DUALIST THEORIES

Some of the major flaws in social theories which treat language as a self-enclosed and self-referential system should now stand exposed. In detaching language from the body, labor, and *praxis*, Saussurean linguistics, structuralist anthropology, post-structuralism, and deconstruction dematerialize language; they liquidate the embodied, expressive, erotic, social, and practical dimensions of language, leaving us with a form without substance.[103] By foregrounding the human body as the site of labor, language and history, I am trying to subvert this idealist move. Anticipating the inevitable charges of "essentialism" this will provoke, it is worth emphasizing again that the body I am describing is an eminently historical one. Not only is it the product of a natural history, it is also a body that—through its *praxis*—transforms itself within biological limits set by natural history.

Human language is part of a behavioral complex with an evolutionary history. It entails unique forms of mediated action based on the human capacity for self-cued *mimesis* and heterotechnic cooperation. Moreover, language is not identical with consciousness and knowledge; on the contrary, it is built upon and presupposes extra-linguistic forms of understanding. Language is dependent on other forms of corporeal and praxic knowledge. As Doyal and Harris put it, "any language depends upon a prior grasp of a range of practical activities which are intelligible to some degree in and of themselves . . . it is activities of this kind, and not language or thought, which constitute the basis for the intelligibility of social life, and of the material world in which social life is lived."[104]

This perspective also plays havoc with Jürgen Habermas's theory of communicative action. Abandoning the idea that an emancipatory politics can be built upon struggles over the control, organization, and disposition of social labor, Habermas has tried to ground critical theory in the formal properties of language. Accepting the claim, made often by Horkheimer and Adorno, that labor is a form of instrumental action designed to dominate and control nature (and hence cannot be the site of emancipatory interests in freedom and reconciliation), Habermas strives to differentiate language and labor in the most thoroughgoing fashion. Whereas work is embedded in instrumental rationality based upon technical rules, communicative action is governed, he suggests, by consensual norms based upon law and morality.[105] While the first sphere is a realm of necessity dominated by the exigencies of technique, the latter is one of potential justice. To develop this argument, Habermas treats language as the key to hominization: "What raises us out of nature is the only thing we can know: *language*," he has argued.[106] But the rub here is that he effectively identifies language with propositional speech, considering the aspiration to rational understanding (as opposed, for example, to erotic or emotional expression) as its essential feature.[107] To this end, he detaches language from the body, sensation, labor, and eros, just as he demarcates it from structures of power and domination. Habermas is interested in the formal properties (or the universal conditions of possibility) that govern all speech. His theory of language, he informs us, will "ignore non-verbalized actions and bodily expressions."[108] In this abstracted, dematerialized concept of language, he locates an ethico-political *telos* toward mutual understanding and social consensus formed in a space free of coercion. Our every sentence is said to involve an interest in being understood, which requires that we appeal by means of rational argument to others as free, reasoning beings. It follows, he contends, that "the utopian perspective of reconciliation and freedom . . . is built into the linguistic mechanisms of the reproduction of the species."[109]

Many commentators have noted the Kantian impulse at work in Habermas.[110] One part of this Kantian move has been under-appreciated, however: the degree to which Habermas partakes of the separation of pure understanding from sensible experience. Yet, as Robin May Schott has argued, a crucial part of the Kantian paradigm is the notion that "the forms of thought . . . are indifferent to the sensible content of experience." Building upon the notion of commodity fetishism developed by Marx and Lukacs, she suggests that the Kantian paradigm mirrors the experience of commodified labor-power: concrete labor is subsumed under the movement of value (abstract labor) which abstracts from its concrete, sensuous characteristics. And this is precisely what Habermas's concept of language entails: abstraction from all the concrete, particular, embodied, erotic, and expressive features of language in order to invest emancipatory possibilities in its formal properties. But this involves a deeply impoverished notion of freedom based on little more than acting in conformity with formal laws.[111] After all, by suggesting that emancipation is not possible in the realm of social labor, and by leaving us with a dehistoricized, ultra-cognitivist theory of language, Habermas so reduces the power of critique and so restricts the concept of emancipation that it is hard to see what sort of "utopian perspective" remains. His "emancipatory politics" involve little more than a gesture toward a noncoercive public sphere where the best argument can prevail—a classically intellectualist construction. Yet, this is the fruit of detaching language from the body, labor, eros, and history. In the next two chapters, I hope to show that there are better ways of theorizing language and liberation—ways that are simultaneously more corporeal and more historical. My argument is developed in dialogue with two great theorists of language, history, and the body: Mikhail Bakhtin and Walter Benjamin.

4

BODY, SPEECH, AND HISTORY: LANGUAGE AND MATERIALISM IN VOLOSHINOV AND BAKHTIN

The "mind" is from the outset afflicted with the curse of being "burdened" with matter, which here makes its appearance in the form of agitated layers of air, sounds, in short, language. Language is as old as consciousness, language **is** practical, real consciousness . . .

—Marx and Engels, *The German Ideology*

In 1929 a great blast was issued against Saussurean linguistics and formalist theories of language and literature. The challenge came from Russia in the form of a pioneering book by Valentin Voloshinov entitled *Marxism and the Philosophy of Language*.[1] Building on Marx's theory of commodity fetishism, Voloshinov described the Saussurean model as an exercise in reification—a sort of violent abstraction from the living activity of people in speech communities. Just as Marx accuses bourgeois economics of trying to efface living labor by attributing its creative powers to capital, so Voloshinov charges Saussure and his formalist followers with trying to erase the living dynamism of speech by conceptualizing language as an abstract, self-sufficient system unconnected to speech and its history (MPL, 77). Severed from labor, value is for Marx a fetish, the spectral image of a forgotten life-activity. The same is true of language when detached from speech: "Linguistic form is merely an abstractly extractable factor of the dynamic whole of speech performance—of the utterance" (MPL, 79).

In Saussure's linguistics, languages are lifeless objects, unchanging economies of meaning. As a result, Saussure builds his theory on the basis of a "finished monologic utterance," an utterance torn from the dynamic continuum of speech (and thus one no longer inviting a response). Dead languages, languages

111

no longer used by any speech community, provide the ideal model for such a linguistics (MPL, 72). Yet, while criticizing Saussurean linguistics as an "abstract objectivism" which detaches language-as-structure from the speech activities of real human subjects, Voloshinov does not endorse a subjectivist view of language as the pure self-creation of autonomous individuals. Rather than invert Saussure's dualism by valorizing the creative process of speech activity (*parole*) at the expense of the systematic features of language (*langue*), Voloshinov seeks to transcend it. He intends to show that the systematic aspects of language are inseparable from the creative flow of speech activity; he sees the abstract (pre-social) individual as a reified construct as much as the self-reproducing language system of abstract objectivism. Language, like labor, is a socially structured process, not an act of individual creation. While individuals shape meanings for themselves, they do so within a social context saturated with prior utterances, structures of meaning, relations of power, and linguistic rules and conventions (MPL, 48–63).

Marxism and the Philosophy of Language seeks a dialectical account of form and content, structure and agency, system and individual as they pertain to language. Yet, refreshingly, Voloshinov does not assume that there is a ready-made Marxist theory of language which merely has to be mobilized against its competitors. Criticizing most "Marxist" interventions in the field for "mechanistic materialism," he insists that a dialectical and materialist theory of language has yet to be developed. Rather than dogmatically proclaim a Marxist philosophy of language, Voloshinov proposes to enact a dialogue between Marxism *and* the philosophy of language in order both to transform linguistics and enrich Marxism. What Voloshinov's friend Pavel Medvedev wrote about Marxist literary theory, applies equally, therefore, to Marxist work in linguistics: "Every young science . . . should value a good opponent much higher than a poor ally."[2] Moreover, this encounter between Marxism and philosophy of language is merely a prolegomenon meant to delineate "basic directions" and "methodological guidelines" for a "genuine Marxist thinking about language" (MPL, xiv, xiii). The result of this dialogue with the dominant trends in linguistics is an often brilliant, original and open-ended work—notwithstanding major problems it leaves unresolved.

SIGNS, UTTERANCES, SPEECH GENRES, AND CLASS STRUGGLE

Marxism and the Philosophy of Language opens with an explosion of concepts whose analytic value remains largely undeveloped. Voloshinov begins with two seemingly straightforward propositions: signs are social phenomena living on the boundaries between individuals; and they are meaningful only in the context of social relations among people. The word, maintains Voloshinov, "is a two-sided act. It is determined equally by *whose* word it is and *for whom* it is meant. . . . I give myself verbal shape from another's point of view, ultimately, from the point of view of the community to which I belong. A word is a bridge thrown between myself and another" (MPL, 86). But the human consciousnesses that come into contact through the word are themselves formed via the medium of signs (be they gestures, words, flags, or stop signs) which have been produced in the course of the social life of a group. There is not, first, a consciousness which then chooses signs to express itself: "Consciousness takes shape and being in the material of signs created by an organized group in the process of its social intercourse" (MPL, 13). Having established that consciousness is both social and material (i.e. that it arises through the materiality of signs within the life of a social group), Voloshinov next addresses the question of the sociomaterial determination of ideological phenomena (often described as the relationship between "base" and "superstructures").

Without pretending for a moment to do justice to this thorny problem, one of the most difficult issues in Marxist theory, let me note that the importance of the base-superstructure metaphor resides in its insistence that ideological conflicts are significantly determined by the practical activities of people organized in a mode of production, social-productive relations and class struggles. This insistence is crucial to combating intellectual idealism (the notion that ideas operate within a self-sufficient world of their own making). At the same time, the metaphor has often been an invitation to some of the crudest and most reductive treatments of culture, religions, art, philosophies, and systems of thought. Voloshinov seeks a nonreductive model of determination. In this respect, his position approximates that of Marx in works like *The German Ideology* which, as one commentator notes, are meant to challenge "the very possibility of distinguishing the material and the ideal as separate spheres in the first place."[3] The material and the ideal form a unity for Marx and Voloshinov. Nevertheless, there are relations of dialectical determination among the internally related elements that constitute a social whole. The problem is to accord sufficient weight to the social relations in which people produce and reproduce the means of material life without reducing everything to these. As Raymond Williams remarks in *Marxism and Literature*: "A Marxism without some concept of determination is worthless. A Marxism with many of the concepts of determination it now has is quite radically disabled."[4]

The most impressive attempts to circumvent the dead-end choice of indeterminacy or reductionism have built upon Marx's claim that a mode of production "is a definite form of activity."[5] Rather than treating the base as a *thing*—for example, the economy, or the forces of production—Marx insists that certain human *practices*, or what he calls "practical activities," exercise a decisive conditioning effect upon others. The base-superstructure metaphor ought to be understood, therefore, not in terms of mechanical causality, but in terms of internal relations of determination within the complex of human activities.[6] Consistent with this, Voloshinov seeks to show that linguistic practice—speech—is conditioned by the nexus of social relations; but he also wants to argue that language plays a unique role in *refracting* (as well as reflecting) these relations (MPL, 18–19, 23).

Relations between base and superstructure, existence and signs cannot be grasped in terms of mechanical causality, therefore. While exploitative relations of productive life will give rise to class conflicts, these struggles are not straightforwardly determined. True, people grouped into antagonistic social classes will invariably find themselves engaged in class conflicts; they will develop some sort of consciousness of their class situation; they will organize, resist, and in some circumstances create political movements, ideologies and parties; they will win and lose battles. All of this constitutes the rich and manifold experience of class. Yet little of this is automatically given by socioeconomic circumstances. Too many other subtle layers of experience intervene for this to be possible—division and unification, modes of self-understanding, competing worldviews, cultures of resistance, forms of organization, histories of victories and defeats, the intervention of other social groups, hopes and betrayals, family life, religion, and popular culture. What signs reflect and refract, therefore, is not a singular socioeconomic fact, but a dynamic process of social interaction between groups and classes whose possibilities are multiple. A single sign, such as a word, reflects and refracts an enormously complex social process: "The word is implicated in literally each and every act or contact between people—in collaboration on the job, in ideological exchanges, in the chance contacts of ordinary life, in political relationships, and so on. Countless ideological threads running through all areas of social intercourse register effect in the word. . . . The word has the capacity to register all the transitory, delicate, momentary phases of social change" (MPL, 19).

Now, this is obviously no simple, reductive notion of the sign. Voloshinov wants to insist upon the fluid dynamism of social life, on the multiplicity of its possibilities, without abandoning all notions of dialectical determination—and without the slide into infinite randomness and contingency (or "arbitrariness") this entails. In this spirit, his notion of the *multiaccentuality* of the sign is designed to capture the dynamics of complex structured social processes.

Different social groups and classes use the same signs, the same words, the same language system, Voloshinov notes. Since a single language or sign system is used by groups with radically different circumstances and life activities, signs become inflected with different and competing meanings as these groups struggle to express their life situations, their outlooks, their aspirations. Conflicts between groups and classes thus interpolate every sign. In Voloshinov's terms, different groups try to ascribe unique *accents* to a given sign: "as a result, differently oriented accents intersect in every ideological sign" (MPL, 23). This notion of the multiaccentuality of the sign enables Voloshinov to focus on the experientially rich and concrete character of language as it actually happens.[7] Rather than mere instantiations of a language system, he theorizes speech in terms of the unique utterances of real individuals involved in specific groups and concrete social relations. "The meaning of a word is determined entirely by its context," he tells us. From here, it is but a short step to the apparently radical judgment of the next sentence: "In fact, there are as many meanings of a word as there are contexts of its usage." Yet, at the very moment when he appears ready to set language adrift in a sea of differences, of infinitely and endlessly new contexts and meanings, Voloshinov changes tack: "At the same time, however, the word does not cease to be a single entity; it does not, so to speak, break apart into as many separate words as there are contexts of its usage" (MPL, 79–80).

But why not, we might ask. Why isn't the unity of the word broken up by an endless proliferation of words? Or, in Voloshinov's own question, "how can the fundamental polysemanticity of the word be reconciled with its unity?" He answers that there is an "identity factor" or "factor of unity" to words. Words have relatively stable, albeit abstract, meanings of the sort we find in a dictionary. And this is because different, contexts interact, they shape, determine, and inform each other. "Contexts do not stand side by side in a row, as if unaware of one another, but are in a state of constant tension, or incessant interaction and conflict" (MPL, 80). Every context, in other words, is intercontextual; it refers to other contexts of meaning. It follows that language is a dynamic field of unique contexts, competing and conflicting evaluations and accents. Yet these contexts, evaluations, and accents are not radically separate; they are in continual interaction, and this interaction constitutes the linguistic sphere. Thus, there is unity in difference—a dynamic, changing unity, an "open totality" (SG, 7) in an always unfinished process of transformation and development. Bakhtin captures this dynamic sense of unity-in-difference of the word in "Discourse in the Novel":

> The word, directed towards its object, enters a dialogically agitated and tension-filled environment of alien words, value judgments and accents, weaves in and out of complex interrelationships, merges with some, recoils from others, intersects with yet a third group. . . .
>
> The living utterance, having taken meaning and shape at a particular historical moment in a socially specific environment, cannot fail to brush up against thousands of living dialogic threads . . . the utterance arises out of this dialogue as a continuation of it and as a rejoinder to it—it does not approach its object from the sidelines.[8]

Language lives, therefore, in "a continuous process of becoming. Individuals do not receive a ready-made language at all, rather, they enter upon the stream of verbal communication" (MPL, 81). Of course, relatively stable meanings are necessary if we are to understand and communicate across a wide range of contexts. But these meanings arise from the "dialectical generative process" of language, they are historical products of the multiple and often conflicting values and accents which permeate speech and which constitute the "theme" of an utterance. For Voloshinov, dictionary-type meanings are the abstract stuff, the raw material for generating thematic utterances (MPL, 100, 101). Moreover, in a particularly fertile argument, he suggests that ruling classes are most drawn to reified and formalistic approaches to language since they seek to impose a static set of meanings on words in order to close off alternative accents and evaluations: "The ruling class strives to impart a supraclass, eternal character to the ideological sign to extinguish or drive inward the struggle between social value judgments which occurs in it, to make the sign uniaccentual" (MPL, 23). In so doing, ruling classes attempt the impossible. At best they can drive other meanings off the public stage of official discourse; but alternative meanings will nonetheless be nourished in unofficial or underground settings, for signs can never be rendered genuinely uniaccentual. "In the ordinary conditions of life," the tensions and contradictions within every sign will be muted. But, "this *inner dialectic quality* of the sign comes out fully . . . in times of social crises or revolutionary changes" (MPL, 23–24). With this argument, Voloshinov connects the struggle over the sign to wider social processes. This is not a Nietzschean contest between individuals intent on imposing their unique wills to power. Instead, Voloshinov sees meanings as connected to the activity of "organized social groups" struggling to accent signs in ways conducive to their organization and self-expression. Ruling classes and dominant groups attempt to impose uniaccentual signs, a single set of meanings that reflect and refract a dominant set of interests. Oppressed groups, on the other hand, struggle to accent signs differently—and, in so doing, express a distinct (and often oppositional) set of interests and meanings. As a result, "sign becomes an arena of class struggle" (MPL, 23).

Voloshinov's concept of the multiaccentuality of the sign is far removed from post-structuralist notions of difference, contingency, and randomness. True, signs and meanings are not singular; they are sites of multiple accents. But this multiaccentuality is not random. Contending accents grow out of structured life situations. Conflicts over accents and meanings reflect and refract struggles over labor, conditions of life, inequality, hierarchy, and social power. Moreover, each group draws upon a reservoir of sociolinguistic meanings which derive from the *speech genres* they have developed in the course of their practical activity.

The concept of speech genres is a crucial one for Voloshinov (and Bakhtin) in terms of moving from the abstract level of a language system to the concrete richness of speech. When we speak we do not simply enter a formal system called language (or *langue*), rather, we enter sites of struggle over meanings. Speech is permeated by social evaluation. But these are not the pristine creations of individuals; instead, social evaluations arise out of the activity of organized social groups. Indeed, many evaluative accents shape the very forms of speech employed by different groups as they develop specialized vocabularies, double entendres, unique expressions, and syntactic structures—all in an effort to shape language according to their social experiences. These evaluative accents congeal in the speech genres of various groups:

> ... an entirely special type of structure has been worked out for the genre of the light and casual causerie of the drawing room where everyone "feels at home" and where the basic differentiation within the gathering (the audience) is that between men and women. ... A different type of structure is worked out in the case of conversation between husband and wife, brother and sister, etc. ... Village sewing circles, urban carouses, workers' lunchtime chats, etc., will all have their own types. Each situation fixed and sustained by social custom, commands a particular kind of organization of audience and, hence, a particular repertoire of little behavioral genres (MPL, 97).

Once more, Voloshinov insists that these multiple speech genres share a common context: the relations of hierarchy appropriate to a particular class structure. "Enormous significance belongs to *the hierarchical factor* in the process of verbal exchange," he writes, and these hierarchical relations are largely "determined by production relations and the sociopolitical order." Speech genres thus grow out of concrete life situations and the repertoire of activities and forms of social interaction these entail. The latter Voloshinov describes as *life genres*—those complexes of behavior (gestures, deference, seriousness, humor, and so on) which reflect and refract a socially structured life situation (MPL, 21, 20–21, 96–97).[9]

A specific individual will inhabit a multiplicity of speech genres, and it is this that gives the individual an enormous range of linguistic possibilities for self-expression. A secretarial worker, for example, will often use a more formal and deferential genre while speaking with her boss, a more relaxed and humorous genre while talking with workmates at lunch, a more politicized genre at a union meeting (e.g., "sisters and brothers"), a more technical genre when attending a discussion of modern art, and so on. Indeed, Medvedev suggests that we are intellectually and culturally richer for the variety of genres we employ (FM, 134).

If the multiaccentuality of the sign is a product of the diverse range of socially structured contexts in which people live their lives, it follows that, rather than arbitrary, speech genres are linguistic expressions of a finite number of concrete social settings as these are determined "by production relations and the sociopolitical order." Consequently, speech genres are highly sensitive to social change. Consider, for example, the innovations in speech consequent upon important social upheavals—the emergence of the black power movement of the 1960s or the women's liberation movement of the 1970s in North America are but two recent examples. When social relations and structures are challenged, and new social movements emerge, these changes are registered in speech. George Orwell's *Homage to Catalonia* offers a beautiful illustration of this point. Describing his amazement at finding Barcelona under the rule of the working class in December 1936, Orwell comments: "Servile and even ceremonial forms of speech had temporarily disappeared. Nobody said '*Señor*' or '*Don*' or even '*Usted*'; everyone called everyone else 'Comrade' or 'Thou,' and said '*Salud!*' instead of '*Buenos dias.*' "[10] In Bakhtin's terms, the workers' revolution in Barcelona had made it possible for the speech genres of the oppressed to occupy greater public space. It follows that speech genres "are the drive belts from the history of society to the history of language" (SG, 65).

Breaking sharply from the formalist position associated with Saussure, *Marxism and the Philosophy of Language* restores speech to its central position in language and society. At the same time, it refuses the idealist move of ascribing pure creative powers to individuals. Individuals *are* creative, for Voloshinov—but within the finite possibilities of the speech genres developed by groups in concrete social settings. Furthermore, by showing how struggles over signs are intrinsic to all class and social struggles, Voloshinov sets out a framework in which ideological and discursive struggles are inseparable from material-practical ones. His pivotal concepts—the utterance, multiaccentuality of the sign, speech genres, and the sign as an arena of class struggle—provide us with powerful means for exploring language and social life. For all these reasons, *Marxism and the Philosophy of Language* remains a vital point of reference for all radical and revolutionary discussions of language. But, like any utterance, it, too, is meant to be interrogated, explored, amended and built upon. And in some areas it ought to be queried most closely.

LURKING DUALISMS: NATURE/CULTURE, ANIMAL/HUMAN, BODY/SIGN

Marxism and the Philosophy of Language generally explores theoretical dualisms in order to transcend them. It pursues one side of a contrastive pair (like *langue/parole*) to the point at which it breaks down and requires the presence of the other. The approach owes something to the method of immanent critique which, proceeding by internal criticism of the concrete body of knowledge in a given field, seeks to preserve their insights and partial truths while overcoming their inconsistencies and internal contradictions. Voloshinov often operates in this way, moving through alternating critiques of each side of the dualism characteristic of contemporary linguistics—abstract objectivism, and individualistic subjectivism.[11] Abstract objectivism rightly sees the systematic aspect of language which precedes the speech activity of any individual, but errs in detaching the language system from the generative activity of speech. Meanwhile, individualist subjectivism correctly emphasizes the creative power of speech, but undermines this insight by failing to see how discourse is structured by socially organized linguistic forms. Voloshinov hopes to integrate the partial truths of each perspective into a richer and more comprehensive theory.

Encountering philosophical dualisms like material/ideal, and individual/social, Voloshinov similarly strives to overcome them. His claim for the embodied character of consciousness, for instance, challenges crude oppositions between the material and the ideal (MPL, 90). In the same spirit, his argument that there exists "a continuous dialectical interplay" between the psyche and ideology refuses to individualize the psyche or to treat ideology as purely systemic and trans-individual (MPL, 39). Voloshinov's point is not that these distinctions are entirely false. Rather, following Hegel and Marx in this regard, he sees them as having a limited truth, as describing "moments" or aspects of real phenomena but as betraying their partiality and incompleteness whenever they are treated as self-sufficient terms which depict phenomena in their full complexity. For critical theory, analysis must work through contrastive distinctions of this sort in order to dissolve them into more complex concepts. Yet, at a number of crucial points, Voloshinov himself falls back upon undialectical antinomies rather than dissolving them through criticism. This is particularly the case where he counterposes nature to history, and the body to consciousness.

The very first pages of *Marxism and the Philosophy of Language* are organized around the opposition between natural phenomena and the world of signs. Natural bodies do not signify, they do not take on special meanings by reference to something else, says Voloshinov. A tool is a tool, a loaf of bread a loaf of bread. Each is self-identical, a natural object, not a sign. Human social reality is thus twofold, consisting of natural phenomena and signs: "side by side with the natural phenomena, with the equipment of technology, and with articles of consumption there exists a special world—*the world of signs*" (MPL, 9, 10). Now, as a point of departure this could be a helpful distinction. It would enable Voloshinov to use the distinction natural phenomenon/sign to point out that signs do not occur in a purely natural way. To acquire meaning, they must be socially organized to that end, they must become part of a sign system. But from here, it would be necessary to show how "natural" phenomena—the material structure of the world, biological history, the human larynx, voice, hands, and so on—are essential to human sign systems. It would be necessary, in other words, to show that signifying activity is conditioned by the "natural," just as the human-natural world is socially mediated. This would involve relaxing the natural phenomenon/sign distinction in ways that capture their complex interrelations, their reconstitution into new forms of human social life. But Voloshinov refuses this move. Instead of providing a point of tension around which to organize a movement in his thought, the distinction natural object/sign operates as a static opposition.

Voloshinov repeatedly falls back on the idea that the physical-biological level of human life is radically removed from the signifying, ideological one. Discussing the individual, he insists that a "rigorous distinction must always be made between the concept of the individual as a natural specimen" and the "ideological-semiotic" concept of the individual, that is, the individual as understood within a system of ideological meanings (MPL, 34). Again, one might argue that this opposition is a useful starting point for understanding the way in which universal biological features of human existence (birth and death, sex and reproduction, hunger and thirst, etc.) are socially mediated. But to insist upon it as a "rigorous distinction" is deeply problematic. It implies a level of natural-biological existence entirely independent of social systems of meaning and signification. In probing the concept of the individual, he maintains that wherever the inner psychic life of an individual is "strongly marked by biological and biographical factors, the further away the inner sign will be from fully fledged ideological expression" (MPL, 35). Put simply, signs for Voloshinov are social, not individual; a fully formed psychic life is a socialized one. He thus sets up two modes of experience—what he calls the "I experience" and the "we experience"—as yet another opposition which rehearses the distinction between nature and language. And he chooses to valorize one of these: the "we experience," the experiential mode which is other-directed, oriented toward dialogue and communication. The "I experience" on the other hand, he describes as inner-directed and self-oriented. The I experience contends Voloshinov, "actually tends toward extermination" as it loses the ideological orientation toward others. Indeed, an individual in the I state regresses from culture to nature, from language and ideology "to the physiological reaction of the animal" (MPL, 88).

These sorts of arguments undercut the dialectical movement at work throughout so much of *Marxism and the Philosophy of Language*. Rather than superseding static dualisms, Voloshinov rehabilitates a set of binary oppositions: nature/sign; biology/society; animal/human by baldly counterposing the natural to the social, the biological to the historical. This counterposition also surfaces in Medvedev's *The Formal Method* with its claim that "the utterance is not a physical body and not a physical event, but a historical event" (FM, 120). But nowhere is this static counterposition more evident than in Voloshinov's earlier book, *Freudianism: A Critical Sketch* (1927).

Voloshinov's attack on Freud posits a rigid distinction between biology and history. The first chapter tells us, for example, that Freud's great error arose from the idea that "a person's consciousness is shaped not by his historical existence but by his biological being, the main facet of which is sexuality."[12] Now, the idea that sexuality is strictly biological is clearly problematic. So is the idea that an individual's biological being is not essential to her historical existence. Yet this is no accidental formulation. On the next page of the text, Voloshinov criticizes Freud because "the three basic events in the life of all animals—birth, copulation, and death— . . . become a surrogate of history" (F, 11). One might readily agree that individual history ought not to be reduced to a purely natural account of these life processes. It matters immensely whether one is born into poverty or abundance, whether one's sexual life takes place in conditions of regimentation and social repression or those of free self-development, and whether one's death is the result of war, hunger, homelessness, or of old age after a lifetime of comfort and fulfillment. All of these are social conditions of physical life. Yet it remains the case that these "biological" aspects are essential parts of individual life history. Voloshinov actually suggests, however, that the psychic conflicts in the lives of individuals do not derive from problems like birth, sexuality, and death, but, instead, from ideological conflicts (F, 88). Once more, one might agree that individual psychic conflicts are inseparable from ideology. The guilt an adolescent or adult feels about sex, for instance, may well have much to do with dominant ideologies. But Voloshinov intends a much stronger meaning than this. Treating individual biological and biographical aspects of life as "animal," he defines consciousness as thoroughly social and ideological—indeed in a remarkable passage in *Marxism and the Philosophy of Language*, he recommends avoiding the term "psychology" entirely: "we should prefer to avoid the word 'psychology' since we are concerned exclusively with the content of the psyche and the consciousness. That content is ideological through and through, determined not by individual, organismic (biological or physiological) factors, but by factors of a purely sociological character" (MPL, 91).

This counterposition of biology and history rehearses a dualism that has plagued Western philosophy. Moreover, it is one that, in an understandable recoil from crude materialism, has also plagued certain Marxist thinkers. Voloshinov is rightly worried about the predominance of "predialectical mechanistic materialism" in much Marxist thought (MPL, iv), about models which employ crude (predialectical) notions of causality and depict phenomena such as human consciousness, language, and meaning as mere reflexes of material processes (understood themselves in the most narrow and reductive sense). One way around this reduction of the sociohistorical to the naturo-material is to dig a gulf between the two realms. This was the move made by the Hungarian Marxist Georg Lukacs in his great work, *History and Class Consciousness*. In the course of a powerful and compelling attack on vulgar materialism, Lukacs sharply separated nature and society by asserting that dialectics applied not to nature but only to the relation between human subjects and their world. Having failed to set forth the nature-society dyad dialectically, Lukacs all too easily collapsed nature into society with his claim that "nature is a social category."[13]

Voloshinov does not absorb nature into society. But rather than showing their interrelationship—how society is naturally conditioned and nature socially mediated—he, too, draws rigid boundaries between the two. Some phenomena are natural, biological and animal in nature; others are social, historical, and human in character. The result is that each sphere serves as a limiting concept for the other: society is the nonnatural, nature is the nonsocial. While his intent, like that of Lukacs, is to avoid mechanical reductionism, the end product is an undialectical dualism. What Gramsci wrote in criticism of Lukacs, applies with equal force to Voloshinov:

> It would appear that Lukacs maintains that one can speak of the dialectic only for the history of men and not for nature. . . . If his assertion presupposes a dualism between nature and man he is wrong because he is falling into a conception of nature proper to religion and to Graeco-Christian philosophy and also to idealism which does not succeed in unifying and relating man and nature to each other except verbally. But if human history should be conceived also as the history of nature (also by means of the history of science) how can the dialectic be separated from nature?[14]

Despite his insistence upon the embodied character of consciousness and the material reality of signs, Voloshinov's dualism leads him to lose sight of the corporeal aspects of language. Rather than seeing human bodies as socially organized and signifying, he insists that "a physical body equals itself . . . it does not signify anything but wholly coincides with its particular given nature" (MPL, 9). While a physical body can be "converted into a sign," Voloshinov treats this as a metamorphosis, a radical change of state. This results in a naturalization (reification) of the "things" we find in human production, like tools and commodities. He tells us that "a tool by itself is devoid of special meaning" and that "the consumer good, as such, is not at all a sign" (MPL, 10). But this will not do. The physical object known as a hammer does not have culturo-technological meaning outside of social relations; to most species it is just another thing. What makes it a tool is its entanglement in a network of human meanings, of shared knowledge and cultural practices that make it recognizable as a tool with specific practical functions. Similarly, a consumer good like bread (Voloshinov's example) is not devoid of significance. Indeed, Voloshinov implicitly recognizes as much when he later argues that a natural phenomenon such as hunger is itself socially mediated—its meaning depends upon whether one is a beggar, a peasant, a bourgeois, or a member of a self-confident group of striking workers (MPL, 88). But if this is so, then a commodity like bread also carries meaning according to the social relations that situate the individual who bakes it, desires it, buys it, eats it, offers it to others, demands it of a capitalist, and so on.

Voloshinov's dualisms of nature and history, body and language result in two reifying tendencies in his thought. On the one hand, "things" (like tools and consumer goods) are naturalized, stripped of their immersion in a world of meanings. At the same time, consciousness and language are significantly dematerialized, separated from nature and the body.[15] As Samuel Weber notes, "Voloshinov's conception of the body remains essentially *naturalistic*. . . . The body is equated with the physical organism and becomes as such the vehicle for the delivery of semiotic material to the psyche." Weber recognizes that Voloshinov creates an opening for a less naturalistic view, that his view of the psyche as a boundary phenomenon existing on the border between the inside and outside of an individual opens up a perspective in which the body is implicated in the signifying and communicative interactions between people. But he argues of Voloshinov that, unlike Bakhtin, "his concept of the body . . . is never reworked in response to the consequences of this theory."[16] Yet, if the important achievements of *Marxism and the Philosophy of Language*—including its effort to transcend undialectical dualisms—are to be preserved, extended, and developed, this will require reworking its concept of the body in exactly this sort of way. And, as Weber intimates, one important source for such a reworking can be found in the writings of Voloshinov's collaborator, Mikhail Bakhtin.

"The Body Needs the Other": Language, Dialogue, and the Body in Bakhtin

The controversies surrounding Bakhtin and his work continue to swirl. Did he write the books attributed to Voloshinov and Medvedev? Was he a Marxist or an anti-Marxist? A Christian or an atheist? A Kantian or a post-structuralist? Often, these debates are conducted in terms of academic models of voice and authorship foreign to the spirit of Bakhtin's thought. But because these controversies shape the field, let me set out some markers for my discussion.

To begin, I am largely uninterested in the debate over Bakhtin's alleged Marxism or anti-Marxism. I believe the textual evidence suggests that Bakhtin did not write any of the major works attributed to Voloshinov and Medvedev: *Freudianism*, *The Formal Method in Literary Scholarship*, and *Marxism and the Philosophy of Language*. I concur with the judgment of Morson and Emerson that "Voloshinov's and Medvedev's works are sincerely Marxist . . . they represent a particularly complex and rewarding form of Marxism, and are among the strongest works on language and literature in our century," and with their further judgment that Bakhtin was not a Marxist.[17] The more significant questions, to my mind, are whether Bakhtin's work can be a fertile source of radical theorizing in the area of language and culture, and whether it might enrich work of Marxist inspiration. I answer "yes" to both these questions. Bakhtin's work grew out of a dialogue with some of the most original Marxist theorizing in the areas of linguistic and aesthetic theory. His own utterances were shaped as responses to his Marxist collaborators, just as they, too, show the imprint of his interventions. The result of this interchange was a burst of theorizing in which each member of the trio published a major work in the course of two years that capped a period of highly charged intellectual discussion and collaboration: Medvedev's

Formal Method (1928), Voloshinov's *Marxism and the Philosophy of Language* (1929), and Bakhtin's, *Problems of Dostoevsky's Poetics* (1929). While Bakhtin's thinking tends to elude the categories of any orthodoxy, it cannot be understood outside this encounter.[18]

Curiously, some of Bakhtin's work prior to his engagement with "the Leningrad Circle" (which included Voloshinov and Medvedev) is especially interesting in terms of the problems I have been exploring to this point.[19] These early philosophical essays, written during the period 1919–1924, are often fragmentary, repetitive, and incomplete—even more so than his published works. The imprint of Bakhtin's early Kantianism remains strong, often frustratingly so, as he struggles with problems that are largely a product of that system of thought. But it is highly significant that the most important of these essays, "Author and Hero in Aesthetic Activity" (1920–1923), strives to break out of the Kantian dualism of mind and world by turning to the body as the site of all experience. This orientation owed much to Bakhtin's lifelong interest in the natural sciences, physics, and biology in particular.[20] These natural-scientific interests aided his effort to overcome Kantian dualism by making the body (and with it language) the point of intersection of individual and world, self and other.

"I am situated," Bakhtin writes, "on the boundary of the world I see."[21] And the world I see is bounded by my seeing body and what it perceives. This makes an experience uniquely mine, since no one else is this body at this place and in this time (which is also the source of tremendous shortcomings of my experience and one of the reasons I need to be "completed" by others). My body is the experiential site of spatiality and temporality; rather than transcendental categories of mind, Bakhtin takes space and time to be modes of embodiment. In the 1930s, he writes that, unlike Kant, he treats space and time "not as 'transcendental' but as forms of the most immediate reality" (FTC, 85 n2). And the most immediate reality for the human individual is his or her body.

Rather than seeing nature and the body as limits, as "others" to history and language, Bakhtin regards them as integral to each. Consciousness and language do not begin where the body ends (as in much of Voloshinov's work); instead, they are modes of my embodied being-with-others. Bakhtin insists, however, that as a body, as a concrete being in particular moments in space and time, I am radically incomplete. The world outside exists for me as a set of fragmentary and partial experiences. Indeed, I can never experience myself as an integral whole since I do not exist for myself as an object in and of the world outside me. In order to attain a richer sense of self, in order to acquire a sense of being-in-the-world, I need the experience of another who can see me from the outside, from a spatiotemporal site other than that of my body. "In this sense," he writes, "one can speak of a human being's absolute need for the other, for the other's seeing, remembering, gathering and unifying self-activity—the only activity capable of producing his outwardly finished personality" (AH, 35–36). In and through others—through their recognition of me, their affirmation of my identity and personality *for them*, their bodily interactions with me, their talk—I overcome the fragmentary character of my limited corporeal experience of self and world and receive a more integral sense of personhood (AH, 12–14, 86, 102).

It is easy to see how this perspective opens on to Bakhtin's celebrated "dialogism," the idea that individuals come into being in and through their communicative interactions with others.[22] And this is how "Author and Hero" is often treated: as an anticipation of his later emphasis on dialogue as the model of self-other relations. But such readings often eclipse Bakhtin's emphasis on the body. For Bakhtin is not simply claiming that each of us is a linguistic being who needs a response from others. He is also insisting that we are *body-selves* whose sense of self coheres only through embodied relations with other body-selves. "Only the other is *embodied* for me axiologically and aesthetically," he states. "In this respect, the body is not something self-sufficient: it needs the other, needs his recognition and his form-giving activity" (AH, 51). This argument rarely figures in interpretations of Bakhtin, but it is a crucial one. For it highlights the embodied character of experience and it takes him to a relationship to which his later writing rarely returns: that between mother and child.

The relation between a child and its mother becomes paradigmatic for Bakhtin's notion of the completion of the body/self through another. While acknowledging that other persons can play an affirming and completing role, he attributes unique importance to the mother:

> . . . as soon as a human being begins to experience himself from within, he at once meets with acts of recognition and love that come to him from outside—from his mother, from others who are close to him. The child receives all initial determinations of himself and of his body from his mother's lips and from the lips of those who are close to him. It is from their lips in the emotional-volitional tones of their love, that the child hears and begins to acknowledge his own proper name and the names of all the features pertaining to his body and to his inner states and experiences (AH, 49).

These acts of love and care from others allow the self to cohere; indeed the self only emerges in and through dyadic relations. And again the mother-child dyad is singled out as the critical one in the development of an individual personality: "The child begins to see himself for the first time as if through his mother's eyes, and begins to speak about himself in his mother's emotional-volitional tones— he caresses himself, as it were, with his first uttered self-expression" (AH, 49). This is both a richly suggestive and deeply problematic line of argument.

The great strength of Bakhtin's argument here is, first, that it transcends the mind/body dualism by instating the corporeal individual, the individual who bodies forth in the world, as the locus of experience. Consciousness, language, and culture are thus attributes of particular kinds of bodies, not extra-natural and extra-bodily events. Second, Bakhtin's argument situates the absent mother at the center of his psychology, theory of language, and concept of individual development. What Nietzsche wants to efface—that we all originate in a mother—Bakhtin chooses to highlight. In marked contrast to the influential theory of Jacques Lacan who treats the mother as a force of nature from which the child must break in order to identify with the father and enter the realm of language and culture, the mother for Bakhtin represents a social relationship, an entry to culture and to language.[23] Third, Bakhtin's discussion also touches on the mimetic moment in language, in particular the idea that the child imitates the emotional-volitional tone of its mother in order to caress itself, to comfort itself with the same sorts of sounds it has heard from her. As a result, the emotional and expressive aspects of language are foregrounded in Bakhtin's account. Yet, while there is much to be commended in this account, there are also some serious limitations which cannot be evaded. These centrally concern Bakhtin's treatment of gender.

While Bakhtin's argument has the merit of alluding to a gendered body, it also tends to naturalize woman as mother, the only form in which women enter his discussion of body and self. Women appear (as mothers) only when he takes up the experience of a developing (male) child. Related to this is a failure to interrogate the concept of "mother" itself. After all, does Bakhtin mean the biological mother? What if this individual is not the child's primary caregiver? What if an aunt, wet nurse, father, older sibling, uncle, grandparent, or someone else plays this role? What if more than one individual parents a child? At one point Bakhtin appears to consider these possibilities, as in his reference above to the child receiving recognition and love "from his mother, from others who are close to him." This formulation opens the door to replacing or supplementing the concept *mother* with that of *primary caregivers*. But he does not see this move through.

There is also an idealization at work here. The mother is largely de-subjectified, effectively reduced to an object (albeit a responsive one) in the world of the child. Bakhtin does not consider what role the child might play in the life of the mother or another caregiver. Indeed, he romanticizes/fetishizes the mother as one who purely and simply loves her child. The mother becomes a fantasy-object, an extension of the desiring body of the (male) child. The mother's love becomes, in Freud's words, "a completely satisfying love-relation, which not only fulfills every mental wish but also every physical need."[24] Rather than seeing a mother (or any primary caregiver) as a complex personality for whom love is only one of a number of emotions constituting her relation to a child, the mother becomes a fantastic object of love (and hate). Bakhtin thus reproduces one of the great shortcomings of much psychoanalytic theory: its failure to pursue Freud's occasional insights into the whole problem of maternal aggression—a phenomenon which unsettles the great emphasis much psycho-analytic thought puts on the socializing role of the father.[25] Bakhtin's insightful and potentially important discussion of the child-mother dyad is marred, there-fore, by a failure to consider the social construction of motherhood and feminin-ity, by a neglect of the ways in which other caregivers might supplant or supplement the biological mother, and by an avoidance of the complex emo-tional responses that comprise the interactions of real mothers and other caregivers with the children in their lives.[26]

These criticisms are not meant to dismiss Bakhtin's attempt to overcome the mind/body dualism, his insistence on the body as the site of interaction between self and other, or his concept of the individual's completion in and through physical (not just discursive) interactions with others—all of which point beyond the dualism plaguing much of Voloshinov's work. It is to urge, however, that these insights can be developed only by overturning his naturalistic concept of the mother (and of the body) and by coming to terms with the way in which gender roles are socially organized and constructed, a problem to which we shall return when discussing Bakhtin's great work on carnival, *Rabelais and His World*.

DOSTOYEVSKY, DIALOGUE, AND THE POLYPHONIC NOVEL

During the six or more years between his work on "Author and Hero" (1920–23) and the appearance of his Dostoyevsky book (1929), Bakhtin's focus shifted increasingly toward language as the key to self-other relations. Undoubtedly, this owed much to the climate of vigorous debate over aesthetic and linguistic ques-tions in post-revolutionary Russia. Moreover, Bakhtin's thought took a "socio-logical" turn during these years—toward a more concrete appreciation of social and historical contexts of self-other relations. As a result, his thinking became less oriented to finding the invariant or transcendental features of human expe-rience, and more attentive to the socially structured situations in which experi-ence takes place. The body, conceived so far in a fairly naturalistic fashion, was largely supplanted by a new and highly social emphasis on language. Language, after all, seems at first glance a more sensitive barometer of social change than does the body. In fact, as we shall see in the next chapter, the body's involvement in language, technology, art, fashion, and so on make it a more complex social indicator than might be supposed. But it is difficult to grasp social processes with a naturalistic notion of the body. In the first instance, then, as Bakhtin's thought became more sociological, he moved away from the body and toward language. As his work developed throughout the 1930s, however, he returned to the body—but via a route influenced by his new attentiveness to sociohistorical context. But in *Problems of Dostoevsky's Poetics*, the body is almost entirely absent; the central organizing concepts of the text are dialogue and polyphony.

In some respects, the Dostoyevsky book is a transitional work. It signals the new importance of language in Bakhtin's thinking, but it lacks the concrete sense of sociohistorical process of his essays of the 1930s. Nevertheless, Bakhtin makes some significant theoretical innovations there which were to inform much of his later work. The great achievement of Dostoyevsky, he argues, was his thorough-going break from the novel as the narrative of a single consciousness. Rather than the unfolding of the narrator's story, rather than the tale of a single voice, Dostoyevsky's novels were organized around the clash, conflict, and interaction of many voices; his novels are multivoiced, or *polyphonic*. Furthermore, the voices that enter a polyphonic novel are internally connected. Dostoyevsky's novels do not bring isolated individual voices into contact for the first time. Always in the process of responding to others, each unique voice resonates with the utterances and accents of others: "In Dostoevsky, consciousness never gravitates toward itself but is always found in intense relationship with other consciousnesses. Every experience, every thought of a character is internally dialogic, adorned with polemic, filled with struggle."[27]

The polyphonic author does not stand outside the novel's characters, or-chestrating their utterances toward predetermined ends; "the author speaks not *about* a character, but *with* him" (PDP, 62, 63). The author of a polyphonic novel frees his or her characters for dialogue. But to do this, the author must allow the dialogue to unfold according to its inner dynamics. To orchestrate the dialogue is to reify; by contrast, in the polyphonic novel, "the author's consciousness does not transform others' consciousnesses (that is, the consciousnesses of the char-acters) into objects. . . . It reflects and re-creates not a world of objects, but precisely these other consciousnesses with their worlds, re-creates them in their authentic *unfinalizability*" (PDP, 68).

Bakhtin's argument for the open-ended and unfinalizable individual seems to anticipate post-structuralist critiques of "the human subject." After all, Bakhtin's concepts of self, consciousness, language, and dialogue are designed to rupture the self-enclosed unity of the bourgeois individual, the self-sufficient, self-inter-ested, utility-maximizing, competitive individual of market economics. However, the polyphonic novel does not trace the dissolution of the self but, rather, the dynamic constitution and reconstitution of selves in and through dialogue. This is why Bakhtin can say that the polyphonic novel "has nothing in common with relativism." Dogmatism and relativism, he suggests, are opposite sides of the same coin. The former closes off dialogue in advance by constituting individuals externally, as objects of monological manipulation, while relativism, on the other hand, so radically separates voices and consciousnesses as to render dialogue impossible (since it makes common language unfeasible). The polyphonic novel strives to transcend both these positions (PDP, 69).

Perhaps most marked off from post-structuralist perspectives is Bakhtin's refusal to repudiate notions of "truth." In opposition to absolutist definitions he posits truth as social and dialogical: "Truth is not born nor is it to be found inside the head of an individual person, it is born *between people* searching for truth, in the process of their dialogic interaction" (PDP,110). Bakhtin advances a sort of dialogical realism which seeks truthfulness in the concrete and manifold richness of social interaction. We are not imprisoned by social texts, therefore, since these are bound up with changing socio-historical contexts. "I am against enclosure in a text," he wrote in one of his last essays (SG, 169). Texts are always refractions of real historical experiences, they originate in that extra-textual world and return to it:

> In the completely real-life time-space where the work resonates, where we find the inscription or the book, we find as well a real person . . . and real people who are hearing and reading the text. Of course these real people, the authors and listeners or readers, may be (and often are) located in different time-spaces . . . but nevertheless they are located in a real unitary and as yet incomplete historical world set off by a sharp and categorical boundary from the *represented* world in the text. Therefore we may call this world the world that *creates* the text. (FTC, 253)

Bakhtin reads the emergence of Dostoyevsky's polyphonic novel in the same spirit. Discussing the "extra-artistic reasons and factors that made possible the construction of the polyphonic novel," he suggests the most important was the impact of capitalist development on Russian society (PDP, 19–20). Bourgeois society, the world of atomized market competition, creates "multi-leveledness and contradictoriness . . . in the objective social world." Dostoyevsky's greatness had to do with his translation, his reflection and refraction, of "the multi-leveledness and contradictoriness of social reality" into a new artistic form—the polyphonic novel (PDP, 28). But Dostoyevsky does not merely reproduce the dynamic interaction among individuals characteristic of a capitalist market society. Rather, he shows individuals trying to break out of their solitariness, he indicates how—contrary to bourgeois individualism—they need others in order to become themselves. The translation of capitalist social experience into artistic form is a critical one; the polyphonic novel exposes the alienated character of individual experience in a bourgeois society.

In constructing a new (dialogical) model of the self, *Problems of Dostoyevsky's Poetics* opens up a rich theory of language built around the concepts of polyphony and dialogue. Yet, Bakhtin's theory of the reflection and refraction of "objective social reality" into artistic form is sketchy at best. Over the course of the 1930s, he tried to give a greater concreteness to his account of the interaction between artistic form and sociohistorical context. As his "sociological turn" continued, he probed the issues of genre and conceptualizations of space-time (or *chronotopes*) in great detail. This investigation would return him the problem of language and the body.

THE TIME OF LABOR AND LAUGHTER:
TOWARD A MATERIALIST THEORY OF THE NOVEL

As the 1930s proceeded, as the stifling repression and terror of Stalinism intensified, Bakhtin seems to have become increasingly concerned about how far a totalitarian regime could go in stamping out dissent and imposing its own monological regime of untruth.[28] The novel now assumed a unique importance in his thought since, in contrast to the monological discourse of a police state, it expresses a polyphonic and dialogical way of seeing the world. The novel, for Bakhtin, stands in defiant opposition to everything that is closed, dogmatic, and finalized; in the face of official discourse and repression it responds with the laughter, irony, and parody of the fool, the rogue and the clown. Occasionally, Bakhtin described it as an *antigenre* because of the way great novels interrogate, even parody, themselves, thereby undermining their own pretensions to finalization. Novelistic consciousness came to represent a reservoir of antitotalitarian impulses.

In the course of developing this view of the novel, Bakhtin also sketched out an enriched theory of language in which the polyphony of great novels corresponds to the inherent multiplicity of language, its dynamic mixing of dialects and accents. Bakhtin moves easily throughout the 1930s from the idea of the polyphonic novel to a theory of language organized around the notions of *polyglossia* and *heteroglossia*. Having conceptualized language as multiple—as the complex unity of different and conflicting dialects—he had arrived at a highly productive approach to thinking about genres (or a hybrid of genres called the novel) that might sustain oppositional attitudes. One of his central concerns in these essays is to account for the transition from the epic to the novel, to explain the social basis of this literary transformation from monological to dialogical representations of human experience.

The epic, argues Bakhtin, is the story of sacred tradition. A narrative of forefathers and beginnings, it cultivates a myth of origins by reciting the story of how a people/nation was founded. Radically distanced from contemporary life, the epic is holy and unchangeable. "It is as closed as a circle; inside it everything is finished, already over," he writes. "One can only accept the epic with reverence, it is impossible to really touch it, for it is beyond the realm of human activity, the realm in which everything humans touch is altered and rethought."[29] But the epic could not entirely displace the dialogical and polyphonic world of life and language. Against its seriousness, there developed a number of comedic genres which contributed to the novel.

While the epic is the story of the national past written in the national language, the novel originates in a world of many languages and dialects, all interacting in "a process of active mutual cause-and-effect and interillumination" (EN, 12). Emerging during an era in European life (the Renaissance and after) when new commercial networks and modes of communication were eroding traditional parochialisms, the novel translated the "polyglot consciousness" of a world resonating with multiple languages into an artistic form which parodies the monological aspirations of previous genres. Against the aspiration of official forms to create literary monuments sealed off from the everyday world of heterogeneity and change, the novel embraces everyday speech; it turns to living language, the speech of the common people in the marketplace and the village square. The novel erodes the distance between literary language and vernacular speech, and between past and present. To the pompous, serious, sacred language of the court or the pulpit, the novel counterposes the laughter of the common people (EN, 21).

Much of Bakhtin's research throughout the 1930s traced the history of *serio-comic* forms which nourished the novel: Socratic irony, Menippean satire, the religious parodies of the Middle Ages, the comedies of Shakespeare, the novels of Cervantes, and Rabelais all figure centrally in his account. All of these "derive from folklore (popular laughter)" which profanes the literary objects of the epic by bringing them close and making them part of the world of the everyday: "Laughter demolishes fear and piety before an object, before a world, making of it an object of familiar contact." Laughter uncrowns, it strips the epic of its robes and ornaments and renders it ridiculous in its commonality—like the emperor who has lost his clothes (EN, 23, 24). By destroying reverence, piety and epic distance, by decrowning and ridiculing everything mythical and monumental, the novel creates a new sense of historical time. The past now becomes part of the present and future; reconnected to everyday life, it becomes fluid and unfinalized and "time and the world become historical" (EN, 30). Yet the history that forms and shapes the characters in the novel does not completely determine them. As products of the daily life of history and society, they, too, are unfinalized. Unlike the characters of the epic, the characters of the novel are capable of self-development, albeit within given sociohistorical circumstances. In this respect, the novel captures the "dialectics of freedom and necessity" that Voloshinov found at work in language and which Bakhtin considered to be at the heart of Dostoyevsky's novels (PDP, 62).

The novel celebrates the multiplicity of languages—what Bakhtin calls "*polyglossia*"—that makes up the world of everyday speech. It uncovers a world immersed in a flow of multiple languages, styles, accents, and world views. Rather than presenting the unitary language of the epic, "the language of the novel is a *system* of languages that mutually and ideologically interanimate one another."[30] The novel is both *polyphonic* (constituted by many voices) and *polyglottic* (composed of many languages, styles, dialects, and accents). It is also parodic. Building upon a rich history of popular parodies—comedic plays, farces, satyr plays—the novel attacks the mystical power of the word. It historicizes and dialogizes the word, stripping it of a fixed, final, and ultimate meaning derived from an ostensible realm of eternal truths: "The parodic-travestying forms . . .

destroyed the homogenizing power of myth over language; they freed consciousness from the direct power of the word" (PHND, 60). By mixing genres, by
parodying itself, by constructing a hybrid genre, the novel mocks the epic and
its claim to eternal truth.

More than representing a polyglot world—a world of many languages—the
novel also depicts *heteroglossia* within a language. It reveals each literary language
as the product of interactions, hybridizations, conflicts, and struggles between
dialects and styles. Behind the myth of a unitary language and the singular
history of a people, it discovers heterogeneity and multiplicity. Beneath the
reified images of official discourse, it reveals "a struggle between languages and
dialects, between hybridizations, purifications, shifts, and renovations" (PHND,
66). The novel opens up the crosscurrents that constitute a language, it lets the
different dialects and styles within a literary language confront and challenge
one another; it depicts language as internally dialogized. We find this conception
most fully developed in Bakhtin's extraordinary essay, "Discourse in the Novel"
(1934–1935).[31]

"Discourse in the Novel" opens with reflections on *heteroglossia*. The "indispensable prerequisite of the novel as a genre" is that it sets in motion "the
internal stratification of any single national language into social dialects, characteristic group behavior, professional jargons, generic languages, languages of
generations and age groups, tendentious languages, languages of the authorities,
of various circles and of passing fashions, languages that serve the specific
sociopolitical purposes of the day, even of the hour" (DN, 263, 262–63). Like
Voloshinov, Bakhtin knows that language has—and must have—internal tendencies towards unification and centralization, that it must be held together by
"centripetal forces." He sees the state and dominant ideological organizations as
the institutional expression of such centripetal tendencies. Unitary language
develops when, through "processes of sociopolitical and cultural centralization,"
these institutions attempt to impose an official langauge with a formal system of
meanings and grammatical rules (DN, 271). And the official view of codified
language has been adopted by "linguistics, stylistics and the philosophy of language," all of which concentrate "on the firmest, most stable, least changeable
and most monosemic aspects of discourse" (DN, 274). Against such formalist
approaches, Bakhtin proposes to consider his object of study "not as a system of
abstract grammatical categories, but rather language conceived as ideologically
saturated, language as a world view, even as a concrete opinion." This means, like
Voloshinov, starting from the utterance and the environment in which it operates. "The authentic environment of an utterance . . . is dialogized heteroglossia,"
he writes. Every utterance takes place in an ideologically charged environment,
one consisting of competing genres, accents, and dialects. Whereas epic and
poetic genres have emphasized the formal and unifying features of language, the
novel deliberately and provocatively emphasizes the decentralizing and centrifugal ones (DN, 271, 272, 272–73).

The close parallels with Voloshinov are striking. While Bakhtin works with a unique vocabulary, his insistence on the evaluative and ideologically saturated nature of all speech and its inherence in the living flow of dialogue are strongly reminiscent of *Marxism and the Philosophy of Language*, as the following passage suggests:

> ...no living word relates to its object in a singular way: between the word and its object, between the word and the speaking subject, there exists an elastic environment of other, alien words about the same subject, the same theme. . . .

> ...The word, directed toward its object, enters a dialogically agitated and tension-filled environment of alien words, value judgments and accents, weaves in and out of complex interrelationships, merges with some, recoils from others, intersects with yet a third group. . . .

> The living utterance, having taken meaning and shape at a particular historical moment in a socially specific environment, cannot fail to brush up against thousands of living dialogic threads. (DN, 276)

Bakhtin's interest is in language as "a living, socio-ideological concrete thing," language which is not the possession of an abstract, monological consciousness, but of an actual human being whose individual consciousness "lies on the border between oneself and the other." His object of study is the word which "is half someone else's" (DN, 293).

This leads him back to ethics. Because the world of the utterance is teeming with evaluations and accents, speech is invariably charged with ethico-political values. "Consciousness finds itself inevitably facing the necessity of *having to choose a language*," he writes (DN, 295). In fact, the world of heteroglossia is a world of choice: since the ideological horizons of speech are always open, every speaker must choose among multiple possibilities for self-expression. Bakhtin sees the human individual as developing *via* a struggle between the "authoritative discourse" of parents, adults, teachers, religious, and political leaders, on the one hand, and "internally persuasive discourse," a discourse which is one's own, which expresses one's values and aspirations, on the other (DN, 342–45). But to develop toward freedom, the individual must break away from the authoritative word; she must manage to de-reify the word by seeing it as a force field of conflicting values and accents, not a magical entity fused with unchanging things. And this is the great achievement of the novel: to have destroyed the mythical epic word by immersing literature in the heteroglossia of everyday speech, to have degraded official literary language by forcing it into contact with the language of fools, rogues, and clowns (DN, 368–69, 401).

The theory of language and the novel that Bakhtin develops in "Discourse in the Novel" surely ranks among the greatest twentieth-century contributions to cultural studies and philosophy of language. Yet, characteristically elliptical, the essay leaves a number of crucial problems hanging. For our purposes, two of these stand out.

The first problem has to do with the conflict between centripetal and centrifugal forces within language. Much of the time, Bakhtin seems to presuppose their existence. But why should these two tendencies be at work within language? Does this speak to a fundamental duality of human life and/or language? Or is it a specifically historical product of certain forms of society? Needless to say, this is an especially important problem when we try to theorize a politics of resistance in Bakhtinian terms.

The second problem I want to flag returns us to the analysis of speech genres. Recall Voloshinov's view that speech genres grow out of "life genres," unique social contexts of life and labor which produce their own shared values and accents. What then of the genres which make up the pre-history of the novel? Where, in Bakhtin's analysis, do the serio-comic popular genres of the rogue, the fool and the clown come from? To say they were there before the novel is an acceptable historical description. But it is not an explanation. Why should these genres have been there? What might have sustained them? And why should they continue to resonate centuries after they first emerged?

Both of these problems speak to a recurring ambiguity in Bakhtin's work, an ongoing vacillation between ontological and historical modes of argument. Yet a purely ontological argument runs the risk of the following circularity: the novel is dialogical because language is characterized by heteroglossia; the parodic-travestying genres of the clown, the fool and the rogue were there because centrifugal forces exist within language. But this sort of ontological argument sits uncomfortably with a more sociohistorical mode of analysis and explanation. In my view, Bakhtin never resolved the tension between these modes of argumentation, between the ontological and the sociohistorical motifs in his thought. Sometimes he rests his case for heteroglossia and the novel on the claim that they are authentic expressions of the essentially dialogical nature of the self; at other times he seems inclined to a more historical account of the emergence of multiple genres, as in his path-breaking essay "Forms of Time and the Chronotope in the Novel" (1937–38).[32]

The "Chronotope" essay, whose methodology is closer to a nonreductive historical materialism than anything else Bakhtin wrote, begins with a brief effort to define its central category: chronotope, whose literal meaning is "time space." A chronotope is the specific artistic form in which time and space are configured and interconnected in a literary work. A story cannot start, never mind develop, without some temporal-spatial indicators. Even if these are enormously vague ("once upon a time, in a land far, far away"), they are nevertheless positioned in some way. Typically, Bakhtin begins his detailed discussion by way of a contrast with the novel. To this end, he chooses a literary form which works with a relatively impoverished chronotope: the ancient Greek romance. This genre serves much the same role as the epic does for the novel—as a counterpoint, a point of comparison and differentiation.

The ancient Greek romance operates as an adventure story. Hero and heroine meet, fall in love, are separated, and must conquer innumerable obstacles and adversities in their struggle to be reunited. The characters in the Greek romance do not develop, time is not filled with their personal growth, crises, and maturation. Their pure love for one another is constant. The story unfolds in terms of the overcoming of external obstacles to their reunification. But not only is biographical time (the time of personal change and development) lacking in the Greek romance, so is historical time. When a new twist in the plot is needed, these are conjured up with words like "suddenly" and "at that moment." The controlling force is chance, not real-life events in historical time (which are not as easily manipulable for purposes of the plot). The Greek romance thus operates with "empty time," a time distanced from actual historical events. The same applies to space. While space is needed for the adventure to unfold, it is stripped of any familiarizing indicators: "For a shipwreck, one must have a sea, but which particular sea (in the geographical and historical sense) makes no difference at all." All adventures in the Greek romance are "governed by an interchangeability of space; what happens in Babylon could just as well happen in Egypt or Byzantium and vice versa" (FTCN, 91, 99, 100).

The chronotope of the ancient Greek romance is constituted by abstract temporal and spatial relations. Biographical and historical time are almost entirely lacking (as are the rhythms of biology and daily life). By contrast, Bakhtin explores a number of other genres whose chronotopes are less abstract. The ancient adventure novel of everyday life, for example, employs concepts of metamorphosis and identity which are drawn from "the treasury of pre-class world folklore" (FTCN, 112). While this gives a greater richness to the chronotope framing these stories, they still lack a sense of the way historical time links moments of crisis and rebirth in the life of the individual to social events. By comparison, the classic Greek biography and autobiography develop a more concrete sense of the social sphere in which individuals live their lives; their chronotope "is constituted by the public square." But this genre so radically socializes and publicizes the individual that his or her life becomes utterly exterior—everything is determined by the public sphere and nothing by processes of personal growth and development. Thus, while they moved out of empty space and time and into the life of an actual human society, ancient biography and autobiography did so by liquidating individuality (FTCN, 112, 131,135). The individual element develops in the Middle Ages with the chivalric romance, but this is a radically subjectivized form, not the individuality of people who develop within the dynamics of social and historical life. Dehistoricized, time in the chivalric romance takes on magical qualities and becomes the plaything of dreams (FTCN, 151–55).

But the Middle Ages was not just the age of the chivalric romance. It was also the epoch of an increasingly sharp differentiation between literary genres, between "high literature" and those "low folkloric and semifolkloric forms that tended toward satire and parody" (FTCN, 158). While a distinction between high and low forms could be made with respect to literature in the ancient world, it was generally less clear-cut. Many Socratic dialogues, for example, put serio-comic forms to work. And, as we have seen, the ancient adventure novel of everyday life drew on folkloric motifs. But, as European feudalism was consolidated, an increasing separation took place between the cultural life of the ruling class and that of the common people. Alongside officially sanctioned high literary forms—or more appropriately, perhaps, *beneath* them—a more distinctive "literature of the dregs of society" emerged. And it was these genres, the literature of the rogue, the clown, and the fool, which provided the literary and artistic reservoir that would nourish the novel.

"The rogue, the fool and the clown create around themselves their own special little world, their own chronotope," writes Bakhtin (FTCN, 159). Their space is that of the public square "where the common people congregate" and their roles are connected intimately with "the public spectacle"—with carnival and festival. Their time is that of public celebration, of masking, parody, and social inversion. During carnival and festival people deliberately stepped out of established social practices: priests and rulers were parodied and ridiculed, fools were crowned, food and wine were consumed in extravagance, people wore masks and abandoned their normal social roles. These public spectacles obeyed unique norms, rules, conventions, and temporalities. The rogue, the clown, and the fool embodied the laughter of the public square. They epitomized "the right to be 'other' in this world, the right not to make common cause with any of the existing categories that life makes available." And by putting on the masks of the clown, and the fool, novelists found a solution to the problem of the position of the author. Through these figures, the author could challenge the separation of high and low, official and popular, by returning to "all unofficial and hidden spheres of human life." And the key to this is focusing on the forbidden body, "in particular the sphere of the sexual and of vital body functions (copulation, food, wine)" (FTCN, 159, 160, 161, 162, 165–66). This provocative line of argument brings us back to an earlier problem: how it is that these images are available for literary representation? What social experiences, what life genres, sustain these popular images and enable them to grow?

Bakhtin's sketchy answer (which is somewhat more developed in *Rabelais and His World*) is in the first instance a deceptively simple one: these parodic images go back "into a folklore that pre-exists class structures" (FTCN, 159). In other words, "the treasury of pre-class world folklore" is replete with images that challenge the serious, official, anti-corporeal high culture of feudal society. But these images continued to develop within medieval popular culture and the folklore of the common people, particularly in their social spaces (the public square and the market place) and social events (festival and carnival). Indeed, toward the end of the Chronotope essay, Bakhtin suggests these events renewed experiences of time appropriate to the rhythms of collective labor and communal consumption in pre-class society. Medieval and early modern carnival and festival are thus ritualized renewals of pre-class chronotopes and forms of experience.

More than any other author, Rabelais is for Bakhtin the writer who encapsulates the carnivalesque experience of time and the world (FTCN, 206). Yet, Rabelais did not single-handedly invent a new chronotope. Instead, in the era of the disintegration of the dominant medieval world view, he revived and renewed folkloric structures of experience dating back to pre-class society. The Rabelaisian chronotope has five defining characteristics derived from ancient folk culture.

The first notable feature about this chronotope is that "time is collective"; it "is differentiated and measured only by the events of *collective life*." Second, the categories of time are organized around those of communal labor, "the phases of agricultural labor and their subcategories," e.g., planting, cultivating, reaping, storing, feasting, and so on. Third, "this is the time of *productive growth*"; time is experienced as a process of birth, death, and rebirth, of generation, degeneration, and regeneration. Crops and seasons come and go; people are born, grow old, and die; young people procreate; new life comes onto the scene. The Rabelaisian chronotope thus entails a generative notion of time, "a pregnant time, a fruit-bearing time, a birthing time and a time that conceives again." This experience of time is, fourth, future-oriented: people "sow for the future, gather in the harvest for the future, mate and copulate for the sake of the future." Fifth, it also involves a concrete and spatialized sense of time. Time is always the time of the earth and nature, the time of the seasons and of planting and harvesting: "Time here is sunk deeply in the earth, implanted in it and ripening in it" (FTCN, 206, 207, 208).

We encounter here a tremendously unified sense of time: biological time, the time of nature, is closely bound up with the temporalities of individual and social life. The separations characteristic of class society (and of capitalism in particular), the alienation of culture from nature and of individual from society, have not yet occurred: "Individual life-sequences have not yet been made distinct, the private sphere does not exist, there are no private lives. . . . food, drink, copulation, birth and death are not aspects of a personal life but are a common affair . . . they are indissolubly linked with communal labor" (FTCN, 209).[33] This is clearly Bakhtin at his most communalistic. He celebrates the communal forms of pre-class life and uses them as a standard by which to criticize the fragmentation of social experience in class society. His discussion here—and in his Rabelais book—is often read as a kind of nostalgic utopianism, a wistful longing for a time prior to individualism, a time when the individual was merely part of the generative time of communal labor and life. I return to this debate below in my discussion of *Rabelais and His World*. For the moment, however, I merely want to note the "negative feature" of folkloric time in Bakhtin's view: its cyclicity. Bakhtin believes that the notion of time as cyclical, as obeying repetitive rhythms drawn from the cycles of the sun, the planets, and the seasons, "limits the force and ideological productivity of this time." The great shortcoming of folkloric time, in other words, is that it cannot develop a profound understanding of "becoming." It treats all events as repetitive and fails to produce a notion of historical growth and development across cyclical time (FTCN, 209–10).

With the emergence of class society, however, social life became internally differentiated. Production, consumption, ritual, celebration, and daily life no longer constituted a unified whole. Food, drink, and sexuality were confined to a "personal" sphere, in the process being driven out of official genres and discourses. Social life also fragmented as individual life-sequences (birth, sexuality, childbirth, death) were linked to specific social classes and subgroups, and, with the development of capitalism, increasingly individualized. Death became a more and more solitary experience: rather than a moment in the continual regeneration of society, it became "an ultimate end." Meanwhile, historical time became attached to reified entities—"the nation, the state, mankind"—and disconnected from the life-sequences of the individual. Yet for all the fragmentation and disintegration of social life, Bakhtin insists that the pre-class sense of unified time was not entirely lost. And he hints at a subtle kind of materialist explanation for this: "in the treasure-house of language and in certain kinds of folklore this immanent unity of time is preserved, insofar as language and folklore continue to insist on a relation to the world and its phenomena based on collective labor" (FTCN, 212–15, 216, 217).

So powerful and enduring was the pre-class experience of time and the world, Bakhtin seems to be saying, that it produced a "treasure-house" of linguistic and folkloric forms which resonate with later experiences of collective labor and communal life. Certainly this reading of Bakhtin is consistent with the concept of "great time" in his last works where he claims that past meanings are always renewable, that "nothing is absolutely dead: every meaning will have its homecoming festival" (SG, 170). Part of Bakhtin's argument in the "Chronotopes" essay seems to rest on precisely this sort of notion of language and folklore as a remembering of past meanings, as a reservoir of unfinalized meanings available for renewal in the future. And yet, as I have hinted, Bakhtin does not seem willing to sever folkloric memory from other forms of social experience. In a particularly interesting section of the "Chronotopes" essay, he discusses the "idyllic chronotope" in the novel which tries to preserve a unified sense of social life by concentrating on a small and familiar "spatial corner of the world" where one generation after another has known the same mountains, valleys, rivers, forests, and homes. With this sort of location in mind, the idyll comes close to capturing folkloric time. But it can do this, he maintains, because it "draws upon the real life of the agricultural laborer under conditions of feudal or post-feudal society—although this life is to one degree or another idealized and sublimated" (FTCN, 226–27).

This is an especially suggestive argument—but it is also a characteristically undeveloped one. Bakhtin seems to be saying that elements of the experience of agricultural laborers in feudal and post-feudal society are continuous with much older forms of pre-class agrarian life. As a result, ancient images and motifs resonate with aspects of life many hundreds (even thousands) of years later. These images and motifs make it possible to offer idyllic portraits of social life in at least some locales within the contemporary world. While this runs the risk of idealizing contemporary conditions, it also enables the novelist to envision a form of life radically different from that of the present. Bakhtin holds that some particularly fruitful reworkings of the idyllic chronotope for purposes of social criticism took place in the eighteenth century (notably in the literary works of Jean-Jacques Rousseau). He sees the idyllic chronotope in the novel as serving a critical purpose and, thus, as more than a nostalgia for images and motifs from the past. While "it was necessary once again to make contact with that lost ideal," this was done "at a new stage of development"; he commends Rousseau, for example, for renewing this chronotope while retaining "individuality" and the "interior aspect of life" (FTCN, 230).

Bakhtin maintains that a whole line of development in the history of the novel, organized around the theme of the destruction of the idyll (and its unified experience of the world), utilized the sort of approach to be found in Rousseau. These works, culminating in the novels of Johann Wolfgang von Goethe, used the idyll to reveal the alienation and fragmentation of modern life; yet, at the same time, they also exposed "the narrowness and isolation of the little idyllic world" (FTCN, 234). In Goethe's work, the theme of alienation from the modern world is joined to the idea that the individual must enter into a process of growth and self-education, one characterized by estrangement from and struggle with an alien social environment. This results in a foregrounding of the problem of becoming—of transformation and development in the life of the individual. But self-transformation is not separated from transformation of the social world. In Goethe's work, as Bakhtin tells us in another essay, we find that the human being's "individual emergence is inseparably linked to historical emergence." The most profound integration of individual growth and historical becoming is to be found, however, in Rabelais who represents "the greatest attempt at constructing an image of *man growing in national-historical time*" (SG, 23, 25).

Rabelais' towering achievement is to have mobilized "the extraordinary force of laughter" for artistic purposes. Of all the elements of the ancient cultural complex, only laughter was not taken over and distorted by the official genres of feudal society. Every other element of artistic and literary life was "sublimated" into the high culture of the ruling class. Official feudal culture tried to coat the whole of society with "a layer of pathetic seriousness" while ignoring (or denouncing) low genres. But, in defiance of the deadly seriousness of officialdom, the comic genres continued to live on in the form of "irony, parody, humor, the joke." As a result, "laughter remained outside official falsifications" and offered an extraordinary resource for social criticism and for new ways of modeling experience (FTCN, 237, 236, 237, 236).

Laughter operates, says Bakhtin, by subverting conventional relationships within language. Irony, humor, parody and the joke all involve "a destruction of linguistic norms for language and thought." Laughter creates distance between things normally found together, and it brings together things customarily found apart. It involves "a constant exceeding of the limits fixed in relationships internal to language" (FTCN, 237). In Voloshinov's terms, laughter breaks down uniaccentuality by setting up comical relations among things, it upsets the boundaries and distinctions so precious to feudal ideologies—distinctions between high and low, refined and vulgar, spirit and body.

For Bakhtin, Rabelais is a *fantastic realist* who uses laughter and parody to counterpose the low to the high, growth and change to *stasis*, the vulgar to the elevated. Feudal ideology had created "an immeasurable abyss" between the word and the body; valorizing the former at the expense of the latter, it depicted the body as sinful and crude. Rabelais' strategy of comic inversion takes over the exaggerated corporeal realism of folklore—its legends of gargantuan human appetites, of gluttony, drunkenness, and sexual license—and mobilizes it to break down the disintegrating world view of the late medieval period. He takes this grotesque body and makes it "a concrete measuring rod for the world." In the face of official asceticism, Rabelais flaunts the vulgar body of wildly exaggerated appetites. Yet, the purpose of this comic operation is not just inversion, but renewal. Rabelais seeks not simply to parody the old world view, but to construct a new one. His literary creation involves a "fusion of the polemical and the affirmative tasks" (FTCN, 170–71, 169).

Before turning to Bakhtin's path-breaking book on Rabelais, I want to bring together a few crucial strands from his "Chronotope" essay. Recall the problem I posed of the tension between ontological and sociohistorical modes of argument in Bakhtin's theory of language. Bakhtin, I suggested, tends to vacillate between seeing dialogue and heteroglossia as essential to language irrespective of context, on the one hand, and treating them as elements of historically generated speech and cultural genres on the other. In principle, these two lines of argument may be reconcilable. But, for historical materialist purposes, the latter argument is especially important. Moreover, Bakhtin's theory of chronotopes—of specific ways of representing the lived experience of time and space—opens up a route to deepening Voloshinov's concept of *life genres*. After all, Bakhtin seems to be saying that chronotopes are profoundly influenced by the structures and rhythms of fundamental life activities: birth and death, labor and consumption, sex and reproduction. This opens the way to a sophisticated materialism in which language, ritual and folklore are seen as integral parts of the life activities that constitute any artistic world view. Speech and literary works (and the chronotopes inherent in them) might then be seen as unique refractions of specific life genres, as entailing conceptions of life, labor, space, time, and the body formed through the everyday sociomaterial practices in which people engage. Thought through in this way, Bakhtin's theory of the chronotope can enrich the theory of life- and speech-genres. More than this, it can be an enabling device in challenging the separation between language and the body so characteristic of post-structuralism and postmodernist theory.

Utopia, Carnival, and the Grotesque Body: Ambiguities of a Bakhtinian Politics

Rabelais and His World is Bakhtin's most famous book—and his most controversial one. Its central thesis is that the serious and comic aspects of human life, which were unified prior to class differentiation and the emergence of the state, crystallized during the Middle Ages in Europe into two separate cultures, philosophies and languages: the official and the popular. The former was institutionally embodied in the Church and the state while the latter took shape in the village squares and the marketplace. Both forms of life had their own rituals and cultural forms. If the Church hierarchy and its preoccupation with sacrifice, penance, and self-abnegation encapsulated official culture, then carnival and popular festivity, with their feasting, drinking, and mocking of rules, norms and conventions, expressed popular culture. Each realm had its linguistic forms: Latin for the official sphere and the vernacular languages of everyday life for the popular.[34] So marked was this distinction, claims Bakhtin, that people in the Middle Ages "participated in two lives: the official and the carnival life" (RHW, 96).

If anything defined carnival, it was "the suspension of all hierarchical rank, privileges, norms and prohibitions" by immersing the world in festive laughter. No person or institution was sacred to festive laughter; it coated all relations in gaiety and celebration. But more than just a moment of decrowning and degrading, carnival also represented rebirth and renewal, and it carried a utopian hope, the desire for a world of equality and abundance (RHW, 10–12). Bakhtin documents the images of "mountains of butter, rivers of milk, and hot pies sprung from the soil like mushrooms" that animate carnivalesque imagery. Similarly, he draws out the carnivalesque legends of a world of equality—"where nobody knows the difference between masters and servants"—to illustrate the popular longing for a world without class exploitation (RHW, 300, 264n41).

In sustaining these utopian aspirations, carnival mobilized the resources of a *grotesque realism of the body* against the rarefied ideology of high feudal culture. It shamelessly celebrated the body as a counterforce to the anti-corporeal spiritualism of official ideology. But the carnivalesque body is not to be confused with the individual body of the isolated bourgeois subject; rather, it represents the individual body in its interconnections with the body of nature and the collective body of the whole people. Just as this monstrously huge body eclipses the body of the individual, so it persists through the births and deaths of generations upon generations of people. In depicting the body as the site of continuous processes of birth, death, and new birth, grotesque realism proclaimed the inevitable death of the status quo. In the face of ruling class claims to eternity, it asserted the materialist premise of the death of all things and the birth of the new; it counterposed the persistence of the body of the people to the passing away of bishops and kings. And it did so in a direct and graphic way by bringing everything into contact with the lower stratum of the body—with eating, drinking, defecating, urinating, copulating, and birthing. Grotesque realism degrades official culture by bringing down to earth everything that is high, spiritual, abstract, and disembodied, by pushing bishops, kings, priests, and lords down to the level of "the lower part" of the body—"the genital organs, the belly and the buttocks." But, while images of degradation dominate the festive activities of carnival, they are not ends in themselves, but means to something new: "Degradation here means coming down to earth, the contact with earth as an element that swallows up and gives birth at the same time. To degrade is to bury, to sow, and to kill simultaneously, in order to bring forth something more and better" (RHW, 21).

The body that serves these symbolic purposes, as I have pointed out, is not the body of the bourgeois individual—it is not one's "own" body, the body as private property. The grotesque body of carnival is expansive, unfinished, transgressive and overflowing. It is defined not by its boundary lines, but its orifices and protuberances: "the open mouth, the genital organs, the breasts, the phallus, the potbelly, the nose." Rather than separated from nature or from the rest of the human community, the grotesque body connects to "the entire material bodily world." In the image of the grotesque body, popular culture drew all aspects of human life back onto "one plane of material sensual experience" (RHW, 26, 19, 367, 381).

And language is one of those aspects of life drawn back to the plane of material sensual experience. The festive popular culture embraced by Rabelais involved a "victory over linguistic dogmatism," over the tyranny of the mystical, monological, and unchanging word. In linguistic terms, this meant the victory of vernacular languages over Latin, of "the language of life, of material work and mores" over that of religion and disembodied scholarship (RHW, 473, 466). As a language cut off from the historical life of the people, Latin could aspire to timelessness. But festive culture knew this language to be dead; it envisioned the rebirth of language through its reconnection with the body of the people. Indeed, Bakhtin sees the reconnection of the body and the word as a central theme of European popular culture of the Middle Ages. In one particularly interesting example, he takes a scene in an Italian comedy involving a conversation between Harlequin and a stutterer. The stutterer struggles to pronounce a difficult word; he trembles, perspires, and loses his breath, his face swells until "it looks as if he were in the throes and spasms of childbirth." Eventually, Harlequin rushes forward headfirst, hits him in the abdomen, and the word is "born." The stutterer, Bakhtin points out, "enacts a scene of childbirth." Moreover, this act of birth requires the collision of upper and lower, of head with abdomen. In this way, language is returned to the body. The word—abstracted and spiritualized by medieval Christianity—is degraded and renewed in its contact with the body and the image of childbirth: "it is a miniature satirical drama of the word, of its material birth, or the drama of the body giving birth to the word" (RHW, 304, 308 309).

Even this brief sketch should give some indication of the enormous power of *Rabelais and His World*. In unearthing rich legacies of popular culture and resistance to officialdom, Bakhtin broke down key prejudices about the common people of medieval Europe. He showed them to be inventive heirs of traditions of popular protest, not merely dominated masses held down by fear and superstition—and, in so doing, he held out hope for resistance and renewal even in the most repressive of circumstances (the allusions to Stalinism are ever-present in his text). More than this, he developed a materialist theory of cultural resistance which emphasizes "the material bodily principle" as the reference point for all attacks on dreary officialdom. For Bakhtin, there is an enduring utopian legacy, deeply rooted in folklore and festive culture, which resists all attempts by ruling classes to deny the demands of the historical body (i.e., the historically developed material aspirations of the common people). And carnival, like the work of Rabelais, is a story of the recurring victory of the people over lies and deadly seriousness, of the ultimate triumph of the claims of bodies over the dreary abstractions of officialdom. In Bakhtin's theory of carnival, as Terry Eagleton puts it, "a vulgar, shameless materialism of the body—belly, buttocks, anus, genitals—rides rampant over ruling class civilities."[35]

Well before the emergence of "history from below" in the 1960s and 1970s, then, Bakhtin was emphasizing the tremendous social, cultural, and linguistic creativity of subaltern classes. More recent scholarship has largely confirmed his views, however much it has modified judgment on specific issues. Peter Burke's *Popular Culture in Early Modern Europe*, for example, documents at length many of the phenomena described by Bakhtin. Burke uncovers a rich popular tradition expressed in "folksongs and folktales; devotional images and decorated marriage-chests; mystery plays and farces; broadsides and chap-books; and, above all, festivals." He draws attention also to the role of parody and mockery in satirical songs and performances, mock sermons, testaments, trials, and baptisms. Like

Bakhtin, he accords pride of place to carnival in nourishing images of a world turned upside down.[36]

Notwithstanding the originality of *Rabelais and His World*, its central theses have been attacked as reckless, irresponsible, even non-dialogical by a number of scholars. Gary Saul Morson and Caryl Emerson, for example, treat the Rabelais book as an aberration at odds with the Bakhtin of dialogue and polyphony. They judge that *Rabelais and His World* is out of step with Bakhtin's philosophy of dialogue in five major respects. First, the work embraces utopianism (albeit of an apolitical sort), a move which Bakhtin elsewhere refuses. Second, it displaces the language and experience of everyday life in favor of the episodic inversions of carnival. Third, it liquidates the personal responsibility of individuals by dissolving them into the collectivity of "the people." Fourth, it devalues memory by valorizing laughter and forgetting. And, finally, it demotes the voice of the individual in favor of the voice of the collective. They conclude that "the unofficial," is as monological as the official and, therefore, that Bakhtin's embrace of Rabelais is inconsistent with his earlier (and later) admiration for Dostoyevsky as the originator of the polyphonic novel.[37]

This critique of *Rabelais and His World* is far from a purely theoretical one. In a substantial review article addressing one particular Marxist reading of Bakhtin, Emerson underlines the political stakes. Challenging radical interpretations which valorize carnival, she bemoans their identification with "the positively dreary, voyeuristic, inevitable tributes to mudslinging, excrement, grotesque orifices and verbal abuse" that run through Bakhtin's book. Rejecting the idea that "a politics of resistance" is to be found in Bakhtin, Emerson suggests that "Bakhtinian carnival is idealist, politically naive, and quite possibly reactionary." As an alternative to those who seek a politics of resistance in Bakhtin, Emerson links him to "pragmatic humanism" and the principle of "democratic preference for rendering differences conversable."[38]

What we have here is another version of an interpretive strategy which seeks, as one critic puts it, "to evade the most radical aspects of Bakhtin's work" by assimilating it "into a liberal schema that he opposed."[39] In examining some of the key problems in the Morson and Emerson reading of "the carnivalesque Bakhtin," I hope to highlight some of these "radical aspects" of *Rabelais and His World*—not to deny the theoretical and political shortcomings of the text, but in order to bring to the fore its most radical and materialist elements.

According to Morson and Emerson, Bakhtin sought in *Rabelais* to endorse the popular against the official, the carnivalesque against the serious. Yet, the text suggests an alternate reading in which carnival figures as a debasing and liberating *moment* in the development of "a new seriousness" oriented toward a classless society (RHW, 439, 471–73). Rather than an end in itself, carnivalesque inversion is said to be a necessary means to a new historical consciousness. But the accent here is on the word *necessary*. A new world view requires a vigorous struggle against the serious, dogmatic, official culture of the ruling class. And this involves a debasing, regenerating inversion which emancipates the oppressed from fear and allows them to envision a new social order.

Bakhtin consistently rejects the notion that carnival is nihilistic. He insists instead that it is ambivalent and regenerating. Carnival, he writes, "uncrowns and regenerates"; carnival images "debase, destroy, regenerate and renew simultaneously" (RHW, 24, 151). But regeneration proceeds by means of overturning and degrading. Bakhtin's is no call to polite conversation and a liberal tolerance of differences. He advocates debasing the spiritualized idealism of official culture and decrowning the figures of authority by bringing them into collision with "the lower bodily stratum," the site of birth.[40] Popular travestying of medieval Christianity "is far removed from cynical nihilism," he contends. "The material bodily stratum is productive. It gives birth. . . . This lower stratum is mankind's real future." This dialectic of debasement and renewal is central to Bakhtin's claim that carnival is not nihilistic; it allows him to talk of carnival's "regenerating flames" (RHW, 378, 463, 394).

Bakhtin insists popular culture could become socially regenerative only by entering the realm of high literature. The greatness of Rabelais is precisely that he reconnected the comedic and the serious, the low and the high. Himself a product of official culture, Rabelais renewed it by debasing it, exposing its absurd seriousness and denial of the body through creative use of the comic reserves of folklore. By bringing it into contact with high culture, Rabelais raised popular culture to a new level. But "in order to achieve this growth and flowering," writes Bakhtin, "laughter had to enter the world of great literature" (RHW, 72, 96). This insistence that laughter "had to enter the world of great literature" is clearly a dialogical one. Just as literature was renewed through its contact with folklore and popular culture, so the latter needed to be enriched by entering the sphere of great literature. But this contact involves an intense social struggle, an ideological clash between radically different world views. In "Discourse in the Novel," for example, Bakhtin commended novelistic prose for its sense of discourse as embedded "in historical becoming and social struggle." Such prose, he continued, "deals with discourse that is still warm from that struggle and hostility, as yet unresolved and still fraught with hostile intentions and accents" (DN, 331). In studying Rabelais, Bakhtin finds speech steeped in "struggle and hostility," and he identifies one side in that struggle (the party of the common people) as capable of producing a new historical consciousness. There is an obvious compatibility here with the Marxian idea that one combatant in the class struggle under capitalism—the working class—embodies historical progress. And it is precisely this moment in Bakhtin's argument—and its associated celebration of debasing and carnivalesque inversion—that seems to so trouble his liberal readers.

Certainly carnival does not simply valorize the extraordinary while devaluing the everyday, as Morson and Emerson claim. When Bakhtin talks of carnival liberating us from "all that is humdrum" in everyday life, he sees the "humdrum"

in terms of the deadening weight of the "conventions, and established truths" of
the dominant world view (RHW, 34). Carnival is itself part of the everyday, it
is its oppositional and subversive side as deposited in rituals, popular speech
genres, languages, and dialects. Similarly, carnival is not just about laughter and
forgetting, it is not a simple devaluation of memory. Instead, it is about the
forgetting of fear as prelude to a kind of remembering in which people reconnect
with utopian images that predate class hierarchy and the state. This sort of
reading allows us to make sense of statements like the following which fly in the
face of the Morson and Emerson position: "The body of the people on carnival
square is first of all aware of its unity in time; it is conscious of its uninterrupted
continuity with time, of its relative historic immortality" (RHW, 255). Rather
than a simple forgetting, carnivalesque laughter involves liberation from the fears
that tie us to class society. Festive time helps us see beyond (and behind) the
"recent" past of class domination so that we might remember a deeper past—one
that allows us to envision a future beyond fear, a future of happiness, equality
and abundance.[41]

The liberal rejection of carnivalesque inversion thus falters at a number of
crucial points. However, there are some serious shortcomings to Bakhtin's theory
of carnival and popular culture, albeit of a different sort than those raised by
liberal critics. One set of problems has to do with gender and the body, another
with problems of hegemony, commercialization, and the deflection of carnival
into hostility against other oppressed peoples.

GENDER AND THE GROTESQUE BODY

Images of pregnancy, childbirth, and the womb proliferate throughout *Rabelais
and His World*. Bakhtin tells us, for instance, that the zone of grotesque realism
"is the fruitful earth and womb." A few pages on he writes: "One of the fundamental tendencies of the grotesque image of the body is to show two bodies in
one: the one giving birth and dying, the other, conceived, generated, and born.
This is the pregnant and begetting body" (RHW, 21, 26). Yet, while pregnancy,
childbirth, and the womb are to be found almost everywhere throughout the
text, women and the specifically female body are rarely present. As we have come
to suspect by now, this absence conceals a tendency to appropriate female procreative power to the male body.

Bakhtin's treatment of women and the female body is a contradictory one.
On the one hand, he accords women a central place in the carnivalesque. He
celebrates the female body—the womb, the pregnant female body, and woman
in the act of childbirth—in a way that is at odds with many traditions in Western
thought. He argues that the popular tradition in late-medieval Europe was not
anti-woman, and he praises it for this. On the other hand, he generally reduces
woman to the womb, treating her purely and simply as a birth-giving body:

The popular tradition is in no way hostile to woman and does not approach her negatively. In this tradition woman is essentially related to the material bodily lower stratum; she is the incarnation of this stratum that degrades and regenerates simultaneously. She is ambivalent. She debases, brings down to earth, lends a bodily substance to things, and destroys; but, first of all, she is the principle that gives birth. She is the womb (RHW, 240).

This is a deeply ambivalent celebration of the female grotesque since what is valorized is not woman as an end in herself, but woman as a means to an end—the giver of new (male) life. The female body is highlighted (like earth or nature) as the ground from which the new is born. Woman is not for Bakhtin an intrinsic part of the new life which is about to enter the world, she is the passing vessel through which new life arrives. This is why he regularly discusses carnival images of the (female) body in terms of "pregnant death" (RHW, 352); necessary as the female vessel is, she must perish so that the new can be born. In this way, Bakhtin faithfully echoes Rabelais' story of the birth of Pantagruel who "was so amazingly large and heavy that he could not come into the world without suffocating his mother."[42]

This twofold association of woman with birth and death prevents Bakhtin's position from becoming merely a romantic celebration of woman as life-giver. Because it signifies death as well as life, the womb is also "the earthly element of terror." "Gay matter is ambivalent," says Bakhtin, "it is the grave and the generating womb." The grotesque body, he continues, "swallows and generates, gives and takes." Because it "swallows," "absorbs" and "takes" at the same time as it gives life, the womb is also associated with the underworld, with hell, and with death (RHW, 91–92, 195, 339, 391, 348–49).

Instead, of probing the sources of these frightening images of women, Bakhtin simply turns to carnivalesque laughter to overcome these fears of the womb. To be sure, he identifies an important aspect of popular attitudes toward pregnancy and childbirth. Rather than privatizing pregnancy and childbirth, for instance, popular culture in early-modern Germany treated them as social events guarded by custom and tradition. A husband was expected to nourish his pregnant wife with meat and wine, rent or buy a bed for her to lie in, hire a nurse if possible, care for her prior to childbirth, be present throughout the delivery, and cater to her afterward. Failure to honor these customs could result in punishment by the courts. Moreover, responsibility extended beyond the husband; all members of society had obligations toward women in pregnancy. Cities passed legislation designed to protect the health of pregnant women, butchers could expect prosecution if they refused to give cheap roast meat to expectant mothers, and pregnant women caught stealing fruit could not be prosecuted. Such laws were buttressed by customs according to which friends, neighbors and relatives would lend swaddling clothes to expectant mothers, and celebrate a safe delivery with gifts such as wine, eggs, and roast meat.[43] These "childbed ales" (where large numbers of people would congregate in the mother's house for some days of eating and drinking) were integral parts of the popular culture discussed by Bakhtin.

In counterposing the large, expansive, open and public body—the "double body" represented by the pregnant, birthing and nursing female—to the self-contained and individualized body of bourgeois society, Bakhtin clearly sides with early-modern popular culture in its celebration of pregnancy and childbirth. (RHW, 318, 322). Implicitly, then, he sides with the people against those early-modern authorities who, with the rise of commercial society, sought to de-publicize pregnancy and childbirth, to put a stop to childbed ales, and to privatize the grotesque female body.[44]

Yet, while much is attractive about Bakhtin's defense of customs which valued pregnancy and childbirth and protected expectant mothers (and in his exuberance toward the pregnant female body), we ought not to lose sight of the restraints these also entailed for women. For just as pregnancy and childbirth were protected, so were contraception and abortion punished, and miscarriages monitored for any evidence of self-induced abortion. There is little doubt that the health and welfare of the child was given priority over that of the mother (even if the ideal was health and well-being for both).[45] The popular attitude toward women which Bakhtin embraces is much more ambivalent than he ac-knowledges. While according unique rights to pregnant women, it also con-strained them. As does his own Rabelais book, early-modern popular culture tended to define women first and foremost as breeders who ought to sacrifice themselves, where necessary, in order to bring forth new life. Women who resisted constraints on abortion were treated "as ungodly, suicidal, murderous, Devil-possessed."[46]

Contradictory and conflicting impulses run through the whole of Bakhtin's treatment of women and carnival. Commenting on his discussion of "figurines of senile pregnant hags" (part of a famous terra-cotta collection), Mary Russo points out that while Bakhtin's description "is at least exuberant," his concept of the female grotesque is "in all directions repressed and undeveloped."[47] One could go further and argue that this repression has to do with Bakhtin's ten-dency to appropriate procreative power to the phallus. He talks at times of "the phallus that generates new life" (RHW, 312; see also 317, 339), lending cre-dence to the claim that he has constructed "a (male) body that has appropriated the feminine while excluding women."[48] Moreover, his discussion of the "mim-icking of childbirth" that characterizes so many of the tricks and comic gestures to be found in European popular culture is thoroughly unreflective about the "womb envy" (and the male desire to appropriate female procreativity) these might be said to reflect.

In the end, then, Bakhtin's "turn to the body" suffers from a failure to interrogate the specific constructions of gendered bodies and relations that run through the popular culture he celebrates. While there is much to commend his critique of idealism via the carnivalesque body, his theory is simply too effusive and celebratory, too inattentive to the problem of hegemony, too focused on just one side of the "dialectic of accommodation and resistance" that characterizes cultures of the oppressed.[49] To develop Bakhtin's powerful analysis of language, culture, and resistance means, among other things, then, to reconstruct it in terms of an analysis which sees carnival and popular culture as a site of the reproduction of dominant social relations, as well as of resistance to them.

POPULAR CULTURE AND RULING CLASS HEGEMONY: THINKING ABOUT CARNIVAL WITH GRAMSCI

Bakhtin often writes as if carnival represents a fully formed world view, a deeply oppositional set of beliefs and social practices that contest official culture right down the line. He tends to describe these two cultures as if they constituted radically different modes of being-in-the-world. As he puts it in the second edition of the Dostoyevsky book, "it could be said (with certain reservations, of course) that a person in the Middle Ages lived, as it were, two lives: one was the official life . . . ; the other was the life of the carnival square" (PDP, p. 129). I do not want to deny the partial truth of this formulation; indeed, I think it is crucial to any critical theory of culture. But unless its partiality is recognized, unless Bakhtin's parenthetical acknowledgment of its limits is elaborated, it will inscribe a romantic populism in which the common people are seen as forever subverting the dominant social order. Such a view flattens out the real tensions and contradictions of popular cultures. Rather than seeing them as complexes of oppositional *and* dominant values, it simply glorifies them as full-fledged alternatives to oppressive and hierarchical world views. A populism of this sort abdicates the need for struggle on the terrain of popular culture—and not simply against the dominant culture—if a genuinely radical, not to say revolutionary, political project is to be constructed. For this reason, any attempt to develop an emancipatory politics on the basis of Bakhtin's theory of language and resistance will have to open the brackets and give full weight to the "reservations" about the duality of cultural life to which he alludes in the passage above.

To begin, we need to be clear that carnival was not sealed off from the upper classes of medieval and early-modern Europe. Monarchs, nobles, clergy, and middle-class professionals all participated in carnival festivities.[50] Rather than two cultures closed off from one another, it is more accurate to see early-modern Europe as consisting of two distinct cultural traditions, only one of which was accessible to the poor, while the ruling class participated in both.[51] To be sure, the poor and the oppressed had their own "hidden transcripts" which mocked the rich and powerful, sustained illicit practices (like theft and poaching), and sustained hopes for vengeance and justice.[52] But carnival was a unique kind of *public* transcript, one in which the elites participated, and it was a more mixed, messy, and ambiguous phenomenon than Bakhtin tends to suggest. Even in situations where one would expect to discover an especially sharp cultural demarcation—like relations between slaves and masters in the American South before the Civil War—we still find a quite dynamic pattern of cultural interchange and interaction between the dominated and the dominators. This is not to understate the brutal facts of oppression; it is to insist, instead, that the resistance of slaves shaped the language and culture of the masters, just as the culture of the masters (particularly their religion) entered into the world of the slaves. What one encounters in these cases is a genuine hybridization or *creolization* of cultures. Without a doubt, something radically new was created by the slaves, but it was something created out of disparate elements which owed something to Africa, something to the culture of the slaveowners, and much to their new conditions of life. One of the foremost historians of slave communities in South Carolina has focused on the unique importance of a slave language (Gullah), constructed from English vocabulary and African grammatical forms, for what it tells us about the creolization of culture: "just as a new language was created out of English words put together in accordance with African grammars, so new cultural forms were put together out of Anglican Christianity, plantation foodstuffs, and white labor systems. But they were all organized according to appropriate African cultural grammars."[53]

And this is the crucial point. Popular cultures do contain unique "cultural grammars," structured ways of seeing and acting within the world that grow out of the life genres of the oppressed. At the same time, these genres are not radically independent of dominant social groups. As much as they embody elements of defiance and contestation, these ways of seeing and acting are constructed within real contexts of power. Outside situations of revolutionary upheaval, the oppressed simply cannot display outright opposition and avoid persecution. As a result, oppositional practices are constructed in ways that minimize danger. Theft is hidden, jokes are told out of earshot of rulers, and more subtle forms of opposition (discourse, dress, gait, etc.) are ambiguously coded. Furthermore, those who resist also accommodate themselves to the power exercised by those above them; not to do so is to invite whippings, confinement, prison, death. When oppositional practices like carnival inversion and parody seize the public stage, they remain rule-governed in ways that do not fundamentally challenge the prevailing relations of power. None of this is to deny the genuinely subversive elements of carnival; it is to insist, however, that *most of the time* these coexist with elements of containment and accommodation.

The fact that carnival did not generally result in any rupture in the overall pattern of social life has led some commentators to emphasize its licensed character as a ritual permitted by authority.[54] This is an important reminder. While authorities often moved to curb carnival, they more often permitted and encouraged it. But to see carnival strictly in terms of ritualized episodes of anarchy and upheaval that reinforced the institutional order is to go too far.[55] Carnival did operate as a safety valve, as a licensed affair for letting off stream in order to return to the business of exploitation and oppression. But the poor and the oppressed also managed to push carnival beyond acceptable limits, occasionally crossing the line where festivity ends and riot begins. Consequently, while providing for a ritualized blowing off of steam, carnival also nourished contestational attitudes and sustained utopian aspirations; it reinforced the dominant order, *and* it hinted at another of equality and abundance. This two-sided nature of popular festivity is nicely brought out in a classic study of "the world the slaves made" in the American South, whose author, Eugene Genovese, cites the view of the African-American abolitionist Frederick Douglass that plantation holidays and celebrations served to keep "down the spirit of insurrection among the slaves." At the same time, he notes the claim of one observer that during these celebrations the slaves were "different beings from what they are in the field; the temporary relaxation, the brief deliverance from fear, and from the lash, producing an entire metamorphosis in their appearance and demeanor." Genovese's perceptive analysis brings together both sides of slave festivities. And, like Bakhtin but with different results, he makes popular laughter central to his assessment:

> Oppressed peoples who can laugh at their oppressors contain within themselves a politically dangerous potential, but the weapons of popular culture also betray a conservative political bias. They direct criticism, as Douglass feared, into channels acceptable to the regime—acceptable because in themselves they pose no direct political threat and may even function as a safety valve for pent-up discontent. Their more dangerous content remains latent so long as the general conditions of life do not generate a crisis that heightens their critical thrust and points it to a political terrain—a crisis that upsets the balance within the bitter-sweet laughter and liberates the anger behind the laughter.[56]

By highlighting the "dangerous" albeit "latent" content of carnival, Bakhtin presents it as something more than manipulation by the ruling class. But in ignoring its "conservative political bias," he evades the problem of carnival's role in reproducing the system, an issue which is central to Gramsci's analysis of folklore, commonsense, and ruling class hegemony.

Gramsci rejects the idea that folklore is "an eccentricity, an oddity or a picturesque element." He urges that it be taken seriously as a "conception of the world and life" in opposition to "official" views of the world. But, unlike Bakhtin, he argues that the folkloric world view lacks integrity; being made up of "different and juxtaposed elements," it remains unsystematic. There are three main reasons for this. First, the collectivity known as "the people" is internally stratified;

rather than representing a unified social group, it constitutes a patchwork, a combination of heterogeneous sections of the population. A reasonably unified and integrated world view can only emerge from the ranks of the subaltern classes if its most progressive sections construct an outlook capable of unifying the people around a coherent political project. Second, folklore draws heavily upon the traditions of official culture. Lacking a fully formed institutional foundation (like schools and churches), folklore, Gramsci writes, "has always been tied to the culture of the dominant class and, in its own way, has drawn from it the motifs which have then become inserted into combinations with the previous traditions." As a result, folklore is "contradictory and fragmentary." Finally, the people lack their own independent forms of political organization and intellectual self-expression for the creation of a genuinely counter-hegemonic outlook. While this becomes possible in the era of the working class movement—with its trade unions, socialist parties, newspapers, cultural organizations and so on—even these run the risk of failing to differentiate themselves adequately from the dominant ideology. In order to do so, popular consciousness must arrive at a "new culture" based upon a synthesis of aspects of "modern culture and popular culture."[57]

Gramsci's analysis involves a twofold rejection of populism and spontaneism. While recognizing a revolutionary potential within the oppressed classes of capitalist society—most significantly within the working class movement—he argues that there are significant obstacles to its actualization. Since dominant classes rule by means of a (dynamic and changing) combination of coercion and consent, they (or social groups allied with them, like priests and intellectuals) exercise an important degree of hegemony over subaltern classes. The securing of a meaningful degree of popular consent involves imposing values specific to the ruling class (and its system of surplus appropriation and political organization), and articulating them with folkloric values and traditions that resonate with aspects of the life-experiences of the majority.

This poses important problems for revolutionary politics. Rejecting the idea that socialism could be foisted upon a reluctant working class, Gramsci defined socialism, following Marx, as the movement for workers' self-liberation.[58] As a result, he could not accept the notion of a revolutionary political project which was not an organic product of the working class movement itself. At the same time, Gramsci rejected spontaneism, the idea that the oppressed are purely and spontaneously oppositional, indeed revolutionary, and thus unaffected by the dominant values and ideas. Recognizing that ruling classes generally win an important degree of consent from the governed, Gramsci did not simply celebrate folklore and popular culture. Instead, he took up a critical attitude toward the "common-sense" knowledge of the mass of the population: there he found a reservoir of alternative values *and* traces of dominant values and ideas. He thus saw the commonsense of the oppressed as an unstable constellation of conservative and contestational ideas:

The active man-in-the-mass has a practical activity, but has no clear theoretical consciousness of his practical activity. . . . His theoretical consciousness can indeed be in opposition to his activity. One might almost say he has two theoretical consciousnesses (or one contradictory consciousness): one which is implicit in his activity and which in reality unites him with all his fellow-workers in the practical transformation of the real world; and one, superficially explicit or verbal, which he has inherited from the past and uncritically absorbed. But this verbal conception is not without consequences. It holds together a specific social group, it influences moral conduct and the direction of will, with varying efficacity but often powerfully enough to produce a situation in which the contradictory state of consciousness does not permit of any action, any decision or any choice, and produces a condition of moral and political passivity.[59]

For Gramsci, as much as folklore and common-sense involve pieces of an alternative view, they also contain sufficient elements of the official outlook to stabilize the dominant relations. Indeed, at decisive moments, verbal adherence to the ruling ideas can produce "moral and political passivity" and a failure to change society even in conditions that are otherwise conducive to such a transformation.[60] Gramsci posits the need, therefore, for a political struggle on the terrain of popular culture. He argues that a revolutionary movement can only be built from within that culture, but that this involves a determined struggle against everything that is backward and reactionary within it, a "struggle of political 'hegemonies.' "[61] In order to mobilize those elements of popular common sense which are potentially emancipatory, the socialist movement must draw upon certain tools of critical self-understanding from the official culture of science and philosophy. An alternative hegemony, or a counter-hegemonic world view, is not there, ready-made for the taking; it must be fought for and constructed from within common sense, by discarding its conservative features and mobilizing, strengthening, and clarifying its oppositional ones.

Bakhtin does occasionally hint at the contradictoriness of popular consciousness. He points out in *Rabelais and His World*, for instance, that the people were not immune from the effects of "medieval seriousness." He suggests that they were impressed by the "seriousness of fear and suffering" projected by the dominant forms of religion and ideology. "It would therefore be a mistake," he says, "to presume that popular distrust of seriousness and popular love of laughter, as of another truth, could always reach full awareness, expressing a critical and clearly defined opposition." Acknowledging the contradictions within popular consciousness, he reformulates the metaphor of people in the Middle Ages living "two lives" by saying that the "two aspects of the world, the serious and the laughing aspect, coexisted in their consciousness" (RHW, 94, 95, 96). This formulation is much closer to Gramsci's notion of popular consciousness as contradiction-ridden. But, unlike Gramsci, Bakhtin tends to treat this as a symptom of cultural immaturity, one which started to disappear near the end of the Middle Ages as laughter entered "the world of great literature" and received a fully formed literary and artistic expression (RHW, 96–97). Among other things, Bakhtin's position here drastically overestimates the power of the novelistic—as if the entry of laughter into the world of literature could automatically defeat official seriousness, fear and superstition.[62] Consequently, he underestimates the sociomaterial and ideological pressures which reproduce domination (and which do not collapse with the appearance of Rabelais). Because he is so attentive to these problems, Gramsci is also more acutely aware of the reactionary aspects of popular culture.

This awareness is crucial when we consider that oppressed social and religious groups such as Jews, Muslims, Turks, and Roma people (commonly known as "gypsies") were generally excluded from carnival; sometimes they were outrightly mocked, occasionally they were attacked. Carnivalesque images often portrayed Jews and Muslims as dogs or pigs, rather than human beings.[63] Similarly, although rituals of inversion often enabled women to dominate and humiliate men, witch trials, too, had a carnivalesque character (even if these were often orchestrated "from above" by the Church). In addition, older unmarried women were often forced to pull a plow through the streets at carnival as a reminder that they ought to take a husband.[64] Carnivalesque activities displayed a propensity to identify outsiders, "others" of ostensibly exotic and sinister origin, as the source of disease, famine, and social tensions. Thus, as much as it mobilized oppositional energies, as much as it ridiculed kings, bishops, nobles, and priests, carnival also ritualized forms of "displaced abjection" whereby, as Peter Stallybrass and Allon White put it, " 'low' social groups turn their figurative and actual power, *not* against those in authority, but against those who are even 'lower' (women, Jews, animals, particularly cats and pigs)."[65]

We find a particularly clear example of the reactionary potential of carnival in the northern United States in the early nineteenth century. Throughout the previous century, New England cities often saw Black-dominated celebrations such as Negro Election Day, which began when slaves accompanied white voters to town and, amidst African-influenced festivities, proceeded to choose Black "governors" and other officials. These popular holidays might last from four to six days and could include African dancing and the crowning of a Black king. While the majority of participants were white, it was Blacks who led the way and whose cultural traditions predominated. Indeed, bourgeois critics especially objected to the racial mixing and preeminence of Black entertainments on such occasions.[66] By the nineteenth century, however, a transformation was underway: popular street culture among those who aspired to be "white," such as the Irish, became increasingly racialized as bands of white working-class youths, many of them with their faces painted black, attacked Black people and their homes and churches, reserving particular hostility for taverns, brothels and theaters where whites and Blacks tended to mix, and for the homes of interracial couples. Commentators were not slow in noting the carnivalesque atmosphere of black-faced white mobs engaged in racial attacks. As a Cincinnati observer expressed it in 1843, race riots were a "festival," a "carnival," indeed, a "Saturnalia."[67]

In an outstanding Marxist study of the social psychology of "white workers" during a crucial period of capitalist industrialization in America, David Roediger points out that black-faced mobs of white working-class youths gave themselves permission to "act black" by enacting the preindustrial permissiveness associated with festivities like Negro Election Day at the same time as they viciously affirmed their whiteness, their differentiation from the very cultural traditions they were reenacting. Such behavior is deeply ambivalent in character; black-faced white crowds were simultaneously identifying with Blacks (who they perceived as enjoying a preindustrial license they were now denied), and affirming their difference as white. But this required a special effort to deny what their actions suggested: a deep and abiding identification with Blacks and the festive cultural traditions of an earlier period. As a result, ambivalent rage exploded in violence and beatings, especially for those who blurred the distinction between Black and white through interracial mixing, sexual relations, and marriage.[68]

This takes us to an issue which simply never surfaces in Bakhtin's theory of popular culture: the cultural transformations induced by the rise of industrial capitalism. Roediger, after all, is drawing attention to an important change in festive social life which accompanied the battle to impose the norms of work, time, and labor discipline appropriate to industrial capitalism. He is suggesting that this transformation witnessed a metamorphosis of the carnivalesque—carnival energies becoming directed at those (Blacks) who represented popular festivity at a time when it was considered an obstacle to the capitalist work ethic. Yet, Bakhtin is singularly uninterested in the cultural transformations associated with the rise of industrial capitalism. This is all the more remarkable since he identifies the marketplace as the carnivalesque social space *par excellence*. Yet, to explore carnival and the marketplace is to place a question mark over the application of Bakhtin's thesis to post-feudal societies. After all, in his treatment of time in the "Chronotopes" essay, Bakhtin argues that "a powerfully and sharply differentiated feeling for time could arise only on a collective, work-oriented agricultural base" (FTCN, 206). What happens, then, to the sense of time in an urbanized, industrial capitalist society? Is it possible for people in such a context to revive "the unified time of pre-class folklore" (FTCN, 208)? What, in short, happens to the carnivalesque in a society subjected to radically different rhythms of life and labor?

Carnival and the Market

It is curious how little attention has been devoted to Bakhtin's account of the marketplace. After all, the marketplace of the early-modern European town was for Bakhtin *the* uniquely carnivalesque space. "The unofficial folk culture of the Middle Ages and even of the Renaissance had its own territory," he wrote, one which constituted "a peculiar second world within the official medieval order and was ruled by a special type of relationship, a free familiar, marketplace relationship" (RHW, 154). Bakhtin spends the better part of a chapter in *Rabelais and His World* exploring the forms of speech characteristic of "the festive marketplace;" hawking and advertising cries—both forms of promoting commodities—figure prominently in his account (RHW, chap. 2). Arguing that uniquely familiar, abusive, and bawdy forms of speech emerged within the marketplace, Bakhtin proceeds to construct this space as the site of liberated speech forms and a unique social subject, a festive collectivity: "Such speech forms, liberated from norms, hierarchies, and prohibitions of established idiom, become themselves a peculiar argot and create a special collectivity, a group of people initiated in familiar intercourse, who are frank and free in expressing themselves verbally. The marketplace crowd was such a collectivity, especially the festive, carnivalesque crowd at the fair" (RHW, 188).

It is important to acknowledge the fundamental insights this analysis provides. The discourse of the early-modern European marketplace did have many of the characteristics Bakhtin enumerates: it was ironic, familiar, coarse, vulgar, and filled with laughter. Moreover, there are good reasons for thinking that in the early-modern period European market towns were spaces in which independent commodity producers and vendors predominated, not large capitalists.[69] To the degree to which this was true, the marketplace did function as a space of independence, a site of social interaction much less inhibited by feudal custom than the village and the manor. Nevertheless, the marketplace was also a space of commodification; however much it may have facilitated the free flow of discourse it was preeminently the site of commodity exchange. Indeed, many French festivals were known as *apport* or *rapport*, literally places where one made purchases. Yet the commercial side of the market rarely impinges on Bakhtin's discussion; it is as if commodities were merely incidental to the free exchange of jokes, insults, and festive speech. And nowhere does Bakhtin even begin to ponder the lives and speech patterns of those who worked the fields, the workshops and proto-factories (not to mention those who were subjected to colonialism) to produce the commodities which circulated within the marketplace. As a result, he offers us a metaphor of the market as an ideal space, as the site of free, familiar, and ironic speech among equals.[70]

Such a typology of the market sets up an all-too-simple opposition between official culture and the festive marketplace. It is true that officialdom often sought to suppress market fairs. In 1781–1782, for instance, standing orders in

England prohibited twenty-four fairs. Ninety years later, the Fairs Act of 1871 led to the abolition of more than seven hundred English fairs in just ten years.[71] The general thrust of state policy, however, was to regulate fairs rather than outrightly abolish them. Authorities hoped to preserve their commercial functions while restraining the popular tumult that often accompanied them. Attempts to regulate England's famous Bartholomew Fair are instructive in this regard. In almost every decade of the Fair's existence, efforts were undertaken to suppress plays and puppet shows (both occasions for satire and attacks on authority). In 1691 and 1708, authorities tried to reduce it from fourteen to three days claiming that its booths were of "extraordinary largeness, not occupied by dealers in goods, merchandise, etc., proper for a fair, but used chiefly for stage plays, music."[72]

What was proper for a fair, in short, was commerce, buying and selling, what was improper was the licentious and anarchic atmosphere of popular entertainment. The problem was that the two were far from easily separable. Selling was itself a kind of street performance: hawking of goods involved banter with the crowd, parodic speeches, and theatrical presentations. Similarly, ballads, broadsheets, almanacs, and images—many of them parodic and satirical—were sold as well as performed. It was well-nigh impossible to determine where business ended and entertainment began. What the authorities undertook was to separate the proper, clean, and orderly from the improper, dirty, and licentious; they hoped, in short, to improve commerce while controlling behavior. And in significant measure they succeeded. Generally speaking, there was a decline of popular recreations as the rhythms of capitalist society began to supplant those of a precapitalist era.[73] But this involved not the decline of fairs so much as their metamorphosis. Increasingly, fairs were defined in commercial terms, as sites for integrating people into a market society. To the degree to which carnivalesque elements persisted, they did so as choreographed performances rather than living elements of social life. It's misleading, therefore, to read the rise of capitalism simply in terms of the suppression of fairs. In France, after all, the period 1871–1903 saw a proliferation of new fairs, largely as a result of the greater extension of the market and new means of transport into rural society.[74] Fairs played a central role in the marketization and commercialization of European life. And there was nothing radically new in this. Fairs had long been a central part of the great trading centers of Holland and Venice, and had come to occupy an increasingly important commercial role in cities like Leipzig, Frankfurt-am-Main, and Lyons. In fact, as industrial capitalism emerged, fairs took on the role of exhibition grounds for new machineries and technologies designed to dazzle and amaze prospective customers and a wider public alike. Appropriately, then, a historian describes the English fair after about 1850 as "the theatre of machines" organized around mechanical rides, electrograph shows, cinema, and the like.[75]

In this context, it is important to note the emergence of the world fair. The first of these was held in London in 1851. Paris soon became the principal site, hosting world fairs in 1855 and 1867, and major expositions again in 1889 and 1900. These fairs were carnivals of commodities and capitalist technology. There were eighty thousand commercial exhibitors at the Paris fair of 1855; fifteen million people visited the city's exposition of 1867; and architectural marvels like the Grand Palais, Trocadero, and the Eiffel Tower were constructed for the fairs of 1889 and 1900.[76] Moreover, by 1900 the state had become a participant in world fairs, using them to create and promote national identities in the age of imperialism.[77] Festive forms associated with carnival and popular culture were increasingly integrated into the circuit of commodities and the creation of patriotic identifications. None of this was unique to Europe. With the expansion of the world market, and the development of national ruling classes intent on capitalist transformations of local societies, carnival was used to similar purpose in other parts of the world. In Caracas, Venezuela, for example, it has been argued that carnival became in the 1870s an instrument of cultural "modernization," as local elites sought to transform it into "a world-system rite" symbolizing the transition from a barbaric to a civilized society (modeled on France).[78]

Because he does not interrogate the two-sided character of the early-modern market (as a site of commerce as well as popular recreation), Bakhtin gives us few tools with which to grasp the transformations which occurred with the rise of capitalism. As new forms of labor discipline were constructed, festive popular culture came under systematic assault from bourgeois reformers as an encouragement to idleness.[79] At the same time, speaking in broad historical terms, the market came to be dominated not by small producers, peddlers, and proprietors hawking their wares in the street, but by large capitalist concerns using advertising and marketing strategies to shape consumer preferences. The fair became increasingly commercialized, drained of its subversive and oppositional undertones, while advertising sought to appropriate the lingering elements of carnival. And during the entry into the age of militarism and imperialism (the year 1870 is a useful benchmark in this regard), these processes intersected with the new spectacle of the world fair and exposition whose "combination of engineering and fantasy" helped fuse bourgeois patriotism with technological awe to create commodified national identities appropriate to an era of intense international rivalry.[80]

If carnivalesque images of equality, abundance and a classless society are to be located after the rise of capitalism, these will not be found by looking for a pristine popular culture sealed off from official society. Mass culture, the culture of the commodity, reigns supreme in modern capitalist society. If elements of carnivalesque subversion and utopian renewal are to be found, it will be in this world of commodities which tolerates no outside. Recognition of this fact has produced no end of pessimistic cultural criticism. It was the great achievement of Walter Benjamin to develop a revolutionary theory that refused to flinch in the face of this daunting fact. Benjamin knew that all prospects for redemption and renewal had to be sought on the terrain of the all-pervasive commodity. The result was a theory drenched in an agonizing appraisal of the difficult prospects for a revolutionary transformation of society. Yet the difficulty of these prospects made the work of developing them all the more urgent. In his efforts to this end, Benjamin produced a series of profound reflections on language, the body, and the commodity. If we are to develop some of the important insights of Bakhtin's theory of language and culture in relation to capitalist society, it will be, I suggest, through the prism of Benjamin's meditations on these issues, meditations which constitute one of the towering achievements of Marxist thought.

CORPOREAL REASON: LANGUAGE, HISTORY, AND THE BODY IN WALTER BENJAMIN'S DIALECTICS OF AWAKENING

An academic conformism today threatens to overwhelm the legacy of Walter Benjamin. This is ironic, given Benjamin's vehement attacks on the way the culture industry, in producing standardized intellectual commodities, transforms critical impulses "into objects of distraction, of amusement, which can be supplied for consumption."[1] Yet, the marketing of a de-clawed Benjamin for the academy is to be expected. After all, more than anyone else, Benjamin taught us to see capitalism's drive to appropriate the radically new and different—in order to sell us the image of novelty while gutting any critical substance. Yet if the appearance of a raggedly provocative but unthreatening Benjamin for the academy comes as little surprise, it also presents a challenge. "In every era," wrote Benjamin, "the attempt must be made anew to wrest tradition away from the conformism that is about to overpower it."[2] It is in this spirit—of turning his thought against conformist readings—that I approach Benjamin's powerful discussions of language and history. I am not the first writer to resist domestications of Benjamin's thought.[3] But this battle must, as Benjamin's aphorism puts it, regularly be fought anew. Moreover, I am mobilizing Benjamin for a most specific purpose: to plunder the resources he offers the project of a critical materialist theory of language.

In wrenching a writer out of his or her context, in using them to intervene in a new setting, we risk distorting the intrinsic structures and rhythms of their thought. But a violent reading, Benjamin insisted, can also be true. The idea of the work as a timeless cultural object is inherently false; it perpetuates the dominant

161

class's myth of a seamless, unitary history. Revolutionary criticism, on the other hand, seeks to explode the monumentalization of cultural products by repositioning past works as resources in the struggles of the present. Revolutionary writers strive to relight the critical charge which official culture has extinguished, or nearly so, in situating these works as pieces in the history of "civilization." This critical operation is not about an arbitrary playing with texts, however. For Benjamin, every authentic reading reactivates the text in translating it into a new context of meaning. A serious reading discovers latent meetings which have yet to be brought to life. But more than this, translation also involves *mimesis*; it requires reconfiguring my experience (as reader/translator) so as to enter the language of another. And in this collision of languages and experiences, present and past, living and dead, an awakening occurs—an immanent transformation that supplements and develops the meaning intended by the author, and gives something unexpected to the translator. "The language of translation," writes Benjamin, "can—in fact, must—let itself go, so that it gives voice to the *intentio* of the original, not as reproduction, but as harmony, as a supplement."[4]

Genuine translation operates like authentic improvisation in jazz, remaking and reconstructing earlier versions while attending closely to their structure. The works to which the revolutionary writer turns are full of unutilized resources, rich sources of meaning which might assist the struggle to change society in the present. But these resources are not easily located, suppressed as they have been by the homogenizing procedures of official culture. Their excavation requires a hyperattentiveness to those moments in which a work from the past speaks urgently to the needs of the present. That this is possible—that a past meaning can be translated and transformed in a new context—has to do both with the unfinished business of human history *and* with the universal features of language which derive for Benjamin from the material structure of experience: our immersion in the language of the material world, "the language of things." All readings refer back to this greater language, and ought to be judged in terms of their ability to make "both the original and the translation recognizable as fragments of a greater language, just as fragments are part of a vessel."[5]

To talk of fragments is particularly appropriate in the case of Walter Benjamin whose works exist largely in fragmentary forms: essays, aphorisms, reviews, unfinished projects. Even his most complete book, *The Origin of German Tragic Drama*, is itself a study of an artistic form that focuses on ruins, on decaying fragments of past objects. Immersed in the decaying fragments of bourgeois culture, Benjamin's thinking resists closure and totalization more vigorously than does that of most major theorists, it evinces a thoroughgoing suspicion of all aspirations to create a total system of thought. Systematically antisystematic, his thinking is the first exercise in negative dialectics.[6] In opposition to capitalism's drive to subsume all facets of existence under the commodity form, revolutionary thought seeks out the gaps in the logic of commodification, those spaces where other meanings are hinted at, in the same way that psychoanalysis probes the hidden meanings of phenomena (like dreams and seemingly chance verbal slips) that clash with their conscious understanding. Truly radical criticism embraces the fragmentary, the seemingly marginal and inconsequential, it aspires to "brush history against the grain" in order to find hidden desires and unfulfilled aspirations which might provide resources for an assault on the totalizing objectives of capital.

Yet, because this antitotalizing critique has so far failed to subvert the rule of capital, Benjamin's writings bear the marks of failure. And they do so self-reflexively. At a very early point, Benjamin saw the recognition of loss as a key to personal and intellectual renewal. "Without the regret for a greatness missed," he wrote of his generation of students, "no renewal of their lives can be possible."[7] And as he turned to politics, his sense of the profound importance of "regret for a greatness missed" became more acute. The historic failings of the Left of Benjamin's age—the defeat of the Paris Commune, the inability to extend revolution outside of Russia and its subsequent degeneration, the failure to block Hitler's rise to power, the defeat of the Spanish revolution—left the stench of barbarism in the very air he breathed. And he was among a very few who immersed his thinking in these brutal facts. The rest of the twentieth century has been no kinder to the utopian impulses of critical thought. Not only can no real revolutionary criticism evade the fact of failure; genuinely revolutionary thinking can take shape only through self-reflection on the trauma which marks it to its core.

There is a facile response to this acknowledgment of traumatic failure, of course: to abandon the revolutionary tradition of the Left. But, for Benjamin, this is to seal one's complicity with barbarism. Instead, his is a call to ethico-political responsibility on the Left, a reminder that past failures decisively mark the present and the future of our work. Benjamin knows that the revolution has thus far failed, and while he thinks against that failure in order to open the space of revolution, he acknowledges it, names it, and mourns its consequences. The very meaning of catastrophe for Benjamin is "to have missed the opportunity."[8] As the slaughters continue, as the mountain of corpses climbs ever higher, as one revolutionary project after another fails, critical theory carries an ever heavier burden. Immersed in catastrophe, critical theory moves in a space filled with loss, and it makes mourning over what has not come to pass—the transition to a new society of freedom—a part of its essential structure. What Benjamin said of Kafka might equally be applied to himself: "To do justice to the figure of Kafka in its purity and its beauty," he wrote, "one must never lose sight of one thing: it is the purity and beauty of a failure."[9]

In what follows, I propose to read Benjamin in terms of the purity and beauty of his failure. I do this as someone who shares this failure. Unlike many commentators on Benjamin, I share his commitment to a revolution against capital. Consequently, I depart sharply from those interpreters who seek to de-radicalize his texts by separating his Marxist politics from his cultural criticism.

At the same time, I make this departure while acknowledging the failings which mark the position from which I do so. Like Benjamin, I do not believe these failings vitiate a Marxist standpoint. But they do impose significant ethico-political obligations on us: they require us to name our failure and to query the possibility of victory. This is not a justification for quietism and a politics of self-amusement, however. Benjamin was decisive in his rejection of "left-wing melancholy" whose "political significance was exhausted," he argued, "by the transposition of revolutionary reflexes . . . into objects of distraction," into routine objects of consumption rather than means of historical transformation.[10] If Benjamin refused to shrink from the horror of the moment in which he wrote—Hitler's victory, the defeat of the Spanish republic, the Hitler-Stalin pact, his own flight from France—if, despite the tragedy that engulfed him, he continued to operate as "a ragpicker, early on, at the dawn of the day of the revolution,"[11] then we who write in his memory ought equally to refuse both facile optimism and a politics of resignation. Among other things, this means resisting all moves to sanctify Benjamin himself, to treat him as the founder of a new doctrine, rather than as an indispensable source for the renewal of critical Marxist thought. Benjamin provides us with some of the most original and profound materialist considerations on language and culture in late capitalism. But his reflections are marked by a failure which we must acknowledge—and share. In the case of Benjamin's work especially, that "old maxim of dialectics" applies: "the surmounting of difficulties through their accumulation."[12]

"A MATERIALISM OF THE WORD": BENJAMIN'S EARLY REFLECTIONS ON LANGUAGE

Benjamin is usually considered to have penned two significant pieces on language: "On Language as Such and On the Language of Man" (1916) and "On the Mimetic Faculty" (1933). Frequently, these are treated as simply two statements of a single philosophy of language.[13] Yet, despite important continuities between these essays, it is impossible to understand the materialist turn Benjamin's thinking took in the years after "On Language as Such" without registering crucial discontinuities. After all, the materialist elements of this early piece coexisted with elements of what he later denounced as an "ahistorical, idealist language mysticism."[14]

"On Language as Such" sets forth an alternative to what Benjamin calls "the bourgeois conception of language."[15] The latter involves a fundamentally instrumentalist outlook: it views language as a set of words used by human beings to communicate their thoughts. In this perspective, language is simply the means by which humans create meanings and exchange them with others. Benjamin posits in contrast a radically noninstrumentalist position. All nature partakes of language, he argues. Indeed, there is a "magic of matter" by which all things, animate and inanimate, communicate with one another. But only "man" has the gift of sound which enables him to name things. And through naming, man comes to know the world in the very language in which God created it (OLS, 323). Human language consists therefore in speaking "the language of things," the hidden language which embodies the fundamental unity of God, man, and world. Rather than a means to an end (the dissemination of human meanings), language for Benjamin *is* the communicative interaction of being with itself; communication takes place *in* language not *through* it (OLS, 315–16). Through their participation in language, humans put into words structures of experience that pertain to the world as a whole. Instead of the creation of human meanings, this original and primordial language involves a *procreation* of meaning, a giving birth to the language of nature through the gift of the human voice. Since the Fall from grace, however, this pure language of things, has been lost; the Adamic word has fractured and fragmented. Human beings now exchange a debased linguistic currency, they use words simply as means to communicate mental thoughts which no longer touch the things themselves. The word has become "a mere sign," a token for representing a mental meaning. Its sensuous ties to things having been radically severed, language has dissolved into rarefied abstractions (OLS, 328).

Yet, all hope of redemption is not lost. While the unity of God, man, and nature has been shattered, it is still possible to locate broken bits of what has been destroyed. But this requires searching for the lingering traces of the forgotten dialogue between human beings and nature. In part because of their concrete, sensuous forms of expression, Benjamin turns first to the plastic arts to find such traces of the language of things: "it is very conceivable that the language of sculpture or painting is founded on certain kind of thing languages, that in them we find a translation of the language of things into an infinitely higher language, which may still be of the same sphere. We are concerned here with nameless, non-acoustic languages, *languages issuing from matter.*" (OLS, 330, author's emphasis) This remarkable formulation captures the intersection of theological and materialist strains in Benjamin's thought. Moreover, it lends credence to those who see Benjamin's theological motifs as a strategic means of highlighting the losses associated with instrumentalized language, rather than as part of a theological linguistics *per se.*[16] By using language symbolically, rather than instrumentally, Benjamin is saying, humans who come after the Fall might enter into the "pure language" of things, nature and God which lies hidden beneath the debased exchanges of human discourse (OLS, 331).[17]

It is not difficult to identify a number of themes in "On Language as Such" which were susceptible to a unique materialist recasting. Benjamin's hostility to "the bourgeois view of language" as a means of exchanging human thoughts echoes Marx's critique of the alienating effects of the extension of the exchange principle into all aspects of human life. Similarly, his critique of a language

abstracted from the concrete and sensuous forms of interaction between people
and nature has points of contact with Marx's criticism of the way capitalism
abstracts from the concrete productive activities of humans and subordinates
them to the rule of "real abstractions" like value, money, and capital. With his
movement in a more materialist direction in the period immediately after writing "On Language as Such," these themes would move to the fore in his thinking about language.

Thanks to the 1985 German publication of volume six of Benjamin's *Works*,
we are in a position to more clearly assess the extent of the changes in Benjamin's
thinking which took place between 1916 and the early 1920s.[18] Largely through
his study of Freud at this time, Benjamin came to place a new emphasis on the
human body, the first indication, it would seem, of his move toward the "anthropological materialism" which figures so importantly in his work from the late
1920s. Whereas the materialism of "On Language as Such" consisted of somewhat mystical invocations of hidden ties between the human mind and the
magic of matter, Benjamin's reflections now came to revolve around the body as
the link between language and things. "The relation of the human form to
language," he wrote at this time, ". . . is the object of physiological study.
Corporeality . . . properly forms part of this study."[19] Henceforth, and particularly in his uniquely Marxist writings after the mid-1920s, this emphasis on
corporeality reshaped his reflections on culture in dramatic ways. This was not
the only major shift in Benjamin's thinking prior to his engagement with Marxism, however. In fact, this move followed upon and interacted with a major turn
away from an older idealist view of history and toward a more messianic one—
a turn which reflected a rethinking of his early political engagements. The interaction between these two distinct intellectual shifts gave a unique shape to
Benjamin's reception of Marxism.

Benjamin had joined the Free German Youth movement as a university
student and taken up a position on its culturalist wing. Whereas the more
politically inclined wing of the movement supported the Social Democratic
Party (SPD), the current with which Benjamin aligned himself focused on education reform and the creation of an autonomous youth culture. Inspired by a
certain reading of Kant's philosophy, the culturalists sought to build a new *ethos*,
a moral spirit (*Geist*) which would usher in an ethical transformation of society.[20]
Benjamin's adherence to this intellectual-political outlook disintegrated after
1914 when Gustav Wyneken, the originator of the youth-culture position, supported German involvement in World War I. Benjamin and his closest associates were shocked by Wyneken's position; indeed two of his friends committed
suicide in a protest against the war. In response, Benjamin broke sharply and
openly with Wyneken and his movement. While continuing to espouse the
ideals of the youth culturalists, he now came to suspect the whole of German
idealism and its rarefied notions of advancing and reforming the German spirit

for leading, as one commentator puts it, "all too easily to the sophistry of the 'ideas of 1914'."[21]

In particular, Benjamin recoiled from the teleological conception of history at the heart of German idealism, which described history as a progressive unfolding of the ethical spirit of the people throughout historical time. Reading historical events in this spirit, as the progressive actualization of an ethical-cultural ideal, Wyneken could describe the barbarism of world war as a necessary moment in the historical unfolding of the true German spirit. Reacting against this conclusion, Benjamin took his distance from progressivist notions of history. Rejecting world views which anticipated a historical realization of an ideal state (since they tended to apologize for the behavior of actual states), he embraced a messianic conception of time in which radical, redemptive change represented not the progress of history, but its disruption. Benjamin thus tried to preserve his ethics by distancing himself from history. While *Geist* was always at work, it did not operate at the level of historical time. The intervention of spirit in human affairs could only occur in nonhistorical (metaphysical) ways which disrupt the continuum of history. Rather than interpret it in terms of a philosophy of history, *geist* could only be grasped in terms of "its metaphysical structure, as with the messianic realm or the idea of the French Revolution."[22]

The problematic relationship between history and metaphysics resurfaces in Benjamin's 1919 dissertation, *The Concept of Criticism in German Romanticism.*[23] The aim of German Romantic criticism, he claims, is not to reconstruct the meaning of a work. Instead, it completes and destroys the work by bringing it into contact with the absolute idea. A finite and specific work of art can only be critically understood through a reading that relates it to the infinite and universal ideas it intends. Criticism is thus a transformative practice, one which destroys the object in its concrete, finite form in order to release it into a sphere of universal principles. Rather than an attentive appreciation of the artistic object, criticism dissolves "the moment of contingency" in the work and transforms it "into something lawful."[24] Yet—and here Benjamin takes his distance from the German Romantics—this critical activity does not actually arrive at the universal object of Beauty and Truth, however much it points to it; it does not accomplish the transition to the realm of the infinite. To suggest otherwise is to replicate the error of German idealism: the idea that particular and universal, profane and metaphysical can be reconciled in real historical time. In an early footnote to his dissertation, Benjamin takes issue with the way "Romantic messianism" demanded "the 'kingdom of God' at this very moment—in time and on earth."[25] As if to underline the point, in a final section added to his dissertation after its submission, he elaborated upon his rejection of "the immediate reconciliation of the conditioned with the unconditioned."[26] Unlike the Romantics, Benjamin continued to insist upon a sharp differentiation of the unconditioned from the conditioned, the absolute from the profane, the messianic from the historical.

Nevertheless, Benjamin still thought in terms of the eruption of the messianic into history. Any critical outlook has to think about the particular in terms of the universal, profane history in terms of redemption. In turning to a messianic notion of time—of a temporality separate from that of history and capable of disrupting the historical continuum—Benjamin continued to judge the world from the standpoint of redemption and to advocate action informed by messianism. But such action could not claim historical efficacy. Messianic action would be antihistorical in form. At this stage, then, Benjamin rubbed shoulders with a sort of anarchist philosophy of the act. In "Critique of Violence" (1921), he embraces "revolutionary violence, the highest manifestation of unalloyed violence by man" as a form of action which completely breaks with the order of myth and law.[27] But this outlook—which separates political action from historical time—raised a problem which continued to dog him after his turn to Marxism: how a political practice might be organized which could mobilize and actualize the messianic forces necessary to break through the flow of historical time. In short, how could the messianic be made flesh? How could the nonhistorical energies of messianic time, the time of human redemption, intervene on the terrain of history?

Materialism and Transcendence: Traces of a Problem

The problem I am posing would be solved easily if we could show that Benjamin simply turned from messianism to materialism.[28] While there is an element of truth to such a claim—Benjamin's messianism *was* incorporated into an increasingly historical and materialist project and thereby transformed—his materialist turn did not in the first instance involve a shift away from, but rather an intensification of messianism. Benjamin's Marxism, in other words, took shape in terms of the complex intersection of his messianic and materialist turns of the period 1915–23. These intersecting moves also shaped his unique attempt to develop a concept of experience appropriate to the critical analysis of bourgeois culture. Two texts of the early 1920s represent these moments in his thinking and the tensions they entailed: the "Theologico-Political Fragment" (1920–21) and his "Outline of the Psychophysical Problem" (1922–23).[29]

The "Theological-Political Fragment" attempts, as its title suggests, to clarify the relationship between theology and politics, or, more aptly perhaps, between the messianic and the historical. In the first instance, Benjamin's clarification of the relationship between these spheres consists merely in a radical demarcation. "Only the Messiah himself consummates all history," he announces, "in the sense that he alone redeems it." But if only the Messiah can consummate history by bringing it to a redemptive resolution, then human action has no messianic or redemptive powers. "For this reason nothing historical can relate itself on its own account to anything Messianic." No historical process tends toward earthly redemption: "the Kingdom of God is not the *telos* of the historical dynamic."[30] This seems to leave Benjamin with a simple binary opposition between the transcendental and the material. Having set up this opposition, however, he undoes it in part by declaring legitimate purpose to human action on the plane of profane historical events. Perhaps under the imprint of his reading of Freud, Benjamin argues that "the order of the profane should be erected on the idea of happiness." He is quick to add, however, that the struggle for happiness does not further the arrival of a redeemed state. In fact, "the quest of a free humanity for happiness runs counter to the Messianic direction" (TPF, 312). Nevertheless, there is a connection between these forces which move in opposite directions, albeit one which shows the impossibility of mapping any relationship between the messianic and the profane. "Just as a force can, through acting, increase another that is acting in the opposite direction, so the order of the profane assists, through being profane, the coming of the Messianic Kingdom," he writes (TPF, 312). Needless to say, this is something less than a compelling solution to the problem. For what the pursuit of earthly happiness accomplishes, he contends, is not a concrete historical goal. Instead it ushers in the downfall of all that is profane. The struggle of a free humanity for happiness is thus an antihistorical one: since happiness cannot be realized by earthly means, to struggle for it is to hasten the destruction of everything profane. Yet this destruction of all earthly kingdoms inadvertently furthers the coming of the Messiah. Consequently, "to strive after such passing [the passing away of all that is earthly] . . . is the task of world politics." And this seems to mean that all profane political commitments are to be repudiated except the destruction of all that exists—an interpretation which gains conviction when he describes the method of such politics as "nihilism," the repudiation of all earthly, human goals (TPF, 313).

Benjamin's perspective here is a radically antipolitical one. Only in abdicating historical-political goals might we further the coming of the messianic state. Yet, as John McCole points out, this kind of nihilist position is fundamentally unstable: it vacillates between fatalistic quietism, a bitter resignation about earthly affairs, on the one hand, and a radical voluntarism which, in rejecting practical political goals, seeks the destruction of all social order on the other.[31] An equally serious problem for Benjamin may have been that his repudiation of the realm of the profane sat uncomfortably with his materialist affirmation of the body and the pursuit of happiness. The sort of materialism toward which Benjamin was moving—what he later called an "anthropological materialism" built around the human body and its technological extensions—entailed a thoroughgoing suspicion of idealist attempts to set up the world of ideas (and ideals) as a transcendent sphere, one beyond the realm of material life. Thus, while wary of resolving the tension between the realms of the messianic and the profane, Benjamin may also have felt the need for a more meaningful relation between them. Indeed, the tenor of "Outline of the Psychophysical Problem," suggests a continuing interest in other ways of theorizing the relation between the body, history, and redemption.

The importance of the "Outline" resides in the increased clarity with which Benjamin tackles the classic mind-body problem of Western philosophy and in his identification of dream-life as the intermediate realm linking the historical and the spiritual. The text opens by asserting the identity of mind and body whose distinction resides simply in their being different "ways of seeing."[32] Benjamin proceeds to define "the form of the historical" as "that of mind and body combined." Indeed "genius" appears in the historical process in the form of "the embodied mind" (OPP, 393). But whereas the body and genius stand in relation to history, this is not the case with spirit and corporeal substance (the body as animated by spirit). Benjamin moves once more into a dualistic mode by positing two distinct spheres, the historical realm of bodies and minds, and the spiritual realm of corporeal substance: "with his body man belongs to mankind; with his corporeal substance to God." Benjamin next discusses the human sphere as one in which, through technology, humanity extends its body in the pursuit of happiness. Nevertheless, he insists again that while "bodily nature advances toward its dissolution," only corporeal substance "advances towards its resurrection" (OPP, 395). Redemption, in short, lies outside the sphere of history.

At this point, however, Benjamin's discussion undergoes a series of shifts that suggest conclusions different from those of the "Fragment." First, he takes up the problem of the body and describes sexuality as constituting, with spirit, one of "the two vital poles" of natural life. Second, discussing "the utter decay of corporeality, such as we are witnessing in the West at the present time," he looks to art (as he had in "On Language as Such") as the mode of experience in which we might recover corporeality and the unity of spirit and nature (OPP, 396). Finally, after a discussion of pleasure and pain and nearness and distance, he turns to dreams as the existential mode of communion between the spiritual and the historical. But such communion is not comprised of instrumental action, it cannot be a goal of waking life. Instead, the free human being, he maintains, is one who follows nature by escaping the forms of consciousness which characterize historical life. The free man is "guided, but like a sleeper. The perfect man lives only in such dreams, from which he never wakes. For the more perfect a man is, the deeper is his sleep" (OPP, 398).

We have here an important move to bridge the gulf between the transcendental and the material, the messianic and the historical. Indeed, after elaborating on dreams, Benjamin discusses Eros as "the binding element in nature," and cites Plato's *Symposium* where Eros is described as "intermediate between the divine and the mortal," as "the mediator who spans the chasm which divides" God and man (OPP, 400). The idea of desire and the dream as connections between the material and the transcendental is one Benjamin would continue to explore across his writings. With his turn to Marxism, his interest in dreams and desire grew as he sought energies and modes of experience that might shatter the reified structures of everyday life. At this point, however, Benjamin had not approached a theory of historical awakening in which dreams are remembered and used as images for historical action. Yet, awareness of this intellectual trajectory provides important insights into his earliest sustained piece of radical modernist criticism, "One-Way Street" (written between 1923–26 and published in 1928). But before looking at that work, I wish to explore his celebrated book of the same year, *The Origin of German Tragic Drama*, for that apparently obscure academic text represents a decisive moment in his rethinking of the problem of materialism, history, and redemption.

CATASTROPHE AND "THE POWER OF THINGS": REDEMPTION AND THE PROFANE REVISITED

To most commentators, *The Origin of German Tragic Drama* appears to have little to do with the problem of materialism and history. The work exhibits no overt traces of an engagement with Marxism. Gershom Scholem said of it, "there is not the slightest evidence of Marxist categories" in the book, a view which has been repeated by critics like George Steiner.[33] Yet Benjamin insisted *Origin* was a "dialectical" work, and I propose to take this claim seriously. *Origin*, I argue, represents a decisive step toward the concept of dialectics that figures centrally in Benjamin's writings of the 1930s. It is the pivotal text in which he developed a theory of practice intended as a complex and esoteric solution to the problem of messianism and history.

The writing of *Origin* (between May 1924 and April 1925) coincided with Benjamin's turn to Marxist politics. The convergence of two events at the time was decisive: his first meeting with the Latvian Bolshevik Asja Lacis with whom he fell in love, and his reading of Georg Lukacs' *History and Class Consciousness*, arguably the most profound and influential work of Marxist philosophy in the twentieth century. Benjamin saw a definite connection between the way he and Lukacs, proceeding from different starting points, arrived at similar conclusions about the unity of theory and *praxis*. For both of them, he wrote, "any definitive insight into theory is bound up with praxis."[34] Given the dualism that had dominated Benjamin's thinking throughout the postwar period, this claim signals a major development. I propose therefore to read Benjamin's book on *Trauerspiel* (German baroque drama) with Lukacs' *History and Class Consciousness* in mind.

History and Class Consciousness represents a profound attempt to renovate Marxist theory in terms of two central categories: reification and totality. Building upon Marx's account of the fetishism of commodities—according to which human practical activity in capitalist society congeals in the form of things (commodities, money, means of production) which come to dominate their

producers—Lukacs argues that a totalizing process of reification pervades modern society. Human practices are systematically objectified as alien, thing-like
structures. Workers lose control of the products of their labor; machines dominate laborers in the process of production; formal bureaucratic regimes admin-
ister people in the public sphere of government and law. As a result, society
assumes the guise of "a second nature" in which human historical processes
take the form of natural laws beyond the conscious direction of humans themselves.[35] Increasingly, natural-scientific methods appropriate to measuring and
manipulating things are applied to the social organization of people. Capitalist
society thus constitutes a wholly reified structure in which things dominate
people. Yet, in the midst of this living hell lurks an emancipatory power.
However, this revolutionary force is not a transcendental one. Since capitalism
constitutes a total system, there is no separate sphere in which messianic
powers might operate; redemptive forces can only be located within this fallen
and debased world of things (commodities and capital). And Lukacs identifies
this force in the proletariat, a class of people whose labor-power is commodified,
who are reduced to administered things (units of labor) in the process of
production, yet whose subjectivity rebels against this general reification. In the
proletariat he finds a unity of opposites—thing and human, nature and history,
subject and object. And for this reason the proletariat can assume the role of
the identical subject-object of Hegel's philosophical system, a subject whose
self-knowledge is simultaneously total knowledge of the objective social world.
In coming to understand themselves as commodities, members of the working
class thereby come to know the inner secret of capitalist society (the logic of
the commodity form).[36]

Benjamin never entirely subscribed to this last part of the Lukacsian schema.
As I argue below, he found the problem of revolutionary subjectivity much more
complex and difficult than its depiction in *History and Class Consciousness*. Nevertheless, much of Lukacs' argument resonates with his own thinking at the
time. In particular, Benjamin was already moving toward a view of modern
society as a nightmare of reification. And, similarly, he was increasingly impelled
toward a position of *immanent critique*—searching for redemptive powers within
the degraded world of the profane, not outside it.

The notion of immanent critique was not something new to Benjamin,
although it assumed a radically new form in the *Trauerspiel* book. In his early
studies of German Romanticism, for instance, he had embraced the idea that
artistic criticism ought to operate immanently, in terms of the symbols and
meaning of the work itself, and not according to external criteria.[37] But any such
notion of criticism repudiates a disconnection between form and content, and
between theory (criticism) and its object—the very disconnection which runs
through Benjamin's thinking about history and the messianic up to this point.
Yet, if artistic criticism is to refuse standards and values external to the art work
itself, should not the same be true for social criticism? What justification could

there be for sociohistorical criticism which turned to metaphysics, to a realm which transcends history? Among other things, *The Origin of German Tragic Drama* was an attempt to extend immanent critique to history—and in so doing to move toward a more dialectical resolution of the problem of materialism and messianism. At the same time, Benjamin remained insistent (against the German Romantics) that criticism could not itself reconcile universal and particular. In the sphere of profane history, everything remains unreconciled. Nevertheless, for the first time since he had broken with German idealism, Benjamin broached the possibility that criticism might identify fragments of redemption in the space of the profane. While criticism could never uncover a total integrated object—a unity of the particular and the universal, the finite and the infinite—it might locate broken bits, shards of redemption, within the reified, historical world.

Origin begins, however, not with *Trauerspiel* itself, but with a dense and difficult "Epistemo-Critical Prologue." The practice of criticism, says Benjamin, performs a "burning up of the husk" (the external form) of an object in order to illuminate its latent truth (OGTD, 31). It does so by assembling conceptual elements that illuminate the object, particularly by bringing together those that lie at extremes to one another. The ideas which embody the latent truth of an object, "come to life," he claims, "only when extremes are assembled around them" (OGTD, 35). Since this may seem obscure, let me illustrate this point with reference to Lukacs. According to *History and Class Consciousness*, the truth of bourgeois society is discoverable only when the extremes of person and thing, subject and object come together—as they do in the proletariat. Benjamin seems to have something similar in mind. *Trauerspiel*, he will argue, expresses the truth of a catastrophic human situation by engineering a collision between extremes such as history and nature, life and death, salvation and ruination. Criticism thus tries to "effect a synthesis between extremes" (OGTD, 41). But what is it that such a synthesis releases? What is illuminated by the critical flame that consumes the husk of a thing? Here Benjamin returns to a central theme of "On Language as Such" by claiming that the truth to which criticism aspires is not a part of empirical reality, rather, it is the lost symbolic dimension of things which was there in "primordial language" and the "primordial form of perception" (OGTD, 36). Criticism seeks to locate those forgotten fragments of the original unity of humans and nature which lie latent in every work of art. But these fragments of utopia can be released only by destroying (burning up) "the false appearance of totality" that the work projects. And here we encounter an important difference in emphasis from Lukacs. For Benjamin there is no total object (or subject) which embodies the truth of history and society. Instead, truth is to be sought in "the merest fragment" to which criticism can attach itself in the course of destroying the false semblance of totality (OGTD, 44).

And this is what makes his decision to study the baroque mourning play so significant. As Benjamin points out, the historical context of the *Trauerspiel* was one of catastrophe: the Thirty Years War which ravaged much of Europe for three decades beginning in 1618. History appears in the baroque as a process of decay and disintegration. And this differentiates the baroque from ancient Greek tragedy which traces the struggle of history against nature, of self-knowing individuals against mythic forces. Rather than a narrative of human struggle against nature, the German baroque is a story of the transformation of history *into* nature. It tells a tale of transience, decay, and death in a world in which there is no hope of salvation. For the Lutheran dramatists of the German baroque, writing in the midst of the Counter Reformation, history represented nothing but historical regress. Not for them was the doctrine of good works, since all human action in a debased world appeared overwhelmingly futile. Theirs were "mourning plays," laments about a world in which death and ruin were the only truths. The baroque, writes Benjamin, "is haunted by the idea of catastrophe." Moreover, it "knows no eschatology," it cannot subscribe to a view of history as culminating in salvation (OGTD, 66).[38] Denied effective means of religious self-expression in a political context where reform (never mind revolution) seemed impossible, the baroque dramatists could only lament their fallen state (OGTD, 79–80, 88). It requires no great leap to see how this historical period could have served Benjamin as a productive analogy for his own. Benjamin, too, experienced a world in ruins; images of decay permeate much of his critical discussion of contemporary culture at the time. [39]

And yet, there were glimmers of redemption in the baroque drama. But these were to be found in "the hopelessness of the earthly condition" not "in the fulfillment of a divine plan of salvation" (OGTD, 81). So thoroughly had God deserted the human world, so bereft of hope was the human condition that "apparently dead objects" now exercised power over human life. Inhabiting a world of extreme reification, people in the baroque drama had become estranged from all the natural sources of life, including their bodies (OGTD, 132, 140). Yet, in divesting the human world of all intrinsic meaning, and in investing power in brute things, these same objects appear as repositories of truth and meaning. In this "pathological state," as Benjamin puts it, even "the most simple object seems to be the symbol of some enigmatic wisdom because it lacks any natural, creative relationship to us." At the extreme point of reification, where social life has been reduced to the purely natural, meaning and truth have deserted human beings to take up residence in the realm of things. This is the fundamental insight of melancholic wisdom. The knowledge of the baroque mourner, "is subject to the nether world; it is secured by immersion in the life of creaturely things." Yet this melancholy "loyalty to the world of things" opens onto a space of fragments of redemption whose objects can be perceived only through an extreme absorption in things which "embraces dead objects in its contemplation, in order to redeem them" (OGTD, 140, 152, 157).

The *Trauerspiel* encounters the messianic in the very depths of the profane, among the decaying ruins of an abandoned world. On a landscape of the dead and dying, it retrieves intimations of a life which once was. At this extreme point of reification, it discovers "the unity of the material and the transcendental object" which characterized the primordial state before the Fall. This is clearly a major shift for Benjamin. In thinking through the problem of the disintegration of culture in bourgeois society, the baroque drama offered him a way to reconfigure the relationship between the messianic and the profane. That is why allegory figures so prominently in his account of *Trauerspiel*. For the baroque drama uses objects to hint at what cannot be named. In a society without hope, where everything living is destined for destruction, hope can only be represented in its opposite—the decaying, the petrified, the corpse. At the heart of the baroque is a profound reversal: history has become nature (a sphere of inevitable decay) and nature has become history (the sphere where meaning still exists, albeit in the form of broken bits of material reality divested of former human meanings). Since the disintegration of the human subject is also the investment of meaning in things, "the profane world is both elevated and devalued" (OGTD, 166, 175).

The baroque mourning play requires a radically unique aesthetic. It cannot employ the conventional symbol in which a particular sign is said to represent and embody a universal.[40] Instead of symbolism—and its implied reconciliation of part and whole—the baroque chooses allegory and its distorted, grotesque, dead, and decaying objects. Allegory refuses to collapse the distance separating the elements of the profane world from the transcendent and the redemptive; it resists all moves to figure this world as one where reconciliation is possible. By seizing upon ruins, dismembered bodies and corpses, it drives home the unredeemed character of historical existence:

> Whereas in the symbol destruction is idealized and the transfigured face of nature is fleetingly revealed in the light of redemption, in allegory the observer is confronted with the *facies hippocratica* of history as a petrified, primordial landscape. Everything about history that, from the very beginning, has been untimely, sorrowful, unsuccessful, is expressed in a face—or rather in a death's head (OGTD, 166).

For this reason, ruins and corpses occupy center stage in the baroque drama. The haphazard accumulation of broken bits of the world speaks to the futility of the human situation. As a result, "it is common practice in the literature of the baroque to pile up fragments ceaselessly, without any strict idea of a goal." This very practice, however, carries through the destructive side of all real criticism. In destroying the appearance of totality, the baroque drama presents objects "in which all ephemeral beauty is stripped off." Stripped bare, exposed as ruins on a petrified landscape, however, these objects provide a "basis for rebirth" (OGTD, 178, 182). In the course of undermining all images of a meaningful world, allegory repositions history as the space in which human action might constitute meaning: "The eternal is separated from the events of the story of salvation, and what is left is a living image open to all kinds of revision by the interpretative artist" (OGTD, 183). By de-mythologizing historical existence, by shattering symbols of reconciliation, allegory reveals a bleak landscape on which new meanings can be written, and thus opens up a space of historical practice. Not that allegory can offer an image of redemption to guide historical action. On the contrary, by showing that objects do not possess transcendent meanings, that profane history knows no metaphysical forces moving toward redemption, allegory simply shows us the alienated, fragmented, reified state of our actual historical existence. It is not that the allegorical object itself contains redemptive power, then, but that in de-mythifying the world, allegory shows us the falsity of all existing claims to meaning. And this recognition—our self-recognition in a world of death and decay—might lead us to act against the reality of a world without hope or transcendent meaning. Hope begins, in short, in the jolting discovery of hopelessness.

Yet, allegory can break down myths of redemption only if it finds ways to shock, to break through the reified patterns of historical life. For that reason, allegories "must constantly unfold in new and surprising ways." Precisely because "it is part of their nature to shock," they quickly become dated (OGTD, 183). Only in the moment of "burning up" can allegory shock us into recognition of the bleakness of historical life. Quoting from Friedrich Creuzer's study of mythologies, Benjamin describes these illuminating moments as being like "the sudden appearance of a ghost, or a flash of lightning which suddenly illuminates the dark night" (OGTD, 163). Ghosts, of course, are forms of afterlife, of that which persists after death. So long as life continues, past sufferings live a spectral existence, as part of the losses which define our condition. And these ghosts can be awakened by attending to "the power of things." The rubble of our historical being—the petrified objects, the smashed and broken things, the piles of corpses— still speak a mute language of broken hopes. So thoroughly have past hopes been destroyed, so brutal have been the catastrophes of history, that only in the midst of the alienated world of things might we receive, in our grief and sorrow, intimations of what has been lost. The time of the baroque is thus a space of mourning. In our lamentations over the state of a deserted world, however, we might find a way to commune with the ghosts of the past, to reenter the world of shattered hopes and broken dreams which is history. Death, in short, may be the point of entry into redemption.[41] And this returns us to the problem of historical time.

History in the baroque obeys no eschatology, no salvation lies at its end. Time is empty—an endless flow of destruction. If meaning is to be found it will be in gathering things together in this space of hopelessness. For this reason space takes priority over time. Distinct temporal moments are spatialized, thrust together side by side on the stage; to the degree to which the baroque wants to depict the interaction of events, "the most radical procedure is to make events simultaneous" (OGTD, 194). In spatializing time, allegory arrests historical movement, destroying all sense of organic growth. As a result, the most important events in the *Trauerspiel* happen at midnight, the hour at which, according to popular opinion, "time stands still like the tongue of a scale" (OGTD, 135). Only in mortifying time, only in destroying organic life, can baroque allegory prefigure redemption. And this is enacted every time severed heads are displayed and goblets of blood consumed. The task of the baroque is thus to raise decay to the highest level of artistic expression. In its dialectic of the extremes, the *trauerspiel* pushes forward "the destruction of the organic" so that truth "might be picked up from its fragments." Yet, in this dialectic of extremes, two attitudes toward the world stand out: the melancholic resignation of the prince, and the worldly intrigue of the courtier (OGTD, 95). In an implicit critique of his own earlier work, and of the dominant attitude among disaffected intellectuals, Benjamin identifies here with the attitude of the courtier. The melancholic stance bemoans the fact that good has deserted this world of unrelenting evil; in so doing it is still defined by the search for a mythical rebirth of good, for a return of God. The courtier, however, proceeds from the most hard-nosed acceptance of God's desertion of earthly existence. Rather than hoping against it, the courtier chooses to take advantage of it. If divine meaning has left this world, then human meaning might come to inhabit it. The courtier proceeds, therefore, toward historical action designed to impart a finite meaning to the profane world. We should not underestimate the significance of this shift in Benjamin's thinking. For, as Julian Roberts puts it, "the *Trauerspiel* book is a recovery of human practice from the desert of religious transcendentism."[42]

Only by recognizing this move toward practice can we understand why Benjamin thought his *Trauerspiel* book had arrived at conclusions similar to Lukacs' *History and Class Consciousness*. After all, Lukacs had attempted to show that "the antinomies of bourgeois thought" which bedeviled philosophy—the undialectical separation of form and content, universal and particular, abstract and concrete—could only be overcome through the practice of a proletarian revolution which changed the structure of social reality. The *Origin* pushed toward a similar conclusion: "Knowledge of good, as knowledge is secondary. It issues from practice," Benjamin argued. If we merely contemplate the world, we will only arrive at knowledge of evil. Knowledge of the good is the knowledge of a practice designed to change reality, it derives from action not contemplation (OGTD, 233). Moreover, earlier in the text, in a theme which reappears across much of his later work, Benjamin suggests that this practical knowledge of the good is a sort of "anthropological, even physiological knowledge" (OGTD, 95).

This position would henceforth occupy a central position in Benjamin's thinking. Rather than the optimistic, evolutionist dialectic in which one social formation organically grows over into another (the vulgar determinism that dominated German Social Democracy), Benjamin was developing a dialectic of pessimism in which the catastrophic collapse of Western culture was the locus of practical possibilities for redemptive action. For this reason, a *ponderacion misteriosa*—a divine intervention in the realm of profane history—appears on the final page of *The Origin of German Tragic Drama*. Yet that intervention is now tied to the profane action of those who intrigue to affect a forsaken world. The *Origin* thus signals a major shift from the position sketched in the "Theological-Political Fragment" and elsewhere. History and redemption, materialism and messianism now meet at the extremes. And this conception of dialectics, fraught with difficulty as it was, would serve to produce some of Marxism's most profound meditations on bourgeois society and the problem of revolutionary agency.

PROFANE ILLUMINATIONS: DREAMS, SHOCKS, AND REVOLUTION

At the time Benjamin was preparing the *Trauerspiel* book for publication, he was also grappling with an artistic current which paralleled his efforts to link cultural criticism and redemption: surrealism. Like Benjamin, the surrealists had come to embrace communism as the political answer to the crisis of bourgeois society, but they, too, feared that Communist membership might compromise their artistic work. In late 1925 and throughout 1926, Andre Breton and his associates debated joining the Communist Party of France (PCF); indeed Breton did briefly join the PCF in 1927.[43]

Part of what held many surrealists back from joining the Communists was their conviction that the Communist Party had an inadequate theory of the emergence of revolutionary subjectivity, one in which proletarian rebellion would grow more or less automatically out of the experience of work under capitalism. For Breton, however, the capitalist labor process with its routinized structures of experience constituted an obstacle rather than a stimulus to revolution. The emergence of revolutionary agency, of a manifest desire for radical change, required the unchaining (*désenchainement*) of people from the routines of bourgeois life. The key was to discover modes of experience qualitatively different from the automatized structure of work. For this reason, the surrealists looked to a whole gambit of experiences beyond the normal and the everyday—dreaming, intoxication, aimless wandering, junk collecting—as sites where repressed libidinal energies might be freed for revolution.[44]

Benjamin was powerfully attracted to the surrealist position. His 1929 essay, "Surrealism, The Last Snapshot of the European Intelligentsia," praised Breton and his colleagues for their effort "to win the energies of intoxication for the revolution."[45] Benjamin was also drawn to the surrealist emphasis on dreams as an alternative mode of experience to the conscious habits of daily life. Yet surrealism erred, in his view, in attempting simply to invert the relationship between dreams and waking life by dethroning consciousness and elevating the dream. In Freudian terms, surrealism proposed to replace the rational with the irrational, reality with the dream, the ego with the id. But Benjamin remained closer to Freud, albeit a fairly radical version of Freud, and to his own dialectic of extremes by trying to bring dreams and waking life into contact with one another. In thinking through the role of dreams in the constitution of revolutionary experience, Benjamin embarked on an immensely fruitful attempt to plunder psychoanalysis for revolutionary purposes. But before making this move, he attempted to find other solutions to the problem of redemption in/from capitalist society. The first of these came in "One-Way Street" which bears the marks of his encounter with surrealism.

"One-Way Street" represents Benjamin's first real effort to create a literary mode appropriate to his revolutionary commitments. The book begins by announcing its break with established traditions of cultural criticism. Benjamin repudiates the "universal gesture of the book" and embraces "the inconspicuous forms" of literature which bridge action and writing—"leaflets, brochures, articles, and placards."[46] Traditional criticism is dead, he declares, and only "fools" lament its decay. Such criticism was "a matter of correct distancing," its practice required that the critic step back from the cultural scene and establish an adequate perspective on things. Today, however, distance has been dissolved. The commodity form penetrates all human relations and practices. Independent literary work is disappearing alongside craft production; each is being conquered by capital. In the bourgeois society of the twentieth century where capital reigns supreme, where corporate newspapers and publishing houses dominate literary production, all writing is a form of advertising (OWS, 476). No longer inhabiting a realm of detached contemplation, literature is now tied to action. Instead of bemoaning this situation, the radical critic must embrace it in the hope of creating slogans and placards which, rather than moving people to purchase and consume, might mobilize them for revolution.

The modern critic finds herself in a world reminiscent of that inhabited by the baroque dramatists. In a powerful section of the book subtitled "Imperial Panorama, A Tour Through the German Inflation," Benjamin analyzes the pathologies of a society of near-total reification. The German Imperial Panorama offers up a modern "petrified, primordial landscape" of ruination where decay at the top of society is destroying the bases of life: "in this society the picture of imbecility is complete: uncertainty, indeed perversion, of vital instincts; and impotence, indeed decay, of the intellect. This is the condition of the entire bourgeoisie." Because "money stands ruinously at the center of every vital interest" meaningful human intercourse is disintegrating: "The freedom of conversation is being lost. If, earlier, it was a matter of course in conversation to take interest in one's interlocutor, now this is replaced by inquiry into the cost of his shoes or of his umbrella." As the commodity form infiltrates all aspects of social life, human relations are completely instrumentalized as are our relations with the natural world. Whereas objects in the natural world were once alive to us,

today "warmth is ebbing from things." Indeed, bourgeois society "has so dena-
tured itself through necessity and greed that it can now receive the gifts of
nature only rapaciously . . . the earth will be impoverished and the land will yield
bad harvests" (OWS, 451, 451–52, 453, 454, 455). The other side of the decay
of our relations with nature and with people is the shriveling of psychic life. As
meaning evaporates from our outer lives, inner life is impoverished. This is why
the great writers of the nineteenth century focus on "the horror of apartments."
They suspect that people are dying in these spaces, that murder is being committed. In the detective novel, which begins in this era with Edgar Alan Poe,
"the bourgeois interior . . . fittingly houses only the corpse" (OWS, 446–47).

In this situation, where death and decay are omnipresent, the traditional
book is absurd. Serious writing now consists in a new effort to "pile up fragments ceaselessly." The task is to improvise, to experiment, to use montage
effects; to juxtapose advertisements, dreams, images of childhood, fragments of
history and fiction in order to create allegories of a society suffocating beneath
the crushing weight of commodities and money. This requires a new mode of
writing oriented to profane illumination of a disintegrating bourgeois order.
Under the influence of both the surrealists and Freud, Benjamin identifies two
types of experience which might open onto these moments of profane illumination: dreams and memories of childhood.[47]

Dream-images and descriptions of dreams punctuate the text of "One-Way
Street" (445, 448, 455, 467). Yet, whereas the surrealists simply valorized dreams
as the alternative form of experience appropriate to the liberation of intoxicating
energies, Benjamin stayed closer to Freud (and to his own dialectic of extremes)
in seeking to bring dream-life and waking consciousness into contact with one
another. While dream elements were crucial to moments of illumination, they
were not illuminating in and of themselves. For this reason, in opposition to the
surrealists, Benjamin cautioned against trying to recount dreams prior to waking
up. Just as Freud had insisted on the importance of transforming the involuntary
ideas of the dream into voluntary ones by acts of remembering and interpreting,
Benjamin too argues that dreams need to be interpreted with certain techniques
of waking life: "only from the far bank, from broad daylight, may dream be
addressed from the superior vantage of memory." In the same spirit, he polemicizes
against the surrealist notion of automatic writing where the writer tries to short-
circuit consciousness by writing so quickly that the mind cannot keep up. "The
more circumspectly you delay writing down an idea," retorts Benjamin, "the
more maturely developed it will be" (OWS, 445, 458).[48]

Benjamin's approach to dreams demarcates his dialectic of extremes from
the surrealist dialectic of inversion. While he does turn to dreams for elements
of experience which might break through the reified structures of bourgeois
consciousness, he insists that dreams must be translated into revolutionary energy by a kind of corporeal knowledge which enlightens *and* activates: "Omens,

presentiments, signals pass day and night through our organism like wave impulses. To interpret them or to use them: that is the question. The two are irreconcilable. Cowardice and apathy counsel the former, lucidity and freedom the latter." Benjamin here counterposes interpretation and action. With Lukacs, he seeks a theory tied to *praxis*. The task of revolutionary enlightenment, he writes in his essay on surrealism, "can no longer be performed contemplatively" (S, 191). The great error of philosophy is that it tries to grasp what is nonconceptual—the sensuous material world, human practical activity, and the language of things—by means of concepts. Real knowledge, a knowledge capable of arriving at truths, involves the destruction of the contemplative standpoint (and the false totalities it creates) in those moments of illumination when truth grips individuals to the core of their being. The challenge is not to ponder dreams as mere pieces of information, but to experience them transformatively, as forms of profane illumination. And this requires a bodily knowledge, a mode of knowing which begins and ends within corporeal life: "To turn the threatening future [depicted in the omen or the dream—[DM] into a fulfilled 'now,' the only desirable telepathic miracle, is a work of *bodily presence of mind*" (OWS, 483, author's emphasis).

"One-Way Street" seeks a new mode of knowledge-experience, a radical praxis in which the body becomes the site of a transformative knowing that arises through physical action—a revolutionary practice, in other words animated by a "bodily presence of mind." The final section of the book, entitled "To the Planetarium," addresses this problem with an overwhelming urgency. Benjamin opens this section by contrasting the ancient ecstatic experience of the cosmos with the modern "optical connection to the universe." Whereas moderns look upon the world as a detached object of contemplation, the ancients felt the cosmos ecstatically, as something which shook them to the depths of their existence. The ecstatic experience has not entirely disappeared, however. Like everything which is repressed, it returns—and with increasing vengeance. Nowhere was this clearer than during the war "which was an attempt at new and unprecedented commingling with cosmic powers." The Great War signaled immense extensions of the human body, new corporeal contacts with hitherto unknown parts of the planet: "Human multitudes, gases, electrical forces were hurled into the open country, high-frequency currents coursed through the landscape, new constellations rose in the sky, aerial space and ocean depths thundered with propellers, and everywhere sacrificial shafts were sunk into Mother Earth." This fantastic burst of technology prefigured a new kind of ecstatic contact with the cosmos. But due to "the lust for profit of the ruling class" who control it, "technology betrayed man." As a result—and here Benjamin's argument resonates with fidelity to Marx—the staggering growth of new productive forces within the bounds of capitalist social relations has brought things to a crisis point where technological extensions of our bodies threaten to eliminate bodily

life itself. Our historical moment thus consists in the collision of extreme possibilities: either a catastrophe of planetary proportions, or a new ecstatic mode
of communal contact with nature. The former was prefigured in the war that
broke out in 1914, while "the revolts that followed it were the first attempt of
mankind to bring the new body under its control" (OWS, 486–87). Benjamin
arrives a decade later at the perspective articulated by Rosa Luxemburg during
World War I: that the choice confronting humanity is socialism or barbarism.[49]
And, like Luxemburg, he looks to "the power of the proletariat" as the key to
social regeneration. Yet, for Benjamin, the socialist revolution will not happen
unless the proletariat is "gripped to the very marrow" by the new cosmic powers
which have been created. And this involves a radical transformation of our
relationship to our bodies and their technological extensions, a revolutionary
process that, as he puts it elsewhere, undertakes "to release the body from traditional collectives and to insert it into new ones."[50]

At just this point, Benjamin pulls his text to a halt. Unlike some commentators, I do not read him as advancing here a crudely materialist position in
which "material processes must somehow penetrate the ideological veil" of bourgeois society.[51] Benjamin does not say revolutionary consciousness will be produced automatically by the collision of technology with old forms of experience.
Indeed, the convulsive movements of the new body-technology nexus, the new
physis, might just as easily culminate in an even more catastrophic war. Benjamin's
problem is that he has not developed a theory as to how "bodily presence of
mind" is to be created. How is a proletariat caught up in the world of bourgeois
decay, a world of impoverished, instrumentalized experience, to grasp the redemptive possibilities of a world in ruins? This problem, I suggest, preoccupied
him for the rest of his life, and comprised the starting point for his famous (and
famously unfinished) Arcades Project. But in grappling with this issue—the
problem of revolutionary subjectivity—Benjamin must have felt the need to
further clarify his relationship to surrealism. And in so doing, he posed some
fundamental problems about experience, memory, language, and dreams which
were to shape his work in decisive ways.

DREAMS, LANGUAGE, AND THE UNCONSCIOUS: TOWARD A THEORY OF EXPERIENCE

The dilemma of Western Marxism concerns how oppressed people are to make
a leap into the realm of freedom. Put simply, how are unfree people to free
themselves? How are they to become capable of an act of self-liberation? In an
important sense, crucial texts in Western Marxism—Gramsci's *Prison Notebooks*,
the surrealists' theory of revolt, and Benjamin's Arcades Project—all respond to
this problem. In the first instance, Benjamin tackled the dilemma frontally.
Following the lead of the baroque dramatists, he sought intimations of redemp-

tion in the very midst of decay and ruin. By destroying myths of reconciliation, by highlighting the separation of the empirical historical world from a redeemed state of truth and beauty, Benjamin sought to depict a barren historical land-scape upon which human actors could write new meanings. But, while this route allowed him to bring together his commitments to materialism and messianic time, it evaded the problem of how human agents immersed in the realm of the profane were to develop an emancipatory practice, how they were to discover a capacity for freedom.

Surrealism was important in this regard because it brought back "a radical concept of freedom" to the European Left. In setting out "to win the energies of intoxication for the revolution," surrealism promoted a "loosening of the self" which is necessary to the revolutionary project (S, 189). Sharing the surrealist conviction that the ordinary modes of experience in capitalist society inhibit, rather than generate, revolutionary consciousness, Benjamin, too, sought to ex-plode bourgeois subjectivity. In contrast to the effects of narcotics or religion, however, the loosening of bourgeois subjectivity required a "profane illumina-tion," a sort of revelatory experience in which the subject finds herself in a radically new, strange, and intoxicating relationship to the world (not simply outside it), one that resonated with older, more practical and playful, modes of being in the world. Yet, while they had posed the problem of freedom and experience, the surrealists were not always equal to it. Indeed, Benjamin criti-cizes Breton and Louis Aragon for their mysticism and irrationalism, for an obsession with omens and fortunetelling which leaves them in "the humid backroom of spiritualism."[52]

Where then do the surrealists more appropriately locate the energies of intoxication? Benjamin leaves no doubt about the matter. Breton, he writes, "was the first to perceive the revolutionary energies that appear in the 'outmoded,' in the first iron constructions, the first factory buildings, the earliest photos, the objects that have begun to be extinct, grand pianos, the dresses of five years ago, fashionable restaurants when the vogue has begun to ebb from them" (S, 181). But what does it mean to speak of such things as containing "revolutionary energies?" While he is vague on the matter, it seems clear that Benjamin shared the surrealist notion (derived from Freud) that such items were heavily invested with libidinal energies. All these sorts of things—old buildings, photos, dresses, and restaurants—were once objects of intense desire. In some cases, they are no longer even repositories of exchange value, as they do not circulate on the market. And even where they still function within the exchange economy (as with a formerly fashionable restaurant), they are no longer objects of excitement, the vogue having "begun to ebb from them." Yet, while they are not objects of current libidinal investment, something of the erotic energies with which they were once invested continues to resonate. Consequently, these things are decay-ing fragments of desire still capable of touching our memories and disappoint-ments. As Breton puts it in the *Manifesto of Surrealism* (1924), a marvelous object "partakes in some obscure way of a sort of general revelation only the fragments of which come down to us: they are the romantic *ruins*, the modern *mannequin*, or any other symbol capable of affecting the human sensibility for a period of time."[53]

In this formulation, Benjamin found bourgeois society presented in the motifs of baroque drama—as a landscape of ruins and corpses (mannequins) littered with fragments of redemption, broken bits of eroticized objects that might be reassembled by a form of dream recollection. If commodities could be treated as baroque ruins, then this meant a new orientation on the recent past of capitalism (which is the goal of the Arcades Project). And this new focus on the recent past returned Benjamin to some fundamental considerations on time. Instead of seeking a point where messianic time might erupt into history, he now found himself searching for a way to awaken the past within the present by bringing its dreams to consciousness. And this meant "constructing" the past as a stimulus to political action, rather than trying to know it contemplatively. Indeed, the surrealist "trick by which the world of things is mastered," he claimed, comes down to substituting "a political for a historical view of the past" (S, 182). This requires treating time not in terms of a temporal flow, but, rather, spatially—by bringing political moments (particularly failed revolutionary ones) from past and present together on stage in order to construct an image of history as a site of unrealized revolutionary possibilities. The field of political action is "a sphere of images and, more concretely, of bodies," not a site of contemplative critique. But "the revolutionary intelligentsia" has failed to grasp this; as a result of having proceeded contemplatively, through rational explanation of the ills of capitalism, it has failed to "make contact with the proletarian masses." In a move beyond "One-Way Street," creating the appropriate political images is now identified as the mediating moment in the body-technology relation necessary to mobilize revolutionary energies: "Only when in technology body and image so interpenetrate that all revolutionary tension becomes bodily collective innervation, and all the bodily innervations become revolutionary discharge, has reality transcended itself to the extent demanded by the *Communist Manifesto*" (S, 192). Two things deserve note here. First, Benjamin's concept of transcendence has been reconciled with his materialism: it is now reality which will transcend itself. Second, the libidinal energies necessary to revolution must be fueled by images, body-images so to speak, which disrupt the consciousness produced by a reified world. In helping him define the problem of images and their relation to the past, Benjamin's engagement with surrealism thus returned him to his earlier concerns with language, memory, and the unconscious.

Perhaps it is not surprising, then, that one of Benjamin's next essays was on Marcel Proust and his *Remembrance of Things Past* (*A la Recherche du temps perdu*, more recently, and more appropriately, translated as *In Search of Lost Time*). For Proust set himself the task of reconstructing childhood experience in all its concrete, sensuous particularities. Benjamin alludes to this, and to his new concern with images that reach into the past, in calling his essay "The Image of Proust." As the title suggests, his concern is twofold: to examine Proust's images, and to construct his own image of Proust. Benjamin is especially interested in Proust's notion of involuntary recollection (*mémoire involuntaire*) which, he says, requires a kind of forgetting. Involuntary recollection requires a rupture with the "purposeful remembering" of waking life.[54] As a purposive member of society I remember to pay my rent, arrive at work on time, keep my appointment with the taxation office, pick up my children from school. Involuntary recollection of the sort in which Proust excels involves forgetting these things; it requires eluding my everyday consciousness so that buried memories might seize me as they do when I sleep. Such memories come as jolts, each one carrying "a painful shock of rejuvenation" as "the past is reflected in a dewy fresh 'instant'" (IP, 211). Proust's memories are saturated with longings for happiness, whose locus is childhood. Indeed, the secret of Proust's images is the "blind, senseless, frenzied quest for happiness" which derived from his childhood (IP, 212). Yet for Benjamin, emancipation from the reified world of the everyday does not involve a simple valorization of childhood. After all, childhood revolves around a fundamental ambiguity. "There is," he writes, "a dual will to happiness, a dialectics of happiness: a hymnic and an elegiac form. The one is the unheard of, the unprecedented, the height of bliss; the other, the eternal repetition, the eternal restoration of the original, the first happiness." Proust, he maintains, is devoted to the latter, to elegiac happiness. This is both his strength and his weakness. His strength because it commits him fanatically to the pursuit of childhood desires, and his weakness because it traps him in a compulsion to repeat rather than to connect past desires with action in the present. Nevertheless, Proust's profound grasp of the sensuous texture of memory, of the way the scent of food can awaken a memory long forgotten, points toward Benjamin's notion of corporeal images. In Proust he finds, in other words, a valiant attempt at depicting "the entire muscular activity of the intelligible body" (IP, 214). And childhood occupies a privileged position in that endeavor.

We can see this by returning to the issue I postponed while discussing "One-Way Street": Benjamin's treatment of childhood. In that work, Benjamin plunges us into childhood experience, he strives to make us feel the world as a child does. Childhood experiences of reading, of time, of touch, of carousels, of collecting, and of hiding come to life in his text. But more than anything else it is *mimesis*, the act of imaginatively entering into material things, becoming one with them in order to acquire their properties *and* impart new meanings to them, that defines all such experiences. The child, he writes:

> knows all the hiding places in the apartment. . . . Here he is enclosed in the material world. It becomes immensely distinct, speechlessly obtrusive. . . . The dining table under which he is crouching turns him into a wooden idol in a temple whose four

pillars are the carved legs. And behind a door, he himself *is* the door—wears it as his heavy mask, and like a shaman will bewitch all those who unsuspectingly enter. (OWS, 465)

Children's play becomes a model of redemptive experience. Radically different from the routine instrumentalism of capitalist labor, play mends some of the broken strands which once tied together humans and nature, people and material objects. Children's play returns the warmth to things, restores the magic to matter, and provides a reentry into the language of things. In so doing, it reestablishes a mimetic relationship to the world. Since "play is always liberating," children are "representatives of Paradise."[55] Benjamin does not advocate a Proustian return to childhood, however. Like Freud, he believes it is vital to grow up. But truly growing up entails relaxing the repressions built up during childhood in order to reclaim the child's aspirations for happiness from the vantage point of a mature adult. Genuine maturity redeems childhood experience.

Benjamin's reflections on his own childhood in "A Berlin Chronicle" (1932) constitute a further refinement of his deliberations on memory and images. And now language returns as a repository of past meanings: "Language shows clearly that memory is not an instrument for exploring the past but its theater. It is the medium of past experience, as the ground is the medium in which dead cities lie." The "real treasure" hidden within the depths of memory are "images, severed from all earlier associations, that stand—like precious fragments or torsos in a collector's gallery—in the prosaic rooms of our later understanding."[56] Whereas autobiography has to do with the flow of time, memory-images have to do with spaces, with "moments and discontinuities" which come "in a flash, with the force of an illumination." Words can trigger these memory-images, those moments of rupture in the flow of narrative time, where discontinuities burst forth. Or, more accurately, some words can—those "that exist on the frontier between two linguistic regions, of children and of adults" (BC, 28, 30, 35). Benjamin is clearly working here with a Freudian model of the mind. Just as there is a conscious level of everyday waking existence where the mind weaves a seamless narrative and censors out repressed and unfulfilled desires, so there is an unconscious level which stores those images, rooted in childhood wishes, which would disrupt this narrative, images which bring together past and present in the theater of memory and leave their traces in language and dreams. To bring these images to consciousness requires shocks which destabilize the structures of waking life and enervate the body: "while our waking, habitual, everyday self is involved actively or passively in what is happening, our deeper self rests in another place and is touched by the shock, as is the little heap of magnesium powder by the flame of the match. It is to this immolation of our deepest self in shock that our memory owes its most indelible images" (BC, 57). As in photography, the memories which make up our deepest self are preserved through flashes that leave their imprint on the unconscious.[57] But, as I have noted, they also leave their traces in words. This claim greatly enriched Benjamin's theory of images and stimulated his most profound meditations on human language, "On the Mimetic Faculty" (1933).

"On the Mimetic Faculty" is Benjamin's most original contribution to a materialist theory of language and he seems to have recognized as much.[58] The text is in many respects a powerful reworking of central themes of "On Language as Such" from the standpoint of his new anthropological materialism. Rather than beginning with the biblical account of the primordial unity of God, man, and nature, Benjamin now starts with nature itself. "Nature creates similarities," he writes, "one need only think of mimicry."[59] In fact, as children's play reveals, human beings possess this mimetic capacity to the highest degree. In modern society the mimetic faculty appears to be in a state of decay; one finds only "minimal residues" of the "magical correspondences and analogies that were familiar to ancient peoples." Nevertheless, we may be witnessing more of a displacement of mimetic activity than its outright decay, Benjamin hints, since we can now locate in language a reserve of "non-sensuous similarities" (OMF, 334).

The new and difficult concept of non-sensuous similarities was crucial for Benjamin's new theory of language, as it was for the major study of bourgeois culture on which he would shortly embark. Compared to the mimetic properties of language, sensuous similarities are not especially mysterious: we observe them when a child pretends to be a tiger, a truck, or a baby; when someone stands still in the dark like a tree in order to remain unseen; or when I make a throwing gesture with my arm to urge someone to toss the rock or ball now. In all such cases the human body is the material medium of sensuous similarities. Alongside such cases, there are also forms of non-sensuous similarity, similarities not expressed overtly through the body—and these are stored in language. Here Benjamin employs the idea of a sort of *linguistic unconscious*, a hidden dimension of language which does not manifest itself in the ordinary course of communicative interaction. The fundamental connection of humans to the world, he seems to suggest, is a sensuous, even erotic one. But capitalism represses this sensuous relationship—which manifests itself most obviously in the play of children—and interposes thoroughly instrumentalized relations. However, just as infantile desires live on in hidden and distorted form in the behavior of adults in bourgeois society, so the corporeal impulses at the root of *mimesis* assume hidden forms within language.[60] It is through language, after all, that we consciously connect ourselves to the world of objects. And traces of our desire for a fuller, more sensuous relationship with the world mark the very words we use.

In the face of thoroughgoing commodification and instrumentalization of the relations between humans and nature, in other words, *mimesis* takes refuge in language. Benjamin has in mind here something more than the phenomenon of onomatopoeia, where the very sound of a word (like "crack") imitates its referent. He suggests that words which lack such obvious resemblances to their referents, even written words, carry traces of non-sensuous similarities. By way of illustration, his discussion of writing leads him to an explicit use of the concept of the unconscious. "Graphology has taught us," he says, "to recognize in handwriting images what the unconscious of the writer conceals in it." But in fact all language contains unconscious images that the speaker/writer means to conceal. Just as analysands in psychoanalysis must find that sleep-like, freely associative state in which to read their own dream-images, slips of the tongue and the like, so a radically materialist theory must approach language with similar intent: to divine the non-sensuous similarities it expresses in distorted form. In this respect, Benjamin seems to be working with Freud's distinction between the manifest and the latent content of the dream-image. Just as the latent content of the dream is carried within its manifest form (which requires a special kind of critical reading), "the mimetic element in language can, like a flame, manifest itself only through a bearer. This bearer is the semiotic element." The dream often seems to be a reproduction of events from daily life which the dreamer uses to provide a coherent account. Critically read, however, this manifest content discloses repressed wishes which consciousness prefers to censor. In similar fashion, the overt content of language, its communicative message (the semiotic element), bears traces of the noncommunicable (the desire for a mimetic relationship with objects and beings in the world). Moreover, just as a psychoanalytic reading of dreams requires the memory flashes of the freely associative state, so a reading of language for traces of non-sensuous similarities must attend to "flashes," to the image that "flits past" (OMF, 335).

A critical materialist theory of language thus requires a new form of the ancient art of reading "what was never written." The age-old practice of storytelling involved interaction among "words, soul, eye, and hand."[61] Yet, in abstracting from bodily practice, the instrumentalization of language and everyday life has repressed these corporeal connections. If these stores of libidinal energy are to be mobilized for revolutionary purposes, then language will have to be read in a radically noninstrumental way: in terms of what has not been spoken or written. Benjamin's later call to "liberate the enormous powers of history . . . which have been put to sleep in the 'once upon a time' of the classical historical narrative," is prefigured here in the idea of emancipating the repressed mimetic elements within language. And this requires a practice of constructing political images, a kind of mimetic activity in which history is remade in memory and the imagination as what it is not at the moment: a sphere of creative human activity.

BODY, HISTORY, AND MEMORY: BENJAMIN VERSUS HABERMAS AND BAKHTIN

In making these claims, I am directly challenging the influential reading of Benjamin's theory of language and *mimesis* developed by Jürgen Habermas whose principal concern is to demonstrate that Benjamin's writings, significant though they are, can offer no guide to political practice. Habermas maintains that Benjamin's thought was animated by a deeply conservative impulse to recuperate a fixed and unchanging store of semantic potential which was originally deposited in myth. The mythical experience of the world rests, after all, upon a primordial unity of people and nature, a set of mimetic practices in which the forces of nature are seen as continuous with the world of human beings. Habermas claims that Benjamin's critique involves a nostalgic effort to recover lingering traces of this ecstatic relation between human beings and nature (and among humans themselves) which is in danger of being forever extinguished.[62] To read him in this way, Habermas treats Benjamin's concepts of language and *mimesis* not as forms of *praxis* which create meaning, but as ways of expressing meanings laid down in the past. This interpretation is certainly consistent with the radical separation between language and labor that defines Habermas's own social theory. But in imposing the same dualistic separation on Benjamin, Habermas impoverishes and deradicalizes the latter's theory of language and *mimesis*. We can see this especially clearly when we return to that form of mimetic activity which is paradigmatic for Benjamin—children's play.

"One-Way Street," for instance, offers up images of play as an intensely mimetic and constructive process: we see children touching foods and letting them roll in their mouths, we see them picking flowers, catching butterflies, building arsenals and zoos in dresser drawers, becoming pieces of furniture, and so on (OWS, 464–66). In all these depictions, mimetic activity is creative and constructive. As Susan Buck-Morss puts it, for Benjamin, "children's cognition had revolutionary power because it was tactile, and hence tied to action, and because rather than accepting the given meaning of things, children got to know objects by laying hold of them and using them creatively, releasing from them *new* possibilities of meaning."[63] Benjaminian *mimesis* is not simply a relic of the past, of the age of myth; *mimesis* can no more come to an end for Benjamin than libido can for Freud. But, whereas it was once a manifest part of human behavior, it now occurs in latent and distorted forms. The mimetic activity we observe in children has, in modern capitalism, come to reside in art, technology, and language. But, like repressed wishes, *mimesis* has assumed disguises that need to be deciphered. That is the task of a particular kind of practice: one which tries to find points of entry into those (distorted) mimetic relations that lurk below the surface of things *in the present*. And this requires recuperating the mimetic activity at work in play and dream-life.

As a form of *praxis, mimesis* generates new meanings. And this has tremendous significance for Benjamin's theory of language. Whereas Habermas sets out to develop a theory of communicative action which ignores "nonverbalized actions and bodily expressions," Benjamin identifies these dimensions of language as decisive to a radically materialist orientation.[64] The bodily, the gestural, and the nonverbal are the largest domain of the mimetic element within language. This is why Benjamin singles out gesture as so crucial to the artistic innovations of Kafka and Brecht. For both of these authors, gesture breaks through the rarefied forms of language, it thrusts the body—whose presence is generally repressed within instrumentalized language—into the center of human life. "Kafka's entire work," claims Benjamin, "constitutes a code of gestures." Moreover, "each gesture is an event—one might even say a drama—in itself." Such gestures are dramatic because they shock modern man whose "body slips away from him," man whose body has become so alien that a cough erupts in him like a foreign creature, an animal.[65] The drama of gesture is an historical one—an index of what has been lost with the decorporealization of language and culture. It is instructive in this regard that Benjamin's program for a proletarian children's theater (which was to be the heart of a revolutionary educational experiment) focused on gesture as the key to disrupting contemplative knowledge and thereby assisting the body (and its mimetic activities) in overcoming the resistances built into rarefied language. "Action and gesture"—and through them "the radical release of play"—define the proletarian children's theater for Benjamin. Indeed, the children's performance, in inverting the relation between hand and head, is for a revolutionary culture what "Carnival was to the ancient cults"—the site where "everything is turned upside down."[66]

One of the reasons Benjamin responded so positively to the epic theater of Brecht had to do with the central role it accords gesture. On the epic stage, gestures serve to disrupt the flow of narrative, to break through the movement of time in order to illuminate that which the temporal flow effaces: "the dialectic which epic theatre sets out to present is not dependent on a sequence of scenes in time; rather, it declares itself in those gestural elements that form the basis of each sequence in time . . . in epic theatre the dialectic is not born of the contradiction between successive moments or ways of behaving, but of the gesture itself."[67]

Such gestures are dialectical because, by disrupting the flow of scenes and actions which recreate the time of everyday history, they cast light on the space of the body and its desires. In so doing, they give rise to "the dialectic at a standstill," the dramatic entry of that which has been repressed—body, Eros, *mimesis*—onto the stage. Gesture is the language of the body and things. Writing of the people of Naples, Benjamin claims that "the language of gestures goes further here than anywhere else in Italy. . . . Ears, nose, eyes, breast, and shoulders are signaling stations activated by the fingers. These configurations return in their fastidiously specialized eroticisms."[68] Yet this erotic language of gestures is slipping away from people in capitalist society. So alienated are we from nature, so strange have our bodies become, that these bases of life seem to belong only to animals. Thus, as Kafka knows, to investigate the past is to discover animals: "animals are the receptacles of the forgotten" (K, 132). Disruptive gestures, gestures which explode the flow of narrative, are designed to jolt us into awareness of what we have forgotten—just like Gregor Samsa's experience upon awakening in Kafka's *Metamorphosis* to discover that he has been transformed into a gigantic insect. Similarly, the enervated gestures of the early Mickey Mouse, by blurring the lines between human, animal, and machine, have the potential to shock viewers into a recognition of the great bodily energies they possess.[69] Gestures embody what language has forgotten, what lives on as its repressed dimension. *Contra* Habermas, the gestures employed by Kafka and Brecht do not reach back to a set stock of past meanings. "The gestures are found in reality," Benjamin insists, moreover, "they are found only in the reality of today."[70] For this reason, Benjamin focused his efforts not on the distant past, the time of myth, but, rather, on the time of capitalism which had reentered the age of myth.

In depicting Benjamin as an essentially nostalgic thinker, one for whom the claims of the past outweigh those of the future, Habermas fails to appreciate the dialectical conception of time that Benjamin found in a series of modernist writers, among them Freud.[71] In psychoanalysis, the past is not an object of simple remembrance and contemplation. Instead, it is an active force in the here-and-now. The past eludes fixity precisely because we relive it in the present, because we struggle with, reinterpret, and remake it. This is not to say that the past is infinitely malleable (psychoanalysis does not subscribe to the thesis of a facile postmodernism that there are no real events). It is to insist, however, that the past can take on new meaning—can become a different kind of force—in the present. We *are* decisively shaped by our pasts, but not rigidly determined by them. Psychoanalysis involves an intervention into the life-history of the individual, a disruption of the way in which the present has (thus far) been determined by the past—and the past by the present. Rather than something laid down once and for all, the past is a site of struggle *in the present*. In trying to remember the past in psychoanalysis, we do so not for its own sake but, rather, because the struggling adult can give a different meaning to events that overwhelmed and traumatized the child. Our relationship to the past is thus determined by our present needs—in particular the need to live healthier psychic lives by mending past wounds.

When we try to reconstruct the past by reinterpreting it from the standpoint of the healing adult we engage in a unique kind of remembering. We do not get free of the past by forgetting it. What has been banished from memory lives on in the unconscious, manifesting itself in the form of neuroses that mask their cause (forgotten traumas). "Wherever there is a symptom there is also an amnesia," writes Freud. This is why neurotics "cannot get free of the past."[72] True, we have to loosen the hold of the historical memory that represses much of the past. But this "forgetting," as with Proust, is about a deeper kind of remembering. What we have repressed, denied, and forgotten haunts us by exercising an unconscious power over us; it returns, albeit in disguised form—as symptoms that mask their underlying cause. Psychoanalysis thus involves a labor of remembrance, a struggle to overcome amnesia, to recall trauma, and to heal its wounds by bringing it to consciousness.

For Marx, too, recorded history has so far been an unconscious process, one driven by blind economic compulsions. The transition to the realm of freedom involves bringing these previously unconscious processes under conscious control. As for Freud, the growth of freedom involves taking over the forces of the past (in this case accumulated in powers of production) and learning to direct them consciously. This is precisely the approach to history that Benjamin advocates in his notes for his Arcades Project. But, like Freud, he believes this requires a difficult and therapeutic labor of remembrance that must continue "until all of the past has been brought into the present in a historic apocatastasis."[73] This labor of anamnesis entails disturbing struggles and collisions. As a character structure laid down in the past senses the traumas it has denied, a battle ensues between primitive impulses to deny and forget and conscious desires to remember, to understand, and to get better. Two different drives for happiness collide: one which seeks happiness through forgetting, the other which seeks it (and an escape from neurotic behavior) by recovering the past. Real insight, therapeutic leaps in self-understanding that overcome intense resistance, have an explosive character. Benjamin tries to capture this with his concept of "dialectics at a standstill." Convinced that revolutionary consciousness cannot arise as a more or less automatic process of daily life under capitalism, Benjamin sought to construct images that could trigger dialectical leaps out of routinized (and neurotic) forms of everyday behavior. But, as should now be clear, this did not entail a project designed simply to recuperate a fixed stock of past meanings. Instead, it involved a praxis through which the past could be remade in the present—by means of coming to a self-understanding which (as for Lukacs) would be self-transforming. Central to this project was the construction of *dialectical images* which, by bringing the past into a jarring relationship with the present, would quickly and dramatically illuminate the petrified landscape of past history. "An image," writes Benjamin, "is that in which the Then and the Now come together into a constellation like a flash of lightening. In other words: an image is dialectics at a standstill." Like a gesture in the epic play, the dialectical image destabilizes the flow of historical time, it uncovers something that the historical narrative represses, and it finds resources in the past for the struggles of the present. In blasting an epoch "out of the reified 'continuity of history,'" historical materialism, says Benjamin, "also blasts open the homogeneity of the epoch. It saturates it with *ecrasite*, i.e., the present" (N, 50, 64).

The struggles of the present transform the past by making a "moment of danger" in the here-and-now the context in which past meanings are reactivated and translated into the language of the present. This is what makes the past so crucial for Benjamin. So long as the ruling class succeeds in imposing its story, its continuous historical narrative, the oppressed will be unable to locate the energies they need for liberation. Just as the neurotic must overcome the resistances imposed by consciousness (and its narrative) in order to locate the frustrated desires for happiness that have produced traumas, so the oppressed class needs to remember (as-yet-unrealized) moments of upheaval, moments when those down below rose against their condition in an effort to realize their dreams of happiness, if they are to remake themselves and their history. The past must be redeemed because we cannot arrive at self-understanding without coming to see history thus far as a field littered with the debris of failed struggles for freedom, as a story of the denial and suppression of the most authentic desires of the oppressed (including the desires of those who came before us and whose past oppression lives on within us). Just as neurotics can be filled by a burning desire to change when they see their pasts as a junkyard of decaying hopes, so the oppressed class will be fired with energy for change if it comes to see history as a site of suffering, oppression and happiness denied. Self-understanding comes, if at all, in the recognition that our lives have been a series of failures and catastrophes, a recognition that can generate the drive to redeem the past by claiming happiness in the here and now. That is why history, for the historical materialist, is not an object of contemplation but a site of struggle to redeem past suffering: "history is not just a science but also a form of memoration (*eine Form des Eingedenkens*). What science has 'established,' memoration can modify. Memoration can make the incomplete (happiness) into something complete, and the complete (suffering) into something incomplete" (N, 61). And this is also why the angel of history, from Benjamin's final text, has its face turned "toward the past." If the cycle of repression is to be broken, it will require facing up to the catastrophe of the past, our pasts, which has piled "wreckage upon wreckage."[74]

Rather than the contemplation of something fixed once and for all, memoration is for Benjamin a constructive activity. It is simultaneously destructive and creative. Rather than an intact object waiting to be recovered, the past is a field of debris whose meaning remains to be constructed. And the revolutionary work of constructing images of the past involves the principle of montage: collecting seemingly insignificant bits and pieces, broken objects and fragments of the past that don't fit the narrative of the ruling class, and assembling them into dialectical images (N, 47, 48). This entails the destructive moment of breaking up the bourgeois historical narrative, shattering its homogeneity. As we have seen in Benjamin's theories of criticism and baroque drama, the truth of a work of art is something latent in it, something disguised by its manifest content, whose realization requires the destruction of its manifest form of appearance. The past, too, appears as a reified totality, a seamless object, which must be shattered if we are to locate fragments of redemption that can be reassembled into dialectical images. Benjamin believes this is the opportunity in the "tremendous shattering of tradition" that capitalism brings about.[75] True, the shattering of tradition has released immense forces of human destructiveness. But this was possible only because tradition contained barbarism. There is no way of separating redemption from barbarism short of completing the shattering of tradition; the attempt to reconstitute precapitalist tradition is the project of a reactionary modernism. The revolutionary task is to enter onto the ground of the destruction of tradition in the recognition that it is a battleground: between those who want to recreate myth by aestheticizing politics (the project of fascism)

and those who hope to politicize art (the project of revolutionary socialism).[76]
This is why Benjamin praises "the destructive character" who reduces what exists
"to rubble": only through the destruction of the past as a grand tradition—and
its reconstruction as a space of suffering, corpses, and debris—might redemption
be possible.[77]

This is not a call to invent whatever meaning for the past we prefer. We
cannot simply redefine a history of pain and oppression as one of pleasure and
liberation. This would be another exercise in forgetting, another effacement of
the suffering which has until now defined history. Benjamin insists upon a
solidarity with suffering as the precondition of the destructive/constructive
attitude toward the past.[78] Suffering is the truth of history, but so is the hidden
drive for happiness. According to the dialectic of extremes, we find the truth
of suffering only when it collides with its opposite: happiness. In constructing
images of history based upon collisions between suffering and dreams of happiness, Benjamin hoped to create images that might literally touch people and
provide a "bodily presence of mind." Again, the analogy with Freud's thought
is useful here. In psychoanalysis, we can never fully know "what really happened" in the past. But, we can know much of the truth about what happened
by the degree to which the psychoanalytic construction of the past is able to
"touch" the individual and assist her self-transformation. Psychoanalytic knowledge is palpable, corporeal; the struggling individual can feel its truths because
they both hurt and inspire.[79] Truth for psychoanalysis is practical, the truth
value of an analysis can only be demonstrated in the practice of the struggling
individual to change herself. "A psychoanalysis is not an impartial scientific
investigation," writes Freud, "but a therapeutic measure. Its essence is not to
prove anything, but merely to alter something."[80] Psychoanalysis shares this
orientation with Marxism. "The question whether objective truth can be attributed to human thinking is not a question of theory but is a *practical* question," says Marx. "Man must prove the truth, i.e., the reality and power, the
this-worldliness of his thinking in practice."[81] Similarly, for Benjamin the truth
of a dialectical construction of history does not reside in providing an accurate
depiction of everything that has happened but, rather, in its capacity to shake
up members of the oppressed class, to fuel their desire to change their situation. Dialectical images acquire truth value in the practice of revolutionary
transformation.

Rather than a romantic longing for the past as a repository of truths, Benjamin adopted the attitude of the junk collector: to grab hold of whatever decaying
things could be salvaged for constructive purposes. This is no easy task, however,
since the past has been constructed as the cultural site of the ruling class. In
recognizing the difficulties involved, Benjamin takes his distance from the more
optimistic attitude toward the past that we find in Bakhtin.

Like Benjamin, Bakhtin sees in language a sedimentation of meanings that
remain accessible to people in the present. Particular linguistic genres—espe-

cially the serio-comic ones—are the repositories of a stock of images (such as the rogue, the clown, and the fool) whose roots go back "into the depths of a folklore that preexists class structures."[82] Moreover, Bakhtin, too, believes that language is a space of memory: "A genre," he insists, "lives in the present, but always remembers its past, its beginning."[83] On top of this, what a genre remembers is not just a stock of formal meanings, but a whole social and material way of life. Since the "whole body" participates in language, a genre includes gesture, intonation, indeed the entire attitude to the world that is embodied in a style of speech.[84] Finally, Bakhtin maintains that meanings are never finalized, that it is always possible to develop and extend them: "There is neither a first nor a last word. . . . Even past meanings, that is those born in the dialogue of past centuries . . . will always change (be renewed) in the process of subsequent, future development of the dialogue. . . . Nothing is absolutely dead: every meaning will have its homecoming festival."[85]

Despite the many obvious points of convergence with Benjamin here, there remain significant divergences.[86] Bakhtin, after all, promotes an unrelentingly optimistic linguistic populism in which the past (via language) offers a treasure chest of carnivalesque genres capable of undoing the monologic discourses and practices of the ruling class. As for Benjamin, the past provides resources for the struggles of the present. But, whereas for Bakhtin the accessibility and integrity of the past are not problematic, for Benjamin they are fraught with the greatest difficulties. And this brings us to Bakhtin's failure to develop a cultural theory appropriate to capitalism. As Benjamin recognizes, capitalism destroys tradition. By reshaping everything according to its own imperatives, it wreaks havoc on old cultural forms. At the same time, it raids images from the past, repackages them, and integrates them into its homogeneous version of past history. In so doing, it presents capitalism as continuous with the very cultural resources it has commodified and debased. Bourgeois society thus creates a mythical sort of historical consciousness—one in which all of history is seen as culminating in the newest cultural forms of the commodity (e.g. technology, architecture, advertising, fashion). Anything that resists this heroic totalizing narrative of the capitalist market—alternate forms of social life, records of suffering and barbarism, episodes of struggle and resistance—is repressed. The past becomes identical with the history of the commodity form. And this presents an enormous problem for remembrance. As Adorno once observed, all reification is a form of forgetting. In the mythico-historical consciousness of modern capitalism, systematic, organized, and compulsive forgetting is the order of the day. We are expected and encouraged to forget the past promises of commodities to bring us enjoyment and of politicians to make life wonderful. For this reason, the treasure chest of cultural resources described by Bakhtin is neither intact nor readily accessible: no longer intact because capitalism has driven a bulldozer over precapitalist cultures and forms of experience; and not readily accessible because in turning everything, including the treasures of the past, into commodities, into petrified objects severed from a connection to past traditions, capitalism annihilates memory. Remembrance, a critical memoration that breaks through the homogenizing forms of bourgeois historical consciousness, is thus the trickiest of operations. It requires blasting open the reified continuum of this mythico-historical consciousness in order to find temporal fissures where fragments of the past might converge with the needs of the present in images that disrupt the mythical structure of experience. This is why Benjamin recommends *dialectics at a standstill*: he hopes to break through reification and to destabilize the apparent continuity of history by making time stand still. By bringing bits of the past onto the stage of the present—a procedure designed to let us glimpse those discontinuous moments when the oppressed have disrupted the "natural" order of things only to be defeated—he hopes to reveal the painful (and potentially therapeutic) truth about the present: that we live in the midst of immense suffering that need not be.

These psychoanalytic dimensions of Benjamin's theory of history and memory give it considerable strengths lacking in Bakhtin's approach. To begin with, Benjamin's theory resists naïve optimism. A simple celebration of the popular against the official will not do since the carnivalesque impulse has been largely appropriated by the commodity. At the same time, Benjamin's commitment to the Freudian notion of the unconscious means that what has been repressed—in this case whole strata of "forgotten" meanings—are nonetheless recuperable. But this requires a difficult practice of recovery which disrupts the experiential forms that dominate everyday life. Agreeing that the carnivalesque lives within language, he insists nonetheless that it has been almost thoroughly commodified, that capital appropriates the erotic longings that erupt in carnival—for food, laughter, sex, togetherness, and community—in order to sell us commodities which regularly betray desire. As with the neurotic who experiences a compulsion to do self-destructive things, capitalism produces a systematic kind of behavior, a deeply ingrained repetition compulsion. The critical task is to liberate the carnivalesque from the commodity, to free desire from its attachment to a compulsion (the eternal return of the commodity). As was the case for the baroque dramatists, however, the one can only be found by entering into the closest contact with the other. Just as the *Trauerspiel* immersed us in devastation and ruin, so Benjamin will take us to the very heart of the petrified landscape of the commodity.

DREAMING OF COMMODITIES: FASHION, FETISHISM, AND UTOPIA

Benjamin intended his unfinished Arcades Project to develop a series of dialectical images designed to break the spell of bourgeois myth.[87] He hoped to conjure up the dreams generated during the childhood of capitalism—the nineteenth century, the era of the first working-class revolutions and the epoch when commodified consumption was significantly extended to the working class—in order to help us awake from our sleepwalk through modern history. These dreams assumed their purest form in Paris, "the capital of the nineteenth century." Benjamin's analysis of these nineteenth-century Parisian dreams involves a series of profound meditations upon language, the body, and the politics of liberation that return us once more to the intersection of Marxism and psychoanalysis in his thought.

In the middle of the 1930s, Benjamin came to see the decisive importance of Marx's concept of commodity fetishism to his own analysis of bourgeois culture.[88] Because workers in capitalist society do not own or control the means of production, argued Marx, their livelihood (and productive life-activity) depends upon the movement of blind and anonymous economic forces (commodities, money, prices, profits, etc.) that elude their control. Similarly, in an unplanned, competitive market system, the survival of individual units of capital (and the well-being of capitalists) equally depends upon the movements of the market— the way in which it prices goods and distributes profits. As a result, alienation and reification inhere in the total structure of modern society. For its inhabitants, "their own movement within society has for them the form of a movement made by things, and these things, far from being under their control, in fact control them."[89] This is why commodity fetishism is not an illusion for Marx, but, rather, an objective social process in which the movement of things (commodities) really does regulate the lives of human beings.

Benjamin recognizes the brilliance with which Marx discovered in capitalism the same dialectical reversal that preoccupied the baroque dramatists: the materialization of human beings, their reduction to objects, and the corresponding animation of things. He finds in Marx a profound reading of capitalism as a self-propelling life of the dead, and of its history as a process made by the blind movement of things. He then sought to extend this analysis by developing the psychoanalytic dimension of commodity fetishism. In so doing, he signaled three significant, and interrelated, moves: first, his break with rationalist models of working-class enlightenment; second, his conviction that workers are not simply duped by capitalism but, rather, are erotically invested in commodities; and, third, his notion that awakening from the spell of the commodity will require submitting to its charms with one eye open, so as to be able to awaken and remember what it was that entranced us—and thereby to dislodge desire from its attachment to the commodity form.

As I have indicated above, Benjamin doubted the power of traditional modes of enlightened critique with their contemplative model of the relationship of human consciousness to the social order. Like the surrealists, he believed little is gained by instructing workers that capitalism is an irrational system in which people are dominated by things. Instead, the problem is to organize forms of experience that generate a new kind of bodily knowledge. Not that Benjamin rejected rational critique. He believed, however, that critical experience had to foster a sort of *corporeal reason*, one that fuses the body and the intellect in a radically new configuration where reason attends to—indeed follows—the messages emanating from the body, since "only the body can generate presence of mind."[90] In order to disrupt the unconscious connections that tie people to a commodified society, reason must connect with images that originate in the unconscious, a suggestion that probably owes something to Freud's contention that visual images are fundamental to memories of childhood.[91] Benjamin's strategy thus entails trying to enter the nexus of erotic investments that people make in commodities in order to undo them from the inside (since they cannot be undone from the outside)—a strategy that involves capturing imagistically the childhood wishes (both individual and collective) that attach to commodities. To this end, he sought a new mode of revolutionary critique, one that is practical and therapeutic in nature, one that lets the irrational speak so that it might be transformed into corporeal reason.

Benjamin's project begins from the premise that, rather than disenchanting the world by replacing myth with science, capitalism has in fact activated tremendous mythic forces. Instead of adhering to gods, however, these mythic powers now pertain to things. In bourgeois society myth is both profaned and strengthened. The fetishism of commodities produces the most amazing investment of symbolic powers and meanings in objects. However, the ancient problem of finding an intermediary link between gods and humans has disappeared in capitalist society. The gods—commodities—are in our midst, we are forever surrounded by them. Consequently, daily life in capitalist society is a sort of sleepwalking, a blind movement through a dream world of fetishes and phantasms. Store windows, shopping malls, billboards, and advertisements all conspire to tell us that happiness, love, meaning, intimacy, romance, sexual fulfillment, and community with others are just a purchase away. Moreover, these images join with primal longings to produce a dense inner world of commodified dream wishes. Every hour of every day, people attend to these wishes by making pilgrimages to the sites of the commodity fetish. These are their true places of worship. Commodities are worshipped as if they were forces of nature endowed with the very powers of life and death. "Capitalism was a natural phenomenon with which a new dream sleep fell over Europe," writes Benjamin, "and with it a reactivation of mythic powers."[92]

As we have seen, Benjamin aims to dissolve myth "into the space of history." But this is not a call to banish fetishes, to tear the veil of appearances off a concealed reality. Like Hegel and Marx, Benjamin sees the phenomenal forms of things as "necessary forms of appearance"—forms in which a reified society necessarily manifests itself in the very structure of human experience. Rather than treating appearances as veils to be pulled aside, dialectical critique for Benjamin involves entering into the heart of these appearances (dreams), to awaken from them, recollect them, and translate the wishes they contain into practical goals of historical action. He summarizes this project with the term *dialectics of awakening,* arguably his most original contribution to the Marxist theory of fetishism.

The dialectics of awakening starts from the Freudian premise that "a dream is a (disguised) fulfillment of a (suppressed or repressed) wish" (ID, 244). But Benjamin extends this claim to include the collective wishes of masses of people in capitalist society. And this is, as he well knew, a most difficult move.[93] He was convinced, however, that capitalism was distinguished by the creation of new modes of *mass* experience. Despite the bourgeois cult of individualism, people were in fact decreasingly individualized. As he put it in "One-Way Street": "A curious paradox: people have only the narrowest interest in mind when they act, yet they are at the same time more than ever determined in their behavior by the instincts of the mass" (OWS, 451). Benjamin took literally the idea of a mass culture of capitalism: masses of people desire the same commodity-images (including those of the culture industry) and invest them with roughly the same hopes. Bourgeois society produces, in short, a tremendous uniformity of desires and wishes, its inhabitants really do dream the same collective dreams. Again, Benjamin follows Freud in claiming that the dream "is continually trying to summon childhood back into reality and to correct the present day by the standard of childhood."[94] And in the case of capitalism, that period of childhood was the nineteenth century.

The opening section of Benjamin's sketch of his Arcades Project, called "Paris, Capital of the Nineteenth Century," is titled, appropriately, "Fourier, or the Arcades." The Paris arcades, after all, were the first real temples for mass viewing of commodities. Glass-enclosed walkways over rows of shops, they constituted "caverns of commodities," a self-contained sphere in which people could commune with the world of commodities—vicariously, through sight (and occasionally touch and smell) or directly, through the sociomaterial act of exchange. And Charles Fourier was the most visionary, the most dream-like of the early nineteenth-century social critics who extrapolated the possibilities of a new society of play and abundance without calling for the overthrow of capital.[95] Both the physical reality of the arcades and the utopian promises of Fourier speak to the enormous hopes aroused by capitalism as a new sociocultural order. Alongside new means of production, capitalism also produced new collective dreams:

> Corresponding in the collective consciousness to the forms of the new means of production which at first were still dominated by the old (Marx), are images in which the new is intermingled with the old. These images are wishful fantasies, and in them the collective seeks both to preserve and to transfigure the inchoateness of the social product and the deficiencies in the social system of production. In addition, these wish-fulfilling images manifest an emphatic striving for dissociation with the outmoded—which means, however, with the most recent past. These

tendencies direct the visual imagination, which has been activated by the new, back to the primeval past. In the dream in
which, before the eyes of each epoch, that which is to follow
appears in images, the latter appears wedded to elements from
prehistory, that is, of a classless society.[96]

This tremendously compressed passage requires some unpacking. To begin
with, Benjamin is saying that the emergence of new means of production gives
rise to hopes that the shortcomings of "the social system of production" might
be remedied by these productive forces themselves. Dreamers (like Fourier who
expresses the hopes of multitudes) desire a radical break with the way things
have been in the recent past. In order to construct images of a new social order,
they reach back (as all dreamers must) to their earliest images of happiness. And
in the case of human society, this means constructing images which draw upon
the experience of pre-class society, of a social order prior to class exploitation.
In this way, past and future converge in a utopian image that might be realized
in the present. Again, the similarity of Benjamin's discussion here with Freud's
conception of fantasy is striking. Fantasy, Freud wrote in "Creative Dreamers
and Day Dreaming,"

hovers, as it were, between three times—the three moments of
which our ideation involves. Mental work is linked to some current impression, some provoking occasion in the present which
has been able to arouse one of the subject's major wishes. From
there it harks back to a memory of an earlier experience (usually
an infantile one) in which this wish was fulfilled; and it now
creates a situation relating to the future which represents a
fulfillment of the wish. . . . Thus past, present and future are
strung together, as it were, on the thread of the wish that runs
through them.[97]

Why, then, is it mid-nineteenth-century Paris that looms so large for Benjamin? Two things are crucial here. First, Paris is the city of the world exhibition:
the world fairs of 1855, 1867, 1878, 1889, and 1900 were designed to entrance
the population with the wonder of commodities and new technologies, to give
them the "lesson of things."[98] Machines, electricity, photography were all enlisted
to generate awe at the immense powers of technology. In the process, the very
physiognomy of Paris was transformed in order to turn it into a city of the
commodity spectacle: the Grand Palais, Trocadero, the Eiffel Tower were all
built as part of the fairs of 1889 and 1900. In these exhibitions, the wishful
dreams of society for a leap into utopia were projected onto the wonders of
commodities, technology, and architecture. Consequently, these expositions were,
in Benjamin's words, "the sites of pilgrimages to the commodity fetish" (PC,

151). But this is only one side of the story. Paris was also, secondly, the site of the two most important working-class uprisings of the nineteenth century: the revolution of June 1848, and the upheaval of 1871 which created the workers' government of the Paris Commune. For Benjamin the Commune was especially important because it represented the moment when the workers' movement broke with Left republicanism—the idea that "the task of the proletarian revolution is to complete the work of 1789 hand in hand with the bourgeoisie"—and came to see a radical break, the establishment of a *workers'* state, as the revolutionary objective (PC, 160). These workers' revolutions were defeated, of course. But their memories, their spirits, continue to haunt the city—which is why that urban engineer, the Baron Georges Eugene Haussmann, pushed the working class out of the city core and into the suburbs (so as to make it more difficult for them to seize the city) and widened the streets (so that troops could be moved quickly to suppress rebellion and so that the erection of revolutionary barricades would be more difficult) (PC, 160). Paris is thus the site of both sides of the utopian dream-wishes generated within bourgeois society: the wish for liberation through commodities (embodied in the world fairs) and the wish for liberation from the rule of commodities (expressed in the failed workers' revolutions). The problem for the modern working class is that these wishes have become conflated as the commodity appropriates revolutionary dreams of a new dawn. The revolutionary physiognomy of Paris—the city of workers' revolution—has become overlaid with the phantasmagoria of commodities: "As a social formation, Paris is a counterimage to that which Vesuvius is as a geographic one: A threatening, dangerous mass, an ever-active June of the Revolution. But just as the slopes of Vesuvius, thanks to the layers of lava covering them, have become a paradisiacal orchard, so here, out of the lava of the Revolution, there bloom art, fashion, and festive existence as nowhere else."[99]

Paris comes to epitomize the dilemma of modern working-class consciousness. The emancipatory impulses of the working class—which have reached their highest forms of expression in this city—have been overlaid with "art, fashion, and festive existence," with a dazzling layer of commodities (and temples for their worship) which function as substitute objects for the gratification of revolutionary desires. It is not lost on Benjamin that the French state made a concerted effort to recruit workers (including foreign workers) to attend the World Fair of 1867 by distributing free tickets, nor that this occurred during the very year in which Marx's *Capital* was published. The incorporation of the working class into commodified culture had become an economic and political project for the ruling class. The fetishistic inversion by which desires for a society of freedom and solidarity became cathected onto commodities was therefore the central political and cultural problem animating the Arcades Project. Benjamin undertook, as a result, to delineate the processes by which the commodity comes to absorb the desire for revolution—so as to locate the gaps in this absorption, the places where the Revolution might still burst through the upper layers of the petrified landscape of bourgeois society. And this meant assisting our "awakening from the nineteenth century" so as to liberate our collective dreams from myth, to clarify and reconstruct them in the space of history as the conscious motives of a revolutionary project.

To accomplish this, Benjamin laid great emphasis on deconstructing the bourgeois cult of the new. In fact, immersion in novelty—which finds its highest expression in fashion—was to play a central role in the Arcades Project. For it was here that dialectical images could be produced: "As in the seventeenth century the canon of dialectical imagery came to be allegory, in the nineteenth it is novelty" (PC, 158). The comparison of fashion with allegory may at first seem far-fetched. But Benjamin believed that here, in fashion, capitalism brought extremes together in ways susceptible of dialectical inversion. Most significantly, fashion brought together images of Heaven and Hell.

The fashion industry is Hell for Benjamin because it is eternal torment. Fashion involves the endless production of novelty—the latest and greatest—which turns out to be nothing but the same thing (exchange value / the commodity) over and over again. Fashion is thus a sort of capitalist repetition compulsion. Just like the neurotic who keeps having the same bad relationship one time after another (each time disguised as something new), the consumer of fashion does the same thing repeatedly (buy the latest products) only to discover that the latest novelty is no different and no better than the last. In the name of an insatiable thirst for the new, fashion addicts us to the eternal return of the same. For this reason, fashion is the "indefatigable agent" of that compulsion for the new which is "the quintessence of false consciousness" in bourgeois society (PC, 158). Our conscious search for novelty is a public enactment of our unconscious desire for happiness (and an unconscious acknowledgment of our profound unhappiness). This is the sense in which Benjamin describes it as "false," since our compulsive desire for fashion is a substitute for a (forgotten) desire for happiness. In developing this analysis of fashion as a repetition compulsion, Benjamin gives two distinctive twists to Freud's theory. First, he radicalizes Freud's insistence that in a sense we are all neurotics, that there are no qualitative distinctions, but only quantitative ones, between neurotics and others (ID, 493). Second, he sees mass production of commodities as producing a neurotic psychic economy, and the latter as providing a continuing stimulus to commodity production itself.[100] Industrial and psychic economies, mass production and mass psychology are thus connected in a collective repetition compulsion.

Yet, this is only one side of Benjamin's analysis. For, at the extreme point of repetition, Hell touches its opposite: Paradise. As for Freud, repetition for Benjamin is a symptom of a desire to escape from the Hell of the same, to heal a wound, to find happiness. The neurotic keeps doing the same thing in Freud's view because that thing represents (in a way he or she wants both to forget *and* to remember) a source of trauma from which they seek relief. Secretly wishing to be relieved of the trauma they have repressed (and which haunts their lives), neurotics keep returning to the same place (e.g. a relationship which stands in for the traumatic situation which has been forgotten). Rather than finding happiness, however, the neurotic is regularly disappointed. Only the leap of recollection which they resist could help free them from the self-destructive cycle of repetition. Instead, they continually reenter this cycle, each time secretly hoping to be freed of what ails them, only to come crashing down in the same Hell once more. Yet, each time, this very disappointment hints at its opposite, at a secret hope to be cured and to find happiness. "Fashion is the eternal recurrence of the new," Benjamin declares. Yet, he asks, "are there nevertheless motifs of redemption precisely in fashion?" (CP, 46) Within the Hell of fashion he seeks traces of a utopian aspiration to be free from the social and psychic illness of capitalism.

As with all images of happiness, those attached to commodities emanate from the past. But these images cannot be derived from the recent past, since we all tend to remember the hardships and oppressions of recent experience. Just as the wish that animates the dream of the individual "always springs from the period of childhood,"[101] so collective wishes, too, reach into prehistoric images associated with classless society (PC, 148). Consequently, fashion engages in great temporal leaps, intent as it is on radically demarcating the new from the recently new. "Every new fashion," writes Roland Barthes, "is a refusal to inherit, a subversion against the preceding Fashion."[102] In refusing to inherit the recent past, fashions often refer to an earlier past, one sufficiently remote (even the 1960s and 1970s will often do today) as to conjure up warm memories of happiness, comfort and well-being. And all such images derived from earlier eras mingle, Benjamin suggests, with elements of "the primeval past." For this reason, there are lingering traces of utopia all around us, especially in those recently outmoded things which so attracted the attention of Breton. That is why Benjamin sets himself the task of a revolutionary reading of the physiognomy of bourgeois culture. All around us he suggests, "deposited in the unconscious of the collective," are intimations of the classless society of prehistory. In the modern city, of which Paris is the exemplar, these intimations "mingle with the new to produce the utopia that has left its traces in thousands of configurations of life, from permanent buildings to fleeting fashions" (PC, 148). Just as the individual unconscious leaves traces of its secret longings in dream-images, jokes, and word slips, so the collective unconscious has deposited its forgotten desires in thousands of forms, from buildings to fashions. Benjamin hopes to reawaken our relationships with these dead objects, to reactivate the erotic energy with which they were infused, so that (like all unfulfilled desires) they might provide the energy for radical change.

Like the world of the baroque, capitalism is a space of death and decay. Capitalism is constantly laying things to rest, pronouncing them dead, long before they expire naturally, so as to replace them with the new. Yet, much as novelty is intoxicating, it is also disturbing; it threatens to dissipate our very identities, tied as these are to memories of the past. As the central character in

Paul Auster's *In the Country of Last Things* puts it, "All around you one change follows another, each day produces a new upheaval, the old assumptions are so much air and emptiness. That is the dilemma. On the one hand, you want to survive, to adapt, to make the best of things as they are. But, on the other hand, to accomplish this seems to entail killing off all those things that once made you think of yourself as human. . . . In order to live you must make yourself die."[103] And this produces a paradox: capitalism kills our old selves, but to stop this process, to stop the flow of time, is itself to stop all change, to die. Capitalism, the society in which "all that is solid melts into air," thus produces a fascination with different forms of death. One of the ways in which people in bourgeois society hold on to their sense of self is by surrounding themselves with reminders—objects, mementos, photographs, and the like—which affirm that they really have existed. This drive is incarnated in the souvenir which encapsulates "the increasing self-alienation of the person who inventories his past as dead possession." Again, the comparison with the baroque is instructive. Whereas the relic was a derivative of the body of the dead person, the souvenir is a reminder of "deceased experience" (CP, 49). But just as the accumulation of souvenirs resembles a piling up of dead objects, so novelty, too, moves ever closer to death. After all, in its drive to be truly new, to escape repetition, bourgeois society can ultimately offer only one genuine novelty, only one thing which cannot be repeated for the individual: death. It is no surprise, then, that as the utopian hopes of capitalist society were challenged by the emergence of a revolutionary workers' movement, black became the dominant color of fashion, at least for the men of official society. Bourgeois society is a society of mourning—for our forgotten pasts, for our unfulfilled wishes, for our deaths which have been foretold as the only real novelty we will experience. Part of Baudelaire's greatness as a poet and an analyst of modernity was to have grasped this, to have seen that the funereal is a constant motif of bourgeois culture. Benjamin cites, for example, the following passage from Baudelaire:

> Is this not an attire that is needed by our epoch, suffering, and dressed up to its thin black shoulders in the symbol of constant mourning? The black suit and frock coat not only have their political beauty as an expression of general equality, but also their poetic beauty as an expression of the public mentality—an immense cortege of undertakers, political undertakers, amorous undertakers, bourgeois undertakers. We all observe some kind of funeral.[104]

Bourgeois society produces an eroticization of death which comes from two different but interrelated impulses: first, the manic desire for novelty which ultimately sees in death that which is truly new and different; and, second, the elegaic desire to stop the constant erosion of our selves by the cult of novelty, the desire to give ourselves the stability of dead objects in which the change-inducing processes of life have been extinguished.

EN-GENDERING THE FETISH: WOMEN, FASHION, AND REDEMPTION

The passage from Baudelaire above speaks largely to male fashion. But Benjamin insisted that the fashion industry centrally involved images of the female body. The emergence of bourgeois society, after all, entailed a deeroticization of the male bodies of the ruling class. Whereas fashion in feudal society was as much the preserve of ruling class men as of women, the rise of capitalism saw a deeroticization of the male body as the dominant male ethos shifted from luxury to industry.[105] The development of the fashion industry principally involved, therefore, the commodification of the female body-image. Yet, this process was more complex than a simple instrumentalization of women. Since commodities are objects of desire, the projection of eros onto women also involves (unstable and contradictory) male identifications with women.

Benjamin's analysis of women, fashion, and prostitutes has sharply divided feminist commentators. Some, like Angela McRobbie and Janet Wolff, see his theory of fashion as reinscribing the "patronizing gaze of the male writer" and as colluding in "a patriarchal construction of modernity."[106] In this interpretation, Benjamin reads the physiognomy of bourgeois culture by directing a conventional male gaze upon the female body. Another group of writers, while acknowledging this moment within his cultural criticism, locates in Benjamin's analysis important resources for the development of feminist critical theory. Eva Geulen, for instance, argues that contemporary feminism "has for the most part avoided the true scope of the gender problematic in Benjamin." In a similar vein, Elizabeth Wilson sees Benjamin as a cartographer of the crisis of the male gaze. The whole point of Benjamin's theory of the capitalist metropolis, she argues, is to trace the "feminization" of men—their transformation into prostitutes of their labor-power who are moved about the city by the circuit of commodities. Benjamin emerges in this view as a brilliant anatomist of male anxiety. Building upon this reading, Esther Leslie argues that Benjamin seeks to explore the potential of the "non-domesticated female bodies" of groups such as "widows, sex murder victims, fashion mannequins, lesbians, female factory workers" in terms of the way they disrupt the capitalist integration of the commodity with the female body.[107] These commentators demonstrate a greater appreciation of the range of motifs, including the psychoanalytic, at work in Benjamin's thinking and they find there significant resources for a critical analysis of gender and sexuality in capitalist society. This is not to suggest that Benjamin avoids a male-centered reading of culture. It is to urge, however, that while engaged in such a reading he destabilizes the male position, exposing its anxieties and the crisis it experiences in the bourgeois urban setting, revealing its simultaneous attraction to and repulsion by its own "feminization." Moreover, Benjamin sees the breakdown of the defensive male ego—and its sustaining myth of the self-made man—as a precondition of revolutionary subjectivity. Male identifications with women as historical actors on a landscape of ruination are decisive to the temporal dislocations involved in revolutionary change.

Not surprisingly, Benjamin's images of women move between polarities. An early text called "The Conversation" (1913), presents women as guardians of the past, as those who speak the incommunicable within language. The female position in language is thereby affiliated with silence and the language of the body, and endowed with redemptive possibilities—themes that figure centrally in the psychoanalytic feminism of Luce Irigaray and Julia Kristeva.[108] A number of other early texts exhibit a similar preoccupation with gender relations. In "The Life of Students" (1914–15), for example, Benjamin criticizes "the dominant erotic convention" of marriage and the family because these restrict the sphere of eros to a narrowly private one. He condemns the deeroticization of the public sphere of culture and the restriction of eros to private acts of procreation between married individuals. Both creation and procreation "are distorted by this separation," Benjamin contends. One result of this distorting separation is that, in the universities, the creative spirit takes the form of male "intellectual autonomy" in the fraternities while relations with women are reduced to "naturalistic" erotic adventures with prostitutes. Culture and nature, male and female, intellect and eros are thus radically separated. The goal of students ought to be "the necessary inclusion of women" in the intellectual realm so as to move toward "a single community of creative persons" united by love.[109] Yet, as Benjamin reacted to the crisis of the student movement—and its leadership's identification of the war with the progress of culture and spirit—he became more skeptical about this image of "a single community of creative persons." After all, such an image promises an actual reconciliation of what is in fact unreconciled—culture and nature, male and female, intellect and sexuality. By the time of his 1916 essay on Socrates, he had moved away from this utopian image. While continuing to idealize female-female love, he criticizes Socrates for sexualizing the spiritual.[110] The Socratic position worries Benjamin because to see the realm of spirit as identical with the realm of nature and sexuality is to enter into myth—as had the students who supported the war.[111] The same position informs his resistance to the messianism of the German Romantics. These writers, after all, celebrated an ideal of androgyny—of the sexual unification of the male and the female. This has long been a problematic move within Western thought, however, since the utopian image of the androgyne is constructed as unifying nature and culture by reintegrating the female into the male, that is, through a move in which the feminine functions as "the other" that enables the male to attain his full humanity.[112] With his turn to Marxism, and to his own unique dialectic of extremes, Benjamin was able to revisit the problem of nature, culture, and the female in a way that avoided naturalizing gender. Now he explored historically constructed oppositions within the images of women appropriate to bourgeois society. Dominant images, he argues, drive women to two extremes: loving mother and mercenary whore. Yet, the collision of these extremes, he intimates, can serve as a lever of social criticism.

One of Benjamin's memoirs of childhood, "Berlin Chronicle" (1931), for example, alternates between the images of mother and prostitute. It is striking how few references there are to men in the text. Yet, it positively overflows with women: nursemaids, whores, servant girls, a teacher, his mother, and grandmother all figure in the narrative. At one level, the text is structured in terms of an opposition between the world of the fathers (which is that of industry, competition and the market) and the world of women (which embodies ancient forms of cultural life).[113] However, by organizing the discussion of the world of women around the pair mother/prostitute, the text insists upon women as historical agents. These women represent hidden dimensions of existence for Benjamin, those places where everyday life melts into something else. Benjamin often describes such experiences in terms of crossing a threshold; this can mean the physical act of entering part of the city where middle-class men do not go, just as it may suggest crossing the line between dreaming and waking life. When we (men) do so, he suggests, we take a step into nothingness, into a dimension whose laws we do not know. Prostitutes are symbols of precisely this threshold crossing: "the places are countless in the great cities where one stands on the edge of the void, and the whores in the doorways of tenement blocks and on the less sonorous asphalt of railway platforms are like the household goddesses of this cult of nothingness" (BC, 11). If whores represent those switching points in the geography of the city where the middle-class male plunges into the realm of the unexpected—and runs the risk of losing his "ownership" of the city—so do mothers for the little boy in the bourgeois interior who is beckoned into a mysterious world by those parts of the house or apartment reserved for his mother and her things.[114] Benjamin recounts a dream in which a ghost had appeared to him. The unknown site on which the ghost operated strongly resembled "the corner of my parent's bedroom that was separated from the rest of the chamber by an arch hung with a heavy, faded-violet curtain, and in which my mother's dressing gowns, house dresses and shawls were suspended. The darkness behind the curtain was impenetrable, and this corner was the sinister, nocturnal counterpart to that bright, beatific realm that opened occasionally with my mother's linen cupboard." Proceeding to describe the linen cupboard with its "sheets, tablecloths, napkins and pillowcases and its "sweet lavender scent," he continues: "These were the hell and paradise into which the ancient magic of hearth and home, which had once been lodged in the spinning wheel, had been sundered" (BC, 54).

The claim that these sites represent both hell and paradise is crucial. Benjamin is not simply affirming the utopian dimension of the female-maternal sphere. He insists that this world is also a living hell. Something ancient and magical is represented by mother and whore. Mysteries of love and sex, production and reproduction, life and death were once unified. Now they have been sundered, wrenched apart. Yet, at the extreme each moves toward its other. The pure idealized love of the mother hints at its opposite, sex as an end in itself, for pleasure rather than procreation, just as sex severed from love (indeed turned into a commodity) points to the other that defines it: love. Benjamin believes there is something profound about these two poles into which the category "woman" is divided because they represent the intersection of the energies of life and death. The pure mother is idealized as life itself (but thereby desexualized) while the whore is sexuality separated from life and reproduction. Benjamin sees these same mythic forces at work in fashion.

One of the great disruptions introduced by capitalism, says Benjamin, was to drive women into industrial production. "The nineteenth century began to use women without reservation in the production process outside the home," he writes. "It did so primarily in a primitive fashion by putting them into factories." The result was a *masculinization* of proletarian women which was expressed politically during the revolution of February 1848 (precursor of the workers' uprising of June of that year) in the movement of working-class women called the "Vesuviennes" who announced that "a revolutionary volcano is at work in every woman who belongs to our group" (PSEB, 93–94). But, after the revolutionary events, the fashion industry laid a layer of glitter over this volcano of female revolutionary hopes. Yet, Benjamin claims, the eruptive power of the revolution still lurks within the interstices of fashion. This power now lies in ruins and fragments, it is to be found only in the broken bits of lava-covered objects that make up the scene of fashion—the body parts of mannequins, yesterday's styles, old advertisements. These shattered bits of the fashion industry represent something more complex than our deception by commodities, however, since they also embody bits of our erotic identifications.

So significant is the eroticization of commodities, says Benjamin, that people in capitalist society secretly want to *be* commodities, that is, to be objects of mass desire. Walk around any major city and you will see people entranced by commodities. One observes them crowding around store windows or making pilgrimages to shopping malls and department stores even, as in the case of "window shopping," when they have no intention to buy. The crowds in the big city are swept up in "the intoxication of the commodity around which surges the stream of customers." The individual desirous of love and recognition soon learns that commodities are objects of mass desire. This triggers a process of identification in which people imagine themselves not simply with commodities (adorned in and surrounded by them), but *as* commodities, as objects of obsessive admiration and desire. The result is a startling "empathy" with the commodity as a central feature of mass psychology in bourgeois society (PSEB, 55–56).

The fashion industry is in the first instance about cultivating a female empathy with the commodity. Women, more than anyone else, are expected to merge with commodities, to transform their body parts into racks for the display of merchandise, to become like mannequins. This tendency reaches its pinnacle in the case of the prostitute who really does merge with commodities, who sells her body (in the same way the wage-laborer sells his or her labor-power). The whore thus represents the truth of the proletariat. If, according to Lukacs, the mysteries of capitalism are solved when self-knowledge and the commodity form coincide in the proletariat, then the prostitute represents this coincidence, this unity of person and commodity, more fully than anyone else. The commodity, says Benjamin, "celebrates its becoming human in the whore" (CP, 42). And since we all secretly want to be commodities, we identify with those who are most thoroughly commodified: prostitutes. The female body is much more than an object of male desire. Men in bourgeois society don't merely "want" women, they secretly desire to *be* women, to be commodified objects of desire. Dream-wishes involve a secret male desire to be feminized. Benjamin believes there is a redemptive force at work here: male identification with the feminine has an emancipatory thrust insofar as we grasp the demythifying character of prostitution.[115] For this reason, perhaps, our society seeks to repress those identifications through a structure of resistances—a social psychology of misogyny and male homophobia which deny this secret longing to be female.

But Benjamin's analysis does not stop here. He is not simply saying that liberation lies in men coming to acknowledge their unconscious feminine identifications. This would merely reinscribe the Romantic ideal of the male attaining his full humanity by appropriating the female image. Rather than idealize existing sexual differences, Benjamin also affirms the way capitalism tends to dissolve them. Just as it sets up ideal images of the feminine as the incarnation of nature and beauty, capitalism simultaneously "masculinizes" working-class women (especially those pushed into the factory), dissolves older family forms, and creates new social spaces for those who reject identification with motherhood and procreation—lesbians, prostitutes, and feminist revolutionaries. Benjamin notes that for Baudelaire "the lesbian is the heroine of modernism" because, in repudiating the role of wife and mother, she affirms the (masculine) creative principle with which men are losing contact (PSEB, 90). But Benjamin also celebrates a more political version of this female repudiation of motherhood. Seizing on the early nineteenth-century socialist-feminist manifesto of Claire Demar, he quotes from its final section: "No more motherhood! No law of the blood. I say: no more motherhood. Once a woman has been freed from men who pay the price of her body . . . she will owe her existence . . . only to her own creativity" (PSEB, 91). For Benjamin the lesbian and the feminist revolutionary are subversive because they break through the naturalized appearance of social life. Capitalism presents its forms of life—production for the market, alienation of the worker from the product of labor, capital's appropriation of surplus value, the idealization of women as incarnations of beauty and their degradation as items of exchange—as forces of nature, not history. But women who repudiate motherhood refuse this reduction to nature, they break with myth by declaring that they are—or can be—agents of their own historical self-development. On the petrified landscape of commodified society, they assert the possibility of historical action—something which is slipping away from working- and middle-class men.

Alongside the emergence of disruptive female agents in the capitalist metropolis, there develops a crisis of masculinity for the majority of men. Commodification, says Benjamin, destroys the classic petty bourgeois ideal of "the self-made man," an ideal which has been especially powerful among the male intelligentsia—writers, artists, and the like. The reality of capitalist modernity is that the petty bourgeois intellectual has become entirely dependent upon capital for his existence. Small, independent means of production disappear with the advance of the large publishing house and the mass circulation newspaper based upon advertising. The *flaneur*—the classic "independent" male intellectual who strolls through the city, soaking up its sights in order to paint or write—is increasingly proletarianized. Baudelaire's greatness was in part to have registered this fact, to have "viewed the literary market without illusions." He "knew what the true situation of the man of letters was: he goes to the marketplace as a *flaneur*, supposedly to take a look at it, but in reality to find a buyer" (PSEB, 33, 34). Baudelaire named this emerging fact in the social life of the "self-made" intellectual: "the unavoidable necessity of prostitution for the poet," his need to find a buyer for his talents, to sell himself like a whore (CP, 53). In destroying the petty bourgeois myth of the self-made man, proletarianization exposes the "feminization" of the male intellectual, his reduction by capital to the circumstances of the prostitute. Rather than a purveyor of the classic male gaze, Benjamin's *flaneur* is an urban male overwhelmed by anxiety and feelings of impotence, a male who, in the categories of bourgeois society, has been "feminized."[116] And yet, Benjamin sees redemptive possibilities on this demythified and barren landscape of people selling their talents and body parts. The recognition that in capitalist society we are all prostitutes shatters the mythical structure of reality, and this allows us to break through the naturalization of history and to enter onto the terrain of historical action. Just like baroque allegory, the destruction of the dream of the self-made man reveals a landscape bereft of beauty and transcendent meaning, a stage full of corpses, body parts, and dead objects awaiting the meanings we have yet to write. As Esther Leslie puts it, "Benjamin is excited by the aura-denying elements of love-for-sale. This acts out and exposes—for therapeutic purposes—the commodity basis of social relations and the solidarity of consumer, seller and consumed."[117] In coming to see ourselves as prostitutes, we grasp the facts of our commodification. And this myth-destroying shock of self-recognition might be used as a trigger for revolutionary action.

Women's fashion and the body of the prostitute are sites of redemptive possibilities since human subjectivity and the commodity fuse most closely there. As always, barbarism and redemption exist side by side. But, unlike giddy postmodernist valorizations of the fashion industry or the life of the prostitute, Benjamin insists that it is primarily a living Hell.[118] It is important to underline this point. Benjamin is not idealizing fashion and prostitution, he is not saying that commodified women are revolutionary *per se*, that they are prophets of liberation. He does not for a moment idealize fashion. The fashion industry is a petrified landscape littered with corpses: of women who have become mannequins, of nonprocreative female bodies who become desirable only insofar as they approximate deadbodies. Fashion, Benjamin argues, "couples the living body to the inorganic world. Against the living it asserts the rights of the corpse." The fetish of commodities is thus "subject to the sex appeal of the inorganic," of the corpse (PC, 153).[119] And, it might be added, this barbarous reality can culminate in the horrific act of the murder of women and prostitutes. Fashion and prostitution are thus at the heart of the dialectic of extremes which characterizes capitalism: sexuality and death, history and nature collide there. Yet, just like the pieces of the broken world of the baroque, the mangled products and body parts of the fashion industry are intimations of a utopian future—if, as in baroque allegory, the shock of demythification and denaturalization drives us onto the barren landscape of historical action. The problem of constructing dialectical images thus involves unearthing "motifs of redemption" that are inextricably bound up with female images. Benjamin means it quite literally, therefore, when he writes that "the eternal is far more the frill on a dress than an idea" (N, 51). Fashion is not revolution, however; it is the commodity masquerading as revolution. As he put it in his last written work: "Fashion has a flair for the topical, no matter where it stirs in the thickets of long ago; it is a tiger's leap into the past. This jump, however, takes place in an arena where the ruling class gives the commands. The same leap in the open air of history is the dialectical one, which is how Marx understood revolution" (TPH, 261). Benjamin's dialectics of awakening is all about this tiger's leap in the open air of history.

THE DIALECTICS OF AWAKENING: BENJAMIN, ADORNO, AND THE TRADITION OF THE OPPRESSED

The world of commodities is for Benjamin a place where Heaven and Hell meet, one where, as in baroque drama and psychoanalysis, redemption can be achieved only via a voyage through the depths of Hell. Only our immersion in the eternal return of the same—which manifests itself in the charred landscape of corpses

and decaying commodities—allows us to approach the point of dialectical reversal. Because it destroys everything fixed and stable and thus renders all tastes and
opinions "antiquated before they can ossify," capitalism repeatedly puts its subjects on trial.[120] Yet, and this is a point lost in postmodernist theory, capitalism
also substitutes the continuity (the oppressive sameness) of the commodity form
for the character structure it destroys. Repetition compulsion becomes the mass
psychology of people in bourgeois society. However, in reaching into the past,
especially the primeval past of classless society, for images of happiness to attach
to commodities, capitalism offers glimpses of utopia. And these, if brought into
explosive contact with the reality of happiness denied, can be the fuel of rebellion. Just like the neurotic who finds it harder and harder to live with his or her
neuroses, the oppressed class, too, regularly rebels against the Hell of the ever-
the-same. Psychoanalysis approaches this problem with techniques (such as free
association and dream analysis) designed to help the analysand experience jarring temporal dislocations. The analytic process works when, feeling the obstacles to their quest for happiness posed by (trauma-denying) patterns of behavior
rooted in the past, people capture the energy invested in repression for purposes
of self-development.

The transformation of psychic forces of repression into energies of emancipation is arguably *the* critical moment in successful psychoanalysis. Revolutionary theory for Benjamin seeks to do the same by constructing dialectical images
saturated with the tensions of existence. Such images make time stand still by
exposing its unspoken secret: that rather than a wonderful world getting better
everyday, we inhabit a world spilling over with unhappiness, a world of broken
dreams. "When thinking reaches a standstill in a constellation saturated with
tensions," writes Benjamin, "the dialectical image appears" (N, 67). Revolutionary criticism mobilizes dialectical images which assault bourgeois mythology—
the myths embodied in its fetishistic use of words like Progress, Freedom and
Happiness—so that its truth content might be released through its destruction.
This is what it means to bring about "the dissolution of 'mythology' into the
space of history": the unrealized (and in this context unrealizable) dream-wishes
generated with the rise of capitalism need to be detached from the mythological
structure of the commodity. Liberation from bourgeois myth involves a dialectic
of destruction and redemption. Just as the individual must reclaim dreams of
happiness as practical goals in her life (by detaching them from myths of a
return to an originary moment of perfect, blissful love, for example), so the
oppressed class must reclaim the libidinal energies it has cathected onto commodities and rechannel them into an emancipatory historical practice. This is
why historical analysis for the revolutionary critic "is not just a science but also
a form of memoration (*eine Form des Eingedenkens*)." But memoration is not
merely recuperation; it involves the remembering agents remaking the meaning
of their pasts by changing their lives in the present. In particular, it means
redeeming past desires for happiness: "Memoration can make the incomplete

(happiness) into something complete, and the complete (suffering) into something incomplete" (N, 61).

But, as we have seen, remembrance is precisely the problem. Reification involves systematic forgetting. This is why Benjamin's attitude toward memory is so much more complex than that of Bakhtin. Moreover, it is not enough to supplant the repressive structures of waking life with the images of the dream. After all, the unconscious is not a pristine realm of freedom; it, too, is profoundly implicated in repression. The psychic forces that tie us to myth are not merely conscious, but deeply rooted in unconscious structures. Benjamin recognizes that these unconscious forces can be exploited for the most oppressive of political purposes (as in fascism). Rational critique remains, therefore, an absolutely indispensable part of the Benjaminian project. Writing of fascism and its cult of primeval experience, for instance, he insists that "all the light that language and reason still afford should be focused upon that 'primal experience' from whose barren gloom this mysticism crawls forth."[121] For this reason, he seeks a mode of experience different from both the dream and ordinary waking life. Just as psychoanalysis (through free association and the use of the sleep-like state on the couch) tries to find a point where dream-images come into contact with the waking powers of rational criticism, so Benjamin hopes to construct forms of experience in which repressed wishes embodied in the collective dreams of a sick culture might be remembered and challenged (as neurotic fantasies) by the powers of reasoned critique. Consequently, images of awakening, of that state in which the waking mind has sufficient contact with its dream-life to remember and analyze its dreams, loom especially large in his theory. Contrasting his approach to the surrealist tactics of Louis Aragon, Benjamin writes: "whereas Aragon remains persistently in the realm of dreams, here it is a question of finding the constellation of awakening." Because bourgeois society requires such a high degree of renunciation, our wishes for happiness take refuge in disguised form in our unconscious dream-life. Imprisoned in our unconscious, libidinal desires can become entangled in the most primitive form of thought: myth. As a result, critical reason is required for purposes of demythification. Benjamin's strategy—designed to assist us in awakening from our dreams and truly remembering them—aligns itself with Freud's position. "It is one of the silent assumptions of psychoanalysis," he claims, "that the antithetical contrast of sleeping and waking has no validity for the empirical form of human consciousness."[122] The dialectics of awakening is oriented to breaking down the antithetical structure sleeping/waking. Just as dreams need to be mediated by the awakened consciousness, so the conscious state needs to be reconnected with the dream-wishes it ordinarily denies. Benjamin seeks, in other words, a dialectics of remembering where the subject recalls her dreams upon awakening, retains its dream-images, and organizes her waking life so as to actualize the desires for happiness the dream contained: "Dialectical structure of awakening: remembering and awakening are most intimately related. Awakening, namely, is the dialectical, Copernican turning of remembrance. It is an eminently composed reversal of the world of the dreamer into the world of the waking."[123]

The reversal of the world of the dream into the world of the waking means shattering the myth upon which dream-wishes have fixated (the eternal return of the commodity) in order to transform the energies invested in myth into powers of historical action. But how is this to happen? How are individuals to be jarred out of the endlessly alternating cycle of (mythical) sleeping life and (forgetful) waking life? In addressing these questions, Benjamin develops a concept of shock experience which is heavily indebted to psychoanalysis.

In a major essay on Baudelaire, for instance, Benjamin turns to *Beyond the Pleasure Principle* where Freud argued that one function of consciousness is to absorb the impact of stimuli from the external environment. Consciousness has a defensive and protective role for Freud; it parries the blows inflicted by reality, smothers them, and weaves a narrative which represses the memory of these sensory shocks and the fears they inspired. Consciousness, in other words, spins a tale of security and stability in a dangerous and frightening world. Nevertheless, these shocks leave effects in the form of memory-traces stored in the unconscious.[124] Moreover, because capitalism involves an acceleration of shock effects—the assembly line, photography, street lighting, film, the movement of crowds hurtling through great cities, bombardment by advertisements, the unfathomable mobilization of science and technology in war—consciousness must become increasingly protective. Yet, this very protectiveness is regularly assaulted by the momentous forces of disintegration released as the capitalist cult of novelty melts down all traditions. And this produces a problem. Our old identifications and desires, the old selves we have left behind, leave traces in the physiognomy of the city and our dwelling places: in outmoded buildings, clothes, art works, photos and so on. Thus, as consciousness absorbs new blows and lets go of old identities, it also regularly confronts monuments to its past dreams and the frustrations they endured. It is these "revolutionary energies that appear in the 'outmoded'" that Benjamin hopes to release through dialectical images which bring hopes from the past into jarring contact with past and present frustrations.

Benjamin seems to be saying that capitalism puts enormous strain on the psyche. On the one hand, it calls upon its most protective and conservative mechanisms to fend off shock and persuade the self that all is well. On the other hand, by accelerating the rate and intensity of shock-experiences, it also forces that conservative mechanism into a process of constant change. But the unconscious does not lose all contact with our older selves and the objects of their desires. For this reason, he recommends a revolutionary form of shock effects that might disrupt our ordinary selves and assist us in seeing truths about our world. This is the source of the affirmative moment in Benjamin's attitude toward film that has bothered many commentators on his "Work of Art" essay. Benjamin need not be read, however, as saying that film is revolutionary per se. Rather, we might read him as saying that technologies of representation which are capable of generating shock effects ought to be utilized for radical purposes. This, it seems to me, is the point of his comparison of the camera with psychoanalysis: "The camera introduces us to unconscious optics as does psychoanalysis to unconscious impulses."[125] The camera, in other words, shows us things we don't otherwise see; it reproduces images which are stored in our "optical unconscious." As Joel Snyder points out, a photograph of an Olympic runner taken at a shutter speed of 1/1000th of a second can show us something we did not consciously "see" while watching the race: the runner with both feet off the ground.[126] And this is true of all forms of experience. We always perceive much more than our consciousness records—including monuments of our past desires. Great jolts of shock can bring these things back to memory. "While our waking, habitual, everyday self is involved actively or passively in what is happening, our deeper self rests in another place and is touched by the shock, as is the little heap of magnesium powder by the flame of the match. It is to this immolation of our deepest self in shock that our memory owes its most indelible images" (BC, 57). What makes film significant is that it is capable of activating the latent dream imagery of the new collective spaces of the capitalist metropolis.[127]

The central purpose of the Arcades Project was to construct dialectical images which would both touch memories stored in the collective unconscious— memories of the utopian hopes epitomized by Fourier's designs for a society in which work becomes play (whose roots reach back to preclass society)—and produce a demythified image of history as ruination. Constructing such images requires rummaging among the ruins of commodities for the dream-wishes and erotic energies that linger on after they have been consigned to the scrap heap of mutilated body parts and decaying objects. The trick is to find the fragments of desire and disappointment that might be joined together for emancipatory purposes. As the narrator of *In the Country of Last Things* puts it: "Everything falls apart, but not every part of every thing, at least not at the same time. The job is to zero in on these little islands of intactness, to imagine them joined to other such islands, and those islands to still others, and thus to create new archipelagoes of matter. You must salvage the salvageable and learn to ignore the rest. The trick is to do it as fast as you can."[128]

There are many obvious difficulties with Benjamin's project. It is not in the least clear, after all, how his explosive dialectics of awakening might be linked with forms of everyday political practice—with strikes, campaigns for public housing, rallies against racial discrimination, struggles to keep a hospital open, or to win equal pay for women. This is not to say that such links cannot be made—indeed Benjamin's strictures are a crucial reminder that all such struggles ought to be joined to a conscious movement for revolutionary social transformation which is fired by utopian imagining—and that this requires preparing a qualitative leap in self-perception and self-understanding. But, at the level of analysis engaged by Benjamin, the concrete problems of modes of political organization and mobilization are elided. This criticism is of a very different

nature, however, from that leveled by Theodor Adorno against Benjamin's concept of dream fetishes. Adorno's misguided critique in fact serves to underline
the importance of what Benjamin was up to.

Reacting to the sections of the Arcades Project devoted to Baudelaire, Adorno
charged that Benjamin had subjectivized Marx's concept of commodity fetishism. By transposing the dialectical image "into consciousness as a 'dream,'" argued Adorno, Benjamin was relinquishing Marx's powerful insight: that "the
fetish character of the commodity is not a fact of consciousness; rather it is
dialectical, in the eminent sense that it produces consciousness."[129] There is an
obvious sense in which Adorno is right. Fetishism is not fundamentally a datum
of consciousness; it is an objective social process in which the products of alienated labor take the form of bits of (capitalist) private property which discover
their social meaning (value) through the unplanned workings of the market
(which operates as if it were a force of nature). But Benjamin does not depart
from the framework of Marx's theory in this respect. His concerns lie elsewhere:
with the other side of the fetish, its function as an object cathected with libidinal
desire upon which dream-wishes are projected. Adorno's criticism seems at first
glance remarkable in its failure even to appreciate what Benjamin is up to here.
Upon reflection, however, this failure appears less surprising. For, as Susan Buck-
Morss has argued, "behind the whole question of whether Benjamin's images
were sufficiently 'dialectical,' the real issue by 1935 between Benjamin and Adorno
was a political one."[130] Not in the least denying the objective social character of
commodity fetishism, Benjamin had become increasingly preoccupied with the
problems that haunted revolutionary activists and theorists of the 1930s—from
Gramsci in his *Prison Notebooks*, to radical surrealists, left-wing syndicalists, and
Trotskyists: the failure of the European revolution after 1917 and the nature of
working-class consciousness in capitalist society. These preoccupations led many
of these theorists to investigate the processes of subjective (or ideological) incorporation of the working class into capitalist society—and the ways in which
these might be resisted. Benjamin shared the concerns of these left-wing radi-
cals. Furthermore, as the Communist parties, the major parties of working-class
opposition, moved during the mid-1930s toward a left populism which embraced the bourgeois myth of history, he felt an urgent need for a radically
different account of the revolutionary process.

During the summer of 1935, Stalin's bureaucracy in Russia directed Communists throughout the West to adopt the tactic of the Popular Front. Having
first been instructed in the late 1920s and early 1930s not to ally with the social
democratic parties in a united front against fascism, the Communist Parties were
now ordered to undertake a dramatic about-face by proclaiming themselves the
representatives of "the people"—not of the working class—dedicated to the defense
of the national interest. To this end, they dropped talk of class struggle, of
fighting for working-class power, and tried to construct alliances with the parties
of liberal capitalism. In so doing, the Communists declared their continuity with

the traditions of bourgeois democracy. Nowhere was this more true than in France where the Communist Party proclaimed itself the heir of the bourgeois revolution of 1789.[131] Benjamin recoiled from the Popular Front. To him it epitomized the very politics responsible for the failure of revolution in Europe: a gradualist progressivism which depicts history as the inevitable transition from one social order to another. By declaring the socialist left the heir of 1789, the Popular Front presented the political project of the working class as the continuation of the bourgeois revolution. No radical break in historical time was envisioned, the working-class movement was summoned simply to take up and complete the original project of the ruling class. Benjamin's impassioned call for a radical notion of fulfilled time, a time which, by brushing history against the grain, recuperates a tradition of the oppressed, is governed by his response to this political moment. Rather than an eccentric return to theology, as some commentators have described it, Benjamin's heightened inflection of messianic motifs involved an explicit political concern: to resist the decline of a distinctly working-class consciousness and the collapse of the Left into a populist progressivism.

Benjamin's letters of the time are full of critical commentary on the Popular Front and the state of the Left. He blames the parliamentary left's embrace of the "national interest" for demobilizing the great French workers' upheaval of the summer of 1936 when more than six million workers undertook mass strikes and factory occupations.[132] Similarly, reflecting on the recent history of the Left in his "Theses on the Philosophy of History," he denounces the politicians of the working-class movement for "betraying their own cause," condemning their "stubborn faith in progress" and their "servile integration" into bourgeois state and society. Turning to the German case—where the defeat of the working-class movement had been most catastrophic—he declares that "nothing has corrupted the German working class so much as the notion that it was moving with the current" (TPH, 258). These concerns were increasingly at the forefront of Benjamin's thinking as he worked at the Arcades Project from 1936 on. In a late 1937 letter to his friend Fritz Lieb, an anti-fascist activist of the Swiss Socialist Left, he attacked the leaderships of the French Communist and Socialist parties for "robbing the workers of their elementary sense of instinctive action."[133] Little surprise, then, that the problem of restoring this sense of instinctive action loomed so large in his dialectics of awakening. Yet, Adorno would have understood precious little of all this. While Benjamin's letters of the time are full of commentary on the French strikes, the anti-fascist resistance in Switzerland, and the politics of the Spanish Civil War, Adorno's correspondence remained remarkably apolitical, seemingly oblivious of the consequences of Hitler's seizure of power or of political events in Spain.[134] As Benjamin deepened his analysis of commodity fetishism in order to better wrestle with the problem of revolutionary experience, he increasingly expressed himself in a language foreign to Adorno. The following notebook entry concerning the Arcades Project, for instance, is unlike anything we find in Adorno's writings: "Would it not be possible," asks Benjamin, "to show from the collected facts with which this work is concerned, how they appear in the process of the proletariat's becoming self-conscious?"[135] Indeed, this had become the central purpose of revolutionary criticism for Benjamin: to assist the working class in coming to political self-consciousness.

Benjamin's focus on fetishes and dreams of commodities was designed to awaken members of the oppressed class to the meaning of the mythical dream world they inhabit. This required the dissolution of bourgeois myth into the space of history—a dissolution which so touches members of the exploited classes that, out of self-recognition in the ruins of defeat and disappointment, they might construct historical images with which to break the cycle of failed revolutions (another form of eternal return). "The task of history," therefore, "is to get hold of the tradition of the oppressed."[136] Yet such a tradition is not an integral thing. It cannot be found in a book or purchased like a commodity. The tradition of the oppressed exists in the form of fragments and ruins which need to be reinvested with meaning—meaning for those who are struggling in the present. Because he did not understand the animating spirit of the Arcades Project, Adorno misread it as an attempt to delineate the objective process of commodity fetishism. But Benjamin was up to something quite different. In a move radically foreign to Adorno, he sought to provide a method by which the oppressed might construct their own tradition, by which they might create an active, revolutionary memory. Rather than subjectivizing the theory of commodity fetishism, Benjamin undertook to extend Marx's theory through a psychoanalytically informed account of commodified dream-images as obstacles to revolutionary class consciousness—obstacles that nonetheless contained fragments of redemption.

And this helps us understand another aspect of the famous debate between Adorno and Benjamin. Adorno criticized the Arcades Project (especially as set out in "The Paris of the Second Empire in Baudelaire") for the way it juxtaposed poetry, history, and economic data. In piling up economic facts next to literary images, he charged, Benjamin implied an immediate and determining relationship between economic base and cultural products, a method which lacks the dialectical category of mediation. Again, Adorno's criticism mistook Benjamin's revolutionary purpose. The category of mediation is of a part with the category of totality: the individual parts of a dialectical whole are already shaped by (mediated through) their relations to the whole (and the rest of its parts).[137] But Benjamin's purpose was not to construct a total picture of the social order; it was to think against the totality that is capitalism, to disrupt its totalizing narrative. Rather than bringing the parts into a seamless, mediated, and integrated relation with one another, this meant making the parts collide in ways that destabilize our normalized experience of capitalism. In arguing for the central role of the concept of mediation (and the notion of totality it entailed), Adorno failed to see that Benjamin's dialectics at a standstill, like Brecht's epic theater, was not about an adequate depiction of an historical totality, but about puncturing the cyclical flow of everyday experience. Benjamin was in search of a dialectical imagery which, rather than providing consciousness with a total picture of the social process, might shock the oppressed, touch their bodily experience, and rechannel energies of collective innervation into historical action.[138] Whatever the weaknesses of Benjamin's method, they were not those identified by Adorno. Much closer to the melancholy attitude of the baroque prince who turns away from the historical realm in despair, Adorno simply failed to understand the commitment to fostering a revolutionary practice that informed the shifts in Benjamin's thinking from the mid-1930s onward.[139]

LANGUAGE AND LIBERATION

Even if I am right to read Benjamin's concept of dialectical images in fundamentally political terms, what relation does any of this have to the problem of language? In following Benjamin's odyssey through arcades, advertisements, world fairs, and dreams of commodities, we seem to have left language far behind. Yet Benjamin did not think so. In his Arcades notebooks, for instance, he wrote, "Only dialectical images are genuine (i.e., not archaic) images; and the place one happens on them is language" (N, 49). What does it mean, however, to talk of language as the place of dialectical images? What could Benjamin intend in suggesting that language harbors secret points of entry into the past, into forms of experiences different from those that dominate waking life? In trying to make sense of these claims, many commentators have invoked Benjamin's debt to messianic notions of time associated with Jewish mysticism. Yet, in so doing, they have often treated his late theory of language in essentially theological terms, as little more than a restatement of his pre-Marxian views. I propose a different tack, however. I intend to take seriously Benjamin's claim that his mature views on language represented "a mimetic-naturalistic theory."[140] Rather than enlisting theology to interpret his linguistic theory, I propose to use psychoanalysis to that end. As I will show, many of the seeming mysteries of Benjamin's mimetic theory of language can be unraveled if we read him through the prism of Freud's dream theory.[141]

Interestingly, Benjamin himself drew attention to this link. In a 1935 letter to Gretel Adorno, he made an intriguing suggestion about the similarities between his and Freud's views on language. "I very much hope you read the contribution by Freud on telepathy and psychoanalysis," he writes. "In the course of his consideration Freud constructs, in passing as he often does his most important thoughts, a connection between telepathy and speech, in which he makes the first a means of understanding—he explicitly points to the realm of insects—phylogenetically the predecessor of the second. Here I find once again the thoughts which are decisively discussed in the small sketch from Ibiza 'On the Mimetic Faculty.'"[142] A number of things are significant about this passage. First, Benjamin again indicates the importance he attached to his short essay on language and *mimesis*. Second, he maintains that Freud holds similar views to his own. Finally, he hints that there are forms of communicative interaction between living things (including insects) and the world that predate speech (and which live on within it). Let us try to unpack this by exploring the possible connections between Freud's theory of dreams and Benjamin's concept of dialectical images—particularly those connections that point to language.

Freud's claim that dreams express unfulfilled wishes (ID, 199, 244) is obviously central to Benjamin's theory of the commodity, dream-wishes and the collective unconscious, as is his insistence that such wishes have their roots in childhood (ID, 705, 746, 757). But rarely have commentators attended to the extent to which major elements of Benjamin's description of dialectical images have their parallels in Freud's dream theory. Freud insists, for instance, that "dreams think essentially in images" and that they do so because the dreaming imagination is deprived of "the power of conceptual speech" and thus "obliged to paint what it has to say pictorially" (ID, 113, 155). Moreover, because they operate imagistically, not conceptually, dreams are under no obligation to obey the law of noncontradiction. Rather than adhere to "the alternative 'either-or' " that dominates the awakened consciousness, dreams—just like baroque allegories and dialectical images—"show a particular preference for combining contraries into a unity." Indeed, dreams can disguise their essential thoughts by making each and every element "stand for its opposite just as easily as itself" (ID, 427, 429, 607–8). The dialectic of extremes is thus a central feature of dreams, even to the extent of opposites passing over into one another. Furthermore, dreams entirely disrupt the narrative flow of linear time. The past is never over for the dream, something that happened in childhood can have tremendous immediacy even in old age. "In the unconscious nothing is past or forgotten," says Freud (ID, 733), everything exists in the mode of now-time. Consequently, dreams operate by way of "a translation of time into space." They take events separated by great stretches of chronological time and resituate them in a space of simultaneity (ID, 534, 424). In all these ways—by employing images rather than concepts, in bringing opposites into the closest contact with one another, by translating time into space—dreams break out of the structures of conscious thought. Indeed, says Freud, they bring thinking to a standstill. Reading Freud's description of this process it is not difficult to imagine Benjamin leaping at the following passage, his heart pounding the way it had when he first read Louis Aragon's *Le Paysan de Paris*. Describing how dreams abandon the ordinary laws of thought, Freud writes, "this abandonment of interest in thought-processes during the night has a purpose: thinking is to come to a standstill" (ID, 730). Here, then, is a direct connection between the structure of dreams and dialectical images. It is almost inconceivable that this passage escaped Benjamin's attention, anymore than those I have cited on images, opposites, and time. Read in relation to *The Interpretation of Dreams*, Benjamin's theory of dialectical images appears to be immersed in psychoanalytic thought. And this connection seems even more compelling when we turn to Freud's comments on language and dreams.

One of the distinguishing features of dreams for Freud is that they represent the victory of concreteness, of a language of the body and its instincts, over abstract forms of thought. This does not mean that dreams cannot employ the language of everyday speech; on the contrary, they often do so. But this is in part, insists Freud, because every language has a repertoire of "concrete terms" which "are richer in associations than conceptual ones." Dreams make use of such words, exploiting the multiple and ambiguous meanings they contain in order to disguise their meanings (ID, 455, 456). In an argument which could be nicely connected with Bakhtin, Freud suggests that popular genres are richer in concrete terms, in words steeped in symbolism. It follows that symbolism is not unique to dreams but is also "to be found in folklore, and in popular myths, legends, linguistic idioms, proverbial wisdom, and current jokes." Moreover, the symbolic connections between things—and Freud is thinking especially of sexual symbols such as a knife or an umbrella representing the penis, or a chest or an oven standing for the uterus—probably refer back to ancient linguistic identities: "Things that are symbolically connected today were probably united in prehistoric times by conceptual and linguistic identity. The symbolic relation seems to be a relic and a mark of a former identity" (ID, 468). Freud appears to suggest here that language expresses the interconnections and symbolic identities among things rather than mechanically mapping names onto things. Prehistoric languages, he argues, expressed erotic-mimetic relations among entities in the world. And bits of these linguistic meanings are still available today, especially in folklore and popular genres, and often come to the fore in dreams. Dreams, in other words, draw upon the ancient and sensuous meanings of words: ". . . the course of linguistic evolution has made things very easy for dreams. For language has a whole number of words at its command which originally had a pictorial and concrete significance, but are used today in a colourless and abstract sense. All that the dream need do is to give these words their former, full meaning or to go back a little way to an earlier phase in their development" (ID, 532).

Rather than speaking in a radically foreign language, dreams employ the ambiguities of the language of everyday life to mobilize the concrete and symbolic meanings effaced by the abstracting tendencies of modern language. Were dreams to speak a language utterly disconnected from any known forms of speech, it would be impossible to interpret them. But, because they use forms of known language which are richly pictorial and imagistic, it is possible for psychoanalysis to translate them into the language of everyday life: "the productions of the dream-work," Freud contends, "present no greater difficulties to their translators than do the ancient hieroglyphic scripts to those who seek to read them" (ID, 457). Indeed, the theme of translation looms large in Freud's theory of dreams. Writing some years later about his dream-book, he maintained that "at that time I learnt how to translate the language of dreams into the forms of expression of our thought language."[143] For Benjamin, all translation refers us back to an originary language, a primary language of *mimesis*, when people spoke "the language of things." Moreover, in his 1915 essay, "The Unconscious," Freud described the unconscious as operating by means of a thing-language, a language based upon "the relations of words to unconscious thing-presentations."[144] The language of the unconscious is vital for redemptive purposes because, as Joel Kovel points out, it draws subjectivity toward a fusion with the organic world of things and other beings.[145] And it is this forgotten dimension of language, I want to suggest, that Benjamin locates in a sort of *linguistic unconscious* thanks to his reading of Freud. Rather than claim that the mimetic-symbolic dimension of language, that dimension which immerses us in the language of things, has been irretrievably lost, Benjamin maintains that it is all around us—in disguised forms that speak to its repression. In fact, his first draft of "On the Mimetic Faculty" employs the Freudian concept of the unconscious to make precisely this point. Discussing the way in which children perceive and create similarities between themselves and the world around them, Benjamin notes that the sphere of similarities has contracted for people in modern society. Nevertheless, he insists:

> It can still be maintained today that the cases in which people consciously perceive similarities in everyday life are a minute segment of those countless cases unconsciously determined by similarity. The similarities which one perceives consciously, for instance in faces, are, when compared to the countless similarities perceived unconsciously or not at all, like the enormous underwater mass of an iceberg in comparison to the small tip one sees projecting above the waves.[146]

Like Freud, then, Benjamin believes unconscious experiences have become repositories of the mimetic relation to the world. And this returns us to his letter to Gretel Adorno. The text which he praises there, and to which he links "On the Mimetic Faculty," is clearly Lecture 30 of Freud's *New Introductory Lectures on Psychoanalysis*. Discussing the fact that in "great insect communities" communication occurs without language or speech, Freud suggests that the nonlinguistic way in which insects communicate is probably "the original archaic method of communication between individuals" which "in the course of phylogenetic evolution" has been replaced by language. Nonetheless, he speculates, "the older method might have persisted in the background and still be able to put itself into effect under certain conditions."[147] It is easy to see why Benjamin should have been so excited by this passage, for it speaks directly to the preservation of an "archaic method of communication," prior to human language, which persists today, albeit "in the background," and which might reemerge "under certain conditions." For Benjamin this is another way of saying that an older language of the body and of things, a language of *mimesis*, lives on in modern language as a repository of a different sensibility, a different mode of experience of self, world, and others, and that this original language might yet become the basis for a radical refashioning of social life.

For much of human history, *mimesis* could be found in ritual and myth. In the modern age, however, it has been driven underground by the ultra-rationalist bourgeois historical consciousness. Yet, since what has been repressed always returns forcefully, albeit in unconscious and potentially damaging forms, mimetic-erotic energies are everywhere around us—attached to commodities, fashions, technology, and systems of power (as in fascism). The language of the body and things has not disappeared, it has simply been displaced. As a result, myth lives on in scientific rationality while eros attaches itself to death rather than to life. These inversions are products of the extreme alienation of capitalism. Yet, they are also the site of possible dialectical reversals. Just as the neurotic often needs to reach a point of emotional collapse before radical change is possible, so it is at the point of greatest sickness that the human agents who populate bourgeois society might find the initiative for a rupture with the existing state of affairs. As in baroque allegory, recognition of the emptiness of the historical landscape might be the point of departure for political action.[148]

Revolutionary possibilities are thus ever-present. This is a central proposition of Benjamin's materialism. However alienated we may be from our bodies and from things, there is always a way back to them—difficult and traumatic as this journey may be. The human historical body—the site of language, *mimesis*, and labor—is the also site of potential revolutionary energies. Yet, before this is denounced as an essentialism of the body, it is crucial to point out that these energies are there for Benjamin because the human body is inherently linguistic and historical (i.e., a site of memories, images, and social desires). This is what Benjamin intended, when he described his overarching theoretical position during the period of the Arcades Project, as an "anthropological materialism." This materialism did not compromise a set of ontological claims about a primary substance called "matter"; rather, it insisted that the body is the point of departure for all of human experience—for language, history, and culture.[149] Like Freud, Benjamin held that psychic repression can never truly eliminate the body, its drives, its dreams and its histories. And the same is true of a society that tries to repress corporeal needs and desires by turning the body into an instrument of production. That is why the proletarian and the prostitute—and, especially, the proletarian as prostitute—figure so centrally in his cultural analysis of capitalism. They are the figures in capitalist society who experience its extreme treatments of the body: on the one hand, they are reduced to the body and nothing else; on the other hand, their bodily needs are systematically discounted and denied. At the same time—and this is especially true of the prostitute and of racial and colonial "others"—their degraded bodies are also sites of projected desire.[150] And there, Benjamin suggests, lie the seeds of revolt.

Not surprisingly, Adorno was eventually to locate his major differences with Benjamin at this nexus. "All of the points on which I differ from you," he wrote Benjamin in 1936, "despite our most fundamental and concrete agreement on everything else, can be grouped together under the heading of an *anthropological materialism* to which I cannot give my allegiance. It is as though for you the measure of concretion were the human body."[151] In an important sense, Adorno was right: the human body *is* the measure of concretion for Benjamin. Indeed, this is why Benjamin's work represents such an important contribution to a materialist theory of language. Yet Adorno, who would draw heavily upon Benjamin's notion of *mimesis*, was unwilling to subscribe to the materialism of the historical body from which that notion originated. There was nothing new about Benjamin's anthropological materialism of the mid-1930s, however. As I have suggested above, his early reading of Freud had impelled him in this direction. Moreover, his interest in surrealism flowed, as we have seen, from the fact that it sought a profane illumination involving the construction of "a sphere of images and, more concretely, of bodies." Indeed, his surrealism essay of nearly ten years earlier had advocated an "anthropological materialism" as the alternative to the "metaphysical materialism" that dominated the official discourse of the Left (S, 192). And this anthropological materialism focused on the historical body, the body as the intersection of desire, labor, image, and technology.

Benjamin understood that bourgeois society tries to efface the human body, beginning with the fetishism of the commodity. Because the products of labor are not regulated and controlled by their producers (and thus establish their value blindly, through the operations of the market), commodities are detached from their origin in the concrete labor of human individuals. And this becomes the model for all the forms of abstraction that characterize bourgeois thought and culture: all along the line, the body is forgotten. Of course, capital must return to the body (people must both produce and consume after all), but this return to the body is a morbid one. It involves the extreme reification in which we are promised happiness by renouncing life, by turning our bodies into means of producing and displaying commodities—indeed by becoming commodities ourselves. Yet—and this is part of the radicalism of Benjamin's thought—capital's strategy is never fully secured. The unfulfilled desires, the disappointed strivings for happiness, are never entirely extinguished. They live on, asserting claims that are reminders of forgotten hopes. These desires originate in the body, and the body (not consciousness) is the place where they are remembered (even if in the form of hysterical symptoms).[152] As the narrator of Jeanette Winterson's novel, *Written on the Body*, puts it: "The physical memory blunders through the doors the mind has tried to seal. . . . Wisdom says forget, the body howls."[153] A precondition of emancipation is that repressed desires must enter into the language of everyday life and that the latter must recover the language of the body and of things. Dreams, as Freud suggests, tend to speak such a language. The challenge is to translate it into the language of waking life. A linguistic task—speaking the language of the body—thus lies at the heart of the revolutionary project. This is what makes Kafka and Brecht so important for Benjamin: they attempt to write a language of the body which brings the forgotten back to consciousness. And that requires staging shock-experiences in which the body asserts its (repressed and forgotten) claims in and through language: "For only the body can generate presence of mind."[154]

Again, it is vital to remind ourselves that the body of which Benjamin speaks is not a piece of personal property abstracted from history and society. For Benjamin, our bodies are extended and transformed by the social relations, technologies, images, and desires through which we produce and reproduce ourselves. This is why he claims that "the collective is a body, too," and why he insists that body and image "interpenetrate" in technology (S, 192). But—and this is where Benjamin departs from a postmodernist like Baudrillard—these historical extensions and modifications of the body do not eliminate it. However abstracted our relations with our bodies become, the historico-material body is always there even if forgotten. *Contra* postmodernism, amnesia is not totality. What has been repressed and forgotten always leaves traces of itself; there is always something to be remembered. And that remembrance—the remembrance of the body, of crushed hopes, of corpses and failed uprisings, of dreams and the ancient meanings of words—is an indispensable part of the project of liberation. Despite its contemporary abstraction and instrumentalization, language carries residues of the mimetic practices from which it emerged. If we can find a way to retrieve these residues, to piece together broken fragments of corporeal meaning and, thereby, awaken forgotten desires, then we will find vast and explosive resources of emancipation. This is what it means to say that the road to liberation runs through the language of the body.

And here we encounter one of the major differences between Benjamin's concept of language and the linguistic theory of Jürgen Habermas. Habermas probes language for those cognitive structures which underpin all discourse, he searches for the rationality implicit in discursive communication. Habermas's position is an ultra-rationalist one. He is uninterested in the corporeal, erotic, mimetic, and affective dimensions of language. And this parallels his hyper-cognitivist approach to psychoanalysis. In Habermas's reading of Freud, analysis becomes an overwhelmingly intellectual preoccupation—a talking through of resistances—rather than a process of bodily emotional struggle, often intensely painful, in which conflicts are restaged. Habermas ignores the fact that the irrational must enter language, that its entry hurts and is thus resisted, and that the conflict between remembrance and resistance involves wrenching collisions between an abstracted (and forgetful) reason and a painful and potentially destructive unreason. Ignoring all of this, treating the analytic procedure as an enlightened dialogue, Habermas reduces psychoanalysis to a science of self-reflection.[155] In so doing, he deradicalizes the materialist impulses at work in Freud's theory. He drops the independent claims of the body and its drives which are so central to psychoanalysis and abandons desires for bodily happiness as the basis of an emancipatory politics. Consigning the drive for happiness to the utopian tradition, Habermas chooses instead the natural law goal of justice.[156]

Habermas's rejection of an anthropological materialism of the sort developed by Benjamin whittles down the emancipatory project into little more than a leftish liberalism. Through his insistent materialism, on the other hand, Benjamin holds to the radicalism of classical Marxism.[157] Rather than a communicative reason implicit within discourse, Benjamin searches out a *corporeal reason*—a reason rooted in the body and its desires for happiness—as the basis of any genuinely emancipatory politics. Recognizing the manifold ways in which irrational impulses could be harnessed to barbarism, however, Benjamin did not advocate an explosive and unmediated politics of the unconscious. Yet, this did not lead him to the anti-corporeal rationalism of Habermas and the liberal tradition. Instead, he sought to return reason to the body, to undo the abstraction of cognition from eros. In this respect, Benjamin's position is close to Marcuse's call for a "libidinal rationality," a rationality rooted in erotic desire and reconciled with the necessities of social labor.[158]

Where Benjamin departs from Marcuse, however, is in trying to work out a critical practice that might contribute to the awakening of such a libidinal rationality. This is why the notion of dialectical images figures so prominently in his work. Benjamin hoped to overcome the limits of contemplative criticism in a critical practice which would awaken forgotten desires for happiness. Critical theory had to find a way to affect body and mind or, more accurately perhaps, to create a "bodily presence of mind." Traditional storytelling knew how to do this; through words it could bring "soul, eye, and hand" into connection.[159] But in a context of extreme alienation from the body, radical techniques are required—like those employed by Kafka and Brecht. The latter's dictum that in epic theater, "the language should follow completely the Gestus of the speaking person," is an apt description of the dialectical reversal that informs Benjamin's strategy.[160] Where language/mind has effaced the body, the dialectics of awakening must begin on the side of the forgotten (the body and its dream-images). Indeed, the construction of dialectical images is itself a mimetic and erotic practice. Mimetic because it aims to reconnect humans and the natural world by creating explosive images of what has been lost in the catastrophe of instrumentalization. And erotic because the reuniting of things which have been rent asunder is in psychoanalysis the very basis of the sexual instincts.[161] But dialectical images are constructed by means of negation—by exposing the catastrophe of the present alongside the dead hopes of the past. In principle, then, the very procedures of dialectical awakening are themselves part of the emancipatory process.

If there is a major weakness in Benjamin's theory of dialectical images it would seem to lie in the difficulties of connecting these with the experience of labor and production. The Arcades Project was focused on images related to consumption. Benjamin recognized, however, that the forms of cultural experience which characterized modernity had their roots in the sphere of production. "The shock experience which the passer-by has in the crowd corresponds," he argued, "to what the worker 'experiences' at his machine."[162] Moreover, production is the central category of his cultural and aesthetic theory of the 1930s in which revolutionary artistic practice requires adopting the standpoint of "the artist as producer."[163] Benjamin did not, however, work out how dialectical images might bring together commodity dream-images with the shock experiences of the assembly line and the tyranny of work in capitalist society. Interestingly, some of the most radical working-class upsurges of this century did occasionally experiment in this direction—and they did so right at the heart of the fashion industry. During the great strikes and union drives of the 1930s in the United States, for example, which took place at the time when the culture industries were being developed, campaigns launched by the International Ladies Garment Workers Union (ILGWU) counterposed the roles of women as both the exploited producers and the targeted consumers of the products of the fashion industry. On a 1933 picket line of Mexican-American dressmakers in Los Angeles described by organizer Rose Pesotta, "the girls came dressed in their best dresses, made by themselves, and reflecting the latest styles." The picketers "marched on the sidewalks like models in a modiste's salon." This direct confrontation of dream-images of fashion with the realities of working women's lives was a tactic regularly employed as the union waged strikes and organized garment workers.[164] More recently, the AgitProp collective of the Labor Community Strategy Center in Los Angeles has developed action pieces influenced by Benjamin. Their 1993 piece *L.A.'s Lethal Air Kills the Dada-Puppen* combines references to dada dolls, Benjamin's image of the artist as producer, "and the longtime Mexican costuming tradition of *cadavera* (dressing up like the living skeleton that honors the memory of the dead) in an action montage of one hundred demonstrators carrying one hundred collectively assembled ready-made dead dolls donning the shriveled-lung bodies and faces of child cadavers."[165]

Regrettably, the possibilities for developing Benjamin's concept of dialectical images in this direction remain largely unexplored. This is principally a fact of political history: we simply lack considerable experience of revolutionary movements which tackled the problems Benjamin addressed. At the same time, however, it is also a fact of the academic reception of Benjamin. We have today a small-scale industry devoted to turning out a Benjaminian fashion. Benjamin appears there not as a revolutionary critic of commodification, but as an ironic commentator on literary and cultural phenomena. But Benjamin was considerably more than that. He was a theorist of the revolutionary Left who confronted some of the central problems of the working-class movement by probing the gaps and fissures in the cultural incorporation of workers into the circuit of the commodity. And he did so by means of a remarkable materialist theory of language. More than any other radical theorist, Benjamin insists upon the bodily, erotic, and mimetic dimensions of language. His anthropological materialism involves an unrelenting refusal to detach language from the body, an insistence that language actually be "seen as part of the body, not its other."[166] The result is a materialist account of language as a site of potential energies of liberation. It is an accomplishment with which we have yet to catch up, and which is in danger of being forgotten in the rush toward tame appropriations of Benjamin. "In every era the attempt must be made anew to wrest tradition away from the conformism that is about to overpower it" (TPH, 255). We ought not let this happen. Benjamin's radically nonconformist thinking about language and liberation deserves nothing less than a critical, revolutionary translation into the debates of the present.

CONCLUSION

Corporeal reason requires learning to read what is written on the body. And as the prisoners in Kafka's *The Penal Colony* know, this does not come easily. The penal officer in Kafka's story explains:

> "Whatever commandment the prisoner has disobeyed is written on his body. . . . This prisoner, for instance . . . will have written on his body: HONOR THY SUPERIORS!" . . . Many questions were troubling the explorer, but at the sight of the prisoner he asked only: "Does he know his sentence?" "No," said the officer. . . . "There would be no point in telling him. He'll learn it on his body."[1]

Learn it on the body. Enlightenment comes for Kafka, if at all, in remembering what has been written on the body. And as Elaine Scarry puts it, "What is 'remembered' in the body is well remembered."[2] Yet, we rarely *know* what the body remembers. So detached from our bodies has modern thought become, so absorbed in the abstracting logic of the commodity, that corporeal knowledge comes as an overwhelming shock, like that eruption of a cough which Kafka calls "the animal." What the body remembers, the modern mind tries to forget: a tortuous story of pleasure and repression, rebellion and defeat which, all too often, does not end well. Yet, this story, written on the body, must be remembered. To forget is to repeat, to perpetuate the cycle of repression.

Body and memory. Sites of domination, they are also the space of slumbering powers of emancipation. But whether those powers will be awakened is a question that transcends theory. To give voice to what the body remembers involves a particular kind of practice. An emancipatory practice—one designed to return the body to language and language to the body—is ill-served, however, by theory which effaces the body, banishing it in order to assign sovereign powers to language. Poststructural linguistics is such a theory. In erasing the laboring body, it reproduces capital's myth of self-birth, the notion that capital can create itself (and infinitely expand) without the mediation of labor. As another myth of self-birth—of language which creates itself outside of bodies and material practices—postmodernist theory naturalizes the actual domination of concrete by abstract labor, body by mind, workers by capital. And these dominations, as we have seen, intersect with those of gender and race, configured as they are around dualisms of mind and body, culture and nature, human and animal. When postmodernist theorists declare "The end of labor. The end of production," when they announce "the end of the scene of the body," they merely lend an apocalyptic rhetoric to the story capital has told for a long time. And when they suggest that in the digital age, "our body often appears simply superfluous . . . since today everything is concentrated in the brain," they efface the laboring bodies whose activities underpin the digitized movements of signs and capital.[3]

This fetishism is not innocent. As one commentator points out, it leads postmodern analysts of the information economy to forget "the teenage girls going blind from soldering circuits in the Philippines, the poisoned groundwater in Silicon valley, the tumors arising in the livers of chip factory workers, the reporters and data-entry clerks paralyzed by repetitive strain injury, and the banalization and cheapening of countless occupations."[4] Nor are these forgettings accidental since, as Adorno reminds us, to reify *is* to forget. Beginning with Saussure's attempt to model language on a fetishistic economics of money and commodities, linguistic idealism reifies as soon as it drops the body out of language. And notwithstanding his criticisms of Saussure, Derrida, too, identifies language with money, offering us economic systems that reproduce themselves without labor (another version of the myth of self-birth), and instructing us that to be a linguistic subject is to be a capitalist (and, therefore, that capitalism always has been and always will be with us). The end result is an uncritical social theory which scorns talk of liberation from the powers of capital.

In order to subvert these idealist moves, I have undertaken a *turn to the body*—and to theorists like Bakhtin and Benjamin for whom language is one of the ways in which humans "body forth" in the world. This turn is not about inverting the dualism of language and body. Rather, following Bakhtin, it is about degrading the abstract and disembodied, bringing low the rarefied language system of postmodernist theory. Rabelais, wrote Bakhtin, "made the top and bottom change places, intentionally mixed the hierarchical levels to discover the core of the object's concrete reality, to free it from its shell and to show its material bodily aspect."[5] If we are to undermine the abstract and disembodied ideas about language that predominate in social theory today, we need just this sort of Rabelaisian move—one which brings mind and language low by making them collide with the material lower bodily stratum.

At the same time, the body itself today stands in need of materialization, or at least the body that appears in so much social theory. In fashionable post-modernism, as Terry Eagleton observes, the body risks "becoming the greatest fetish of all."[6] Postmodern body-talk fetishizes by reducing bodies to signs. Clinging to linguistic abstractions, it refuses contact with natural, biological and laboring bodies. Defetishizing theory subverts these moves by making the top and the bottom change places, as the first step toward displacing their hierarchical relation. And this requires starting from the biological body, the body which links us to nature and animality, and showing how the human body remains a part of nature even as it enters culture and the time of social history. Like mind, language is an attribute of a particular hominid species which has evolved on the same biological principles as have ants, chimps and squirrels. In developing historical bodies, bodies they shape and extend through technology, language, and culture, humans do not leave biology behind. They simply lay down new orders of time and new structures of activity that require specific explanatory principles. Crucially, of course, this new temporal order is also the time of human freedom, the site upon which we develop new capacities and potentialities by extending our biological bodies into culture.

Historical materialism is fundamentally an account of the dynamics specific to the social life of creatures who make their own history by extending and reshaping their bodies, and of how the productive activity of those bodies crystallizes into structures of exploitation where society is divided into classes. Marx sees the historical dynamics of class society in terms of fundamental conflicts over exploitation and resistance to it. Voloshinov's theory of word and utterance, his notion that class society involves a struggle over the sign, is an invaluable application of this Marxian insight to the philosophy of language, an insight Bakhtin retains in his notion of the *heteroglossia* inherent in all languages. But Bakhtin does not equate the heterogeneity of language with an endless proliferation of differences and a radical destabilization of all structures of meaning. Rather, he sees language as bound up with and shaped by concrete forms of life—of labor, time, festival, and the social body. And he sees class societies as entailing a fundamental divide between official and popular genres. In the latter—in the carnivalesque genres associated with the rogue, the fool, and the clown—he finds immense resources of popular resistance to oppression. This is a finding we can ill afford to surrender.

In their insistence on the struggle over the sign and the richness of popular genres, Voloshinov and Bakhtin repudiate poststructuralist notions of an all-determining language system. They position language as a site of struggle where the oppressed have significant resources with which to challenge structures of domination. Yet Bakhtin's celebration of carnival comes at a real cost: a blindness

to capital's capacity to commodify the carnivalesque. By integrating Freud's notion
of the unconscious into his theory of commodity fetishism, by teasing out the
hidden erotic connections that tie us to commodities, Walter Benjamin draws
attention to capital's ability to sell us dream-images of the commodity. He shows
how modern society both activates and represses our desires for bodily, erotic,
mimetic ties to the world of people and things. At the same time, Benjamin
understands that capitalism betrays these desires, forcing them to take refuge in
our dream-life. Moreover, he holds that in the mass culture of the commodity,
the oppressed dream together—of a world of equality and abundance, a world
beyond the divisions of class, a world in which people and nature are reconciled.
Benjamin believes these frustrated collective dreams—both promoted and repressed by capitalism—have a potentially disruptive power. To realize that power,
however, the dreams of the oppressed must be translated into a language of
revolutionary action, which involves activating the forgotten side of language,
the language of bodies and things that bourgeois and postmodern theory have
repressed. And this requires the shock of dialectical images which bring to
knowledge the frustrated desires the body remembers—and which expose the
emptiness of the story consciousness tells itself. Only in the shock of self-
recognition on the empty landscape of history, a space of ruins and shattered
desires, will we be able to find the energies for revolutionary action.

Benjamin's theory of body, history, and language is a major achievement in
Marxist thought. It provides a means of incorporating the insights of Voloshinov
and Bakhtin without taking over the romantic populism toward which Bakhtin
gravitates. Like Gramsci, Benjamin believes a struggle must be waged on the
terrain of popular discourse and experience. Benjamin supplements Gramsci,
however, in suggesting that the political problem is not simply to dislodge the
hegemony of ruling class ideas but, in fact, to destabilize our unconscious
identifications with the commodity form itself. At the same time, Benjamin
lacks the concrete considerations that Gramsci developed in the course of his
involvement in political organizations and mass struggles; Benjamin's stunning
formulations lack an operational dimension. Gramsci's considerations on hegemony, political organization, mass action, and popular consciousness are pre-
mised on the idea that mass organizations and parties of the oppressed are the
"historical laboratory" in which counter-hegemonies are formed, "the crucibles
where the unification of theory and practice, understood as a real historical
process, takes place."[7] Bringing together Gramsci's theory of political organization and counter-hegemony with Benjamin's views on body, language and memory
is not fundamentally a problem of theory, however, so much as it is a problem
of practice.

While we are a long way from the development of such a practice at the
moment, it should now be clear that the postmodern fetish of language points
us entirely in the wrong direction. The materialist approach to language explored
across these studies at least points us toward emancipatory possibilities. And

they remind us, I hope, of our practical obligations to the struggle for human liberation, the struggle of prisoners to read what has been written on their bodies, the struggle to liberate labor and desire. While challenging the fetishes of capital that postmodernism reinscribes, this book is also meant as a reminder of those practical obligations to the actual flesh-and-blood battles against capital that people wage everyday. For, as Benjamin put it, fetishes and myths will continue "as long as there is a single beggar."[8]

NOTES

INTRODUCTION

1. Like many commentators, I am using the generic term "postmodernist social theory" to describe that work which, taking post-structuralist critiques of "humanism" as their point of departure, attempt to inscribe language—whether as discourse, text, or writing—as the central determinant of human existence. In my view, the relations between postmodernist art and postmodernist theory are strained and difficult ones. My focus, however, is on social theory that operates in a postmodernist register. Among the best explications of the theoretical underpinnings of postmodernism are Peter Dews, *Logics of Disintegration: Post-Structuralist Thought and the Claims of Critical Theory* (London: Verso, 1987); Gillian Rose, *Dialectic of Nihilism: Post-Structuralism and Law* (Oxford: Blackwell, 1984); Frederic Jameson, *The Prison-House of Language* (Princeton: Princeton University Press, 1972); Allan Megill, *Prophets of Extremity: Nietzsche, Heidegger, Foucault, Derrida* (Berkeley: University of California Press, 1985); Richard Harland, *Superstructuralism: The Philosophy of Structuralism and Post-Structuralism* (London: Routledge and Kegan Paul, 1988); J. G. Merquior, *From Prague to Paris: A Critique of Structuralist and Post-Structuralist Thought* (London: Verso, 1986). For recent critiques of postmodernist theory see Teresa Ebert, *Ludic Feminism and After: Postmodernism, Desire and Labor in Late Capitalism* (Ann Arbor: University of Michigan Press, 1996), and Terry Eagleton, *The Illusions of Postmodernism* (Oxford: Blackwell, 1996). On the economic and cultural moment of postmodernism see David Harvey, *The Condition of Postmodernity* (Oxford: Blackwell, 1989), and Fredric Jameson, *Postmodernism or, The Cultural Logic of Late Capitalism* (London: Verso Books, 1991).

2. Andrew Parker, "Mom," in *Sexual Difference*, Special Issue of the *Oxford Literary Review* 8, nos. 1–2:102.

3. Susan Bordo, "Feminism, Postmodernism and Gender-Scepticism," in *Feminism/Postmodernism*, ed. Linda J. Nicholson (New York: Routledge and Kegan Paul, 1990), p. 145. The question of the body in Foucault's thought—and, of his relation to postmodernist theory—is too large an issue to take up here. I tend to be sympathetic, however, to those critics who believe the body-self is a stumbling block in Foucaultian thought. In this vein see Ladelle McWhorter, "Culture or Nature? The Function of the Term 'Body' in the Work of Michel Foucault," *Journal of Philosophy* 86 (1989): 608–614, and Gad Horowitz, "The Foucaultian Impasse: No Sex, No Self, No Revolution," *Political Theory* 15, no. 1 (February 1987): 61–80.

4. On this point see Caroline Bynum, "Why all the Fuss about the Body? A Medievalist's Perspective," *Critical Inquiry*, 22 (Autumn 1995): 4.

5. Jacques Lacan, *Ecrits: A Selection*, trans. Alan Sheridan (New York: W. W. Norton, 1977), p. 65.

6. Jacques Derrida, "Structure, Sign and Play in the Discourse of the Human Sciences," in Jacques Derrida, *Writing and Difference*, trans. Alan Bass (Chicago: University of Chicago Press, 1978), p. 280; Judith Butler, *Bodies That Matter: On the Discursive Limits of "Sex"* (New York: Routledge and Kegan Paul, 1993), p. 49.

7. Vicki Kirby, *Telling Flesh: The Substance of the Corporeal* (New York: Routledge and Kegan Paul, 1997), p. 120. This is an important critique of post-structuralist body-talk, especially as it figures in some feminist theory. Kirby attempts to use Derrida's version of deconstruction against these anticorporeal theorists. While this is an interesting move—and one which develops lines of argument which Derrida clearly does open up—I believe, as I argue in chapter 2, that Derrida's position, too, collapses into a new kind of idealism.

8. I understand critical materialism to be the practice of materialist critique. I judge this practice to be the essence of Marx's theoretical work. For later works in this tradition see Patrick Murray, *Marx's Theory of Scientific Knowledge* (Atlantic Highlands: Humanities Press, 1988); Theodor Adorno, *Negative Dialectics*, trans. E. B. Ashton (New York: Seabury Press, 1973); and Max Horkheimer, "Materialism and Metaphysics," in Max Horkheimer, *Critical Theory*, trans. Matthew J. O'Connell and others (New York: Herder and Herder, 1972), pp. 10–46. It should go without saying that the "proof" of materialist criticism cannot be found outside the process and results of critical practice itself.

9. Adorno, *Negative Dialectics*, p. 22.

10. Henry Mayhew, *London Labour and the London Poor* (London: Frank Cass, 1861–62), 1:2.

11. Jonas Frykman and Orvar Lofgren, *Culture Builders: A Historical Anthropology of Middle-Class Life*, trans. Alan Crozier (New Brunswick, NJ: Rutgers University Press, 1987), p. 223.

12. Himani Bannerji, "Gender, Race, Class and Socialism: An Interview," *New Socialist*, 3, no. 1 (February–March 1998). See also Anne McClintock, *Imperial Leather: Race, Gender and Sexuality in the Colonial Contest* (New York: Routledge and Kegan Paul, 1995), esp. chs. 2, and 4.

13. Frantz Fanon, *Black Skin, White Masks*, trans. Charles Lam Markmann (New York: Grove Press, 1967), p. 167.

14. Karl Marx, *Capital*, vol. 1, trans. Ben Fowkes (Harmondsworth: Penguin Books, 1976), pp. 128, 138, 150.

15. For one of the most important treatments of this issue see Alfred Sohn-Rethel, *Intellectual and Manual Labour: A Critique of Epistemology* (London: MacMillan Press, 1978).

16. Hal Foster, *The Return of the Real: The Avant-Garde at the End of the Century* (Cambridge, MA: MIT Press, 1996), p. 96. Regrettably, Foster tends not to see that Jean Baudrillard's work is an exemplar of just this trend.

17. I use the term *vulgar deconstruction* to mark my recognition that not all deconstructionists are committed to a simpleminded textualization of social life. Indeed, there are readings of Derrida's remark to this effect which move in a materialist direction; I will explore the implications of these in chapter 2. But as many commentators have pointed out, straightforwardly idealist renderings of deconstruction—or what I have called "vulgar deconstruction"—dominate within literary criticism in particular and much cultural studies generally.

18. See Theodor Adorno, *Aesthetic Theory*, trans. Robert Hullot-Kentor (Minneapolis: University of Minnesota Press, 1997), p. 45.

19. Jacques Derrida, "Deconstruction and the Other," in *Dialogues with Contemporary Continental Thinkers*, ed. Richard Kearney (Manchester: Manchester University Press, 1984), p. 121. As I show in chapter 2, Derrida argues that capitalism has always already been there and, therefore, that it always will be.

20. I borrow the term "language-body" from Luce Irigaray, *Marine Lover of Friedrich Nietzsche*, trans. Gillian C. Gill (New York: Columbia University Press, 1991), p. 65. I return to Irigaray's argument in chapter 1.

21. For a discussion of the body as an indeterminate constancy see Carol Bigwood, "Renaturalizing the Body (with the Help of Merleau-Ponty)," *Hypatia* 6, no. 3 (Fall 1991): 54–73.

22. Terry Eagleton, *The Ideology of the Aesthetic* (Oxford: Basil Blackwell, 1990), p. 199.

23. Indeed, this was a central feature of the "vulgar Marxism" associated with Karl Kautsky. See, for example, Massimo Salvadori, *Karl Kautsky and the Socialist Revolution*, trans. John Rothschild (London: Verso, 1979), pp. 23–24

24. Sigmund Freud, *The Interpretation of Dreams*, trans. James Strachey, vol. 4 of the Penguin Freud Library (Harmondsworth: Penguin Books, 1976), p. 719. Thus, Monique David-Menard is correct when she writes that "one cannot rely on the idea of a bodily sensorimotor system that would be independent of the history of the symbolization of the desiring body," but she errs in not recognizing the reversibility of this statement: the symbolizing desiring body is also always a bodily sensorimotor system. Failure to see this produces a recurring dualism throughout her interesting study. See Monique David-Menard, *Hysteria from Freud to Lacan: Body and Language in Psychoanalysis*, trans. Catherine Porter (Ithaca: Cornell University Press, 1989), p. 66.

25. On Darwin's radical materialism see Adrian Desmond and James Moore, *Darwin: The Life of a Tormented Evolutionist* (New York: Time Warner, 1991). For Freud's radical materialism see William J. McGrath, *Freud's Discovery of Psychoanalysis: The Politics of Hysteria* (Ithaca: Cornell University Press, 1986).

26. Mikhail Bakhtin, *Speech Genres and Other Late Essays*, trans. Vern W. McGee (Austin: University of Texas Press, 1986), p. 6, hereafter cited in the text as SG.

27. Mikhail Bakhtin, *Rabelais and His World*, trans. Helene Iswolsky (Bloomington: Indiana University Press, 1984), p. 21

28. Rainer Nagele, *Theater, Theory, Speculation: Walter Benjamin and the Scenes of Modernity* (Baltimore: Johns Hopkins University Press, 1991), p. 14.

29. Mikhail Bakhtin, "Forms of Time and Chronotope in the Novel," in Bakhtin, *The Dialogic Imagination*, ed. Michael Holquist (Austin: University of Texas Press, 1981), p. 171.

30. Among important recent materialist-feminist studies which insist upon a turn to real, natural-historical bodies, albeit by way of a more sympathetic engagement with postmodernism than my own, I would single out Vicki Kirby, *Telling Flesh;* Elizabeth Grosz, *Volatile Bodies: Toward a Corporeal Feminism* (Bloomington: Indiana University Press, 1994); and Rosemary Hennessy, *Materialist Feminism and the Politics of Discourse* (New York: Routledge and Kegan Paul, 1993). For Marxist-feminist work which has influenced my thinking see Himani Bannerji, *Thinking Through: Essays on Feminism, Marxism and Anti-Racism* (Toronto: Women's Press, 1995); Dorothy E. Smith, *Texts, Facts, and Femininity: Exploring the Relations of Ruling* (New York: Routledge and Kegan Paul, 1990); and *Writing the Social: Critique, Theory, and Investigations* (Toronto: University of Toronto Press, 1999). An especially spirited polemic against postmodernist feminism is Teresa L. Ebert, *Ludic Feminism and After.* While this is an important and powerful book, I don't share Ebert's suspicion of all discussion of bodies and desires—indeed, I attempt to show below how these issues can be taken up in historical materialist terms. In this regard, I also wish to acknowledge an important work by Helga Geyer-Ryan, *Fables of Desire: Studies in the Ethics of Art and Gender* (Cambridge, Eng.: Polity Press, 1994), which explores gender and class through the prism of the work of Walter Benjamin. I would also like to note the important discussions of embodiment in Susan Bordo, "'Material Girl': The Effacements of Postmodern Culture," and her "Bringing Body to Theory"; Carol Bigwood, "Renaturalizing the Body (with the help of Merleau-Ponty)"; and Iris Young, "Throwing Like a Girl," "Pregnant Embodiment," and "'Throwing Like a Girl': Twenty Years Later" all in *Body and Flesh: A Philosophical Reader*, ed. Donn Weldon (Malden, MA: Blackwell, 1998). See also Susan Bordo, *Unbearable Weight: Feminism, Western Culture and the Body* (Berkeley: University of California Press, 1993). The importance of Maxine Sheets-Johnstone's *The Roots of Thinking* (Philadelphia: Temple University Press, 1990) for my work will become obvious in chapter 3. Among feminist engagements with psychoanalysis which explore the materialist dimensions of Freudian thought I have particularly benefited from Marcia Ian, *Remembering the Phallic Mother: Psychoanalysis, Modernism and the Fetish* (Ithaca: Cornell University Press, 1993); Madelon Sprengnether, *The Spectral Mother: Freud, Feminism and Psychoanalysis* (Ithaca: Cornell University Press, 1990); and Naomi R. Goldenberg, *Returning Words to Flesh: Feminism, Psychoanalysis and the Resurrection of the Body* (Boston: Beacon Press, 1990).

31. For evidence that medieval views of the body were often much more material in nature see Bynum, "Why all the Fuss about the Body?"

32. Edward W. Said, *Orientalism* (New York: Vintage Books, 1979), p. 42.

33. See Fanon, *Black Skin, White Masks*, pp. 165–80; and also Said, *Orientalism*, pp. 232–33, 312–16. Neither Fanon nor Said, however, adequately explore the feminization of the bodies of the racially oppressed. Said does, however, refer to this question in passing (see pp. 6, 207). For interesting and sympathetic, but by no means entirely compatible, readings of Fanon on gender see McClintock, *Imperial, Leather*, pp. 360–68, and Ato Sekyi-Oto, *Fanon's Dialectic of Experience* (Cambridge, MA: Harvard University Press, 1996), pp. 211–35. For discussions of the racialized female body see Angela Davis, *Women, Race and Class* (New York: Vintage Books, 1983); Dionne Brand, *Bread Out of Stone*

(Toronto: Coach House Press, 1994), pp. 27–49; and Himani Bannerji, *Thinking Through*, pp. 33, 61–62, 100. For a very rich Marxist treatment of the social psychological dynamics of racism in the United States and the attraction and repulsion of whites towards Blacks as representatives of the body and eros see David R. Roediger, *The Wages of Whiteness: Race and the Making of the American Working Class* (London: Verso Books, 1991).

34. Kelly Oliver, *Womanizing Nietzsche: Philosophy's Relation to the "Feminine,"* (New York: Routledge and Kegan Paul, 1995), p. 105.

35. The maternal body ought not simply be identified with that of the birth-mother. Class and racial inequalities often mean that working-class women do some or much of the mothering of children from higher social strata. For an important treatment of this issue with respect to Freud's omissions in this regard, see Jim Swan, "*Mater* and Nannie: Freud's Two Mothers and the Discovery of the Oedipus Complex," *American Imago* 31, no. 4 (1974): 1–64.

36. See in particular Naomi R. Goldenberg, *Returning Words to Flesh*; Marcia Ian, *Remembering the Phallic Mother;* and Madelon Sprengnether, *The Spectral Mother*. Interestingly, while these authors are deeply critical of Freud's work, they all look to a critically reconstructed psychoanalysis for a way of "thinking through the body." Ian in particular (pp. 202–28) calls for a rejection of Lacanian idealism and a return to Freud's materialism

37. Goldenberg, *Returning Words to Flesh*, p. 36.

38. This is the problem with some of the later work of Luce Irigaray who, in a utopian move, attempts to locate an ethics of sexual difference which would reconcile woman and man, angel and body. See Irigaray, "Sexual Difference," in *The Irigaray Reader*, ed. Margaret Whitford (Oxford: Blackwell, 1991), pp. 165–277. For some interesting critical observations on this move see Kari Weil, *Androgyny and the Denial of Difference* (Charlottesville, VA: University Press of Virginia, 1992), pp. 165–69.

39. Charles Merewether, "To Bear Witness," in *Doris Salcedo* (New York: New Museum of Contemporary Art, 1998), p. 20.

40. Walter Benjamin, "Franz Kafka," in Benjamin, *Illuminations: Essays and Reflections*, ed. Hannah Arendt (New York: Schocken Books, 1968), p. 122.

CHAPTER 1

1. For a representative sample of such interpretations see David B. Allison, ed., *The New Nietzsche: Contemporary Styles of Interpretation* (New York: Delta Books, 1977), and many of the essays in *Nietzsche as Postmodernist: essays pro and contra*, ed. Clayton Koelb (Albany: State University of New York Press, 1990). A perceptive assessment of key themes in such readings is provided by Ernst Behler, *Confrontations: Derrida, Heidegger, Nietzsche*, trans. with an afterword by Steven Taubeneck (Stanford: Stanford University Press, 1991).

2. Walter Kaufmann, *Nietzsche: Philosopher, Psychologist, Antichrist*, 4th ed. (Princeton: Princeton University Press, 1974), p. 167; R. J. Hollingdale, *Nietzsche: The Man and His Philosophy* (London: Routledge and Kegan Paul, 1965), p. 88. I do not mean to commend these studies uncritically, but both works, much like Arthur Danto's *Nietzsche As Philosopher* (New York: MacMillan, 1965), have the merit of grasping the central importance for Nietzsche of the challenge posed by Darwinism. Behler's valuable study (cited in endnote

1 of this chapter), on the other hand, has one mention of Darwin—and this is in reference to a famous statement by Freud!

3. Both Marx and Freud take up the revolutionary impact of Darwinism in highly creative ways. I will have something to say about Darwin and Marx in the next chapter. For an introduction to Freud's response to Darwin see especially Frank J. Sulloway, *Freud, Biologist of the Mind* (Cambridge, MA: Harvard University Press, 1992).

4. Friedrich Nietzsche, *Untimely Meditations*, trans. R. J. Hollingdale (Cambridge: Cambridge University Press, 1983), p. 140. Further references to this work will be given in the text and indicated with the abbreviation UM.

5. In fact, Kant's treatment of the thing-in-itself and objects of experience involved a fundamental ambiguity between his realist commitments and the transcendental idealism of his critical philosophy. On this point see George Schrader, "The Thing in Itself in Kantian Philosophy," in *Kant: A Collection of Critical Essays*, ed. Robert Paul Wolff (New York: Anchor Books, 1967), pp. 172–88. I should add that in his second and third critiques—on morality and aesthetic judgment—Kant tried to go beyond the problem of knowledge per se.

6. Immanuel Kant, *Critique of Pure Reason*, trans. Norman Kemp Smith (New York: St. Martin's Press, 1965), p. 127.

7. Ibid., pp. 59, 61.

8. Let me underline here that I don't believe this confrontation with Darwin to be the single animating impulse in Nietzsche's thought. My claim, rather, is that this confrontation gives a bold, materialist charge to his critique of philosophy.

9. See Peter Bergmann, *Nietzsche, "the Last Antipolitical German,"* (Bloomington, IN: Indiana University Press, 1987), pp. 110–13. The question as to how much Nietzsche understood of Darwin's central argument, as opposed to the views of his popularizers, remains a point of debate. Arthur Danto, *Nietzsche as Philosopher*, pp. 223–5, is bemused by Nietzsche's alleged "anti-Darwinism," which he sees as largely ironic in tone. R. J. Hollingdale, *Nietzsche*, pp. 89–90, portrays Nietzsche as largely grasping and accepting Darwin's central views, as does Irving M. Zeitlin, *Nietzsche: A Re-examination* (Cambridge: Polity Press, 1994), pp. 5–7, 127–32. Daniel C. Dennett believes that Nietzsche's "acquaintance with Darwin's ideas was beset with common misrepresentations and misunderstandings" [*Darwin's Dangerous Idea: Evolution and the Meanings of Life* (New York: Simon and Schuster, 1995), p. 182.]. My own view is that Nietzsche did grasp the revolutionary import of Darwin's anti-teleological thrust, which he embraced, but was troubled deeply by all notions of evolution as leading to some kind of "progress" and "improvement" of the human species. As I will show below, Nietzsche's major concerns about Darwinism are of a *political* nature. For Nietzsche's later shifts away from the perspectives of his first book, *The Birth of Tragedy*, see Peter Levine, *Nietzsche and the Modern Crisis of the Humanities* (Albany: State University of New York Press, 1995) pp. 110–11.

10. Hollingdale, *Nietzsche*, pp. 88, 89.

11. Friedrich Nietzsche, *The Gay Science*, trans. Walter Kaufmann (New York: Vintage Books, 1974), pp. 85, 116. Further references to this work will be given in the text and indicated with the abbreviation GS.

12. Friedrich Nietzsche, *The Will to Power*, pp. 266, 270, 289. Further references to this work will be given in the text and indicated with the abbreviation WP. Given the problems surrounding these unpublished manuscripts, I shall use them only to supplement lines of argument clearly found elsewhere in Nietzsche's published writings.

13. Friedrich Nietzsche, *Beyond Good and Evil*, trans. Walter Kaufmann (New York: Vintage Books, 1989), p. 19. Further references to this work will be given in the text and indicated with the abbreviation BGE.

14. Friedrich Nietzsche, *Daybreak: Thoughts on the Prejudices of Morality*, trans. R. J. Hollingdale (Cambridge: Cambridge University Press, 1982), p. 27. Further references to this work will be given in the text and indicated with the abbreviation D.

15. See, for example, the section entitled "Anti-Darwin" in Friedrich Nietzsche, *Twilight of the Idols*, published in one volume with *The Anti-Christ*, trans. R. J. Hollingdale (Harmondsworth: Penguin, 1990), pp. 85–86. Further references to this work will be given in the text and indicated by the abbreviation TI. See also "Against Darwinism" and the two entries entitled "Anti-Darwin" in *The Will to Power*, pp. 343–44, and 361–65. For one representative sample of the confusion regarding passages such as these see Danto, *Nietzsche as Philosopher*, p. 223 who writes: "it is hard to see why Nietzsche wished to count himself an anti-Darwinian."

16. The expression "socialist dolts" can be found in *Beyond Good and Evil*, p. 118.

17. Nietzsche, *The Will to Power*, p. 344; and *On The Genealogy of Morals*, trans. Walter Kaufmann and R. J. Hollingdale, published in one volume with *Ecce Homo* (New York: Vintage Books, 1989), pp. 78–79. Further references to this work will appear in the text indicated by the abbreviation GM.

18. Nietzsche, *Twilight of the Idols*, p. 86.

19. See also *Thus Spoke Zarathustra*, trans. R. J. Hollingdale (Harmondsworth: Penguin Books, 1961), p. 220 where Nietzsche calls for a "new nobility." Further references to this work will be indicated in the text with the abbreviation Z.

20. Nietzsche, *Ecce Homo*, trans. Walter Kaufmann, published in one volume with *On the Genealogy of Morals* (New York: Vintage Books, 1989), p. 327. Further references to this work will be given in the text and indicated with the abbreviation EH. On this theme see also *Twilight of the Idols*, p. 54.

21. For a noteworthy exception see Bruce Detwiler, *Nietzsche and the Politics of Aristocratic Radicalism* (Chicago: University of Chicago Press, 1990).

22. For the critique of the central importance ascribed to self-preservation see also *The Will to Power*, pp. 344–45.

23. Of course, there is an ironic moment to these declarations; but Nietzsche knows full well that there is more to it than that, that he has been trying to construct an argument, to persuade (without this self-knowledge there would be none of the tension required for irony and, indeed, self-parody). And it is the persuasiveness, or lack thereof, of these exclamations that concerns me at the moment.

24. Dennett, *Darwin's Dangerous Idea*, p. 466.

25. This is especially true of the Nietzsche promoted by Michel Foucault. For a representative sample of views which attach central importance to the will to power see the essays collected in David B. Allison, ed., *The New Nietzsche*.

26. As he says about *Twilight of the Idols*, p. 32.

27. Dennett, *Darwin's Dangerous Idea*, p. 465.

28. Stephen Jay Gould, *An Urchin in the Storm: Essays about Books and Ideas* (New York: W. W. Norton, 1987), p. 48.

29. ———. *The Panda's Thumb: More Reflections in Natural History* (New York: W. W. Norton, 1982), p. 28.

30. Gilles Deleuze, *Nietzsche et la philosophie* (Paris: Presses Universitaires de France, 1973), p. 48.

31. Lacking knowledge of the (genetic) mechanism of biological inheritance, Darwin too lapsed occasionally into Lamarckian reasoning, as Christopher Wills points out in *The Wisdom of the Genes: New Pathways in Evolution* (Oxford: Oxford University Press, 1991), pp. 68–69.

32. Gould, *Urchin*, p. 70; see also *Panda's Thumb*, pp. 83–84.

33. Nietzsche, *Beyond Good and Evil*, pp. 151, 209, 111.

34. The reference to intoxication takes us back to Nietzsche's embrace of the Dionysian over the Appolonian "moments" in the emergence of human culture. Although Nietzsche seems to believe that both are necessary, it is the latter that he holds to be imperiled.

35. Claudia Crawford, "Nietzsche's Physiology of Ideological Criticism," in *Nietzsche as Postmodernist*, p. 165. See also Richard Brown, "Nihilism: 'Thus Speaks Physiology,'" in *Nietzsche and the Rhetoric of Nihilism: Essays on Interpretation, Language and Politics*, eds. Tom Darby, Béla Egyed, Ben Jones (Ottawa: Carleton University Press, 1989), pp. 133–44.

36. Alexander Nehemas, *Nietzsche: Life as Literature* (Cambridge, MA: Harvard University Press, 1985), p. 181.

37. Henry Staten, *Nietzsche's Voice* (Ithaca: Cornell University Press, 1990), pp. 125, 126. This is a study of first-rate importance. Although Staten's "psychodialectical" approach is driven by different concerns than those I have raised, it converges with my own view on a number of crucial points.

38. See Michael Tanner, "Introduction" to Friedrich Nietzsche, *The Birth of Tragedy*, trans. Shaun Whiteside (Harmondsworth Penguin Books, 1993), p. xiii. Notice also Nietzsche's invocation of *Birth of Tragedy* in the final section of *Twilight of the Idols*, p. 120.

39. Eric Blondel, *Nietzsche: The Body and Culture*, trans. Sean Hand (Stanford: Stanford University Press, 1991), p. 219.

40. This, in my view, is the key to understanding Nietzsche's mystical ramblings about "eternal return"; to will a change, to will something different, would be to get caught up in the flux of temporality. Endless change as staying in the same place is the key to eternal recurrence.

41. Rodolphe Gasché, "*Ecce Homo* or the written body," *Oxford Literary Review*, 7 (1985): 9, 10, 23, 22.

42. Ibid., p. 11.

43. Staten, *Nietzsche's Voice*, pp. 100–104.

44. Again, Staten is one of the few commentators to have picked up on this point. An insightful, but only partially successful, attempt to grapple with Nietzsche's fascination with asceticism is Charles E. Scott, "The Mask of Nietzsche's Self-Overcoming," in *Nietzsche as Postmodernist*, esp. pp. 222–29.

45. Martin Heidegger, *Nietzsche, Vol. III: The Will to Power as Knowledge and as Metaphysics*, ed. David Farrell Krell (San Francisco: Harper and Row, 1987), p. 46.

46. Ibid., p. 80. At times, Heidegger wants to fault Nietzsche for encouraging biologistic and Darwinistic interpretations. See, for example, ibid., p. 86.

47. Michel Haar, "Heidegger and the Nietzschean 'Physiology of Art,'" in *Exceedingly Nietzsche: Aspects of Contemporary Nietzsche Interpretation*, eds. David Farrell Krell and David Wood (London: Routledge and Kegan Paul, 1988), p. 15.

48. Ibid., p. 19.

49. As quoted by David Farrell Krell, *Daimon Life: Heidegger and Life-Philosophy* (Bloomington, IN: Indiana University Press, 192), p. 17.

50. Martin Heidegger, *Early Greek Thinking* (New York: Harper and Row, 1975), pp. 64–65.

51. See Krell, *Daimon Life*, p. 21.

52. Martin Heidegger, "What Calls for Thinking," in Heidegger, *Basic Writings*, ed. David Farrell Krell (San Francisco: Harper Collins, 1977), p. 357.

53. Martin Heidegger, *Being and Time*, trans. John Macquarrie and Edward Robinson (New York: Harper and Row, 1962), p. 291.

54. Martin Heidegger, "Letter on Humanism," in *Basic Writings*, pp. 203, 204, 206.

55. For a useful overview see Ellen Kennedy, "Nietzsche: Woman as Untermensch," in *Women in Western Political Philosophy*, eds. Ellen Kennedy and Susan Mendus (Brighton: Wheatsheaf Books, 1987), pp. 179–201.

56. Staten, *Nietzsche's Voice*, p. 64.

57. Peter Sloterdijk, "Eurotaoism," in *Nietzsche and the Rhetoric of Nihilism*, pp. 110–11.

58. Jacques Derrida, *Spurs: Nietzsche's Styles/Eperons: Les Styles de Nietzsche*, trans. Barbara Harlow (Chicago: University of Chicago Press, 1979), pp. 65, 51. My own view is that Derrida is insensitive to this movement in Nietzsche's thought because he, too, is a philosopher in flight from "origins,"—that is, birth, mother, body. I return to this point in the next chapter.

59. For the argument that Nietzsche was fully aware he was constructing a new myth by which many could live, see Stanley Rosen, "Remarks on Nietzsche's Platonism," in *Nietzsche and the Rhetoric of Nihilism*, pp. 145–63, and Levine, *Nietzsche and the Modern Crisis*, p. 126.

60. Allan Megill, *Prophets of Extremity: Nietzsche, Heidegger, Foucault, Derrida* (Berkeley: University of California Press, 1985), pp. 101, 102.

61. See, for example, Friedrich Nietzsche, "On the Pathos of Truth" and "On Truth and Lies in a Nonmoral Sense," in *Philosophy and Truth: Selections from Nietzsche's Notebooks of the early 1870s*, trans., and ed. Daniel Breazeale (New Jersey: Humanities Press, 1979). For a useful discussion of language in Nietzsche which focuses heavily on his early writings see Alan D. Schrift, "Language, Metaphor, Rhetoric: Nietzsche's Deconstruction of Epistemology," *Journal of the History of Philosophy*, no. 3, (1985):371–95. See also J. P. Stern, "Nietzsche and the Idea of Metaphor," in *Nietzsche: Imagery and Thought*, ed. Malcolm Pasley (Berkeley and Los Angeles: University of California Press, 1978).

62. This point is brought out nicely by Claude Lévesque, "Language to the Limit," in *Nietzsche and the Rhetoric of Nihilism*, pp. 45–53.

63. Stern, "Nietzsche and the Idea of Metaphor," p. 72.

64. Lévesque, "Language to the Limit," p. 47.

65. Nietzsche, "Oedipus Talks of the Last Philosopher with Himself," in *Postponements: Women, Sensuality, and Death in Nietzsche* by David Farrell Krell (Bloomington, IN: Indiana University Press, 1986), pp. 39–40.

66. Danto, *Nietzsche as Philosopher*, p. 97.

67. Louis A. Sass, *Madness and Modernism: Insanity in the Light of Modern Art, Literature, and Thought* (New York: Basic Books, 1992), p. 184. Sass's book is of a largely provisional and exploratory nature. Especially suggestive, in my opinion, are his brief references (pp. 543–44n.74–75) to Benjamin and Lukacs in terms of understanding the modern condition.

CHAPTER 2

1. For an interesting effort to detach Saussure from post-structuralist readings see Leonard Jackson, *The Poverty of Structuralism: Literature and Structuralist Theory* (London and New York: Longman Group, 1991), chap. 1.

2. Jacques Derrida, *Given Time: I. Counterfeit Money*, trans. Peggy Kamuf (Chicago: University of Chicago Press, 1992), p. 84.

3. It is also the case, as I explain below, that for Derrida this new era was always already there.

4. The weakness of Saussure's argument here is, as I argue below, that he doesn't connect speech to gesture and bodily communication in general.

5. Françoise Gadet, *Saussure and Contemporary Culture*, trans. Gregory Elliot (London: Century Hutchinson, 1989), p. 59.

6. David Holdcroft, *Saussure: Signs, System and Arbitrariness* (Cambridge, Eng.: Cambridge University Press, 1991), pp. 125, 126. It is worth noting that Holdcroft's discussion converges with some key points made by John M. Ellis in his critique of Derrida in *Against Deconstruction* (Princeton: Princeton University Press, 1989), especially pp. 50-64. Holdcroft is insufficiently attentive, however, to the problems entailed when treating the opposition male/female as if it is of the same order as the opposition hot/cold.

7. This is not to deny that they have a use-value, only that use-value is irrelevant outside its entanglement in exchange-value (and the value relations this presupposes).

8. Karl Marx, *Capital*, vol. 1, trans. Ben Fowkes (Harmondsworth: Penguin Books, 1976), p. 163.

9. Karl Marx, *Grundrisse*, trans. Martin Nicolaus (Harmondsworth: Penguin Books, 1973), p. 146. Further citations from the *Grundrisse* are given in the text and indicated as G.

10. Elaine Scarry, *The Body in Pain: The Making and Unmaking of the World* (Oxford and New York: Oxford University Press, 1985), p. 260.

11. Marx, *Capital*, 1:165.

12. Karl Marx, *Capital*, vol. 3, trans. David Fernbach (Harmondsworth: Penguin Books, 1981), p. 516.

13. Paul J. Thibault, *Re-reading Saussure* (London: Routledge and Kegan Paul, 1997), p. 205.

14. Ferruccio Rossi-Landi, *Language as Work and Trade: A Semiotic Homology for Linguistics and Economics*, trans. Martha Adams and others (Amherst: Bergin and Harvey Publishers, 1983), p. 50.

15. V. N. Volosinov, *Marxism and the Philosophy of Language*, trans. Ladislav Matejka and I. R. Titunik (Cambridge, MA: Harvard University Press, 1986), p. 81.

16. Maurice Merleau-Ponty, *The Visible and the Invisible*, trans. Alphonso Lingis (Evanston, IL: Northwestern University Press, 1968), pp. 89, 92, 95. For similar arguments see Theodor Adorno, *Negative Dialectics*, trans. E. B. Ashton (New York: Seabury Press, 1973), esp. "Introduction."

17. See especially Michael Ryan, *Marxism and Deconstruction: A Critical Articulation* (Baltimore: Johns Hopkins University Press, 1982), and Bill Martin, *Matrix and Line: Derrida and the Possibilities of Postmodern Social Theory* (Albany: State University of New York Press, 1992). One of the most interesting materialist readings of Derrida—but one which does not attempt a connection with Marx—is Vicki Kirby, *Telling Flesh: The Substance of the Corporeal* (New York: Routledge and Kegan Paul, 1997).

18. Among the most powerful critiques of Derrida in this regard are M. C. Dillon, *Semiological Reductionism: A Critique of the Deconstructionist Movement in Postmodern Thought* (Albany: State University of New York Press, 1995); Peter Dews, *Logics of Disintegration: Post-Structuralist Thought and the Claims of Critical Theory* (London: Verso, 1987); and Gillian Rose, *Dialectic of Nihilism: Post-Structuralism and Law* (Oxford: Blackwell, 1984).

19. Andrew Parker, "Between Dialectics and Deconstruction: Derrida and the reading of Marx" in *After Strange Texts: The Role of Theory in the Study of Literature*, eds. Gregory S. Jay and David L. Miller (University of Alabama Press, 1985), p. 156.

20. See, for example, J. Claude Evans, *Strategies of Deconstruction: Derrida and the Myth of the Voice* (Minneapolis and Oxford: University of Minnesota Press, 1991), chap. 10.

21. As a number of commentators have pointed out, Derrida conflates signs with signifieds in a fashion which shows enormous confusion with respect to Saussure's argument. For Derrida's discussion see especially *Of Grammatology*, trans. Gayatri Chakravorty Spivak (Baltimore and London: Johns Hopkins University Press, 1974), pp. 29-65, hereafter cited in the text as OG; and *Positions*, trans. Alan Bass (Chicago: University of Chicago Press, 1981), pp. 18-22, hereafter cited as P. For a discussion of Derrida's conceptual slippages and confusions in this area see Ellis, *Against Deconstruction*, pp. 50-64.

22. See Derrida, "Différance," in his *Margins of Philosophy*, trans. Alan Bass (Chicago: University of Chicago Press, 1982), pp. 1-27. For those familiar with the writings of the later Heidegger, Derrida's debt to the Heideggerian concept of Being should be clear, especially when Heidegger crosses out the word Being to emphasize that it is no-thing.

23. Jacques Derrida, "Signature Event Context," in *Margins*, p. 318. Further citations from this article will be indicated as SEC in the text.

24. I won't dwell on Derrida's confusions, but I should note here (*a*) that he has once again collapsed the distinction between signifieds (concepts) and referents; and (*b*) that he has also taken for granted that reference is severed if we talk about something that is not visibly "there." Why this should be so—why we cannot talk about an absent or nonexistent object, person, or relation without "severing" reference—is nowhere explained.

25. Again note the entirely curious idea that reference entails some sort of physical presence, a recurring confusion in Derrida's work.

26. Derrida, "Différance," p. 26n26.

27. Jacques Derrida, *Given Time: I. Counterfeit Money*, trans. Peggy Kamuf (Chicago: University of Chicago Press, 1992), pp. 23-31, 37-45. Hereafter cited in the text as GT. Derrida is taking issue here particularly with Marcel Mauss and his classic study *The Gift: The Form and Reason for Exchange in Archaic Societies*, trans. W. D. Halls (London: Routledge and Kegan Paul, 1990). In much of his argument, Derrida seems to be developing and extending a reading sketched out by Georges Bataille's interpretation of the gift in, for example, *The Accursed Share*, vol. 1, trans. Robert Hurley (New York: Zone Books, 1991), pp. 67-71.

28. Derrida discusses this remark at length in *Spurs: Nietzsche's Styles*, trans. Barbara Harlow (Chicago and London: University of Chicago Press, 1979), pp. 123-43.

29. Jean Baudrillard, *The Transparency of Evil: Essays on Extreme Phenomena*, trans. James Benedict (London: Verso Books, 1993), p. 58.

30. Jacques Derrida, *Specters of Marx: The State of the Debt, the Work of Mourning, and the New International*, trans. Peggy Kamuf (New York: Routledge and Kegan Paul, 1994), pp. 53, 54, hereafter cited in the text as SM.

31. Jean Baudrillard, *For a Critique of the Political Economy of the Sign*, trans. Charles Levin (St. Louis: Telos Press, 1981), p. 87, hereafter cited in the text as FC; Baudrillard, *Symbolic Exchange and Death*, trans. Iain Hamilton Grant and Mike Gane (London: Sage Publications, 1993), p. 20; and *Transparency*, p. 34.

32. Karl Marx and Frederick Engels, *The German Ideology*, 3rd ed. (Moscow: Progress Publishers, 1976), pp. 48, 49.

33. Marx, *Grundrisse*, p. 228.

34. Karl Marx, *Early Writings*, trans and ed. T. B. Bottomore (New York, Toronto, London: McGraw-Hill, 1964), p. 161.

35. At this stage in his work, Baudrillard assumed three forms taken by products (and social stages corresponding to these forms): use-value; exchange-value, and sign-value. Later, he adds a fourth stage—the "fractal" one. On this see *Transparency of Evil*, p. 5, hereafter cited in the text as TE.

36. For an important critique of Baudrillard's views on the Gulf War see Christopher Norris, *Uncritical Theory: Postmodernism, Intellectuals and the Gulf War* (London: Lawrence and Wishart, 1992), esp. chap. 1, and postscript.

37. Jean Baudrillard, *Fatal Strategies*, trans. Philip Beitchman and W. G. J. Niesluchowski (New York and London: Semiotext(e)/Pluto, 1990), p. 25.

38. Thomas Keenan, "The Point is to (Ex)Change It: Reading *Capital* Rhetorically," in *Fetishism as Cultural Discourse*, eds. Emily Apter and William Pietz (Ithaca and London: Cornell University Press, 1993), pp. 152-85, hereafter cited in the text as TPEI.

39. Note that Marx considered this distinction of such import that he claimed it as his own discovery—a rare moment in his writings—and that he describes it as "crucial to an understanding of political economy": Marx, *Capital*, 1:132.

40. I deliberately use the notion of a "responsible reading" here since this is something that Derrida regularly invokes both to counter the idea that deconstruction licenses any reading, and to show how one might derive an ethics from deconstructive premises. While I think Derrida generally fails on these counts, I accept his commitment to reading responsibly/responsively.

41. Marx, *Capital*, 1:128, hereafter cited in the text as C.

42. Or so it does in the case of "world money."

43. Karl Marx, *A Contribution to the Critique of Political Economy*, trans. S. W. Ryazanskaya (Moscow: Progress Publishers, 1970), p. 49.

44. There will often be a further subdivision of surplus-value into rent paid to a landowner.

45. Karl Marx, *Capital*, vol. 3, trans. David Fernbach (Harmondsworth: Penguin Books, 1991), p. 516, hereafter cited in the text as C3.

46. Jacques Derrida, *Glas*, trans. John P. Leavey, Jr. and Richard Rand (Lincoln and London: University of Nebraska Press. 1986), p. 209. Hereafter cited as GL.

47. Sigmund Freud, "Fetishism," in Freud, *On Sexuality*, vol. 7 of the Penguin Freud Library, trans. James Strachey (Harmondsworth: Penguin Books, 1997), pp. 351-57.

48. This is an overriding theme of Derrida's *Spurs: Nietzsche's Styles*, trans. Barbara Harlow (Chicago and London: University of Chicago Press, 1979).

49. Kelly Oliver, *Womanizing Nietzsche: Philosophy's Relation to the "Feminine"* (New York and London: Routledge and Kegan Paul, 1995), pp. 70, 66.

50. Luce Irigaray, *Marine Lover of Friedrich Nietzsche*, trans. Gillian Gill (New York: Columbia University Press, 1991), p. 65.

51. Oliver, *Womanizing Nietzsche*, pp. 104-5.

52. Again, one of the most important efforts in this direction is Kirby, *Telling Flesh*.

53. Richard Harland, *Superstructuralism: The Philosophy of Structuralism and Post-Structuralism* (London: Routledge and Kegan Paul, 1987), p. 147.

54. Adorno, *Negative Dialectics*, pp. 10, 177, 181.

55. Max Horkheimer, "Materialism and Metaphysics," in Horkheimer, *Critical Theory*, trans. Matthew J. O'Connell and others (New York: Herder and Herder, 1972), pp. 28, 32.

56. Adorno, *Negative Dialectics*, p. 33.

57. Karl Marx and Frederick Engels, *The German Ideology*, 3rd rev. ed. (Moscow: Progress Publishers, 1976), pp. 45, 46, hereafter cited in the text as GI.

58. It is here, in the analysis of the laboring body and its repression within dominant theoretical discourses, that one of the most fruitful dialogues between Marxism and at least some currents in feminism might be developed. An emancipatory theory returns us to labor and childbirth/child-rearing not to essentialize these but because, as Freud taught us, that which has been repressed must be remembered and worked through if we are to expand the realm of freedom.

59. See Jairus Banaji, "From the Commodity to Capital: Hegel's Dialectic in Marx's *Capital*," in *Value: The Representation of Labour in Capitalism* (London: CSE Books, 1979), pp. 14-45.

60. Adorno, *Negative Dialectics*, p. 5.

61. Ibid., pp. 23, 179.

62. Henry Staten, *Derrida and Wittgenstein* (Oxford: Basil Blackwell, 1985), p. xvi. Similarly materialist readings of Derrida are offered by Horst Ruthrof, *Semantics and the Body: Meaning from Frege to the Postmodern* (Toronto: University of Toronto Press, 1997), pp. 5-7; and Vicki Kirby, *Telling Flesh*, p. 54. These interpretations offer the most promising direction for those working in a deconstructive vein but, as should be clear, I think deconstruction is fundamentally compromised by it idealism.

63. Derrida, "Fors. Les mots anglés de Nicolas Abraham et Maria Torok," as cited in Christopher Johnson, *System and Writing in the Philosophy of Jacques Derrida* (Cambridge: Cambridge University Press, 1993), p. 90.

64. Peter Dews, *Logics of Disintegration: Post-Structuralist Thought and the Claims of Critical Theory* (London: Verso Books, 1987), p. 19.

CHAPTER 3

1. On this point see Max Horkheimer, "On the Problem of truth," in *The Essential Frankfurt School Reader*, eds. Andrew Arato and Eike Gebhardt, (New York: Continuum Books, 1982), especially pp. 409–414.

2. See, for example, Steven Rose, R. C. Lewontin, and Leon J. Kamin, *Not in Our Genes: Biology, Ideology and Human Nature* (Harmondsworth: Penguin Books, 1984); Stephen Jay Gould, *The Mismeasure of Man* (New York: W. W. Norton, 1981); and R. C. Lewontin, *Biology as Ideology: The Doctrine of DNA* (Toronto: Anansi Press, 1991). In making these points, I do not mean to suggest that Darwin himself was free from racist and sexist prejudices. On the contrary, one finds these regularly throughout *The Descent of Man* in particular. I insist, however, that these do not contaminate the core elements of his theory.

Indeed, like the authors mentioned above, I argue that Darwinism can provide powerful ammunition against attempts to concoct biological bases for social inequalities.

3. Vicki Kirby, *Telling Flesh: The Substance of the Corporeal* (New York: Routledge and Kegan Paul, 1997), p. 98.

4. Karl Marx, *Early Writings*, ed. T. B. Bottomore (New York: McGraw-Hill, 1964), pp. 163–4.

5. Max Horkheimer, "Materialism and Metaphysics," in Horkheimer, *Critical Theory: Selected Essays*, trans. Matthew J. O'Connell and others (New York: Herder and Herder, 1972), p. 34.

6. A motif that recurs in his writings. See, for example, Theodor Adorno, "On the Fetish Character in Music and the Regression in Listening," in Adorno, *The Culture Industry: Selected Essays on Mass Culture*, ed. J. M. Bernstein (New York: Routledge and Kegan Paul, 1991), pp. 30–31.

7. See Barbara Ehrenreich and Janet McIntosh, "Biology Under Attack," *The Nation* 264, (June 9, 1997): 11–16. A recent confrontation with anti-Darwinism in Western social theory, and philosophy is Daniel C. Dennett, *Darwin's Dangerous Idea: Evolution and the Meanings of Life* (New York: Simon and Schuster, 1995).

8. Karl Marx to Ferdinand Lassalle, 16 January 1861, in Karl Marx and Frederick Engels, *Selected Correspondence*, 2nd. ed. (Moscow: Progress Publishers, 1965), p. 123.

9. Adrian Desmond and James Moore, *Darwin: The Life of a Tormented Evolutionist* (New York: Warner Books, 1991).

10. Cited by Desmond and Moore, *Darwin*, p. 314.

11. Charles Darwin, *The Descent of Man and Selection in Relation to Sex* (Princeton: Princeton University Press, 1981), 1:153. There are two independently numbered volumes in this book which will be cited hereafter in the text as DM.

12. Charles Darwin, *The Origin of Species by Means of Natural Selection* (New York: Avenel Books, 1979), p. 458; hereafter cited in the text as OS.

13. Cited by Desmond and Moore, *Darwin*, p. 505. In *Descent*, this conclusion is rendered in more careful language: "some extremely remote progenitor of the whole vertebrate kingdom appears to have been hermaphrodite or androgynous" (207).

14. Paul H. Barrett, ed., *Metaphysics, Materialism and the Evolution of Mind: Early Writings of Charles Darwin*, with commentary by Howard E. Gruber (Chicago: University of Chicago Press, 1980), pp. 186, 189.

15. Cited in Desmond and Moore, *Darwin*, p. 236; Barrett, *Metaphysics, Materialism and Evolution of Mind*, p. 79. There are times when Darwin does use the rhetoric of progress (e.g. *Origin*, p. 459), but he seems to intend a fairly "soft" sense. In any case, these appear to involve rhetorical and ideological commitment at odds with the theoretical core of his position.

16. Helena Cronin, *The Ant and the Peacock* (Cambridge: Cambridge University Press, 1991), p. 287. I say that this is *one* central notion to evolutionary biology. Too often things are left here, as if genes did not require organisms and organisms did not require environments. One current of evolutionary thought—often associated with "complexity theory"—holds that natural selection does not proceed according to purely random variations; that, instead, certain functional patterns are likely to emerge given the structural features of life forms. For an introduction to these views see Roger Lewin, *Complexity: Life at the Edge of Chaos* (New York: Macmillan, 1992). A provocative development of these ideas is offered by Robert Wesson, *Beyond Natural Selection* (Cambridge, MA: MIT Press, 1991).

17. Richard Dawkins, *The Selfish Gene* (Oxford: Oxford University Press, 1976). While there is some good science in parts of this book, Dawkins is regularly guilty of what Dennett, *Darwin's Dangerous Idea*, (pp. 81–82) has called "greedy reductionism"—attempting to inflate the range of a given level of theoretical explanation. Dawkins' ideological attacks on the "unnatural" welfare state (p. 126) are a glaring case in point.

18. Lewontin, *Biology as Ideology*, p. 48.

19. Richard Levins and Richard Lewontin, *The Dialectical Biologist* (Cambridge, MA: Harvard University Press, 1985), p. 93.

20. For a wonderful and learned (but jargon-free) introduction to such views see Jonathan Weiner, *The Beak of the Finch: A Story of Evolution in Our Time* (New York: Vintage Books, 1995).

21. Weiner, *The Beak of the Finch*, p. 282; John Tyler Bonner, *The Evolution of Culture in Animals* (Princeton: Princeton University Press, 1980), and *Life Cycles* (Princeton: Princeton University Press, 1993).

22. Stephen Jay Gould, *The Panda's Thumb: More Reflections in Natural History* (New York: W. W. Norton, 1982), p. 24.

23. Robert Padgug, "Sexual Matters: On Conceptualizing Sexuality in History," in *Forms of Desire: Sexual Orientation and the Social Constructionist Controversy*, ed. Edward Stein (New York: Routledge and Kegan Paul, 1992), p. 51.

24. See Cronin, *The Ant and the Peacock*, pp. 145–72.

25. Karl Groos, *The Play of Animals: A Study of Animal Life and Instinct* (London: Chapman and Hall, 1898), as cited by Cronin, *The Ant and the Peacock*, p. 157.

26. See the intriguing discussion in Cronin, *The Ant and the Peacock*, chap. 8, and for a fascinating discussion of a particularly dramatic "selection event" see Weiner, *The Beak of the Finch*, pp. 71–81.

27. Lynn Margulis and Dorion Sagan, *Mystery Dance: On the Evolution of Human Sexuality* (New York: Summit Books, 1991), p. 33.

28. W. C. McGrew, "The Female Chimpanzee as a Human Evolutionary Prototype," in *Woman the Gatherer*, ed. Frances Dahlberg (New Haven and London: Yale University Press, 1981), p. 54. On Chimpanzee sexuality generally see Jane Goodall, *Through a Window: My Thirty Years with the Chimpanzees of Gombe* (Boston: Houghton Mifflin, 1990), chap. 9.

29. Gould, *Panda's Thumb*, p. 132.

30. For the view that the "savanna hypothesis" is probably false see James Shreeve, "Sunset on the Savanna," *Discover* (July 1996).

31. C. O. Lovejoy, "Hominid Origins: The Role of Bipedalism," *American Journal of Physical Anthropology* 52 (1980): 250.

32. The development of the opposable thumb is especially important in this regard. See John Napier, "The Evolution of the Hand," *Scientific American* 207, no. 6 (1962): 56–62.

33. Donna Haraway has cautioned us about some of the biases built into primatology in her *Primate Visions: Gender, Race, and Nature in the World of Modern Science* (New York: Routledge and Kegan Paul, 1989). These are vitally important cautions. But Haraway also recognizes the importance of critical scientific work in this field, such as that of Adrienne Zihlman whose research figures centrally in a number of arguments I develop below.

34. McGrew, "The Female Chimpanzee," pp. 45–51; Jane Goodal, "Tool-using in Primates and Other Vertebrates," *Advanced Studies of Behaviour* 3 (1970): 195–249; Richard E. Leakey and Roger Lewin, *People of the Lake: Mankind and its Beginnings* (New York: Avon Books, 1978), pp. 120, 124–5, 131–2.

35. Richard B. Lee and Irven Devore, *Kalahari Hunter-gatherers: Studies of the !Kung San and Their Neighbours* (Cambridge, MA: Harvard University Press, 1976); Leakey and Lewin, *People of the Lake*, pp. 95–99.

36. Nancy Tanner and Adrienne Zihlman, "Women in Evolution. Part I: Innovation and Selection in Human Origins," *Signs: Journal of Women in Culture and Society*, 1 (1976): 600.

37. For further suggestions in this direction, see Adrienne L. Zihlman, "Women as Shapers of the Human Adaptation," in *Woman the Gatherer*, p. 109. On women as hunters see, for example, Agnes Estioko-Griffin and P. Bion Griffin, "Woman the Hunter: The Agta," in *Woman the Gatherer*, pp. 121–52. For a discussion of the politics of this hypothesis see Haraway, *Primate Visions*, chap. 14.

38. Leakey and Lewin, *People of the Lake*, pp. 116–20.

39. Ibid., p. 120.

40. Glynn L. Isaac, "Food Sharing and Hominid Evolution: Archaeological evidence from the Plio-Pleistocene of East Africa," *Journal of Anthropological Research* 34 (1978): 311–25. Isaac initially used the term "home base," but switched to "central foraging place" to avoid modern connotations of the word "home."

41. Gould, *Ever Since Darwin*, p. 72.

42. Ibid., p. 68.

43. It is also in the reproductive interests of males to do so, even if their interest in this regard is not quite so strong. See Meredith F. Small, *Female Choices: Sexual Behavior of Female Primates* (Ithaca: Cornell University Press, 1993), pp. 197–98.

44. Ibid.

45. Tanner and Zihlman, "Women in Evolution," p. 606.

46. It may also be the case that the development of homoerotic and homosexual attractions played an important role in encouraging cooperation among males. For speculations to this effect see Daniel Rancour-Laferriere, *Signs of the Flesh: An Essay on the Evolution of Hominid Sexuality* (Bloomington, IN: Indiana University Press, 1985), chap. 47.

47. Karl Marx, *Capital*, vol. 1, trans. Ben Fowkes (Harmondsworth: Penguin Books, 1976), p. 493n4.

48. J. Desmond Clark, "African Origins of Man the Toolmaker," in *Human Origins*, eds. G. L. Isaac and E. R. McCowan (California: W. A. Benjamin, 1976), pp. 17–25; Kathy D. Schick and Nicholas Toth, *Making Silent Stones Speak: Human Evolution and the Dawn of Technology* (New York: Simon and Schuster, 1993), pp. 67–82; Leakey and Lewin, *People of the Lake*, pp. 83–86. Throughout this discussion I use traditional descriptions of hominid types—such as *habilis* and *erectus*. A growing body of evidence suggests, however, that there were many hominid types (perhaps as many as twenty) coexisting at times; certainly, there was no simple, linear progression from one to the next.

49. See Norman Geschwind, "The Organization of Language and the Brain," *Science* 170 (1970): 940–44; Sherwood L. Washburn, "Tools and Human Evolution," in *Culture and the Evolution of Man*, ed. M. F. Ashley Montagu (New York: Oxford

University Press, 1962), p. 18; Philip Lieberman, *Uniquely Human: The Evolution of Speech, Thought and Selfless Behaviour* (Cambridge MA: Harvard University Press, 1991), pp. 20–27.

50. Merlin Donald, *Origins of the Modern Mind: Three Stages in the Evolution of Culture and Cognition* (Cambridge, MA: Harvard University Press, 1991), p. 97.

51. Schick and Toth, *Making Silent Stones Speak*, pp. 227–40; Clark, "African Origins of Man the Toolmaker," pp. 29–33; Donald, *Origins of the Modern Mind*, pp. 112–14. For some recent complications concerning the dating of *erectus* fossils, migration out of Africa, and the spread (or absence) of the Acheulean tool kit in areas where *erectus* fossils have been found see James Shreeve, "Erectus Rising," *Discover*, (September 1994): 78–89.

52. John C. Eccles, *Evolution of the Brain: Creation of the Self* (London: Routledge and Kegan Paul, 1989), p. 67.

53. See the interesting discussion of this point in Charles Woolfson, *The Labour Theory of Culture: A Re-examination of Engels's Theory of Human Origins* (London: Routledge and Kegan Paul, 1982), pp. 38–41. See also B. B. Beck, *Animal Tool Behaviour: The Use and Manufacture of Tools by Animals* (New York: Garland STPM Press, 1980), p. 218.

54. See Shick and Toth, *Making Silent Stones Speak*, pp. 293–301; Michael A. Corbalis, *The Lopsided Ape: Evolution of the Generative Mind* (New York: Oxford University Press, 1991), pp. 46, 64.

55. Noam Chomsky, *Rules and Representations* (New York: Columbia University Press, 1980), pp. 76–79, 222–3; Chomsky, *Language and Politics* (Montreal: Black Rose Press, 1988), pp. 25–6; John Lyons, *Chomsky*, 3rd. ed. (London: Fontana Books, 1991), pp. 24–26.

56. Sue T. Parker and Constance Milbrath, "Higher Intelligence, Propositional Language, and Culture as Adaptations for Planning," in *Tools, Language and Cognition in Human Evolution*, eds. Kathleen R. Gibson and Tim Ingold (Cambridge: Cambridge University Press, 1993), pp. 326–7.

57. Nicholas Toth and Kathy Schick, "Early Stone Industries and Inferences Regarding Language and Cognition," in *Tools, Language and Cognition*, p. 352.

58. Maxine Sheets-Johnstone, *The Roots of Thinking* (Philadelphia: Temple University Press, 1990), p. 374.

59. Donald, *Origins of the Modern Mind*, pp. 88, 89.

60. Lev Vygotsky, *Thought and Language*, ed. Alex Kozulin (Cambridge, MA: MIT Press, 1986), pp. 80–83, 89–91; Vygotsky, *Mind in Society*, eds. Michael Cole, Vera John-Steiner, Sylvia Scribner, Ellen Souberman (Cambridge, MA: Harvard University Press, 1978), pp. 21–28.

61. Andrew Lock, "Language Development and Object Manipulation: Their Relation in Ontogeny and Its Possible Relevance for Phylogenetic Questions," in *Tools, Language and Cognition*, p. 292.

62. Sheets-Johnstone, *The Roots of Thinking*, p. 311. It is important to emphasize that Sheets-Johnstone is not insensitive to questions of sex and gender; the Darwinian body that informs her account does not efface sexual difference.

63. Mark Johnstone, *The Body in the Mind: The Bodily Basis of Meaning, Imagination, and Reason* (Chicago: University of Chicago Press, 1987), especially chap. 8.

64. The idea of the body as a "semantic template" is developed by Sheets-Johnstone, *The Roots of Thinking*, e.g., p. 6.

65. Ferdinand de Saussure, *Course in General Linguistics*, trans. Wade Baskin (New York: McGraw-Hill, 1959), pp. 65–69, 73–78, 111–14. Saussure here moves back and forth between the trivial and the idealist sense of "arbitrariness" in the relationship of signifiers to both signifieds and real world referents. For a discussion of the way in which Derrida and others inflate this see John M. Ellis, *Against Deconstruction* (Princeton: Princeton University Press, 1989), pp. 19–21, 45–64.

66. David F. Armstrong, William C. Stokoe, and Sherman E. Wilcox, *Gesture and the Nature of Language* (Cambridge: Cambridge University Press, 1995), pp. 182–85.

67. For arguments that syntax is what defines human language see Curtis G. Smith, *Ancestral Voices: Language and the Evolution of Human Consciousness* (Englewood Cliffs: Prentice Hall, 1985), p. 159, and Armstrong, Stokoe and Wilcox, *Gesture and the Nature of Language*, p. 19.

68. Kathleen R. Gibson, "Tool Use, Language and Social Behaviour in Relationship to Information Processing Capacities" in *Tools, Language and Cognition*, p. 252.

69. Ibid., p. 255.

70. See Kathleen R. Gibson, "Comparative Neurobehavioural Ontogeny and the Constructionist Approach to the Evolution of the Brain, Object Manipulation, and Language," in *Glossogenetics: The Origin and Evolution of Language*, ed. Eric de Grolier (Chur: Harwood Academic Publishers, 1983), pp. 48–49. As should be clear, I favor a Vygotskyian developmental psychology over the Piagetian version employed by Gibson. For Vygotsky's critique of Piaget see his *Thought and Language*.

71. Peter Reynolds, "The Complementation Theory of Language and Tool Use," in *Tools, Language and Cognition*, p. 422.

72. Ibid., p. 412.

73. Ibid., p. 423.

74. Karl Marx and Friedrich Engels, *The German Ideology*, 3rd rev. ed. (Moscow: Progress Publishers, 1976) p. 49.

75. Reynolds, "The Complementation Theory," p. 423.

76. The ostensible lateralization of language and praxic skills on the left side of the brain has encouraged many theorists to suggest a close link between language and toolmaking. See, for example, Diane Kimura, "Neuromotor Mechanisms in the Evolution of Human Communication," in *Neurobiology of Social Communication in Primates*, ed. H. D. Steklis and M. J. Raleigh (New York: Academic Press, 1979); Philip Lieberman, *The Biology and Evolution of Language* (Cambridge, MA: Harvard University Press, 1984), pp. 57, 67–68; Lieberman, *Uniquely Human: The Evolution of Speech, Thought and Selfless Behaviour* (Cambridge, MA: Harvard University Press, 1991), pp. 104–6; William H. Calvin, *The Throwing Madonna: Essays on the Brain*, rev. ed. (New York: Bantam Books, 1991); and Michael C. Corballis, *The Lopsided Ape: Evolution of the Generative Mind* (New York: Oxford University Press, 1991), esp. chaps. 4–8. The verdict on these arguments, however, is far from clear. See, for example, the important questions raised by Donald, *Origins of the Modern Mind*, pp. 62–67, 71–93.

77. See Robin Dunbar, *Primate Social Systems* (London: Croom Helm, 1988). This perspective is expanded and developed in Dunbar, *Grooming, Gossip and the Evolution of Language* (Cambridge, MA: Harvard University Press, 1996), chap. 4.

78. Dunbar, *Grooming, Gossip and the Evolution of Language*, p. 78.

79. A. N. Meltzoff, "Imitation, Objects, Tools, and the Rudiments of Language in Human Ontogeny," *Human Evolution* 3 (1988): 60.

80. Elizabeth Visalberghi, "Capuchin Monkeys: A Window into Tool Use" in *Tools, Language and Cognition*, p. 147; Christophe Boesch, "Aspects of Transmission of Tool-Use in Wild Chimpanzees," in *Tools, Language and Cognition*, pp. 171–83.

81. Donald, *Origins of the Modern Mind*, p. 171. See also the interesting discussion of experiments in this area in Karen Wright, "The Tarzan Syndrome," *Discover* (November 1996): 92, 94. These experiments have little to do with the "clambering hypothesis" discussed in Wright's article.

82. See the discussion of this point in Antonio R. Damasio, *Descartes' Error: Emotion, Reason and the Human Brain* (New York: Avon Books, 1994) pp. 226–40.

83. Meltzoff, "Initation, Objects, Tools," p. 47.

84. See for example Jan Bremmer and Herman Roodenburg, eds., *A Cultural History of Gesture* (Ithaca: Cornell University Press, 1992).

85. Donald *Origins of the Modern Mind* (p. 179) argues for toolmaking as the original "self-cued mimetic skill."

86. One of the most vigorous advocates of this position is Gordon Hewes. See, for example, "Language in Early Hominids," in *Language Origins*, ed. R. Wescott (Silver Spring, MD: Linstock Press, 1974), pp. 1–33; "The Current Status of the Gestural Theory of Language Origin" in *Origins and Evolution of Language and Speech*, eds. S. Harnard, H. Stekils, J. Lancaster (New York: New York Academy of Sciences, 1976), pp. 482–504; "The Invention of Phonemically-Based Language," in *Glossogenetics: The Origin and Evolution of Language*, ed. Eric de Grolier (Chur: Harwood Academic Publishers, 1983), pp. 143–62.

87. John Bowlby, *Attachment and Loss: Vol. 1: Attachment* (New York: Basic Books, 1969). With Bowlby, I want to insist that the term mother here applies "to the person who mothers the child and to whom he becomes attached" (p. 29n1).

88. Anne Fernald, "Human Maternal Vocalizations to Infants as Biologically Relevant Signals: An Evolutionary Perspective," in *The Adapted Mind: Evolutionary Psychology and the Generation of Culture*, eds. Jerome H. Barkow, Leda Cosmides, and Jooh Tooby (New York and Oxford: Oxford University Press, 1992), p. 404.

89. Ralph Greenson, "The Mother Tongue and the Mother," *International Journal of Psycho-Analysis* 31 (1950): 18–23. On this point, see also the remarks by Doris F. Jonas and A. David Jonas, "Gender Differences in Mental Function: A Clue to the Origin of Language," *Current Anthropology* 16 (December 1975): 628–29.

90. See the discussion of this issue by Rancour-Laferriere, *Signs of the Flesh* chap. 18. It is important, nonetheless, not to romanticize the mother-child bond, since it is also a site of aggression. This point has been drawn out from a psychoanalytic perspective by Madelon Sprengnether, *The Spectral Mother: Freud, Feminism and Psychoanalysis* (Ithaca: Cornell University Press, 1990).

91. Bruce Richman, "Did Human Speech Originate in Coordinated Vocal Music?" *Semiotica* 32 (1980): 235.

92. Ibid., p. 240.

93. Dunbar, *Grooming, Gossip and the Evolution of Language*, p. 26.

94. Donald, *Origins of the Modern Mind*, p. 186. See also Rancour-Laferriere, *Signs of the Flesh*, pp. 238–41.

95. Richman, "Did Human Speech," p. 242.

96. Alexander Marschack, "Some Implications of the Paleolithic Symbolic Evidence for the Origin of Language," *Current Anthropology* 17 (June 1976): 281.

97. Sheets-Johnstone, *The Roots of Thinking*, p. 149. For a recent example of this sort of dualism see Robbins Burling, "Primate Calls, Human Language, and Nonverbal Communication," *Current Anthropology* 34 (1993): especially 25–30.

98. Philip Lieberman, "On the Evolution of Human Language," in *The Evolution of Human Languages*, eds. John A. Hawkins and Murray Gell-Mann (Redwood City: Addison-Wesley Publishing, 1992), p. 22.

99. Grover S. Krantz argues the former position in "Sapienization and Speech," *Current Anthropology* 21 (December 1980): pp. 773–79. A number of critics have argued, however, that the evidence is far from clear. See the comments on Krantz's article in ibid., pp. 779–90.

100. Donald, *Origins of the Modern Mind*, p. 249.

101. Leslie A. White "On the Use of Tools by Primates," *Journal of Comparative Psychology* 34 (1942): 371, 372.

102. This position need not read back into history the sort of dynamic development of productive forces that characterizes capitalism—with its drive to revolutionize the means of production in order to increase relative surplus-value. The ahistorical nature of this view has been exposed by Ellen Meiksins Wood. See, for example, Meiksins Wood, "From opportunity to Imperative: The History of the market," *Monthly Review* 46, no. 3 (July-August 1994).The way in which productive forces develop or stagnate is very much determined by the social relations of production and exploitation that prevail. Nevertheless, human toolmaking cultures are distinguished by their capacity for retention and development of new productive forces, a capacity which is socially organized in a given historical context. For a discussion of forces of production in terms similar to mine see Tim Ingold, "Tool-use, sociality and intelligence," in *Tools, Language and Cognition*, chap. 19, and Gyorgy Markus, *Language and Production: A Critique of the Paradigms* (Dordrecht: D. Reidel Publishing, 1986), pp. 79–80.

103. The fact that some post-structuralist theories talk about language in terms of "desire" does not undermine my point. Remarkably, even desire has been dematerialized in these accounts, becoming little more than the metaphysical search of signifiers for signifieds, of signs for referents, as subjects try to overcome an ontological "lack" which is constitutive of their being. On this point see M. C. Dillon, *Semiological Reductionism: A Critique of the Deconstructionist Movement in Postmodern Thought* (Albany: State University of New York Press, 1995), chap. 6.

104. Len Doyal and Roger Harris, "The Practical Foundations of Human Understanding," *New Left Review* 139 (May–June 1983): 64. This is an important article, although the authors' reliance on Martin Heidegger undermines their own position in ways they seem not to grasp.

105. Habermas has drawn this distinction, albeit with a fair bit of imprecision, in a number of works. For different versions see *Toward A Rational Society*, trans. Jeremy J. Shapiro (Boston: Beacon Press, 1970), pp. 91–92; *Knowledge and Human Interests*, trans. Jeremy J. Shapiro (Boston: Beacon Press, 1971), p. 42; *Theory and Practice*, trans. John Viertel (Boston: Beacon Press, 1973), chap. 4; *Communication and the Evolution of Society*, trans. Thomas McCarthy (Boston: Beacon Press, 1979), pp. 97–99; *The Theory of Com-*

municative Action, trans. Thomas McCarthy, vol. 1, pp. 9–15; *The Philosophical Discourse of Modernity*, trans. Frederick G. Lawrence (Cambridge: Polity Press, 1987), pp. 75–82.

106. Habermas, *Knowledge and Human Interests*, p. 314.

107. Habermas often seems uncertain as to whether he wants to argue that the orientation toward rational understanding is a universal feature of language—the implication of the "universal pragmatics" he advances in *Communication and the Evolution of Society*—or whether it emerges in modernity with its supposed "disenchantment" of the lifeworld. The latter view tends to dominate in *The Theory of Communicative Action*.

108. Habermas, *Communication and the Evolution of Society*, p. 1.

109. Habermas, *The Theory of Communicative Action* 1:398.

110. For some of the most important criticisms of Habermas see the essays by Heller, Giddens, and Schmid in *Habermas: Critical Debates*, eds. John B. Thompson and David Held (Cambridge, MA: MIT Press, 1982); Joel Whitebrook, "Reason and Happiness: Some Psychoanalytic Themes in Critical Theory," in *Habermas and Modernity*, ed. Richard J. Bernstein (Cambridge, MA: MIT Press, 1985), pp. 140–60; and Olivia Blanchette, "Language, the Primordial Labor of History: A Critique of Critical Social Theory in Habermas," *Cultural Hermeneutics* 1 (1974): 325–82. Many, although not all, of these critics raise the issue of Habermas's Kantianism, a problem which is discussed also by Thomas McCarthy, *The Critical Theory of Jürgen Habermas* (Cambridge, MA: MIT Press, 197), pp. 325–28, 379–80. For Habermas's (to my mind unconvincing) denial that his is a Kantian approach see *Communication and the Evolution of Society*, pp. 21–25.

111. Robin May Schott, *Cognition and Eros: A Critique of the Kantian Paradigm* (University Park: Pennsylvania State University Press, 1993), pp. 126–28.

CHAPTER FOUR

1. V. N. Volosinov, *Marxism and the Philosophy of Language*, trans. Ladislav Matejka and I. R. Titunik (Cambridge, MA: Harvard University Press). Throughout this book I use the conventional English spelling of Voloshinov. I also attribute *Marxism and the Philosophy of Language* to Voloshinov, while recognizing the influence of Mikhail Bakhtin. In my judgment, however, Bakhtin was not the author of this book. Indeed, I follow Gary Saul Morson and Caryl Emerson in believing that Voloshinov's book exercised an important influence on Bakhtin despite the clear differences between the positions of each of these theorists. See Gary Saul Morson and Caryl Emerson, *Mikhail Bakhtin: Creation of a Prosaics* (Stanford: Stanford University Press, 1990), pp. 115–17, 195, 205–7. Further references to *Marxism and the Philosophy of Language* will be given in the text and indicated by the abbreviation MPL followed by the page number.

2. P. N. Medvedev (and Mikhail Bakhtin), *The Formal Method in Literary Scholarship*, trans. Albert J. Wehrle (Cambridge, MA: Harvard University Press, 1985) p. 174. While the publishers treat Bakhtin as the coauthor or primary author of this work, I attribute it to Medvedev. This book will hereafter be cited in the text as FM.

3. Derek Sayer, *Marx's Method: Ideology, Science and Critique in 'Capital'* (Sussex: Harvester Press, 1979), p. 4.

4. Raymond Williams, *Marxism and Literature* (Oxford: Oxford University Press, 1977), p. 83.

5. Karl Marx and Frederick Engels, *The German Ideology*, 3rd rev. edn. (Moscow: Progress Publishers, 1976), p. 37.

6. For efforts to work out a nonreductive theory of base-superstructure relations see Raymond Williams, "Base and Superstructure in Marxist Cultural Theory," in Williams, *Problems in Materialism and Culture* (London: Verso Books, 1980); and Melvin Rader, *Marx's Interpretation of History* (New York: Oxford University Press, 1979), esp. chap. 1. See also Bertell Ollman, *Alienation: Marx's Conception of Man in Capitalist Society* (London: Cambridge University Press, 1971), chap. 3. For an insightful rethinking of the terms of the base-superstructure problem see Ellen Meiksins Wood, "Rethinking Base and Superstructure," chap. 2 of her *Democracy Against Capitalism: Renewing Historical Materialism* (Cambridge: Cambridge University Press, 1995).

7. In this regard, Voloshinov's efforts join those of E. P. Thompson more than thirty years later in his attempt to reorient Marxist thought by insisting that class is not a structure or a thing, but a process, that is, that class actually "happens." See E. P. Thompson, *The Making of the English Working Class* (New York: Vintage Books, 1963) pp. 9–10.

8. Mikhail Bakhtin, "Discourse in the Novel," in *The Dialogic Imagination: Four Essays by M. M. Bakhtin*, ed. Michael Holquist (Austin: University of Texas Press, 1981), pp. 276–77. This essay is hereafter cited in the text as DN.

9. While the translators of *Marxism and the Philosophy of Language* use the term "behavioral genres," I prefer the translation adopted by Morson and Emerson (p. 291): "life genres." I should also point out that there are moments when Voloshinov, in tune with older currents within Marxism, tends to reduce these genres to those of class experience narrowly conceived. My own view is that the concept of life genres can be mobilized with respect to a wide range of social experiences organized according, for example, to sexual orientation, ethno-racial identity, and gender, to name some of the most important. The task is then to show the ways in which these are also (but not merely) constitutive of class experience.

10. George Orwell, *Homage to Catalonia* (Harmondsworth: Penguin Books, 1966), pp. 8–9.

11. As should be clear, I am discussing fundamental theoretical or philosophical dualisms here. There are other kinds of dualities (or contrastive pairs) which play a very different role in human life, deriving as they often do from fundamental physical and corporeal experiences (e.g., hot/cold, light/darkness, danger/safety, birth/death).

12. V. N. Voloshinov, *Freudianism: A Critical Sketch*, trans. I. R. Titunik (Bloomington, IN: Indiana University Press), p. 10, italics deleted. Further references to this book will be given in the text and will be cited as F.

13. Georg Lukacs, *History and Class Consciousness*, trans. Rodney Livingstone (London: Merlin Press, 1971), pp. 130, 34. It is worth noting that the claim that "nature is a social category" has a partial validity—so long as it is linked with (and not merely juxtaposed to) the proposition that society is a natural category. Taken together, these propositions could serve to illuminate the complex interrelationship of nature and society—something Lukacs does not do.

14. Antonio Gramsci, *Selections from the Prison Notebooks*, trans. Quintin Hoare and Geoffrey Nowell Smith (New York: International Publishers, 1971), p. 448.

15. Again, these are tendencies that predominate within the most dualistic parts of *Marxism and the Philosophy of Language*. There are also countertendencies, lines of argument that move in a more dynamic and dialectical direction, which are well worth building upon.

16. Samuel Weber, "The Intersection: Marxism and the Philosophy of Language," *Diacritics* 15 (1985): 98n9.

17. Morson and Emerson, *Mikhail Bakhtin*, p. 117.

18. Indeed, even Bakhtin's late work continues to employ Marxist categories like reification ("The materialization of man under conditions of class society carried to its extreme under capitalism," Mikhail Bakhtin, "Toward a Reworking of the Dostoevsky Book," Appendix to *Problems of Dostoevsky's Poetics*, ed. and trans. Caryl Emerson [Minneapolis: University of Minnesota Press, 1984], p. 298), and to refer to Marx: "Karl Marx said that only thought uttered in the word becomes a real thought for another person and only in the same way is it a thought for myself," *Speech Genres and Other Late Essays*, trans. Vern W. McGee (Austin: University of Texas Press, 1986), p. 127. None of this makes Bakhtin a Marxist; but it is evidence of a continuing dialogue with Marxist thinking. I suspect that Bakhtin's English-language biographers may be right to see a "commitment to a kind of socialism" in his thought, but this remains an open question. See Katerina Clark and Michael Holquist, *Mikhail Bakhtin* (Cambridge, MA: Harvard University Press, 1984), p. 77.

19. On the Leningrad Circle, see Clark and Holquist, *Mikhail Bakhtin*, chap. 4.

20. See Michael Holquist, "Bakhtin and the Body," *Critical Studies* 1, no. 2 (1989): 19–42. See also Bakhtin's reference to attending a 1925 lecture by Ukhtomsky (or Uxtomskij) in "Forms of Time and of the Chronotope in the Novel," In *The Dialogical Imagination*, p. 84 n1. Further references to this essay will be given in the text and cited as FTCN.

21. Mikhail Bakhtin, "Author and Hero in Aesthetic Activity," in *Art and Answerability: Early Philosophical Essays by M. M. Bakhtin* (Austin: University of Texas Press, 1990), p. 8. This essay is hereafter cited in the text as AH.

22. It is important to remember that "dialogism" is a term rarely used by Bakhtin even if it is a useful shorthand for summarizing some of the central themes of his writings (e.g., the polyphonic novel, language and heteroglossia, speech genres, and so on). Michael Holquist has used the term in the title of his book, *Dialogism: Bakhtin and His World* (London and New York: Routledge and Kegan Paul, 1990).

23. For an excellent discussion of the effacement of the mother in psychoanalytic theory (particularly that of Freud and Lacan)—and also for how certain psychoanalytic insights might be used to overturn this effacement—see Madelon Sprengnether, *The Spectral Mother: Freud, Feminism and Psychoanalysis* (Ithaca: Cornell University Press, 1990).

24. Sigmund Freud, "Leonard Da Vinci and a Memory of His Childhood" in *The Standard Edition of the Complete Psychological Works of Sigmund Freud*, trans. James Strachey et al. (London: Hogarth, 1974), 11:117.

25. See Sprengnether, *The Spectral Mother*, pp. 27–38, 59–80, 118.

26. In discussing femininity and motherhood as socially constructed, I do not mean to suggest that they are *pure* social constructs. Some recent theory, particularly that of a post-structuralist persuasion, has acted as if there are not corporeal distinctions among people. While some "identities" are highly constructed socially—nationality, ethnicity, race, and sexual orientation figure prominently here—there are actual physico-anatomical

features which do play a real role in shaping identities and which, for instance, prevent nearly half of humankind from being biological mothers.

27. Mikhail Bakhtin, *Problems of Dostoevsky's Poetics*, ed. and trans. Caryl Emerson (Minneapolis: University of Minnesota Press, 1984), p. 32. Further references to this work will be given in the text and cited as PDP.

28. Both Voloshinov and Medvedev were arrested and jailed during the 1930s; it appears they were either murdered by the state or died in prison. Bakhtin was arrested in 1929 and was ultimately sentenced to "internal exile" rather than a prison term.

29. Mikhail Bakhtin, "Epic and Novel: Toward a Methodology for the Study of the Novel," in Bakhtin, *The Dialogical Imagination*, pp. 16, 17. Further citations from this essay will hereafter be given in the text and indicated with the abbreviation EN.

30. Mikhail Bakhtin, "From the Prehistory of Novelistic Discourse," in Bakhtin, *Dialogical Imagination*, p. 47. Further references to this essay will hereafter be given in the text and cited as PHND.

31. See Mikhail Bakhtin, "Discourse in the Novel," in Bakhtin, *Dialogical Imagination*. Further references to this essay will by given in the text and cited as DN.

32. Mikhail Bakhtin, "Forms of Time and the Chronotope in the Novel," in Bakhtin, *Dialogical Imagination*.

33. Note, however, that Bakhtin also connects "the battle against nature" and "war" with the pre-class society of communal labor (FTCN, p. 209).

34. Mikhail Bakhtin, *Rabelais and His World*, trans. Helene Iswolsky (Bloomington, IN: Indiana University Press, 1984), pp. 6, 73–96, 465–66. Further references to this work are given in the text and cited as RHW.

35. Terry Eagleton, *Walter Benjamin or Towards a Revolutionary Criticism* (London: Verso Books, 1981), p. 150.

36. Peter Burke, *Popular Culture in Early Modern Europe* (New York: Harper and Row, 1978), pp. 24, 122–24, 179–96.

37. Morson and Emerson, *Mikhail Bakhtin*, pp. 94–95, 225–6, 224, 227, 228.

38. Caryl Emerson, "Getting Bakhtin, Right and Left," *Comparative Literature* 46 (1994): 291, 297, 299, 300, 301. Emerson has returned to the issue of Bakhtin and carnival in her book *The First Hundred Years of Mikhail Bakhtin* (Princeton: Princeton University Press, 1997), chap. 4. In the course of reviewing (largely Russian) debates over the Bakhtinian carnivalesque, she does not signal any movement one way or another in her own views.

39. Ken Hirschkop, "A Response to the Forum on Mikhail Bakhtin," in *Bakhtin: Essays and Dialogues on His Work*, ed. Gary Saul Morson (Chicago: University of Chicago Press, 1986), pp. 74, 79.

40. However, as I shall point out below, in ignoring the fact that it is female bodies which give birth, Bakhtin often appropriates procreative power to the male body.

41. This is one of a number of points at which Bakhtin's theory could be strengthened and developed by way of a dialogue with psychoanalysis, a dialogue which Bakhtin and his circle generally refused.

42. Francois Rabelais, *Gargantua and Pantagruel*, trans. J. M. Cohen (Harmondsworth: Penguin Books, 1955), p. 174.

43. Ulinka Rublack, "Pregnancy, Childbirth and the Female Body in Early Modern Germany," *Past and Present* 150 (February 1996): 84–110.

44. Ibid., p. 102.

45. Ibid., p. 90.

46. Ibid, p. 92. Rublack also emphasizes that these biases were not imposed by male doctors and officials against the wishes of midwives, mothers, and other women, but that these female groups shared this procreative bias. It is worth pointing out here too that Bakhtin's ambivalence toward the womb invites a psychoanalytic reading. For one interesting example of the latter see Ruth Ginsburg, "The Pregnant Text. Bakhtin's Ur-Chronotope: The Womb," *Cultural Studies* 4 (1993): 165–76. While I believe that one can learn much from such readings, I am reluctant to reduce Bakhtin's ambivalence to such an interpretation. It seems to me that the ambivalence of the popular culture I have described is an indispensable part of the story.

47. Mary Russo, *The Female Grotesque: Risk, Excess and Modernity* (New York: Routledge and Kegan Paul, 1994), p. 63.

48. Ginsburg, "The Pregnant Text," p. 167.

49. I borrow the term "dialectic of accommodation and resistance" from Eugene D. Genovese, *Roll, Jordan, Roll: The World the Slaves Made* (New York: Vintage Books, 1972), p. 658.

50. Burke, pp. 25–28, 61, 104, 109. For the participation of the English gentry in popular festivity see Robert Malcolmson, *Popular Recreations in English Society, 1700–1850* (London: Cambridge University Press, 1973), pp. 68–71.

51. Ibid., p. 28.

52. For an important treatment of this issue see James C. Scott, *Domination and the Arts of Resistance: Hidden Transcripts* (New Haven: Yale University Press, 1990). Scott's interesting discussion is deeply flawed, however, by a thoroughly inaccurate reading of Gramsci's concept of hegemony.

53. Charles Joyner, *Down by the Riverside: A South Carolina Slave Community* (Urbana and Chicago: University of Illinois Press, 1985), p. 239. For the term "creolization of culture" see p. xx.

54. Terry Eagleton makes this point in *Walter Benjamin, or Towards a Revolutionary Criticism*, p. 148, as does Ranajit Guha, *Elementary Aspects of Peasant Insurgency* (Delhi, India: Oxford University Press, 1983), p. 30.

55. See Max Gluckman, *Rituals of Rebellion in South-East Africa* (Manchester: University of Manchester Press, 1954); and Victor Turner, *The Ritual Process: Structure and Anti-Structure* (Chicago: Aldine Press, 1969), esp. chap. 2.

56. Genovese, *Roll, Jordan, Roll*, pp. 577, 580, 584. Genovese's important study is marred by an unhelpful and sometimes misleading use of the concept of "paternalism" to characterize relations between masters and slaves.

57. Antonio Gramsci, *Selections from Cultural Writings*, trans. William Boelhower (Cambridge, MA: Harvard University Press, 1985), pp. 191, 189, 195, 194, 191.

58. For Marx's version of the principle of working class self-emancipation see the "Provisional Rules" which he drafted for the First International ("the emancipation of the working classes must be conquered by the working classes themselves") in Karl Marx, *The First International and After: Political Writings*, vol. 3, ed. David Fernbach (Harmondsworth: Penguin, 1974), p. 82. For a detailed discussion of this principle in Marx's thought see Hal Draper, *Karl Marx's Theory of Revolution, Volume 1: State and Bureaucracy* (New York: Monthly Review, Press, 1977), esp. chap. 10.

59. Antonio Gramsci, *Selections from the Prison Notebooks*, ed. and trans. Quinton Hoare and Geoffrey Nowell Smith (New York: International Publishers, 1971), p. 333.

60. Indeed it seems clear that Gramsci believed precisely this had occurred during Italy's "two red years," 1919–1920. See Paolo Spriano, *The Occupation of the Factories: Italy 1920*, trans. Gwyn A. Williams (London: Pluto Press, 1975); and Gwyn A. Williams, *Proletarian Order: Antonio Gramsci, Factory Councils and the Origins of Communism in Italy 1911–1921* (London: Pluto Press, 1975).

61. Gramsci, *Selections from the Prison Notebooks*, p. 333.

62. See Ken Hirschkop, "Bakhtin, Discourse and Democracy," *New Left Review* 160 (November–December 1986): 111; and Michael Gardiner, *The Dialogics of Critique: M. M. Bakhtin and the Theory of Ideology* (New York: Routledge and Kegan Paul, 1992), p. 176. There are obvious reasons for this overestimation. In the political context of Stalinist Russia in the 1930s and 1940s with its regime of terror and repression, the popular culture of laughter and defiance must have seemed infinitely more progressive than an authoritarian official culture of lies and intimidation. Understandable as this bias is, it does not render Bakhtin's uncritical celebration of popular culture serviceable for political purposes.

63. Burke, *Popular Culture*, pp. 48–49, 167, 200; Peter Stallybrass and Allon White, *The Politics and Poetics of Transgression* (Ithaca: Cornell University Press, 1986), p. 53.

64. Burke, *Popular Culture*, pp. 164, 168, 200.

65. Stallybrass and White, *Politics and Poetics*, p. 53. On carnival and suspicion of "outsiders" see Malcolmson, *Popular Recreations*, p. 83, and Burke, *Popular Culture*, p. 177.

66. See Joseph P. Reidy, "Negro Election Day and Black Community Life in New England," *Marxist Perspectives* 1 (1978): 102–17; Shane White, "Pinkster: Afro-Dutch Syncretization in New York City and Hudson Valley," *Journal of American Folklore* 102 (January–March 1989); and David R. Roediger, *The Wages of Whiteness: Race and the Making of the American Working Class* (London: Verso, 1991), pp. 23–24, 101–103.

67. As cited by Roediger, *The Wages of Whiteness*, p. 108.

68. Ibid., p. 106.

69. See, for example, Rodney Hilton, "The Small Town as Part of Peasant Society" and "Women in the Village," in Hilton, *The English Peasantry in the Later Middle Ages* (Oxford: Clarendon Press, 1975). See also Eugen Weber, *Peasants into Frenchmen: The Modernization of Rural France, 1870–1914* (Stanford: Stanford University Press, 1976), pp. 407–412.

70. Indeed, this would be another sense in which Bakhtin could be compared to the nineteenth-century utopian socialists who hoped to create an ideal marketplace where only free and equal transactions might occur. Gardiner, *The Dialogics of Critique* (p. 187), makes the comparison in a different sense. For a critique of free market socialism see David McNally, *Against the Market: Political Economy, Market Socialism and the Marxist Critique* (London: Verso, 1993).

71. Stallybrass and White, *Politics and Poetics*, pp. 33, 177.

72. As quoted by Ian Starsmore, *English Fairs* (London: Thames and Hudson, 1975), p. 13.

73. See Malcolmson, *Popular Recreations*, chs. 6 and 7.

74. Weber, *Peasants into Frenchmen*, p. 408. On fairs as sites for immersing peasants in the patterns of a market society see Weber, ibid., pp. 411–412.

75. Starsmore, *English Fairs*, chap. 5; see also chs. 3 and 4.

76. Susan Buck-Morss, *The Dialectics of Seeing: Walter Benjamin and the Arcades Project* (Cambridge, MA: MIT Press, 1991), pp. 83–86.

77. Ibid., p. 89.

78. I am relying here on the interesting study by Robert H Lavenda, "The Festival of Progress: The Globalizing World-System and the Transformation of the Caracas Carnival," *Journal of Popular Culture* 14 (Winter 1980): 465–75. For another study which looks at commercialization of carnival in a postcolonial society, albeit largely in descriptive terms, see Renu Juneja, "The Trinidad Carnival: Ritual, Performance, Spectacle and Symbol," *Journal of Popular Culture* 21 (Spring 1988): 87–99.

79. See, for example, David Underdown, *Revel, Riot and Rebellion: Popular Politics and Culture in England 1603–1660* (Oxford: Oxford University Press, 1985), pp. 47–72; Malcolmson, *Popular Recreations*, chs. 6 and 7; E. P. Thompson, *Customs in Common: Studies in Traditional Popular Culture* (New York: New Press, 1991), chs. 3, 5, and 6.

80. The expression "combination of engineering and fantasy" comes from Starsmore, *English Fairs*, p. 95. Again, I am not suggesting that the oppositional elements of carnival were entirely appropriated, simply that they became bound up with commodification in new and complex patterns. For an optimistic reading see Abner Cohen, *Masquerade Politics: Explorations in the Structure of Urban Cultural Movements* (Berkeley: University of California Press, 1993).

CHAPTER 5

1. Walter Benjamin, "Left-Wing Melancholy," in Benjamin, *Selected Writings, Volume 2: 1927–1935*, eds. Michael Jennings, Howard Eiland, and Gary Smith (Cambridge, MA: The Belknap Press of Harvard University Press, 1999), p. 424.

2. Walter Benjamin, "Theses on the Philosophy of History," in Benjamin, *Illuminations*, ed. Hannah Arendt (New York: Schocken Books, 1968), p. 255. This piece will henceforth be cited in the text and indicated by the abbreviation TPH.

3. Especially noteworthy English-language efforts to reclaim Benjamin as a revolutionary theorist of the Left are the following: Terry Eagleton, *Walter Benjamin or Towards a Revolutionary Criticism* (London: Verso Books, 1981); Julian Roberts, *Walter Benjamin* (London: MacMillan, 1982); and Susan Buck-Morss, "Walter Benjamin: Revolutionary Writer," *New Left Review* 128 (1981): 50–75, and 129 (1981): 77–95.

4. Walter Benjamin, "The Task of the Translator," in *Illuminations*, p. 79.

5. Ibid., p. 78.

6. As is argued persuasively by Susan Buck-Morss, *The Origin of Negative Dialectics: Theodor W. Adorno, Walter Benjamin, and the Frankfurt Institute* (New York: The Free Press, 1977). At the same time, what I describe below as Benjamin's "dialectic of extremes" is resistant to the central role that the concept of mediation often plays in Theodor Adorno's version of dialectics. On this point see Michael W. Jennings, *Dialectical Images: Walter Benjamin's Theory of Literary Criticism* (Ithaca: Cornell University Press, 1987), pp. 30–32, and Rainer Nagele, *Theater, Theory, Speculation: Walter Benjamin and the Scenes of Modernity* (Baltimore: The Johns Hopkins University Press, 1991), p. 87.

7. Walter Benjamin, "The Life of Students," in Benjamin, *Selected Writings, Volume 1: 1913–1926*, eds. Marcus Bullock and Michael W. Jennings (Cambridge, MA: The Belknap Press of Harvard University Press, 1996), p. 46.

8. Walter Benjamin, "N [Re Theory of Knowledge, Theory of Progress]," in *Benjamin: Philosophy, Aesthetics, History*, ed. Gary Smith (Chicago: University of Chicago Press, 1989), p. 66.

9. Walter Benjamin, "Some Reflections on Kafka," in *Illuminations*, pp. 144–45.

10. Walter Benjamin, "Left-Wing Melancholy," *Selected Writings*, 2: 424.

11. Walter Benjamin, "An Outsider Makes His Mark," in Benjamin, *Selected Writings*, 2:310. While this is used as a description of his friend Siegfried Kracauer, it seems clear Benjamin identified himself with such a role.

12. Walter Benjamin, *Understanding Brecht*, trans. Anna Bostock (London: New Left Books, 1973), p. 43.

13. For instance, the widely used English-language volume of Benjamin's writings which contains these two pieces, *Reflections: Essays, Aphorisms, Autobiographical Writings*, ed. Peter Demetz (New York: Schocken Books, 1986) runs these essays side by side without indicating the considerable gap between the periods of their respective composition.

14. Walter Benjamin, "Privileged Thinking," in *Selected Writings*, 2:570. I do not mean to deny the continuing importance of Jewish messianism in Benjamin's efforts to renovate Marxism. But these theological motifs were "profaned," brought into the closest contact with historical materialism. When Gershom Scholem objected that Benjamin had gone "much too far" with his "elimination of theology," and when he criticized his friend for looking at Kafka's work "only from its most *profane* side," he intuited correctly just how far Benjamin had moved from the more idealist and theological orientation of his earlier work. See Gershom Scholem, ed., *The Correspondence of Walter Benjamin and Gershom Scholem 1932–1940*, trans. Gary Smith and Andre Lefevre (New York: Schocken Books, 1989), pp. 123, 126. Especially illuminating in this regard is Benjamin's 1931 review "Theological Criticism," *Selected Writings*, 2:428–32. For one of the better treatments of these issues see Rolf Tiedemann, "Historical Materialism or Political Messianism? An Interpretation of the Theses 'On the Concept of History,'" in *Benjamin: Philosophy, Aesthetics, History*, pp. 175–209.

15. Walter Benjamin, "On Language as Such and the Language of Man," in *Reflections*, p. 318. Further references to this essay are given in the text and cited as OLS.

16. See, for example, Max Pensky, *Melancholy Dialectics: Walter Benjamin and the Play of Mourning* (Amherst: University of Massachusetts Press, 1993), pp. 55–59.

17. As we shall see, allegory replaces symbolism as the repository of noninstrumental meanings in Benjamin's later thought.

18. Walter Benjamin, *Gesammelte Schriften*, vol. 6, ed. Rolf Tiedemann and Herman Schweppenhauser (Frankfurt am Main: Suhrkamp Verlag, 1985). Further references to the German edition of Benjamin's Works will be indicated with the abbreviation *GS*. According to Gershom Scholem, while at the University of Bern, Benjamin participated in a seminar on Freud and wrote a paper on the Freudian theory of the drives. See Scholem, *Walter Benjamin. Die Geschicte einer Freundschaft* (Frankfurt: Suhrkamp, 1975), p. 75.

19. Ibid., p. 66.

20. The best English-language discussion of Benjamin and the Free German Youth movement is provided by John McCole, *Walter Benjamin and the Antinomies of Tradition* (Ithaca: Cornell University Press, 1993), chap. 1. See also Richard Wolin, *Walter Benjamin: An Aesthetic of Redemption* (New York: Columbia University Press, 1982) pp. 4–13.

21. McCole, *Walter Benjamin*, p. 56.

22. Benjamin, "The Life of Students," p. 37.

23. Among some of the better treatments in English see Bernard Witte, *Walter Benjamin: An Intellectual Biography*, trans. James Rolleston (Detroit: Wayne State University Press, 1991), chap. 3; Rodolphe Gasché, "The Sober Absolute: On Benjamin and the Early Romantics," *Studies in Romanticism* 31 (Winter 1992): 433–53; and David Ferris, " 'Truth Is the Death of Intention': Benjamin's Esoteric History of Romanticism," *Studies in Romanticism* 31 (Winter 1992): 455–80.

24. Walter Benjamin, "The Concept of Criticism in German Romanticism," in *Selected Writings*, 1:182.

25. Ibid., pp. 185–86n3.

26. Ibid., p. 181.

27. Benjamin, "Critique of Violence," in *Reflections*, p. 300.

28. This in fact is the misleading title of chapter 4 of Wolin's *Walter Benjamin*, entitled "From Messianism to Materialism." However, Wolin's discussion (e.g., pp. 115–18) demonstrates a more complex reading.

29. The dating of the "Theologico-Political Fragment" has been a matter of some dispute. Theodor Adorno argued that this text was among the last Benjamin wrote, and thus needed to be dated alongside Benjamin's "Theses on the Philosophy of History." The editors of Benjamin's works favor the earlier dating, a view which I endorse. Adorno's position may have involved a wishful attempt to weaken the significance of Benjamin's turn to political engagement, a point to which I shall return.

30. Walter Benjamin, "Theological-Political Fragment," in *Reflections*, p. 312. Further citations from this piece will be given in the text and indicated as TPF.

31. McCole, *Walter Benjamin*, pp. 67–69, especially pp. 68–69n47.

32. Benjamin, "Outline of the Psychophysical Problem," in *Selected Writings*, 1:393. Further references to this essay are given in the text and cited as OPP.

33. Scholem as cited by George Steiner, "Introduction" to Walter Benjamin, *The Origin of German Tragic Drama*, trans. John Osborne (London: Verso Books, 1977), p. 15. Steiner registers his assent with this view on the same page. Further citations from this work will be indicated in the text with the abbreviation OGTD.

34. Benjamin to Scholem, September 1925, as cited by Wolin, *Walter Benjamin*, p. 112.

35. Georg Lukacs, *History and Class Consciousness*, trans. Rodney Livingstone (London: Merlin Books, 1971), pp. 83–109.

36. Ibid., pp. 197–206.

37. See Benjamin, "The Concept of Criticism in German Romanticism," p. 159.

38. For this reason, those critics are right who suggest that the *Trauerspiel* book ought more appropriately to be entitled *The Origin of the German Mourning Play*.

39. See McCole, *Walter Benjamin*, p. 128.

40. See Nagele, *Theater, Theory, Speculation*, pp. 88–89.

41. For an insightful discussion of mourning in Benjamin's thought see Eduardo Cadava, "Words of Light: Theses on the Photography of History," *Diacritics* 22 (Fall–Winter 1992): 84–114.

42. Roberts, *Walter Benjamin*, pp. 147–48. See also Pensky, *Melancholy Dialectics*, pp. 19–23, 79, 114, 133, 137.

43. See Mark Polizzotti, *Revolution of the Mind: The Life of Andre Breton* (New York: Farrar, Strauss and Giroux, 1995), chap. 9.

44. See Margaret Cohen, *Profane Illumination: Walter Benjamin and the Paris of Surrealist Revolution* (Berkeley: University of California Press, 1993), pp. 107–10 for an interesting discussion of this concept.

45. Walter Benjamin, "Surrealism, The Last Snapshot of the European Intelligentsia" in *Reflections*, p. 189, hereafter cited in the text as S.

46. Walter Benjamin, "One-Way Street," in *Selected Writings*, 1:444, hereafter cited in the text as OWS.

47. For the time being I confine my discussion to the question of dreams; I return to memories of childhood in the next section.

48. For a fuller discussion of these issues see Cohen, *Profane Illumination*, pp. 174–78.

49. Rosa Luxemburg, "The Crisis of German Social Democracy," in *Selected Political Writings of Rosa Luxemburg*, ed. Dick Howard (New York: Monthly Review Press, 1971), p. 334.

50. Walter Benjamin, "Program for Literary Criticism," in *Selected Writings*, 2:290.

51. Cohen, *Profane Illumination*, p. 183.

52. This is a recurring theme in Benjamin's attempt to develop a unique cultural critique. For this reason, I find that Wolin goes too far in connecting Benjamin with irrationalist currents. See Richard Wolin, "Experience and Materialism in Benjamin's Passagenwerk," in *Benjamin: Philosophy, Aesthetics, History*, pp. 213, 218, 219. Like Freud, I would argue, Benjamin was attempting to explore many of the phenomena familiar to irrationalism—for example, dreams and images—without abandoning rational critique. In correcting (p. 219) an earlier error in which he claimed that Benjamin sided with the surrealists and against Freud in valorizing the manifest content of dream-images (see *Walter Benjamin: An Aesthetic of Redemption*, p. 127), Wolin still insists unnecessarily on a strong strain of irrationalism in Benjamin's thinking.

53. Andre Breton, *Manifestoes of Surrealism*, trans. Richard Seaver and Helen R. Lane (Ann Arbor: University of Michigan Press, 1969), p. 16.

54. Walter Benjamin, "The Image of Proust," in *Illuminations*, p. 202, hereafter cited in the text as IP.

55. Walter Benjamin, "Old Toys," in *Selected Writings*, 2:100 and Benjamin, "Notes to Theses on History," as quoted by Susan Buck-Morss, *The Dialectics of Seeing: Walter Benjamin and the Arcades Project* (Cambridge, MA: MIT Press, 1989), p. 265.

56. Walter Benjamin, "A Berlin Chronicle," in *Reflections*, pp. 25–26. This essay will hereafter be cited in the text and indicated with the abbreviation BC.

57. Walter Benjamin, "A Short History of Photography," *Screen* 13 (Spring 1972): 7.

58. See, Gershom Scholem, ed., *The Correspondence of Walter Benjamin and Gershom Scholem 1932–1940*, pp. 28, 169–70, and see generally the correspondence in *Gesammelte Schriften*, 2:951–55.

59. Walter Benjamin, "On the Mimetic Faculty," in *Reflections*, p. 333. Further references to this essay will be given in the text and cited as OMF.

60. While there is an important degree of speculation in my discussion here, I hope it will gain persuasive power in the course of my argument below about the absolute centrality of psychoanalytic categories to Benjamin's Arcades Project. Sigrid Weigel, too, sees "On the Mimetic Faculty" as involving a psychoanalytic reformulation of Benjamin's language theory. See her *Body- and Image-Space: Re-reading Walter Benjamin*, trans Georgina Paul with Rachel McNicholl and Jeremy Gaines (New York: Routledge and Kegan Paul, 1996), p. 136.

61. Walter Benjamin, "The Storyteller," in *Illuminations*, p. 108.

62. Jürgen Habermas, "Walter Benjamin: Consciousness-Raising or Rescuing Critique," in *On Walter Benjamin: Critical Essays and Reflections*, ed. Gary Smith (Cambridge, MA: MIT Press, 1988), pp. 110–111.

63. Buck-Morss, *Dialectics of Seeing*, p. 264, author's italics.

64. Jürgen Habermas, *Communication and the Evolution of Society*, trans. Thomas McCarthy (Boston: Beacon Press, 1979), p. 1.

65. Walter Benjamin, "Franz Kafka," in *Illuminations*, pp. 120, 121, 126, 132.

66. Walter Benjamin, "Program for a Proletarian Children's Theater," trans. Susan Buck-Morss, *Performance* 1, no. 5 (March–April, 1973): 30, 31, 32. On this project see also Asja Lacis, "A Memoir," *Performance* 1, no. 5, pp. 24–27; and Hans-Thies Lehmann, "An Interrupted Performance: On Walter Benjamin's Idea of Children's Theatre," and Gerhard Fischer, "Benjamin's Utopia of Education as *Theatrum Mundi et Vitae*: On the Programme of a Proletarian Children's Theatre" both in *'With the Sharpened Axe of Reason': Approaches to Walter Benjamin*, ed. Gerhard Fischer (Oxford: Berg, 1996), pp. 179–200, 201–217.

67. Walter Benjamin, "What Is Epic Theatre? [First Version]," in *Understanding Brecht*, p. 12.

68. Walter Benjamin (with Asja Lacis), "Naples," in *Selected Writings*, 1:421.

69. A point made nicely by Miriam Hansen, "Of Mice and Ducks: Benjamin and Adorno on Disney," *South Atlantic Quarterly* 92, no. 1 (Winter 1993): 44. See also Walter Benjamin, "Mickey Mouse" and "Experience and Poverty," in *Selected Writings*, 2:545, 734–35.

70. Walter Benjamin, "Studies for a Theory of the Epic Theatre," in *Selected Writings*, 2:23.

71. See the important treatment of this issue by Helga Geyer-Ryan, *Fables of Desire* (Cambridge, UK: Polity Press, 1994), chap. 2.

72. Sigmund Freud "Five Lectures on Psychoanalysis," in *Two Short Accounts of Psychoanalysis*, trans. James Strachey (Harmondsworth: Penguin Books, 1991), pp. 43, 40. Habermas understands the core of Freud's argument here (see his *Knowledge and Human Interests*, trans. Jeremy Shapiro [Boston: Beacon Books, 1971], chap. 10, but he gives it his characteristically ultra-rationalist twist by deemphasizing the body and the role of the drives in Freud's theory. On this point see Joel Whitebrook, "Reason and Happiness: Some Psychoanalytic Themes in Critical Theory," in *Habermas and Modernity*, ed. Richard J. Bernstein (Cambridge, MA: MIT Press, 1985), pp. 140–60.

73. Walter Benjamin, "N [Re The Theory of Knowledge, Theory of Progress]," in *Benjamin: Philosophy, Aesthetics, History*, p. 46. Further references to this crucial notebook will be given in the text and indicated as N.

74. Walter Benjamin, "Theses on the Philosophy of History," in *Illuminations*, p. 257, hereafter cited in the text as TPH.

75. Walter Benjamin, "The Work of Art in the Age of Mechanical Reproduction," in *Illuminations*, p. 221.

76. For one of the most insightful sets of reflections on this theme see Susan Buck-Morss, "Aesthetics and Anaesthetics: Walter Benjamin's Artwork Essay Reconsidered," *October* 62 (Fall 1992): 3–41.

77. Walter Benjamin, "The Destructive Character," in *Reflections*, p. 303.

78. See, for instance, Walter Benjamin, "Julien Green," in *Selected Writings*, 2:331.

79. Sigmund Freud, "Constructions in Analysis," in *the Standard Edition of the Complete Psychological Works of Sigmund Freud*, trans. James Strachey (London: Hogarth Press, 1953), 23:262.

80. Sigmund Freud, "Analysis of a Phobia in a Five Year Old Boy," in *Case Histories I*: 263.

81. Karl Marx, "Theses on Feuerbach," in Karl Marx and Frederick Engels, *The German Ideology* (Moscow: Progress Publishers, 1976), p. 615.

82. Mikhail Bakhtin, "Forms of Time and Chronotope in the Novel," in Bakhtin, *The Dialogical Imagination*, trans. Caryl Emerson and Michael Holquist (Austin: University of Texas Press, 1981), p. 159.

83. Mikhail Bakhtin, *Problems of Dostoevsky's Poetics*, ed. and trans. Caryl Emerson (Minneapolis: University of Minnesota Press, 1984), p. 106.

84. Mikhail Bakhtin, "Toward a Reworking of the Dostoevsky Book," in *Problems of Dostoevsky's Poetics*, p. 293.

85. Mikhail Bakhtin, "Toward a Methodology for the Human Sciences," in Bakhtin, *Speech Genres and Other Late Essays*, trans. Vern W. McGee (Austin: University of Texas Press, 1986), p. 170.

86. One of the few interesting attempts to bring Bakhtin and Benjamin into contact with one another is Terry Eagleton's *Walter Benjamin*.

87. The existing notebooks also contain a series of theoretical and methodological considerations relevant to the analysis that informs these images.

88. See Benjamin to Scholem, May 20, 1935, in *The Correspondence of Walter Benjamin and Gershom Scholem 1932–1940*, p. 159.

89. Karl Marx, *Capital*, vol. 1, trans. Ben Fowkes (Harmondsworth: Penguin Books, 1976), pp. 167–68.

90. Walter Benjamin, "The Path to Success, in Thirteen Theses," in *Selected Writings*, 2:147.

91. Sigmund Freud, *The Psychopathology of Everyday Life*, vol. 5 of the Penguin Freud Library, trans Alan Tyson (Harmondsworth: Penguin Books, 1975), pp. 86–88.

92. Walter Benjamin, *Gesammelte Schriften* V: 494. Notebook K of Benjamin's Arcades Project, from which this passage is drawn, is entitled "Dream City and Dream House; Dream of the Future, Anthropological Materialism, Jung."

93. See H. D. Kittsteiner, "Walter Benjamin's Historicism," *New German Critique* 39 (Fall 1986): pp. 193–94.

94. Freud, "Fragment of an Analysis," p. 107.

95. See, for example, Charles Fourier, *Design for Utopia: Selected Writings*, ed. Frank E. Manuel (New York: Schocken Books, 1971).

96. Walter Benjamin, "Paris, Capital of the Nineteenth Century," in *Reflections*, p. 148. Hereafter references to this work will be given in the text and cited as PC.

97. Sigmund Freud, "Creative Writers and Day-Dreaming," *The Standard Edition of the Complete Psychological Works of Sigmund Freud*, vol. 9:147–48.

98. Rosalind H. Williams, *Dream Worlds: Mass Consumption in Late Nineteenth-Century France* (Berkeley: University of California Press, 1982), p. 58.

99. Walter Benjamin, *Gesammelte Schriften* 5:1056, as cited by Buck-Morss, *Dialectics of Seeing*, p. 66.

100. Walter Benjamin, "Central Park," trans. Lloyd Spencer, *New German Critique* 34 (Winter 1985): 36. Further citations from this piece will be given in the text and indicated as CP.

101. Freud, "Fragment of an Analysis," p. 107.

102. Roland Barthes, *The Fashion System*, trans. Matthew Ward and Richard Howard (New York: Hill and Wang, 1983), p. 273.

103. Paul Auster, *In the Country of Last Things* (New York: Penguin Books, 1987), p. 20.

104. As cited by Walter Benjamin, "The Paris of the Second Empire in Baudelaire," in Benjamin, *Charles Baudelaire: A Lyric Poet in the Era of High Capitalism* (London: New Left Books, 1973), p. 77. Further references to this essay are hereafter given in the text and cited as PSEB.

105. J. C. Flugel, *The Psychology of Clothes* (New York: International Universities Press, 1930), p. 111.

106. Angela McRobbie, "The *Passagenwerk* and the Place of Walter Benjamin in Cultural Studies," in McRobbie, *Postmodernism and Popular Culture* (London: Routledge and Kegan Paul, 1994), p. 113; Janet Wolff, "Memoirs and Micrologies: Walter Benjamin, Feminism and Cultural Analysis," *New Formations* 20 (1993):122.

107. Eva Geulen, "Toward a Genealogy of Gender in Walter Benjamin's Writings," *The German Quarterly* 69 (Spring 1996): 168; Elizabeth Wilson, "The Invisible Flaneur," *New Left Review* 191 (January–February 1992): 106–110; Esther Leslie, "On Making-up and Breaking-up: Woman and Ware, Craving and Corpse in Walter Benjamin's *Arcades Project*," *Historical Materialism* 1 (1997): 75.

108. Walter Benjamin, "The Metaphysics of Youth," in *Selected Writings*, 1:6–10. On the connections to Kristeva and Irigaray see Weigel, *Body- and Image-Space*, p. 85.

109. Benjamin, "Life of Students," pp. 43–44.

110. Walter Benjamin, "Socrates," in *Selected Writings*, 1:53–54.

111. Note that at this stage, Benjamin accepted the identification of sexuality with nature, a position which he came to reject as he developed his analysis of capitalist culture.

112. For a first-rate study of this question see Kari Weil, *Androgyny and the Denial of Difference* (Charlottesville: University Press of Virginia, 1992). See also Thais E. Morgan, "Male Lesbian Bodies: The Construction of Alternative Masculinities in Courbet, Baudelaire, and Swinburne," *Genders* 15 (Winter 1992): 37–57.

113. See Witte, *Walter Benjamin*, pp. 143–47.

114. One of the abiding problems that runs through Benjamin's intriguing discussions of women is that they are constructed from the standpoint of the male. While there is a powerful charge to his notion of secret male identifications with women, he does not interrogate female identifications themselves.

115. This point is touched on from slightly different directions by Miriam Hansen, "Benjamin, Cinema and Experience: 'The Blue Flower in the Land of Technology'," *New German Critique* 40 (1987): 215–16; and Rey Chow, "Benjamin's Love Affair with Death," *New German Critique* 42 (1989): 80–83.

116. Wilson, "The Invisible Flaneur," pp. 108–110. Again, this is not to deny the operation of the male gaze in many of Benjamin's analyses, it is simply to point out its complications.

117. Leslie, "On Making-up and Breaking-up," p. 83.

118. On this point see the important discussion of female prostitution in Ryan Bishop and Lillian S. Robinson, *Night Market: Sexual Cultures and the Thai Economic Miracle* (New York: Routledge and Kegan Paul, 1997), chap. 8.

119. Benjamin's analysis of this linking of eros and the dead is developed, along with some of its latent feminist implications, in Christine Buci-Glucksmann, *La raison baroque: De Baudelaire a Benjamin* (Paris: Editions Galilee, 1984), especially part II, chapter 1. The sociohistorical context in which Benjamin confronted the link between women and death has been discussed by Maria Tatar, *Lustmord: Sexual Murder in Weimar Germany* (Princeton: Princeton University Press, 1995).

120. Karl Marx and Frederick Engels, "Manifesto of the Communist Party," in Marx, *The Revolutions of 1848, Political Writings: Volume 1*, ed. David Fernbach (Harmondsworth: Penguin Books, 1973), p. 70.

121. Walter Benjamin, "Theories of German Fascism," *New German Critique* 17 (Spring 1979): 128.

122. As cited by Cohen, *Profane Illumination* p. 54.

123. Benjamin, *Gesammelte Schriften*, 5:1058.

124. Walter Benjamin, "On Some Motifs in Baudelaire," in *Illuminations*, pp. 161–63.

125. Benjamin, "Work of Art," p. 237.

126. Joel Snyder, "Benjamin on Reproducibility and Aura: A Reading of 'The Work of Art' in the Age of Its Technical Reproducibility," in *Benjamin: Philosophy, Aesthetics, History*, p. 160. On the optical unconscious see also Benjamin, "A Short History of Photography," p. 7.

127. See Walter Benjamin, "Reply to Oscar A. H. Schmitz," in *Selected Writings*, 2:16–19.

128. Paul Auster, *In the Country of Last Things*, p. 36.

129. Adorno to Benjamin, 2 August 1935 in *Aesthetics and Politics*, p. 111.

130. Buck-Morss, *Origin of Negative Dialectics*, pp. 144–45.

131. On the Popular Front see Fernando Claudin, *The Communist Movement: From Comintern to Cominform* (Harmondsworth: Penguin Books, 1975), pp. 166–241; E. H. Carr, *Twilight of the Comintern, 1930–35* (New York: Pantheon Books, 1982), chap. 18; Duncan Hallas, *The Comintern* (London: Bookmarks, 1985), chap. 7.

132. For very useful treatments see Phillipe Ivornel, "Paris, Capital of the Popular Front or the Posthumous Life of the 19th Century," *New German Critique* 39 (Fall 1986): 61–84; and Chryssoula Kambas, "Politische Aktualitat: Walter Benjamin's Concept of History and the Failure of the French Popular Front," *New German Critique* 39 (Fall 1986): 87–98.

133. As quoted by Kambas, "Politische Aktualitat," p. 93.

134. Buck-Morss, *Origin of Negative Dialectics*, pp. 137–39.

135. Benjamin, *Gesammelte Schriften*, 5:1033.

136. Ibid., p. 1236.

137. See, for example, Istvan Meszaros, *Lukacs' Concept of Dialectic* (London: Merlin Press, 1972), chap. 6.

138. For excellent treatments of Benjamin's notion of bodily experience see Susan Buck-Morss, "Aesthetics and Anaesthetics," and Miriam Bratu Hansen, "Benjamin and Cinema: Not A One-Way Street," *Critical Inquiry*, 25, no. 2 (Winter 1999): 306–343.

139. See Roberts, *Walter Benjamin* p. 172.

140. Benjamin, *Gesammelte Schriften*, 2:950.

141. It is arguable, of course, that Benjamin found in Freud another thinker influenced by Jewish mysticism. This is an intriguing idea which deserves further investigation. It is, however, beyond the range of this study and of my own competence. For the classic study of Freud in this regard see David Bakan, *Sigmund Freud and the Jewish Mystical Tradition* (Boston: Beacon Press, 1975).

142. Benjamin, *Gesammelte Schriften*, 2:952.

143. Freud, "Fragment of an Analysis," p. 44.

144. Sigmund Freud, "The Unconscious," in *On Metapsychology*, vol. 2 of the Penguin Freud Library, ed. Angela Richards (Harmondsworth: Penguin Books, 1984), p. 210.

145. Joel Kovel, "Marx, Freud and the Problem of Materialism," in Kovel, *The Radical Spirit: Essays on Psychoanalysis and Society* (London: Free Association Books, 1988), p. 318.

146. Walter Benjamin, "Doctrine of the Similar (1933)," *New German Critique* 17 (1979): 65.

147. Sigmund Freud, *New Introductory Lectures on Psychoanalysis*, vol. 2 of the Penguin Freud Library (Harmondsworth: Penguin Books, 1973), p. 86.

148. This argument is developed especially forcefully in Benjamin, "Experience and Poverty," in *Selected Writings*, 2:731–36.

149. See, for example, the section of the Arcades Project entitled "p anthropologischer Materialismus, Sektengeschichte," *Gesammelte Schriften*, 5:971–81.

150. See Bishop and Robinson, *Night Market*, chap. 5; Ann Laura Stoler, "Carnal Knowledge and Imperial Power: Gender, Race, and Morality in Colonial Asia," in *Gender at the Crossroads of Knowledge: Feminist Anthropology in the Postmodern Era*, ed. Micaela di Leonardo (Berkeley: University of California Press, 1991); Sharon Tiffany and Kathleen Adams, *The Wild Woman: An Inquiry into the Anthropology of an Idea* (Cambridge, MA: Schenkman, 1985).

151. *Gesammelte Schriften*, 7:864.

152. For an interesting discussion of the way in which the body thinks and talks through hysterical symptoms see Monique David-Menard, *Hysteria from Freud to Lacan: Body and Language in Psychoanalysis*, trans. Catherine Porter (Ithaca: Cornell University Press, 1989).

153. Jeanette Winterson, *Written on the Body* (Toronto: Vintage Books, 1992), p. 130.

154. Benjamin, "The Path to Success," p. 147.

155. See Jürgen Habermas, *Knowledge and Human Interests*, chap. 10.

156. See the excellent discussion of these issues in Joel Whitebrook, "Reason and Happiness," esp. pp. 155–58.

157. By classical Marxism I mean that political tradition, associated with Marx, Engels, Rosa Luxemburg, the early years of the Bolshevik Revolution, with Antonio Gramsci, and with much of the libertarian socialism of the anti-Stalinist left generally.

158. Herbert Marcuse, *Eros and Civilization: A Philosophical Inquiry into Freud* (Boston: Vintage Books, 1962), p. 182.

159. Walter Benjamin, "The Storyteller," *Illuminations*, p. 108.

160. Bertolt Brecht as quoted by Nagele, *Theater, Theory, Speculation*, p. 156.

161. On this point see Freud, "Beyond the Pleasure Principle" in Freud, *On Metapsychology*, vol. 11 of the Penguin Freud Library (Harmondsworth: Penguin Books, 1984), p. 332.

162. Walter Benjamin, "On Some Motifs in Baudelaire," *Illuminations*, p. 176.

163. Walter Benjamin, "The Artist as Producer," in *Reflections*, pp. 220–38. See also Roberts, *Walter Benjamin* pp. 152–61.

164. Rose Pesotta, *Bread upon the Waters* (rpt. 1944, Ithaca: ILR Press, 1987), pp. 33–34, 359–60.

165. Lian Hurst Mann, "Subverting the Avant-Garde: Critical Theory's Real Strategy," in *Reconstructing Architecture: Critical Discourses and Social Practices*, Thomas A. Dutton and Lian Hurst Mann, eds. (Minneapolis: University of Minnesota Press, 1996), pp. 302–3.

166. Geyer-Ryan, *Fables of Desire*, p. 120.

CONCLUSION

1. Franz Kafka, *The Penal Colony: Stories and Short Pieces*, trans. Willa and Edwin Muir (New York: Schocken Books, 1961), p. 197.

2. Elaine Scarry, *The Body in Pain: The Making and Unmaking of the World* (Oxford: Oxford University Press, 1985), p. 109.

3. Jean Baudrillard, *Symbolic Exchange and Death*, trans. Iain Hamilton Grant and Mike Gane (London: Sage Publications, 1993), p. 20; Baudrillard, *Fatal Strategies*, trans. Philip Beitchman and W. G. J. Niesluchowski (New York and London: Semiotext(e)/ Pluto, 1990), p. 25; and Baudrillard, "The Ecstasy of Communication," in *The Anti-Aesthetic: Essays in Postmodern Culture*, ed. Hal Foster (Port Townsend, Wash: Bay Press, 1983), p. 129.

4. Doug Henwood, "Info Fetishism," in *Resisting the Virtual Life: The Culture and Politics of Information*, eds. James Brook and Iain A. Boal (San Francisco: City Lights, 1995), p. 164. See also David McNally, "Marxism in the Age of Information," *New Politics* 6, no. 4 (Winter 1998): 99–106.

5. Mikhail Bakhtin, *Rabelais and His World*, trans. Helene Iswolsky (Bloomington, IN: Indiana University Press, 1984), p. 403.

6. Terry Eagleton, *The Illusions of Postmodernism* (Oxford: Blackwell, 1996), p. 25.

7. Antonio Gramsci, *Selections from the Prison Notebooks*, trans. Quinton Hoare and Geoffrey Nowell Smith (New York: International Publishers, 1971), pp. 333, 335. For some considerations on Gramsci's discussion of language and political action see David McNally, "Language, History and Class Struggle," in *In Defense of History: Marxism and the Postmodern Agenda*, eds. Ellen Meiksins Wood and John Bellamy Foster (New York: Monthly Review Press, 1997), pp. 26–42.

8. Walter Benjamin, "Notes (IV)," in Benjamin, *Selected Writings, Volume 2: 1927– 1934*, eds. Michael W. Jennings, Howard Eiland, and Gary Smith (Cambridge, MA: The Belknap Press of Harvard University Press, 1999), p. 688.

INDEX

Abstract labor, 5, 6, 52, 53, 67, 68, 109
Adorno, Gretel, 219, 222
Adorno, Theodor, 56, 75, 76, 77, 80, 108, 195, 230, 263n29; his debate with Benjamin, 216–19. *See also* Negative dialectics
Advertising, 158, 179
Allegory, 175–77, 210; and bourgeois novelty, 202
Aragon, Louis, 183, 213, 220
Arcades, 199. *See also* Benjamin, Walter
Auster, Paul, 204

Bakhtin, Mikhail, 1, 9, 10, 11, 55, 109, 123–59, 194–96, 221, 230, 231; authorship of texts, 255n.1; and the body, 124–25, 127, 142; comparison with W. Benjamin, 194–96, 213; concept of the chronotope, 129, 134–39, 140; concept of truth, 128–29; in context of Stalinism, 130, 143, 260n. 62; dialogism, 125; early Kantianism, 124; and gendered

body, 126–27, 146–49; on laughter, 140, 145, 146, 147, 154; mature theory of language, 132–34; relation to Marxism, 123, 257n. 18; theory of the novel, 130–34; theory of the utterance, 132, 133; works: "Author and Hero in Aesthetic Activity," 124, 125, 127; "Discourse in the Novel," 115, 132–34, 145; "Forms of Time and the Chronotope in the Novel," 134, 137, 138, 140, 155; *Problems of Dostoevsky's Poetics*, 124, 127; *Rabelais and His World*, 127, 136, 138, 141, 143, 144, 146, 156
Bannerji, Himani, 4
Baroque drama, 174–75, 176, 193, 211; and bourgeois society, 184. *See also Trauerspiel*
Barthes, Roland, 203
Baudelaire, Charles, 204, 205, 209, 210, 214
Baudrillard, Jean, 65, 225, 246n35; and virtual economy, 63, 64, 65, 66
Benjamin, Walter, 1, 8, 10, 13, 14, 109, 158–59, 161–208, 230, 232, 233; aesthetic criticism, 172–73,

271

Benjamin, Walter *(continued)* 193; anthropological materialism, 169, 223, 224, 228; application of Freudian categories to analysis of capitalism, 202, 214–15; Arcades Project, 182, 184, 192, 196, 201, 202, 215, 216, 217, 218, 219, 223, 227; on commodity fetishism, 197–201, 216, 224; corporeal reason, 180–81, 196, 226; critique of irrationalism, 264n. 52; dialectical images, 192, 194, 211, 212, 219, 220, 220–21, 226–27; dialectics, 171, 178; dialectics at a standstill, 190, 192, 196; dialectics of awakening, 199, 211, 113, 215, 219, 226; dialectic of extremes, 180, 194, 207, 211, 220, 261n. 6; disagreements with T. Adorno, 216–19; on empathy with the commodity, 208–9; on eroticization of commodities, 197, 198, 208; on fashion, 202–5, 208–11; on the *flaneur*, 210; and Freud's dream theory, 219–223; and Freud's influence on his thought, 166, 169, 179, 180, 186, 188, 194, 196, 198, 199, 213, 214; on gesture, 189–92; and immanent critique, 172, 173; involvement in Free German Youth, 166; and Jewish mysticism, 262n. 14, 269n. 141; on language and *mimesis*, 187–88, 222–23, 225, 226; on "the language of things," 162, 165, 181, 222; on linguistic unconscious, 187, 222; and G. Lukacs, 171–72, 178; memory and recollection, 185–86, 193, 196, 212–13, 225; and messianism, 167–69, 183, 217; play and childhood experience as models, 185–86, 187, 190, 222; on profane illumination, 181, 183; program for a proletarian children's theater, 190; and prostitutes in capitalist society, 205, 207, 209, 210, 211, 223; on psychoanalysis and revolution, 179,

188, 191–94, 197, 212, 213, 215; relation to surrealism, 178, 180, 183, 224; on shock-experience, 186, 214, 227; theory of dreams, 170–71, 178–81, 213; theory of the image, 184, 186, 188, 199; on time, 184; on tradition, 193, 195; and tradition of the oppressed, 211, 218; and translation, 168, 170, 171; turn to Marxism, 168, 170, 171; on women and bourgeois society, 205–11, 267n. 114; works: "A Berlin Chronicle," 186, 207; "The Concept of Criticism in German Romanticism," 167; "The Conversation," 206; "Critique of Violence," 168; "The Image of Proust," 185; "The Life of Students," 206; "On Language as Such and the Language of Man," 164–66, 170, 173, 187; On the Mimetic Faculty," 164, 187, 220, 222; *One-Way Street*, 171, 179, 180, 181, 184, 185, 189, 199; *Origin of German Tragic Drama*, 162, 171, 173, 177, 178; "Outline of the Psychophysical Problem," 168, 170; "Paris, Capital of the Nineteenth Century," 199; "Surrealism, Last Snapshot of the European Intelligentsia," 178; "Theological-Political Fragment," 168, 170, 178; "Theses on the Philosophy of History," 217; "The Work of Art in the Age of Mechanical Reproduction," 214

Biology, 2, 11. *See also* Evolutionary biology; Modern Darwinism; Natural selection

Bipedalism, 87

Blondel, Eric, 33

Bodies of meaning, 9, 97

Body, in bourgeois thought, 4–5, 11; in postmodernist theory, 2, 5, 11, 141; and word in Bakhtin, 142–43. *See also* Bourgeois body; Carnivalesque body; Female body; Grotesque

body; Historical body; Laboring body; Maternal body
Bonner, John Tyler, 84
Bourgeois body, 5, 11
Brecht, Bertolt, 190, 191, 219, 225, 226
Breton, Andre, 178, 183, 203
Buck-Morss, Susan, 189, 216
Burke, Peter, 143
Butler, Judith, 3

Carnival, 136, 141, 142, 144, 149–50; Benjamin's views on, 190; and capitalism, 156, 261n. 80; debate over Bakhtin's theory of, 144–46; and race, 154–55; its two-sidedness, 153–55. See also Bakhtin, Mikhail
Carnivalesque body, 142
Cassagnac, Granier de, 4
Chimpanzees, 86, 88, 90, 91, 96
Chomsky, Noam, 94
Chronotope. See Bakhtin, Mikhail
Classical Marxism, 269n. 157
Commodity fetishism, 6, 9, 12, 66–70, 111, 197; Benjamin's theory of, 197–201; differences between Benjamin and Adorno on, 216. See also Fetishism
Communist Party (of France), 178, 217
Critical materialism, 4, 10, 74, 236n. 8; in Benjamin, 188. See also Materialist critique
Critical theory, 4, 7, 8, 12, 80, 119, 163

Damasio, Antonio, 98
Darwin Charles, 8, 9, 18, 77, 80, 96, 247n. 2; Descent of Man, 81; on human speech, 103–5, 106, 107; Marx's attitude toward, 76; Origin of Species, 76, 80, 82, 83, 84; radical implications of his theory, 81–82; theory of sexual selection, 85–86
Darwinian body, 97

Darwinism, 26, 36, 76, 77, 79; Nietzsche's relation to, 15–27; and phenomenology, 98
deconstruction, 1, 6, 44, 45, 46, 55, 73–74, 76, 108; and dialectics, 56; idealism of, 77; and Nietzsche, 16; vulgar deconstruction, 237n. 17. See also Derrida, Jacques
Defetishizing critique, 231; in Marx, 74–75; opposed by Derrida, 46, 57, 66, 71, 74
Deleuze, Gilles, 15, 18, 27
Demar, Claire, 209
Derrida, Jacques, 1, 3, 7, 9, 10, 12, 45, 46, 69, 230; against defetishizing critique, 46, 57, 66, 71; concept of différance, 58–59, 60, 72; and the gift, 60–62, 76; and language, 59, 61; and Marx, 56–57, 66; on money, 62–63, 66; on Nietzsche, 15, 18, 40, 72, 243n. 58; and Saussure's linguistics, 47–48, 50, 57–58, 245n. 21, 245n. 24; on the subject, 61; theory of capitalism, 63; on woman, 72. See also Deconstruction
Degradation, 10; as Bakhtinian strategy, 142, 144–45
Desire, and the commodity, 197, 199; in Benjamin's analysis of capitalism, 170–71; in postmodern thought, 2, 8, 254n. 103
Dews, Peter, 77
Dialectical criticism, 69; in Benjamin, 198
Dialectical images. See Benjamin, Walter
Dialectics, 56, 75, 164; Benjamin's concept of, 171, 178. See also Negative dialectics
Dialectics at a standstill. See Benjamin, Walter
Donald, Merlin, 95, 103
Dostoyevsky, Fyodor, 128, 129, 131, 144
Douglass, Frederick, 151
Dreams. See Benjamin, Walter; Freud, Sigmund; Surrealism
Dunbar, Robin, 101, 102

Eagleton, Terry, 8, 143, 231
Embodied knowledge, 97
Emerson, Caryl, 144
Engels, Frederick, 64
Epic theater. *See* Brecht, Bertolt
Eros, 39, 170
Evolutionary body, 9
Evolutionary biology, 79, 80, 82, 83, 248n. 16. *See also* Modern Darwinism; Natural selection
Exchange abstraction, 5, 6

Fanon, Frantz, 5, 238n. 33
Fascism, 193, 213, 216, 223
Female body, 5, 11, 12; in Bakhtin, 126–27, 146–48
Feminist theory, 11, 12; and Benjamin, 205–6; and materialist feminism, 238n. 30
Fetishism, of commodities, 6, 9, 12, 54, 66–70, 171; Derrida's theory of, 57, 67, 71–72; Freud's theory of, 71; of money capital, 12, 54; in Saussure's linguistics, 52, 54. *See also* Commodity fetishism
Feuerbach, Ludwig, 64
Folklore, Bakhtin's theory of, 135, 136, 138, 140; Gramsci on, 151–54
Foucault, Michel, 15, 18, 263n. 3
Fourier, Charles, 199, 200, 215
Freud, Sigmund, 3, 8, 9, 76, 77, 120, 126, 191, 192, 202, 225, 232; theory of fetishism, 71; works: *Beyond the Pleasure Principle*, 214; "Creative Dreamers and Day Dreaming," 200; *The Interpretation of Dreams*, 221; *New Introductory Lectures on Psychoanalysis*, 222; "The Unconscious," 222

Gasché, Rodolphe, 33
Geist, 166, 167
Generativity, and human language, 94, 102, 119; and human tool-making, 100, 102

Genovese, Eugene, 151
German Romanticism, 167, 172, 206
Gesture, 95; and language, 98, 103
Geulen, Eva, 205
Gibson, Kathleen, 99–100
Goethe, Johann Wolfgang von, 139
Gould, Stephen Jay, 26, 27, 84–85, 87
Gramsci, Antonio, 232; on folklore and popular culture, 151–54; on Lukacs, 122; *Prison Notebooks*, 182, 216
Groos, Karl, 85
Grotesque body, 140, 141, 142, 147; as female, 147
Grotesque realism, 142
Gullah, 150

Haar, Michel, 36
Habermas, Jürgen, 108–9, 225–26; his interpretation of Benjamin, 188–91
Haeckel, Ernst Heinrich, 18
Haraway, Donna, 249n. 33
Hegel, G. W. F., 6, 40, 119, 172, 198
Heidegger, Martin, 18, 58, 60; on Nietzsche, 35–38
Heteroglossia, 130, 132, 133, 134, 140
Historical body, 7, 9, 223, 231
Historical materialism, 76, 231; and Bakhtin, 134. *See also* Materialist conception of history
Holdcroft, David, 50, 51
Hollingdale, R. J., 15–16, 18
hominids, 250n. 48; archaic *homo sapiens*, 93; *homo erectus*, 92; *homo habilis*, 92–93, 94; *homo sapiens*, 93; Neanderthals, 93
Horkheimer, Max, 74, 80, 108
human language, and the body, 99; emergence of, 94–96; origins, 99
Hume, David, 16, 17

Idealism, 2, 4, 76; in Derrida, 73;
German idealism, 167; and
Nietzsche, 33, 34, 38, 40–41, 43.
See also Linguistic idealism; New
idealism; Postmodern idealism
Imperialism, 11, 12
Information economy, 46
Irigaray, Luce, 72–73, 206, 239n. 38

Johnstone, Mark, 97

Kafka, Franz, 14, 163, 190, 225, 226,
229
Kant, Immanuel, 16–20, 25, 29, 30,
57, 124, 240n. 5
Kantianism, and Bakhtin, 124; in
Habermas, 109
Kaufmann, Walter, 15, 16
Keenan, Thomas, 66–67
Kirby, Vicki, 3, 80
Kovel, Joel, 222
Kristeva, Julia, 206

Labor Community Strategy Center,
227
Laboring body, 2, 3, 4, 5, 9, 13, 66,
75; in Marxism and feminism,
247n. 58; and postmodern theory,
230
Lacan, Jacques, 1, 3, 126
Lacis, Asja, 171
Lamarck, Jean Baptiste, 27
Lamarckianism, 27, 28; and Darwin,
242n. 31
Lewontin, Richard C., 83
Leslie, Esther, 205, 210
Liberal materialism, 8
Libidinal body, 8
Life genres, 117, 134, 140, 141, 256n.
9
Linguistic idealism, 2, 3, 4; in
Nietzsche, 34; and post-structuralism,
108
Lukacs, Georg, 56, 109, 121–22, 192,
209; and Benjamin, 171–72, 177,

180; *History and Class Consciousness*,
121, 171–72, 173, 177
Luxemburg, Rosa, 182

Marcuse, Herbert, 226
Marx, Karl, 3, 8, 9, 42, 52, 54, 56,
64, 77, 101, 109, 119, 152, 191,
198, 199, 211; *Capital*, 52, 67, 68,
70, 91, 201; on the commodity,
5, 44, 53, 68–69; on credit, 63;
and Darwin, 80–81; *The German
Ideology*, 64, 111, 113; on tech-
nology, 91
Mass culture, 158
Materialism, 74, 80; of the body, 143;
and Derrida, 73, 74; in Marx, 75.
See also Critical materialism; Liberal
materialism; Historical materialism;
Materialist critique
Materialist conception of history, 85,
107. *See also* Historical materialism
Materialist critique, 4, 74. *See also*
Critical materialism
Maternal body, 12, 13, 239n. 35; in
Bakhtin, 136–37. *See also* Mother
Mayhew, Henry, 4
McCole, John, 169
McRobbie, Angela, 205
Medvedev, Pavel, 112, 117, 120, 123,
258n. 28
Megill, Alan, 40
Memory, Bakhtin's theory of, 138,
146; in Benjamin, 185–86, 193,
196, 212–13, 225
Mendel, Gregor, 82
Merleau-Ponty, Maurice, 56, 77, 96, 97
Mimesis, 102, 103, 108; Benjamin's
theory of, 187–88, 222–23; and
language, 106, 126; and translation,
162
Modern Darwinism, 82. *See also*
Evolutionary biology
Money, 53; Baudrillard on, 65–66;
Derrida's concept of, 62; Marx's
theory of, 69; in Saussure's
economics of language, 52

Morson, Gary Saul, 144
Mother, 12–13; in Bakhtin, 126; in
  Benjamin, 207–8. *See also* Maternal
  body
Multiaccentuality of the sign, 114,
  116, 117, 118

Natural history, 8
Natural selection, 80, 81, 83, 86, 89,
  97
Negro Election Day, 154–55
Negative dialectics, 56, 162
Nehemas, Alexander, 31
New idealism, 1, 2, 3, 6, 7, 10
Nietzsche, Friedrich, 1, 10, 12, 62,
  126; aristocratic biology, 27;
  aristocratic radicalism, 23; and
  asceticism, 34–35; on the body,
  24, 27, 29–32, 35; and Darwin,
  15–27; death of God 21, 23, 29;
  on "the herd," 24, 25, 28, 29; his
  idealism, 33, 34, 38, 40–41, 43;
  and interpretation, 30, 32, 33; and
  Kant, 16, 18, 30; and Lamarckianism, 27, 28; on language, 41; and
  materialism, 30, 32, 33; on
  morality, 29; new slavery, 23; on
  race, 27, 28; on the self, 31, 32; the
  superman, 28, 29, 31; on truth, 30,
  41; will to power, 23, 24, 25, 26,
  30, 33, 44; on women, 35, 38–40,
  72; works: *The Anti-Christ*, 35;
  Birth of Tragedy, 25, 32; *Day Break*,
  20; *Ecce Homo*, 33; *The Gay Science*,
  18, 21, 24, 31, 38, 42; *Genealogy of
  Morals*, 28, 32, 34; *Thus Spoke
  Zarathustra*, 28, 30–31, 33, 34;
  Untimely Meditations, 19, 21, 22,
  28, 35

Oliver, Kelly, 12, 72, 73
Orwell, George, 118

Paris Commune, 163, 200
Phenomenology, 96
Philosophy of consciousness, 2, 16,
  17

Plato, 11, 36, 40; his *Symposium*, 39,
  170
Polyglossia, 130, 131
Polyphonic novel, 128, 129, 131
Popular culture, 143, 147–48, 149;
  in Bakhtin, 142, 153; Gramsci's
  theory of, 151–52; transformation
  under late capitalism, 156–57.
  See also Folklore; Mass culture
Popular Front, 216–17
Postmodern idealism, 3
Postmodernism, 1–3, 6, 7, 11, 212,
  225, 235n. 1; and the body, 2, 11,
  141; and Nietzsche, 16, 25; and
  virtual economy, 63
Post-structuralism, 1, 2–3, 6, 12, 76,
  128, 230; model of language, 65,
  108, 141; and Nietzsche, 16, 25;
  and Saussure's linguistics, 47
Praxis, 93, 95, 96, 108; in Lukacs and
  Benjamin, 171, 181; and *mimesis*,
  189–90
Pregnancy, 147–48
Prostitutes, 4; in Benjamin's analysis
  of capitalism, 205, 207
Proust, Marcel, 184–85, 191
Psychoanalysis, 3, 8, 126, 162–63,
  191–93, 194, 211, 212

Rabelais, Francois, 11, 131, 142–48,
  154, 230; as fantastic realist, 140.
  See also Bakhtin, Mikhail
Rée, Paul, 18
Reification, 195, 197; and Benjamin's
  theory of baroque drama, 174;
  Lukacs' account of, 172; in
  Saussure's linguistics, 55, 111
Repetition compulsion, 3; and
  capitalism, 196, 202, 212
Reynolds, Peter, 100, 101
Ricardo, David, 52
Richman, Bruce, 105
Roberts, Julian, 177
Roediger, David, 155
Ross-Landi, Ferruccio, 55
Rousseau, Jean-Jacques, 139
Russo, Mary, 148

Said, Edward, 12
Salcedo, Doris, 13–14
Sass, Louis A., 43
Saussure, Ferdinand de, 1, 9, 10, 44,
    45, 46, 69, 97, 111, 230; definition
    of language, 47; on linguistic value,
    48–54; and the sign, 48, 49, 51
Scarry, Elaine, 53, 229
Scholem, Gershom, 171, 262n. 14
Schott, Robin May, 109
Self-birthing capital, 70, 230
Self-birthing male, 12, 39–40, 72–73
Sexual selection. See Darwin, Charles
Sheets-Johnstone, Maxine, 95, 96, 106
Sign language, 98
Smith, Adam, 51
Social Darwinism, 22
Social Democratic Party (of Germany),
    166, 177
Sociobiology, 79. See also Vulgar
    Darwinism
Socrates, 36, 206
Speech genres, 116–17, 118, 134, 141,
    195
Stallybrass, Peter, 154
Staten, Henry, 31, 39, 77
Stern, J. P., 41
Strauss, David, 19, 25, 26
Surrealism, 178, 180, 216; concept
    of freedom, 183; and dialectic of
    inversion, 180; and dreams, 178–79,
    180. See also Aragon, Louis; Breton,
    Andre
Syntax, 99, 106, 107

Thibault, Paul, 54
Tool-making, 92, 93; apes and
    humans, 100, 101, 102; and
    language, 94, 99
Tools, 88, 91; Acheulean tool-kit, 93,
    93, 95; and chimpanzees, 88; in the
    fossil record, 91–92
Trauerspiel, 171, 173, 174, 175, 177,
    196; as mourning plays, 174

Utopia, 212; in Bakhtin, 137, 141,
    143, 146; and Benjamin's theory of
    fashion, 211; in Fourier, 199

Voloshinov, Valentin, 1, 9, 55, 112–
    23, 127, 131, 132, 133, 140, 231;
    arrest of 258n. 28

Wallace, Alfred, 85
Weiner, Jonathon, 84
Weber, Samuel, 122–23
Western Marxism, 182
White, Allon, 154
Williams, Raymond, 113
Wilson, Elizabeth, 205
Winterson, Jeanette, 224
Wolff, Janet, 205
Wood, Ellen Meiksins, 254n. 102,
    256n. 6
World fairs, 157–58, 200
Wyneken, Gustav, 166, 167